PAST OR PORTAL?

Enhancing Undergraduate Learning through Special Collections and Archives

Edited by Eleanor Mitchell, Peggy Seiden, and Suzy Taraba

Association of College & Research Libraries
A division of the American Library Association
Chicago, 2012

3062787820

The paper used in this publication meets the minimum requirements of American National Standard for Information Sciences–Permanence of Paper for Printed Library Materials, ANSI Z39.48-1992. ∞

Library of Congress Cataloging-in-Publication Data

Mitchell, Eleanor, 1950-
  Past or portal? : enhancing undergraduate learning through special collections and archives / Eleanor Mitchell, Peggy Seiden, Suzy Taraba.
    pages cm
  Includes bibliographical references.
  ISBN 978-0-8389-8610-3 (pbk. : alk. paper) -- ISBN (invalid) 978-0-8389-9443-6 (ebook) -- ISBN (invalid) 978-0-8389-9447-4 (kindle) -- ISBN (invalid) 978-0-8389-9453-5 (pdf)
  1. Academic libraries--Relations with faculty and curriculum--United States--Case studies. 2. Libraries--Special collections--Case studies. 3. Library orientation for college students--Case studies. 4. Research--Methodology--Study and teaching (Higher)--Case studies. 5. Archives and education--Case studies. I. Seiden, Peggy, 1954- II. Taraba, Suzy. III. Title.
  Z675.U5M5577 2012
  025.5'677--dc23

                      2012006254

Printed in the United States of America.

Inset cover image from The University of Hawaii at Hilo's Christensen Photographic Collection

16 15 14 13   5 4 3 2

Table of Contents

THE PROGRAM

THE WORK

ABOUT THE AUTHORS

Introduction

Eleanor Mitchell, Peggy Seiden, and Suzy Taraba

Undergraduate engagement with the rich holdings of special collections and archives in colleges and universities, public and special libraries, is a powerful trend in higher education. Not so long ago, many special collections librarians and archivists feared that the omnipresence of digital resources would render archives and special collections obsolete, at least in the public eye. The reality could hardly be more different: as it turns out, readily available digitized materials often whet researchers' appetites for the "real thing." Digital surrogates complement and enhance the use of physical materials. (And, of course, many archives and other materials are now born digital.) Archivists and special collections librarians have found that their reading room visits, requests for class instruction, and the general fascination of students and scholars with artifacts from the past and other unique or uncommon materials, have all soared as their collections have become easily discoverable online. The democratization of learning enabled by the internet spread quickly to archives and special collections: the old stereotypes of the off-limits treasure room and the inaccessible archives are now long gone. Once populated almost exclusively by senior faculty and graduate students in the throes of dissertation research, today archives and special collections reading rooms are equally likely to be filled with undergraduates.

Why teach undergraduates using resources in special collections and archives? Can't they just find everything they need on the internet? Answers to these questions abound in the case studies presented in *Past or Portal? Enhancing Undergraduate Learning through Special Collections and Archives.*

Unlike the rekeyed, disembodied texts found in cyberspace, the resources of archives and special collections can teach students about the history of printing and publishing, the materiality of the text and its container, and how readers of the past approached a book or document. Students discover that the text is only one of many aspects of a physical artifact that they can learn to "read." They develop research and interrogatory skills that take them far beyond modern reprints of a text into a deeper understanding of the artifact. They come to understand that the author of the text is only one of many people responsible for the presence of an archival document, photograph, or book in their hands. They encounter artists' interpretations of the book as a medium of communication. All the "stuff" of special collections and archives—archival collections, rare books, photographs, ephemera, realia, artists' books, scrapbooks, and more—offers a wealth of possibilities for new approaches to teaching and learning. Special collections and archives engage and empower undergraduates as well as enhance their learning experiences. These materials are far more than mere survivors of the past; they are truly portals to new ways of learning and thinking.

Past or Portal? provides a host of examples of the effective involvement of undergraduates with primary sources found in archives and special collections in nearly fifty different institutions. We hope that it will inspire librarians and faculty who are new to teaching using these resources, as well as those who have been using similar methods for years. The impetus for the volume came from several places. In the late 1990s, Susan M. Allen, then

Director of Libraries and Media Services at Kalamazoo College, conducted a survey on special collections in Oberlin Group libraries. Her findings are detailed in "Rare Books and the College Library: Current Practices in Marrying Undergraduates to Special Collections" (*Rare Books and Manuscripts Librarianship*, Spring 1999, 13:110-119). This article was an early inspiration for us. In the intervening years, the visibility and importance of special collections in undergraduate education grew as humanities and social science curricula evolved to include greater emphasis on undergraduate research and widespread digitization projects began to make archives and special collections more easily and broadly accessible. We, the editors of this volume, witnessed and participated in these changes on our own campuses; newsletters from research libraries and other Oberlin Group libraries frequently contained captivating articles documenting student engagement with these collections. In 2007, the Association for Research Libraries published a lavish tome highlighting its members' special collections.[1] This volume sparked a discussion on the Oberlin Group's directors' email distribution list concerning whether a similar compendium of special collections in liberal arts colleges might be warranted. At the 2009 Oberlin Group Meeting, Peggy Seiden, College Librarian at Swarthmore, raised the possibility of a volume containing case studies of undergraduate use of special collections. Her follow up inquiry to the Oberlin Group library directors yielded a great deal of interest. Eleanor Mitchell, Director of Library Services at Dickinson College, and Suzy Taraba, Head of Special Collections and University Archivist at Wesleyan University, offered to join her as co-editors. Despite the flowering of this educational trend, relatively little on the topic has been published in the library and archives literature. This book is one attempt to address the need for models that offer best practices, creative approaches, and solutions to commonly experienced challenges.

In the Spring of 2010, we put out a call for one-page abstracts of case studies involving teaching undergraduates using archives and special collections. Our call was distributed via several email distribution lists devoted to archives, special collections, and college libraries, as well as by word of mouth. The response was overwhelming: nearly one hundred case studies were proposed. Our original hope for about thirty solid case studies proved to be a significant underestimation. We expanded the acceptances to nearly fifty that were truly compelling, and those authors were asked for fuller case studies.

Past or Portal?: Enhancing Undergraduate Learning through Special Collections and Archives presents forty-seven case studies from a wide range of institutions. All of the case studies explore undergraduate learning that is directly connected to archives and special collections. While the resources and approaches of each institution differ, most of the case studies are easily adaptable to other collections. The case studies are grouped in four sections: The Artifact, the Pedagogy, the Program, and the Work. Although many of the case studies could easily fit in more than one of these categories, they have been written to stress the aspects that relate to the section to which they have been assigned.

THE PROGRAM

Case studies in the Program section address broad, multi-disciplinary approaches to undergraduate involvement with archives and special collections. Anne Marie Lane offers practical tips on starting and expanding a program of teaching using rare books, based on her successful, wide-ranging efforts at the University of Wyoming, Laramie. Suzy Taraba analyzes the extensive outreach at Wesleyan University and explores the challenges of sustaining an ambitious program.

Collaboration between faculty and librarians is crucial in achieving desired goals at several institutions. At Augustana College, the library offers faculty stipends to encourage in-depth research in special collections, resulting in the development of courses directly connected to the holdings. Faculty at Oberlin College describe their efforts to develop a book studies program, one of the few such programs in a liberal arts college. Creative use of technology is the key to introducing large numbers of University of California undergraduates to research using primary sources, where an annual undergraduate research prize is a special incentive for students. An intensive course, "Incunabula to PDFs: What is the Future of Libraries?," is a collaboration between the Honors Program and Special Collections at Iowa State University.

All of these programs have in common serious efforts to infiltrate as much of the curriculum as possible. The program case studies go far beyond the expected English, history, and art classes to engage students and faculty in disciplines as diverse as aquatic entomology, astronomy, computer science, costume design, dance, mathematics, pharmacy, and visual literacy. They offer models for building and sustaining similar programs at other institutions.

THE PEDAGOGY

The chapters in the section on pedagogy focus on innovative and effective methods to teach using the materials and processes of special collections and archives. Some, such as the chapter on the archival research course in the History department at University of Wyoming, describe semester long, structured projects through which students delve deeply into research methods and critical analysis of sometimes conflicting primary sources. At the University of Oregon, students throughout their freshman year seminar write and document their own university experience, some beginning even before arriving at school, and they use Web 2.0 tools as creators rather than consumers. In a first year writing course at Dartmouth, the exploration of the novel, *The English Patient,* along with archival materials about a Dartmouth student who served in the Second World War, leads to a better understanding of the novel and the process of primary source research. A semester-long seminar in architectural history at Connecticut College centers on archival materials about the campus and its architecture. The chapter on Emory University "specifically explores the pedagogy of teaching first-year composition students ..., using the literature collections housed in the Manuscript, Archives, and Rare Book Library (MARBL). By putting first-year composition students quite literally in touch with the materials of literary creation, instructors open new avenues for students to engage with and understand the writing process."

Other chapters describe modules or assignments used within academic courses. At the University of Colorado at Boulder, librarian and science faculty collaboration has, over the last decade, developed an active learning model which engages undergraduates in both the history and relevance of science through the use of realia. At the University of Minnesota, Archives and Special Collections staff have developed and honed three instructional modules to become a flexible, reusable "tool kit" for use across the curriculum to teach research skills and strategies using primary materials. In the chapter on the University of Chicago's program, five approaches to integrating manuscripts and rare books into creative writing classes are shared; this chapter underscores the need for special collections to reach new populations, and the value of these activities in providing inspiration to young writers.

The programs and approaches span the curriculum. At University of the Pacific, students in an experimental psychology course read diaries and analyze the emotional states of the writers; three interrelated assignments in a jazz seminar call upon the multi-format resources of their rich Dave Brubeck collection. Descriptions of creative approaches to faculty and student outreach provide replicable examples for readers of this volume. Professor Victoria Levine, at Colorado College, calls upon the collection of archival sound recordings of Indo-Hispanic folklore in both a music theory and a Southwest Studies course. Offered by the Department of Anthropology at Harvard, the year-long course Archaeology of Harvard Yard "makes extensive use of the Harvard University Archives' services and collections as students literally uncover Harvard history," beginning with an actual archaeological dig on the campus and proceeding to artifact analysis and presentation. At the University of Illinois, the archivist is advisor to and heavily involved in the Ethnography of the University Initiative; for courses across the curriculum, in such varied disciplines as anthropology, English, kinesiology, and urban planning, archives staff identify resources, teach classes, and consult on assignments and research papers.

Some of the programs in this section make extensive use of digital technology to enhance teaching and learning. *Nebraska U: A Collaborative History* is an initiative through which students in courses, such as Douglas Seefeldt's Digital History, engaged in archival research and built the digital archive, making University of Nebraska history discoverable through the web. The chapter from the University of Vermont demonstrates how students in an American Ethnic Studies course utilized an unfinished digitized archival collection in an online class while they contributed to its production.

The focus of these chapters is on pedagogy; the reader will find much that is replicable and adaptable in the examples from a variety of institutions of different sizes, populations, and locales, and with a range of archival and special collections.

THE ARTIFACT

While the eleven case studies in the section on the artifact often employ innovative teaching methods and are part of larger programs, their essential focus is on the objects themselves, their contexts, and what they can tell us. Even though the artifact is central, many of techniques employed in helping students to understand them is transferable to similar—and sometimes wildly different—objects.

Featured artifacts range from medieval manuscripts to ultramodern artists' books. Eric Johnson unpacks a medieval manuscript at Ohio State University to teach students what the book has to offer even if they can't read the text. At Oxford, students "speed-date" with medieval manuscripts, figuring out as much as they can by careful observation. Toni Bowers and her students at the University of Pennsylvania prepared a transcript of their final class on the "Pamela Craze," in which they explore what they learned through a semester-long investigation of Richardson's popular novel and its many spinoffs. Two different case studies from Johns Hopkins investigate reading and libraries in the late Middle Ages to the Early Renaissance and in the 19th century. The case study from Wake Forest uses a novel pedagogical approach, with a librarian "embedded" in a class, to introduce students to the materiality of Renaissance texts.

At Eastern Carolina University, students research the history of their state through the "North Carolina artifact assignment," which involves intensive study and contextualizing of a single document. Programs and courses at St. John's University and Skidmore take artists' books as their jumping off point. At Colorado College, two librarians from different departments taught a short, intensive course exploring the history and future of the book using a hands on approach. Finally, Michael Paulus presents the "sources continuum," exploring the relationships among primary, secondary, and tertiary sources, and how a given artifact can exhibit the properties of different types of sources at different times. This case study offers a new theory of archival epistemology that is guaranteed to open students' (and librarians' and faculty's) eyes.

THE WORK

The programs described by the twelve institutions who contributed to "The Work" vary significantly. The authors of these chapters each write about programs where students are involved directly in the work of special collections as part of coursework, as student workers, or in internships. The impact of these experiences on students' choices of majors and careers is documented in Jim Gerencser's analysis of former special collections interns at Dickinson.

While undergraduates may not possess the level of expertise of special collections librarians or archivists, their work experiences touch on nearly every aspect of special collections work from collection building through exhibit curation and programming. Steve Rice's historiography students at Ramapo College initiated the development of a collection of American history textbooks from the nineteenth and twentieth centuries. At the University of Delaware, a student collected oral histories to document an African-American neighborhood adjacent to the campus.

The growth of service-learning within the college curriculum has provided another avenue for students to engage with special collections. While most projects described in these case studies were focused on collections within the home institution library, several projects provided assistance to affiliated collections. As part of the service-learning component of a public history course at the University of Hawaii Hilo, students worked with a collection of 8000 images that was donated to the Northern Hawaii Education and Research Center. At Tulane, again as part of a service-learning requirement, history students worked with the Amistad Research Center with the goal of gaining an introduction to archival studies, as well as "a better understanding of the need to preserve and make accessible the historical record of underrepresented peoples."

In some case studies, students contributed many hours to rehousing and processing archival materials. As Dickinson's Malinda Triller notes, the development of finding aids and basic metadata to accompany collections presents its own challenges when done by students with minimal training. Working at an entirely different level, Rachel Buurma's student assistants at Swarthmore are involved in developing rich descriptive database of paratextual information in early English novels, a project which enables a much deeper engagement with the materials than typically allowed by a semester-long project.

Several of these case studies discuss class projects to develop exhibits. The scope of these projects ranges from major exhibits to one or two cases. At Bryn Mawr College, students curated an exhibit on Medieval Books of Hours and, at Carleton College, students worked with materials at the other end of the time continuum—artists' books. An intern working with the Ulysses S. Grant papers at Mississippi State wrote about researching and curating a small exhibit based upon a single postcard. Often these exhibits had both a physical and virtual presence.

Nearly all of these case studies describe projects that are the result of collaborations among students, librarians or archivists and faculty. In many cases faculty and students contributed to authoring the chapters. They are honest accounts which detail the challenges as well as the rewards in undertaking these projects.

Past or Portal? includes case studies to interest just about everybody. We hope that you will find this collection useful and inspiring!

NOTES

1. Philip N. Cronenwett, Kevin Osborn, Samuel A. Streit, eds. *Celebrating research: rare and special collections from the membership of the Association of Research Libraries.* (Washington, DC: Association of Research Libraries, c2007).

THE
ARTIFACT

The History and Future of the Book, a Half-Block Course at Colorado College

Steve Lawson and Jessy Randall

INTRODUCTION

In January of 2010, we (Steve Lawson, Humanities Liaison Librarian and Jessy Randall, Curator of Special Collections) co-taught a half-credit class at Colorado College entitled The History and Future of the Book. Using CC Special Collections materials, we examined the development of technologies of the written word, from clay tablets and sheepskin scrolls to the manuscript codex, early printed book, modern printing, and digital text. During the course of the course (as it were), we expected our students to question the ways reading, writing, and preserving texts intersect with identity, memory, and history. We also incorporated a hands-on experience at The Press at Colorado College—and all this in just nine days. The subject matter and learning goals for the class are not unique, but this integration of the press, the highly compressed timeline for the class, and the collaborations we realized across the college are worth discussing in the context of bringing Special Collections and undergraduates together in a meaningful way.

COLORADO COLLEGE

While we believe that the lessons of our experience are widely applicable, Colorado College has several advantages when it comes to teaching a course like The History and Future of the Book. The College follows an unusual academic calendar called "The Block Plan." Each semester is divided into four "blocks" of three and a half weeks duration. During a block, students take only one class and faculty likewise teach one class. Classes usually meet for three hours

in the morning, and sometimes also have afternoon sessions such as labs.

In addition to the eight full blocks, during January the College has a "half-block" at the end of winter break. These half-block courses are optional for students and carry a half-credit. It was this half-block option that made our course possible. Since we are both full-time librarians, it was unlikely we could neglect our regular responsibilities for a full block during the regular year, but during half-block the campus is significantly quieter. Instead of doing catch-up projects during that time, we took on co-teaching The History and Future of the Book. (This meant, of course, that our catch-up projects multiplied about a thousandfold by the time we were back at our desks, but that was a consequence we were willing to accept.)

PREHISTORY OF THE COURSE

We had long wanted to collaborate on a course on book history, first discussing the idea in 2003. Both of us have experience with special collections, handling and researching old or rare books, and working with students individually or in small groups to explain topics touching on the history of books, or the material nature of books as objects. Neither of us had taught a course in book history, though we had both done extensive library instruction and Jessy had taught a community college course on children's literature.

At Colorado College, librarians do not have faculty status, and for-credit courses taught by college staff are rare (though not unknown). Already determined to collaborate with each other in the library, we realized that we would have to be prepared to collaborate with a professor or even an entire academic department in order to find a sponsor who would shepherd our course through the approval process. After talking to a few professors in likely departments, we found that we would have the strongest support from Carol Neel, a professor of history who took it upon herself to ensure that the course would happen and would be listed under the history department's offerings. Carol has long-standing ties to the Press at Colorado College and was eager to find opportunities to get more students involved with the Press. The process strengthened informal ties between the library and the history department in general, and, more specifically, led to a fruitful working relationship for us with Professor Neel.

An early step toward teaching our course was embedding ourselves in Neel's Cultures of the Book class, a First Year Experience class taught over two blocks in the fall of 2008. This was a history course for first year students with a strong book history element; the class read writers from St. Augustine to Milan Kundera and viewed films including *The Name of the Rose* and *Fahrenheit 451*. An experience at the Press at Colorado College was part of the class; using a text from manuscript material in Special Collections along with their own expertise, the students designed and printed a small book about American slang of the past and present.

We attended Neel's class as often as we could while still seeing to our work in the library. In the classroom, under the leadership of Neel, we found ourselves in dual roles of student and teacher, sometimes nearly simultaneously. We might know a great deal about one day's topic and next to nothing about another. Overall, though, the experience gave us a great deal of insight as to what it was like to hold a class on the block plan. Our half-block, offered a year and a half later, focused more on the book as object and current-day reading technologies; our syllabus ended up being quite different from Neel's.

But our embedding experience was invaluable: we took away from it a sense of the myriad ways a class can work, and a feeling of confidence that we could actually develop and teach our course.

ASSIGNMENTS AND DISCUSSIONS

As we began writing our syllabus we realized that a chronological approach was too simplistic for our purposes. Instead, we organized our time thematically, with readings and discussions covering the book as object (starting with the question "What is a book?"), the history of reading technologies, books and owners, digital literature, preservation and loss, and bibliomania. Our overview text was David Pearson's *Books as History* (Oak Knoll, 2008) and we chose additional readings from major authors in the field of book history (Nicholson Baker, Nicholas Basbanes, John Carter, Robert Chartier, Richard Clement, Robert Darnton, Daniel Traister) and also included extremely current opinion pieces and articles, some of which were published during the time the course was running. Since this was a course about books and reading, we made sure to read an actual start-to-finish *book*, and chose a novel, Ray Bradbury's *Fahrenheit 451*.

Our first written assignment also functioned as a "get to know you" exercise. We asked our students to read John Scalzi's response to the internet meme "15 Things About Me and Books" (http://www.scalzi.com/whatever/003906.html) and to write similar lists that would give us all an idea of the place books held in that person's life. Responses were posted to the class's courseware page.

When we discussed the book as object we asked the students to delve into the anatomy of books (using John Carter's *The ABC of Book Collecting*) to describe the physical characteristics of particular books. We had a motley collection of 19th and 20th century books which we handed out to the students for them to describe. When we told them to write two pages describing their books, some of our students looked at us askance thinking they wouldn't be able to fill up even one page, but most found that it was easy to complete the assignment once they started trying to describe the paper, the type, the binding, and (in some cases) the dust jacket, even without getting into the condition of their books. We talked about the difference between describing a book for identification purposes vs. commercial ones, and even held a mock book auction one morning during our discussion of bibliomania. (One of our students experienced auction fever and overbid his imaginary budget!)

Our most unusual, exciting, and popular assignment was surely the project at the Press, which was a manageable, bite-size printing project—a small accordion-fold book, made by letterpress printing a single large sheet and dividing it into three strips. Each student was responsible for choosing and typesetting a quote about books or reading, and each student received two copies of the finished product. This project only succeeded because Colin Frazer, the printer at the Press at the time, did most of the preparation and post-printing work; if our students had had to do everything, only a simple broadside project would have been feasible.

We designed our other assignments to be both academic and practical. Early in the course, we asked our students to *handwrite* a short response paper to the night's reading; instead of sharing these via electronic means (as we shared much of our work), we had the students bring their handwritten responses to class, place them on our large seminar table, and then walk around the room looking at them. This brought us a concrete understanding of the difference between disseminating electronic texts vs. physical ones. Some students did the bare minimum; others made beautiful, crafted text-objects for us to admire.

Thinking like librarians, we designed a final project that wasn't a paper but rather a plan for a small imaginary exhibition of five items on some aspect of book history. This seemed a good way to allow them to get deeper into particular subjects that interested

them, and indeed, their topics ranged widely, from early Korean government documents to digital poetry. We expected them to provide images of the items in the imaginary exhibition, exhibition labels for them, and a short overview or exhibition introduction. They gave five-minute presentations on their exhibitions on the last day of class.

Our least successful assignment was probably a speculation paper. After reading *Fahrenheit 451*, we asked the students to speculate about the future of books and reading. Instead of the creative, well-thought-out arguments we expected, we mostly received grand statements about our students' love of physical books.

REFLECTIONS AND EVALUATION
Student Learning

In the planning process for the class, we had to agree on learning outcomes, readings, assignments, approaches to the material, and so on. Defining our learning outcomes was an extremely valuable exercise for us, because it helped us define, for ourselves, just what we wanted to accomplish. We stated our learning outcomes in this way in the syllabus:

Upon successful completion of the course, students will be able to :

- Use specialized vocabulary for describing and discussing books as objects;
- Set type and operate a printing press as a novice printer to gain a greater understanding of the creation of hand-set books;
- Draw conclusions and make predictions about the future of books and reading which are grounded in an understanding of both the history of the book and the contemporary situation;
- Use specific historical examples from the history of the book to propose and support a proposition about books, printing, reading, or the like.

Because we were explicitly interested in talking about the future, we were often challenged to keep class discussions based in facts or in the actual texts that we read instead of unsupported speculation. In addition, we became aware of a sense of self-satisfaction among our students, a feeling that we were "the people of the book" and therefore superior to non-readers. If we'd understood this right away and looked at it critically, it might have made for a good discussion: *Are readers morally superior to non-readers? Why do some people think that? What are the flaws in that argument?* But instead we allowed the feeling to snowball, so that as the class went on some of our students seemed to think that simply by stating their beliefs or emotions about books—their love for the smell of the pages, etc.—they'd please us and earn a good grade.

A useful term for us throughout the class was *affordances*, visual clues to the function of an object. We asked, *What are the affordances of a paper-and-binding book compared to the affordances of a text on a Kindle or a computer screen.* As it happened, we had one student in the class who owned a Kindle and used it regularly. We tried not to push him into speaking for all Kindle users, but we often found ourselves turning to him when the class needed a different point of view. In future years we plan to use a college-purchased Kindle and/or iPad or other device students could take turns using to better inform our discussion of the affordances of different reading technologies.

Ironically, though our students generally claimed to prefer paper-and-binding books to digital reading devices, they seemed reluctant to use paper-and-binding books in their research for their class assignments. But perhaps this is not so ironic—they generally agreed that paper-and-binding books were preferred for certain kinds of reading, such as pleasure reading or novel reading, whereas reading for research was quite different.

Collaboration

The class was valuable for us as a chance to collaborate in new ways. (We believe our team-teaching was valuable to the students, too.) We had collaborated on library work in the past, but the kind of collaboration that goes into planning, teaching, and grading a brand new course is different than the kind of collaboration that we had done before. We had a strong, even daunting sense of responsibility and accountability toward our as-yet-unmet students—these would be OUR students, and we would be able to run the course exactly as we pleased. Ironically, we realized after we'd finished teaching the course that we never scheduled a library instruction session for our students—something that would have benefited them greatly. So an unintended bonus of teaching the class was a greater understanding of the difficulty CC faculty have in scheduling library instruction.

In the classroom, our collaboration was less planned-out and more intuitive. Typically, we would discuss in advance which of us would be responsible for which lectures or discussions that we would lead. But a lively seminar class typically breaks down those established boundaries, and we needed to be sensitive to each other as well as the class as a whole.

There were times when we disagreed in class, in a friendly way—for example, when we asked the class "What is a book?". A lively discussion followed. At one point, Jessy differentiated between a *book* (a physical object) and a *text* (the words of a particular version of *The Wizard of Oz*, for example, which might be published or distributed in various ways). Steve defined book more broadly, saying that if he read a text on a Kindle, he would still say that he had read a book. In advance of the class, this sort of disagreement seemed like something to avoid, but during the actual discussion it had no negative effect, and possibly even gave our students implicit permission to disagree. More important, our friendly, respectful disagreement served as a model for the discussion—we genuinely wanted to know each other's views, and were willing to rethink our own statements. We were also able to live with a certain amount of ambiguity and multiple possible answers, just as we expected our students to be.

Collaboration continued outside of the classroom, as we needed to be attuned to each other's standards when dealing with students. When it came to grading, we had to explicitly discuss our standards and rationales, but this need for consistency and agreement was also important when talking to students about their assignments informally. We kept each other abreast of what we had told students about their proposals or drafts, so that students wouldn't get a mixed message from the two of us. Because we had already been collaborating so intensely on the course, there were few times when we differed about the advice or grades that we gave to students. In cases where we did differ, we had to accept that speaking with one voice was more important that one person getting his or her way. (We always leaned toward the higher grade when we differed on grades.)

One of the hazards of collaboration is scheduling. To accommodate the printer's schedule, we began our printing project toward the end of our course, but in retrospect we wish we could have visited the Press much earlier. Because we hadn't yet seen the actual printing presses when we discussed the invention of movable type, our students were a bit lost; five minutes at the Press would have made it abundantly clear how movable type works.

When the students filled out evaluations on the last day of class, they all remarked upon the benefits of having two instructors; none saw team-teaching as a minus, a result which surprised at least one of us. Because we didn't speak with one voice, the students understood that we didn't expect them to receive just one view of the history and future of the book. A solo instructor, of course, could also make this clear, but it is easily apparent when two instructors regularly offer different views, ask different questions, and geek out in different ways.

FUTURE OF THE COURSE

The History and Future of the Book supports CC's minor in The Book (the past, present, and future of the written word in its material form); the minor, like the half-credit class, was offered for the first time in the 2009-2010 school year. It requires students to take courses in Art, English, and History. The fact that the minor is now official seems to indicate that there will be continued demand for our half-block class.

Indeed, when we taught the class again in January 2012, we had 24 students (compared to 16) and had to reserve a larger classroom and rework the printing project to accommodate the larger group. Our syllabus changed dramatically, as we expect it will every time. In 2012, we read Geraldine Brooks's *The People of the Book* instead of Bradbury, and were able to pass a Kindle and an iPad around the classroom. We focused less on predicting the future and more on how the different material forms of the written word help books make their meaning.

FURTHER READING

For more information about this course and CC's book minor, including full syllabi, please visit: http://www2.coloradocollege.edu/library/index.php/SpecialCollections/BookMinor/

Rebooting the Old North State: Connecting Undergraduates with State Focused Special Collections Materials

L.K. Gypsye Legge, Matthew Reynolds, and Dale Sauter

HISTORY

In 2001, Joyner Library's Special Collections Department, the Verona Joyner Langford North Carolina Collection and the East Carolina University's Department of English, jointly developed the "North Carolina Artifact Assignment" to demystify special collections and encourage students to engage actively in meaningful historical research early in their college careers. The assignment requires second semester English composition students to select an artifact that focuses on an aspect of North Carolina history and put it into its historical context. Since its beginning, the project has proven quite successful and now reaches more than 1,000 students per year. In its recent history, the project has seen some changes. These changes include digitization of a variety of artifacts, changes to instructional spaces, shifts in the assignment's scheduling and topical focus, and the introduction of online bibliographic instruction components.

INTRODUCING THE ASSIGNMENT

As mentioned above, the assignment asks second semester English Composition students to select an artifact from either the library's North Carolina Collection or Special Collections and write a 4-6 page research paper that puts the student's chosen object into its historical context. Before the selection process takes place, students attend library instruction sessions in the library's smart classrooms. The sessions include a review of available resources, finding aids, and specialized procedures for researching in a special col-

lections setting. Two separate orientation sessions are warranted as Joyner's Special Collections and North Carolina Collection units, though having a similar collection focus, differ somewhat in the availability and uniqueness of their materials. While Special Collections consists almost entirely of unique archival materials, none of which circulate, the North Carolina Collection exists as a blended collection that includes secondary resources that are available for borrowing. At the end of the instruction sessions, students are taken to the two collections for a brief tour. After attending the initial orientation, many English Department instructors opt for a second in-house work session, staffed with additional personnel, to aid students with artifact selection and to answer any questions.

An example of how an artifact is put into greater historical context is the connection made by ECU student D.J. Fussel III, who discovered and wrote about a photograph in a local state-focused magazine from the 1970s. The article featured an image of two vintners, both related to Fussel, as well as a written account of how they operated their winery. During the research process he delved deeply into both primary and secondary resources and was so inspired by his work that he decided to change his major to History and also won an undergraduate writing award for his essay, "From Vines to Wine: The Story of Duplin Winery."[1]

THE ARTIFACTS

The foundations for all these activities are the items

themselves. For the purposes of this assignment an artifact is a typically considered a primary source such as map, image, newspaper article, or manuscript greater than 40 years old that is viewed in physical or digital form. Examples of recently cited artifacts include an 1883 biography of a former slave, a 1909 North Carolina railroad map, and a 1969 newspaper article focusing on the draft lottery for the Vietnam War and quoting North Carolinians.

While the majority of each department's holdings are physically available, it was recognized that asynchronous digital access for student researchers would be beneficial. Digital access could help overcome common "impediments" of using special collections materials, particularly given the high volume of use by 1,000 students annually, the risk of damage to fragile items, and the fact that space in the "search rooms" is at premium. Additionally, digital access to materials reduced student concerns of working under the direct supervision of a Special Collections representative, with pencils only and white gloves on occasion, long waits for requested items, and negotiating limited service hours. Digitized materials also give students a chance to interact with these materials in a consequence-free environment. They can be downloaded, manipulated, and if changed beyond recognition can be downloaded fresh again. Undergraduates are very interested in taking possession of their research materials and in an environment where they are unable to check out the item, a digital surrogate allows them the ownership that they crave.

As a first step, over 500 rare materials related to North Carolina were digitized from both the Special Collections and the North Carolina Collection and mounted on the Web in 2003 as the Eastern North Carolina Digital Library [ENCDL].[2] More recently, the library's digitization efforts have expanded dramatically and the ENCDL is now part of a much larger digital repository that allows students direct access via the library catalog or via links to digitized items through finding aids. This expanded Digital Collection is searchable through a robust metadata that finds or presents item information in a variety of ways including an assigned subject cloud, a keyword search box and collection browsing.

The Digital Collections user interface goes beyond giving students simple access to the item through the use of user-generated tags and comments. It is now possible for visitors to the Web pages to better identify or classify an item's subject matter or historical context that may not be discerned with top down assigned subject headings. For example, an image of a child who has had polio[3] may have been identified by an archivist as a 1956 image of a three year old, but an Allied Health major may see an early example of physical therapy in the leg braces worn, or occupational therapy in the toys in the image. Not all students will engage with an item at any level beyond the assignment, but the possibility is there so that with online access the engagement and contribution can be immediate and provide a sense of ownership for the student researchers.

CHALLENGES AND CHANGES IN LIBRARY INSTRUCTION

Several challenges have presented themselves throughout the lifetime of the project, including changes in instruction locations, scheduling of the assignment during the semester, shifts in the assignment's focus, and making the most out of sometimes short contact times with students during bibliographic instruction sessions. Maintaining flexibility and open communication between both library units and the English Department faculty has been key to continued success of the program.

The first challenge was shifting the locations for student instruction sessions. In the past, North Carolina Collections orientations were taking place in the aforementioned space while those for Special Collections took place in their reading room. Now, however, all student orientation sessions are conducted in rooms specifically designed for bibliographical instruction that are shared with the library's Reference Department. These facilities include smart podiums, advanced projecting equipment, and computing terminals for all students. Access to computers was of paramount importance so students could complete guided exercises showing them how to navigate the departments' various finding aids.

The large presence of unique materials in Special Collections warrants that research regulations must be more rigorous and intense than in the North Carolina Collection. Therefore, one compromise instituted with the location change was to bring all students to the Special Collections reading room during the last fifteen minutes of the orientation sessions. It was felt that this additional visit was important in order to give students a sense of location. It also afforded the opportunity for staff to introduce necessary research tools such as the Special Collections' reference book collection and other features of the department, including public computers and security lockers.

Finding an appropriate time to complete the assignment during the semester has also proved to be a challenge. Due to the more involved procedures required for research in Special Collections, staff-to-student ratio problems, and competition with the Reference Department for classroom space, the English instructors were asked to stagger the due dates for the assignments throughout their semester schedule. In the case of the North Carolina Collection, this scheduling change reduced collection stress and made time for secondary resources checked out by students to be returned and reshelved in time for the next set of classes to begin work. It was also requested of the instructors to limit the number of students in their class to fifteen who chose to use Special Collections (versus the unlimited North Carolina Collection) for their project. The typical class size is approximately twenty-five students. These changes, along with the offer by both Special Collections and North Carolina Col-

lection staff to provide follow-up sessions upon request to any students and instructors who needed review, greatly helped increase the efficiency of the procedures involved in completing the project.

The project has also had two changes in its focus that have required some minor modification of bibliographic instruction sessions and relevant sample artifacts that were shown to students. Both changes resulted from new textbook adoptions within the Department of English in support of the English Composition course. The first was a change to a reader that featured essays that focused on the theme of citizenship. Fortunately, the reader defined citizenship broadly, allowing for students to focus on anything from volunteerism or historic preservation, to civil rights and beyond. One popular series of artifacts related to this theme is the Greensboro Record's daily newspaper articles covering the 1960s Greensboro lunch counter sit-ins and ensuing racial confrontations and political changes.

More recently, a second reader has been introduced that focused on career issues, and asked students to choose an artifact that related to their chosen vocation and write an article that would be suitable for inclusion in a trade journal associated with that vocation. Nursing and public health majors particularly enjoy the images of truck-based tuberculosis x-ray machines, viewing them as investigatory tools for research on changes in disease, technology, and rural medicine. Though helping the students find proper artifacts that fit within this changed assignment framework was sometimes difficult, especially with certain new professions such as computer programming or physical therapy, staff and students working creatively and collaboratively could find appropriate sources. It is recognized that the focus of the assignment will continue to change over time, but the broad and varied nature of our collections can continue to meet future challenges.

The last, and perhaps most daunting challenge, has been finding ways to maximize the impact of the contact time with students. Over the years library instructors have found that fitting all lessons into a 50 minute presentation is difficult. This is especially true for Special Collections' sessions, as there are so many more procedures of which students need to be aware before beginning research. One resolution to this has been the recent creation of a series of video tutorials using Adobe's Camtasia software package. Though the tutorials were designed primarily with the freshman project in mind, they were also made to be of value to long-distance researchers and first time in-house researchers who are not familiar with the collections and procedures.

In light of the limited interaction time with composition students, it is now possible to have students view the tutorials focusing on basic procedures and research skills before the instruction session, allowing library instructors to focus on answering questions, engaging students in guided exercises, and showing more examples of artifacts that would serve as an ideal focus for their projects. In the case of the North Carolina Collection, compulsory viewing of the tutorials was facilitated by the addition of a short online quiz, the results of which were automatically emailed to the instructor. An added value of these tutorials is the opportunity for students to review procedures and the use of finding aids at the time of need should they find themselves with questions when engaging in independent research.

IMPLEMENTATION SUGGESTIONS

As shown above, the proven flexibility of the assignment and continued success both positively reflect on the value of the relationships developed with not only the students involved in the project, but their faculty as well. The key to success is to meet with faculty in other departments with the well-developed proposal that highlights the value of writing across the curriculum through the use of Special Collections resources. Furthermore, it is beneficial to collaborate with them to create an assignment flexible enough to withstand small changes in focus but simple enough that it that can be easily implemented and incorporated into the syllabi for lower-level university courses that are taught primarily by adjunct faculty or temporary graduate assistants. By making clear to the faculty and graduate students the value of such an assignment and the fact that it would be easy to fold into their curriculum, librarians can ensure that use of primary sources is an integral part of the students' college experience.

CONCLUSION

This project has shown that special collections libraries can develop engaging programs in collaboration with other campus departments to create active student researchers. This value is stressed by one of our library instructors who seeks to inspire students in instruction sessions by informing them that "… even undergraduate students can make an original contribution to knowledge through use of primary sources that perhaps no one else has used before."[4] Any way that we can encourage use of the library and its facilities and reduce or remove students' lack of knowledge about, or the trepidation that often accompanies, approaching primary sources moves us all closer to meeting our shared mission.

NOTES

1. http://www.ecu.edu/cs-lib/reference/instruction/DuplinWinery.cfm

2. http://digital.lib.ecu.edu/historyfiction/

3. http://digital.lib.ecu.edu/2763

4. York, M., reiterated in personal communication via email, Tuesday, June 29, 2010.

Teaching by the Book: The Culture of Reading in the George Peabody Library

Gabrielle Dean

First, there is a gasp or sigh; then the wide-eyed viewer slowly circumnavigates the building. In the George Peabody Library, one of the Johns Hopkins University's rare book libraries, I often witness this awe-struck response to the architecture. The library interior, made largely of cast iron, illuminated by a huge skylight and decorated with gilded neo-Gothic and Egyptian elements, was completed in 1878 and fully expresses the aspirations of the age. It is gaudy and magnificent, and it never fails to impress visitors.

The contents of the library are equally symbolic and grand, but less visible. The Peabody first opened to the Baltimore public in 1866 as part of the Peabody Institute, an athenaeum-like venture set up by the philanthropist George Peabody; it originally included a lecture series and an art gallery in addition to the library and the renowned conservatory. The library's collection was built with Peabody's generous bequest, augmented by book donations from community benefactors. These early acquisitions were oriented towards the "best works on every subject" so that the library would be "well furnished in every department of knowledge, and of the most approved literature."[1] The library was open "for the free use of all persons who may desire to consult it," although its materials did not circulate.[2] The Peabody became the de facto library for the new Johns Hopkins University when it opened up a few blocks away in 1876, and the librarians purchased books with their academic neighbors in mind. The collection, as it grew, reflected these local conditions.

This collection in its splendid house was the core of an undergraduate seminar I taught called "Read-ing Culture in the Nineteenth-Century Library," which examined the intersections of the public library movement, nineteenth-century book history and popular literature in order to describe the culture of reading in nineteenth-century America. I designed this semester-long course with two complementary aims in mind.

First, I wanted to develop a new model for teaching American literature. Instead of proceeding from a set of texts deemed significant by twenty-first century critics, our syllabus drew from the Peabody's collections to gain insight into what was actually purchased, promoted and read in the nineteenth century. Moreover, there was no artificial separation between the texts we examined and their material contexts. My own research focuses on the print culture environments of American literature, but I have found it difficult in the past to present this history in my American literature courses due to the logistical constraints of the regular classroom. Studying the library's collections in the library itself, students had access not just to the words on the page but to the pages themselves—plus their illustrations, inscriptions and bindings. By extension, the physicality of the books was intimately tied to the physical features of the library space. The course offered students an "inside out" view of American literary history—one that originated in literature as it was read in its own time, and as represented by its material traces in the Peabody.

Secondly, I wanted to initiate new avenues of library use. The challenges that face many special collections outreach efforts are amplified in the case of the Peabody. The Peabody is glamorous indeed, but it is located about 2.5 miles from the Hopkins Homewood campus where students in the arts and sciences, engineering and education are based. The 15-minute ride on the free campus shuttle is a stretch for busy undergraduates with back-to-back classes. Most of the Rare Book and Manuscript department's rare book class sessions take place in the main campus library, even when they involve books from the Peabody. Moreover, many researchers prefer to read digitized versions of books and periodicals rather than make a trip to the library; this phenomenon will increase as more and more "medium rare" books become available online. As a result, most of the Peabody's visitors are tourists, community groups and advanced researchers. So I designed this course to generate familiarity with and excitement about the Peabody, through the course itself and through its after-life, a student-curated exhibit of Peabody books to be displayed both in the main campus library and online. In short, I wanted the course to illuminate the Peabody from the "outside in"—to bring attention to the collection through a sharper sense of what this utterly amazing library meant to nineteenth-century readers.

COURSE DESIGN: A BALANCING ACT

The course was cross-listed in English and the Program in Museums & Society. As an English course, it would need to provide insight into literary history and guidance in reading literature; as a Museums & Society course, it had to address issues related to material culture and institutional collection-building. It was also designated a "W" course, which meant it had to incorporate a certain amount of writing instruction, feedback and revision. Finally, there was the location issue: I wanted class to meet at the Peabody itself, despite the difficulty this would create for students. This variety of curricular needs and goals made planning rather tricky.

In view of the location issue—crucial to making the Peabody more visible from the "outside in"—I set a weekly meeting schedule so students would have to travel as infrequently as possible. I also planned to shift to project-related class sessions in week 10 of our 15-week semester, so that students would have time in class to conduct research for their exhibits.

These scheduling adaptations, necessary as they were, put additional pressure on my goal to teach nineteenth-century American literature from the "inside out." I could not assume that students would have the background that would make this perspective intelligible. The benefit of teaching literature in the usual way is that students already know how to proceed: you crack open your anthology or reprint; you read, discuss and write about the assigned texts. Students might also have prior experience with the modes of interpretation native to this method—formal, historical or theory-based criticism. But an approach to literature that develops out of reading culture and the material book? That was likely to be unfamiliar. If I wanted to convey the impact on nineteenth-century reading practices of the inter-connected phenomena of increased literacy, increasingly cheap printed matter and public libraries, I was going to have to illustrate those changes against a historical backdrop.

So the course began with a whirlwind introduction to the material history of the book—from Sumerian clay tablets and papyrus scrolls, to parchment manuscript codices, to early printed books and engravings on paper. We then decelerated to spend several weeks examining the "everyday" reading of the seventeenth, eighteenth and nineteenth centuries: bibles, almanacs, chapbooks, grammars and other books for children, periodicals, gift books and cheap novels. Along the way, we read articles (these were on e-reserve, accessible through the course management system and the library website) about the early modern book market, "intensive" and "extensive" reading, and the history of child literacy.[3]

Having landed in the nineteenth century, we switched our focus over the next three weeks to the history of libraries. Here the point was to show how nineteenth-century public libraries responded to and supported the spread of literacy and affordable reading matter, but also put certain restrictions on reading. Some historical background was again necessary: first, a summary of library history from ancient times to the present; then a look at eighteenth and early nineteenth-century social libraries, exemplified by some wonderful marked-up and dog-eared catalogues of mechanics, subscription and circulating libraries, along with books that had been featured in them. This class was taught by a guest lecturer with expertise in the history of libraries. Then we spent two weeks reading about the advent of the public library movement and some of the social dilemmas it stirred up. One such dilemma, about appropriate reading for young women, was illustrated with a brief examination of sentimental novels—a class of reading matter that did not pass muster in many public libraries even though it was wildly popular.

This background on public libraries set us up to investigate the Peabody itself in more detail over the course of the next two weeks. We ventured into the Peabody archives to learn how the library fit into the larger social mission of the Institute; this session was led by the Peabody Institute archivist and the head of our special collections department. We read about the Peabody's early collection policies. And we explored the building, to understand how the Peabody's architecture brought "new" technology to a socially progressive vision that was, paradoxically, grounded in the past. That is, both the building and the collection were oriented towards the cultural legacies that the founders wanted to pass on.

During this examination of the Peabody, students were encouraged to start thinking about their final projects—the task that took up the remaining five weeks of the semester. These last classes were largely devoted to project research, writing, peer review and individual conferences with me and with another curator, a specialist in the early modern pe-

riod, who advised them on pre-1800 items in their collections. For our last meeting, students gave short presentations on their exhibit projects.

ASSIGNMENTS: THREE COMPLEMENTARY PIECES

The big unknown in the course design was the student-curated exhibit. Would we collectively create one exhibit, or would students make their own? Would the exhibit actually be installed by semester's end, or would students simply prepare the materials for it? How would the digital and physical versions of the exhibit relate? Weighing these options in conversation with the head of the Program in Museums and Society, I realized I would have to let students design their own final projects—collaboration on such a labor-intensive project requiring on-site research would be impossible in terms of scheduling. I also figured that a variety of topics would do a better job of "advertising" the Peabody to exhibit viewers. This decision led to the next: if students were going to build individual exhibits from scratch, there was no way we could also have the exhibit installed by the end of the semester. So students would create portfolios of exhibit materials in the spring, which I would then steer into readiness for display in the fall. I would make selections from their collections for the physical exhibit, and digitize images of their entire collections for a new exhibit platform that colleagues in the library were starting to put into place.

With these basic parameters in mind, I developed guidelines for the exhibit project and two complementary assignments. Given that the exhibit would require "practical" writing for a non-academic audience, I wanted one assignment to exercise academic writing skills. And I also wanted one assignment to be somewhat creative and personal—something that would help students approach the exhibit project with ingenuity and an individualized sense of "reading culture."

The assignment that addressed this last aim was a commonplace book—a reading diary. Students would record each week a selection of passages from the assigned reading and add their own commentary. Since the keeping of commonplace books was an established practice in the nineteenth century, this exercise would help them understand historical reading practices and see their own reading practices in historical context. Of course, it was also intended to encourage students to do the reading and ask questions—particularly important tasks since our weekly meetings had to accommodate time for looking at books as well as discussion. As often happens with journal assignments, students did not document their command of the reading as much as I would have liked, but the ways they used the assignment to explore their own ideas were closer to the original function of commonplace books than I had anticipated. In keeping with our focus on books as material objects, I also asked them to consider carefully the forms of their books. One student wrote hers as a blog; two others chose to handwrite their entries to get the feeling for "old-fashioned" composition.[4] I collected their commonplace books twice during the semester and gave my feedback in letters, another kind of everyday writing practice in the period under study.

The grading criteria for the commonplace books were relatively relaxed; accordingly, I wanted the more academic assignment—with higher stakes in terms of grading—to be somewhat familiar while also targeting the largely unfamiliar course topics. The "Poe in periodicals" paper, due at mid-term, drew on student experience with the essay genre but also asked them to think about literary "content" in new ways. Students chose one of four magazine issues edited by Edgar Allan Poe, with multiple contributions by Poe.[5] They then read the print and electronic versions of their selected issue; the print versions were available to them in the main campus RBMS reading room for several weeks before the due date, and the electronic versions were accessible through ProQuest's *American Periodical Series*

Online. After reading the magazines in these different forms and locations, students had to write an argument-driven essay comparing the two versions by, first, identifying important differences, especially in the pieces by Poe; then describing how those differences changed their experience of reading; and, finally, discussing the implications for contemporary libraries of these different textual states and readerly practices.

The final assignment—the exhibit project—switched the emphasis from the students' own experiences reading historical materials to the reading experiences of nineteenth-century library patrons themselves. Each student created a book collection from the Peabody's holdings focused on a topic that would have been meaningful to the Peabody's readers in the first decades of its existence. Students then interpreted their collections through a set of materials, turned in and revised on a staggered schedule, and gathered together into a final portfolio.

First, students had to write a proposal outlining a topic and the historical grounds for the collection. Then they had to find visually appealing and intellectually representative books within the range of this topic; this involved some review of catalog search techniques plus several chaperoned practice sessions paging books from the closed stacks. In addition to the proposal, the portfolio elements included 1) a "finding aid"—a survey of the collection and a brief description of its historical context; 2) an exhibit brochure, which translated the finding aid research into a form that would appeal to a public audience; and 3) labels for each book in the collection of 12 to 20 items. Using actual finding aids and exhibit materials as models, we discussed the writing conventions governing each portfolio element and techniques that would make their collections—the result of their own recently acquired expertise—interesting to non-specialists. Through peer review, conferences and revision, we also looked at titling, item order and connections between items.

IN THE END: SWEET SUCCESS (AND SOME SWEAT)

The final student collections were, in a word, fantastic. Each of the students interpreted the Peabody in light of her own interests and background knowledge—and each touched on an exemplary aspect of the Peabody's collection. One student who fell in love with the children's books we examined early in the semester created "Once Upon a Time: Fairy Tales in the George Peabody Library." Her collection raised questions about the Peabody's definition of its own readership: children were not allowed in the library, so why so many fairy tale books? Her research pointed to the deep connections between the Peabody and Hopkins—where the emerging discipline of anthropology may have encouraged Peabody librarians to buy books about international folklore. A philosophy major created "The Stewardship of a Republic: Ancient Rome and Baltimore." Noting that "ancient Rome occupied a prominent place" in the American imagination in the nineteenth century, she assembled books that showed how the Peabody fed this interest both with specialized works for researchers and more general books for students and lay readers, and speculated that this interest developed because "the lessons of history were especially relevant to nineteenth-century Americans, looking for guidance for their unique situation in the world—a growing, independent power, in the hands of a broad populace." A major in the Writing Seminars focused on a related phenomenon, the American interest in the nature of their new nation, in "Go West, O Pioneers! America's Obsession with the Wilderness." She illustrated what she was learning in another English class about American nature writing with books from the Peabody that demonstrated the many facets of this fixation: explorers' accounts of the riches of the West, "souvenir" books celebrating the American landscape, travel guides for adventurous tourists and stories about "cowboys and Indians"

aimed at youthful readers. My one science major surprised us all by focusing not on science, but religion. For "Under One Roof: Religious Books in the George Peabody Library," she looked at the changing definitions of and relationships between faiths from the seventeenth century through the early twentieth century, in holy books, theological tomes and texts for practitioners—not just the Christian and Jewish books that would have been used most often by local readers in this period, but books pertinent to Islam, Buddhism and Hinduism. The Peabody's ecumenical acquisition policies and multiple communities of readers, both scholarly and popular, led to a collection that, unintentionally, set an "interfaith" precedent long before there was such a thing as an "interfaith center."

Launching any new class takes time, and it is especially true of a course that incorporates experimental methods and assignments! This course took several months to prepare. During the semester, I also spent many hours pulling representative books and working one-on-one with students. After the semester was over, I continued the work by shepherding their wonderful collections into forms tailored to the actual exhibits. Planning around a digital exhibit platform that was simultaneously under development put an additional variable into the equation; ultimately, I decided to photograph many of the students' collections so that the digital exhibit will be ready to mount as soon as the platform is established.

Now that the groundwork has been laid, I am eager to teach the course again. I will do a few things differently next time: find a way to include a nineteenth-century "domestic" novel in the reading; keep the student collections smaller. And, if they are available, I will add to the roster of guest speakers by inviting my wonderful former students to tell us what they know. I want to thank them especially for their hard work, imagination and enthusiasm for learning "by the book."[6]

APPENDIX 3.1
Reading Culture in the Nineteenth-Century Library

Museums & Society / English 389.355
Spring 2010
Peabody Library, Thursdays 2-4:20

Dr. Gabrielle Dean, gnodean@jhu.edu
Office: MSEL M-level, #9, by appointment
Office phone: 410-516-8540; cell 954-512-9194

Reading takes place within a complex cultural context that requires literacy, the production and distribution of textual materials, and specific ideas about time and space. But because it is part of the everyday fabric of life, the culture of reading is hard to identify and define. In this course, we will recover one small piece of the historical culture of reading by investigating the relationship between reading and libraries in nineteenth-century America, with a focus on the George Peabody Library.

In the nineteenth century, the culture of reading was shaped by numerous social patterns. In order to account for this variety, our inquiries will draw from multiple subject areas, including American literary history, the history of the material book and the history of libraries. This interdisciplinary approach will provide insight into a crucial but often obscure feature of nineteenth-century American life.

In addition, this class will offer you first-hand experience doing research with rare books and manuscripts. Our examination of reading culture in the nineteenth-century library will culminate in a double exhibit: a *digital* exhibit of small collections that you curate individually, and a *physical* exhibit of selections from your collections to be displayed at the Eisenhower Library in fall 2010. Students will need therefore to balance traditional academic approaches with curatorial goals. Suggested prerequisites include a background or strong interest in nineteenth-century U.S. literature and/or history; research and writing skills; and an ability and willingness to work as a group.

COURSE REQUIREMENTS

Attendance and participation: Attendance is mandatory because this is a discussion- and project-oriented class. If you need to miss class due to illness or some other unavoidable crisis, please let me know as soon as possible. If you are unable to reach me, contact a classmate. You are responsible for informing yourself of missed material and assignments, and for handing in work on time.

Participation is vital to your success in this course. We will operate as a seminar, so you are expected to add your voice to our conversations. Please come to class ready to think, question, brainstorm, discuss, investigate, and work cooperatively as part of a team.

Readings: Readings are accessible online (use link), via e-reserve (**E**), or will be circulated in class (**C**). Background readings, on e-reserve or regular reserve (**R**), are not required; I have provided them to help you pursue topics that you might find interesting or useful, especially for your final project. You should complete the week's readings before class so that you will be able to participate.

Please note that, as the semester progresses, our learning modality will shift from reading-intensive to project-based methods. In the last few weeks of the course, you will be creating your own reading lists.

Writing assignments: The three writing assignments for the course ask you to engage a range of styles, from the informal to the academic to the practical.

1. Commonplace book. A commonplace book is a collection of passages that a writer copies from other texts, adding commentary. Yours may take any form that you wish—a longhand journal, a set of loose sheets, a blog—and may be organized and embellished in any way you like. It should contain passages that you select from our readings, along with your own interpretations of and responses to those passages. In addition, I will give you four or five brief writing assignments to include in your commonplace book. More details to come. Due 2/25, 4/8 and 5/13.

2. Magazine analysis. You will choose an issue of a magazine edited by Edgar Allan Poe from the 1830s, read the whole issue, then write a 5-page argument-driven essay about it, addressing in part the different experiences of reading in print and online. More details to come. Due 3/12.

3. Exhibit portfolio. Your final project will consist of a portfolio of materials related to a small collection of rare books that you identify, research and prepare for exhibition. The portfolio includes an exhibit proposal, a finding aid for your collection, an exhibit brochure with a bibliography, and labels for the objects. More details to come. Due 5/13.

EVALUATION
Participation   20%
Regular attendance is the foundation of participation. Your participation grade will also be based on the amount of attention and active engagement you demonstrate in class, by asking questions, volunteering your ideas, discussing your classmates' ideas, and responding to my inquiries. If you are curious about your level of participation or would like guidance about how to improve, please ask me.

Commonplace book   20%
Your commonplace book should contain thorough, thoughtful responses to the brief assignments; a selection of passages that shows the breadth of your reading and your understanding of course topics; commentary that raises and pursues challenging questions; creativity and care in the form and organization of the commonplace book; and evidence of effort. You do not need to use formal, academic prose in your commonplace book, but you should pay attention to style and mechanics.

Poe in Periodicals essay 20%
Your essay should make a clear and interesting argument, backing it up with persuasive evidence. Your essay's structure should help your reader follow your ideas, in both the overall organization of the essay and at the level of paragraphs and sentences. Style and mechanics count. Preliminary writing assignments will also affect your final grade.

Exhibit portfolio   40%
Your proposal, finding aid, brochure and labels will be graded for the depth and accuracy of your research, your creative exploration of materials, and the quality of your writing, particularly how well you take care of your audience's needs. Only the final version of the portfolio will be graded, but I will take into account the attention you give to revision, as well as the feedback you provide to your peers.

You must complete all three of the course writing assignments to pass the class. **There are no examinations for this class.**

CLASS POLICIES AND PROCEDURES
Deadlines: Unless otherwise noted, assignments are due at the beginning of class on the day they are due. Late assignments will be accepted, but penalized.

Ethics: Collaboration with classmates is encouraged in this class, especially for the final project; we will discuss how to share work fairly and how to define your own contributions to a group endeavor. Regardless of whether you work on your own or with others, all work you do for this class should reflect your own efforts; any assistance you receive or sources you use need to be acknowledged. Academic misconduct includes but is not limited to plagiarism, forgery, unauthorized collaboration, unfair competition, improper use of the Internet, reuse of assignments, alteration of graded assignments, and lying. If you have questions about this matter as it relates to this course, please consult with me. For general information on such topics as reporting academic misconduct and ethics procedures in the case of suspected misconduct, see "Academic Ethics for Undergraduates" at http://www.jhu.edu/~advising/ethics.html and the Ethics Board website, http://ethics.jhu.edu.

Conduct and esprit de corps: Please show your respect for your classmates and instructor by silencing cell phones, MP3 players, etc. in class and by refraining from non-class related internet activity during class.

Many of us will be dependent on the JHU shuttle for transportation to Mt. Vernon, which may cause delays. Please let me know if you are going to be late for this or another reason. See the JHU shuttle page at http://www.parking.jhu.edu/shuttles_jhmi_homewood.html for more information.

Because we meet in the Peabody Library and will spend most class periods examining rare materials, we cannot have food or drinks in the classroom.

Please feel free to talk with me about your questions and ideas; drop by my Eisenhower office any time on Mondays, Tuesdays or Fridays, visit me at the Peabody on Wednesdays or Thursdays, or make an appointment via email. I've provided my cell number above but please use it only for last-minute notifications about a tardiness or absence.

I look forward to an interesting, productive and fun semester. Welcome!

Week 1, January 28. Introductions.
Introduction to the course. Overview of assignments and introduction to commonplace book assignment. Pre-modern reading culture and the "Gutenberg revolution."

Background
Lotte Hellinga, "The Gutenberg Revolution," from *A Companion to the History of the Book*, 207-219. **E**

In class
Manuscript pages, bibles, books of hours, chain books. Printer's type, engraving plates. Introduce commonplace book assignment.

PART 1: READING CULTURE
Week 2, February 4. The history of reading.
Reading as a historical phenomenon. Also: introduction to Poe in Periodicals assignment.

Reading
John Feather, "The British Book Market 1600-1800," from *A Companion to the History of the Book*, 232-246. **E**

Stephen Colclough, "Readers: Books and Biography," from *A Companion to the History of the Book*, 50-62. **E**

Steven Roger Fischer, "The 'Universal Conscience,'" from *A History of Reading*, 253-305, focus on 255-262 and 266-292. **E**

In class
Bibles, almanacs, chapbooks, and other examples of "intensive" vs "extensive" reading.

Week 3, February 11. Literacy and the invention of childhood.
Literacy education and children's reading.

Reading
Fred Lerner, "The Rising Generation," from *The Story of Libraries: From the Invention of Writing to the Computer Age*, 154-167. **E**

A.-M. Chartier, "The Teaching of Literacy Skills in Western Europe: An Historical Perspective," from *The Cambridge Handbook of Literacy*, 451-467, focus on 455-464. **E**

Go to Early English Books Online (EEBO) at

http://eebo.chadwyck.com/home and do a subject search for "readers" (no quotation marks). You should get a few dozen results. Choose 3 to read. Be sure to note bibliographic information so that we can find them again.

Begin reading an issue of one of the periodicals Poe wrote for and edited; see assignment description for information about how to access the magazine online.

In class
Primers and children's books.

Week 4, February 18. Rewriting reading.
Commonplace books, gift books, periodicals and the circulation of text. Guest: Earle Havens, Curator of Early Modern Rare Books and Manuscripts.

Reading
Lucia Knowles, "Commonplace Books" http://www1.assumption.edu/users/lknoles/commonplacebook.html

Earle Havens, "Eighteenth Century" and "Nineteenth Century," from *Commonplace Books: A History of Manuscripts and Printed Book from Antiquity to the Twentieth Century*, 81-97. **E**

Go to Yale University's Beinecke Rare Book and Manuscript Library's Digital Image Collection at http://beinecke.library.yale.edu/digitallibrary/ and search for the keyword "commonplace book" (no quotation marks). You should get several pages of results. Browse and choose a few pages from a commonplace book to read. Be sure to note bibliographic information so we can find them again.

Isabelle Lehuu, "Leaflets of Memory: Giftbooks and the Economy of the Gaze," from *Carnival on the Page: Popular Print Media in Antebellum America*, 76-101. **E**

Continue reading your issue of the Poe periodical.

In class
Commonplace books, diaries and other manuscript books. Giftbooks, annuals and prize books.

PART 2: LIBRARIES FOR THE PEOPLE
Week 5, February 25. Mechanics' libraries, subscription libraries, circulating libraries.
Quick summary of library history through the 18th century. Early "public" libraries. Guest: Elliott Shore, Director of Libraries and Professor of History, Bryn Mawr College.

Reading
Wayne A. Wiegand, "Libraries and the Invention of Information," from *A Companion to the History of the Book*, 531-543. **E**

Joseph Lawrence Yeatman, "Literary Culture and the Role of Libraries in Democratic America: Baltimore, 1815-1840," *The Journal of Library History* 20.4 (Fall 1985): 345-367. **E**

Elizabeth McHenry, "'An Association of Kindred Spirits': Black Readers and Their Reading Rooms," from *Institutions of Reading: The Social Life of Libraries in the United States*, 99-118. **E**

Background
James Green, "Subscription Libraries and Commercial Circulating Libraries in Colonial Philadelphia and New York" from *Institutions of Reading: The Social Life of Libraries in the United States* (Amherst: University of Massachusetts Press, 2007): 53-71. **R**

In class
Pictures and plans of libraries. Handbooks, manuals, periodicals, novels.

Commonplace book part 1 due, in class, 2 pm. Please see assignment description for information about what this set of writings needs to include.

Week 6, March 4. The public library movement.

The origins of the public library and nineteenth-century Anglo-American ideas about social welfare.

Reading

Trustees of the Public Library of the City of Boston, *Upon the Objects to be Attained by the Establishment of a Public Library*, http://www.mcmillanlibrary.org/history/report_of_trustees.html

Paul Sturges, "The Public Library and Reading by the Masses: Historical Perspectives on the USA and Britain 1850-1900," http://www.ifla.org/IV/ifla60/60-stup.htm

Harriet Beecher Stowe, *Uncle Tom's Cabin* (1851), chapters I and II. Please also read one other article in the electronic version of *The National Era* for June 5, 1851. VOL. V, NO. 23, which you can reach via the library catalog. http://proquest.umi.com/pqdweb?did=220224221&sid=1&Fmt=10&clientId=5241&RQT=309&VName=HNP

Susan Warner, *The Wide, Wide World* (1850), chapter 1. http://ufdcweb1.uflib.ufl.edu/ufdc/?m=hd1J&i=74739

Dr. Donna Campbell, *Literary Movements:* Domestic or Sentimental Fiction, 1820-1865 http://www.wsu.edu/~campbelld/amlit/domestic.htm

Background

Earle Havens and Pierre-Alain Tilliette, eds., *The Extravagant Ambassador: The True Story of Alexandre Vattemare, the French Ventriloquist Who Changed the World.* At GPL.

In class

Novel serializations and reprints.

Week 7, March 11. Space, gender and class in the public library.

Reading

Excerpts from William Frederick Poole, *Remarks on Library Construction,* 1884. Read at googlebooks:
http://books.google.com/books?id=K46UkImxzy8C&dq=remarks+on+library+construction&printsec=frontcover&source=bl&ots=tbDlQ9QSSo&sig=lL9e2o1gpq5KBby9OkdmnzEATnQ&hl=en&ei=7ik5S8i5BZGHlAfWypSTBw&sa=X&oi=book_result&ct=result&resnum=1&ved=0CAoQ6AEwAA#v=onepage&q=&f=false 1-13.

Excerpts from Mary Antin, *The Promised Land,* 1913. Read at googlebooks: http://books.google.com/books?id=NhwEAAAAYAAJ&dq=mary+antin+promised+land&printsec=frontcover&source=bn&hl=en&ei=0SU5S_LLAYuQlAfhkJyiBw&sa=X&oi=book_result&ct=result&resnum=4&ved=0CBkQ6AEwAw#v=onepage&q=library&f=false 256-259, 337-355.

Abigail A. Van Slyck, "Giving: The Reform of American Library Philanthropy," from *Free to All: Carnegie Libraries & American Culture, 1890-1920,* 1-43. **E**

Alexis McCrossen, "'One Cathedral More' or 'Mere Lounging Places for Bummers'? The Cultural Politics of Leisure and the Public Library in Gilded Age America," *Libraries & Culture* 41.2 (2006): 169-188. **E**

Background

John Willis Clark, *The Care of Books. An Essay on the Development of Libraries and their Fittings, from the Earliest Times to the End of the Eighteenth Century,* 1901. On googlebooks.

Donald E. Oehlert, *Books and Blueprints: Building America's Public Libraries,* 1991. At GPL.

In class

Field trip to Enoch Pratt? Or, last questions regarding the assignment due tomorrow?

March 12. Poe in Periodicals essay due, 5 p.m.

Bring your paper to Gabrielle's office in Eisenhower Library (M-level, office #9) or email it to me.

March 18. Spring break, no class.

PART 3: THE PEABODY LIBRARY
Week 8, March 25. Founding history.
The origins of the Peabody Library and its collection. Introduction to final project.

    Guests: Cynthia Requardt, Curator of Rare Books and Manuscripts, and Tracey Melhuish, Peabody Archivist.

Reading
George Peabody's founding letter, dedication address, excerpts from the annual reports of the Peabody trustees, and early librarian correspondence. **C**

Francis T. Barrett, "A Great Catalogue, being an Appreciation of the Catalogue of the Library of the Peabody Institute, Baltimore," *Library* 1894 s1-6: 69-73. **C**

John Dorsey, *Mr. Peabody's Library: The Building, the Collection, the Neighborhood.* **C**

To look at
"Desiderata" books, library plans and other samples from the archives.

Week 9, April 1. Architecture and collections.
The Peabody Library as "cathedral" and state-of-the-art engineering. Collections within collections.

Reading
Charles Belfoure, "Peabody Institute 1857" and "Peabody Institute 1875" in *Edmund G. Lind: Anglo-American Architect of Baltimore and the South.* **E**

Phoebe Stanton, "The Peabody," from James D. Dilts and Catharine F. Black, eds., *Baltimore's Cast-Iron Buildings and Architectural Ironwork.* **E**

David Farris, "John Pendleton Kennedy: A Finding Aid." **C**

Background
Mary Ellen Hayward and Frank R. Shivers, Jr., "The Reign of the Romantics, 1829-1878," from Hayward and Shivers, eds., *The Architecture of Baltimore: An Illustrated History*, 98-149. **E**

In class
Pictures of and tour of the library. Discuss possible exhibit themes. Spend time researching project.

PART 4: BOOKS AT AN EXHIBITION: COLLECTIONS FROM THE PEABODY LIBRARY

Week 10, April 8. Project research.
Collection tools as stages of research: catalog entry, finding aid, exhibition catalog, scholarly article.

Reading
Wikipedia, "Pictures at an Exhibition" http://en.wikipedia.org/wiki/Pictures_at_an_Exhibition#Gallery_of_Hartmann.27s_pictures

In class
Listen to an orchestral arrangement of Modest Mussorgsky's 1874 piano suite called "Pictures at an Exhibition" and discuss the exhibition project. Look at finding aids and library exhibit catalogs. Spend time researching materials for your finding aid.

Commonplace book part 2 due, in class, 2 p.m.

Week 11, April 15. Individual student conferences.
Instead of meeting as a group this week, I will meet with you individually for 20 minutes. We'll discuss your exhibit proposal and the draft of your finding aid.

Exhibit proposal and draft of finding aid due.

Week 12, April 22. Peer exchange.
In class
Bring three copies of your finding aid, exhibit catalog and labels to class for peer review and discussion.

Week 13, April 29. Student collection presentations.

In class

Collection presentations. Should we make this open to the public?

Week 14, May 6. No class. Exam period. Optional conferences.

Week 15, May 13. Final exhibit portfolio due. Final commonplace book due.

ADDITIONAL TITLES OF INTEREST ON RESERVE

Matthew Battles, *Library: An Unquiet History* (New York: Norton, 2003).

Dee Garrison, *Apostles of Culture: The Public Librarian and American Society, 1876-1920* (New York : Free Press, c1979).

Fred Lerner, *The Story of Libraries: From the Invention of Writing to the Computer Age* (New York: Continuum, 1998).

Konstantinos Staikos, *The Great Libraries from Antiquity to the Renaissance*, trans. Timothy Cullen (New Castle DE: Oak Knoll Press, 2000).

John Tebbel, *Between Covers: The Rise and Transformation of Book Publishing in America* (New York: Oxford, 1987).

NOTES

1. George Peabody, *Letter from George Peabody, Esq. to the Trustees for the Establishment of an Institute in the City of Baltimore* (Baltimore: John D. Toy, 1857), 5.

2. Peabody, 5.

3. Please see syllabus in the appendix for details. The syllabus included here reflects the original plans for the course; the actual schedule changed when the university closed for a week in February due to record snowfalls.

4. One student even chose to use loose sheets of unlined paper so that the ultimate "book" could be detached from its chronological composition and reorganized thematically.

5. The magazines were the *Southern Literary Messenger* II.1 (December 1835), *Burton's Gentleman's Magazine* V. 3 (September 1839) and V.4 (October 1839) and *Graham's Lady's and Gentleman's Magazine* XVIII.4 (April 1841).

6. I would also like to thank Elizabeth Rodini, Associate Director of the Program in Museums and Society, for her support setting up the class. Heartfelt thanks also to my guest lecturers: Paul Espinosa, Peabody Library Assistant; Earle Havens, Curator of Early Modern Rare Books and Manuscripts; Cynthia Requardt, recently retired Kurrelmeyer Curator of Special Collections; Tracey Melhuish, Project Archivist, Peabody Institute; and Elliott Shore, *Constance A. Jones Director of Libraries and Professor of History, Bryn Mawr College. This class and the ensuing exhibit could not have happened without the help of Paul Espinosa and the rest of the rare books team, especially Amy Kimball, Heidi Herr and student photographer extraordinaire Julie DePasquale, and the collaboration of our conservation department headed by Sonja Jordan-Mowery.*

The Scholar's Bookshelf: Recreating a Premodern Library for the Classroom

Earle Havens, Ph.D.

I think as a sensory experience the books themselves win it hands-down. Once the students are exposed to the strangeness of old books, then the strangeness of the text and the thinking behind it becomes more evident....I want them to walk around, browse the books, and see what they can find.

~ Walter Stephens, The Charles S. Singleton Professor of Italian, Johns Hopkins University

OVERVIEW

During the Spring 2010 semester an upper-level undergraduate seminar entitled "Writing and Wonder: Books, Libraries, and Discovery, 1250-1550" was team-taught by myself and two senior professors in the Department of German & Romance Languages & Literatures within the Krieger School of Arts and Sciences at Johns Hopkins University. While it was based in the romance languages, this inherently interdisciplinary seminar was also cross-listed with the departments of Classics, English, History, and the History of Art. With the support of a $5000 "Technology Fellows" grant from the Sheridan Libraries' Center for Educational Resources, we identified and selectively digitized portions of fifty rare books from the libraries' collections. All were produced during the late Middle Ages and Renaissance and would have formed much of the "standard furniture" of a strong fifteenth or early sixteenth-century private scholarly library. (Figure 4.1) Among the books were medieval illuminated manuscripts, incunabula, and sixteenth-century books touching a variety of themes

relevant to premodern scholarship: ancient Greco-Roman texts, medieval theological and philosophical titles, and Renaissance scholarly and literary works ranging from bibles and biblical glosses, to chronicles and histories, major works of political theory, natural history, and imaginative literature. This rich and complex archive of major and minor works were all physically gathered together and placed on an "open reserve" shelf that was available for students enrolled in the seminar to browse in a secure reading room throughout the course of the semester. This, allied with a digital platform for selective browsing on-line, facilitated extensive consultation of the various textual and unique physical attributes of these works—historical bindings, provenance inscriptions, contemporary manuscript annotations, illuminations and graphic illustrations, typography, &c.—both during, and also well beyond, the normal operating hours of the rare book reading room.

Initially we deployed our technology grant to procure professional digital imaging for significant portions of books in the collection. The remainder of our technology grant was used to hire two graduate students to assist in post-production tagging, splicing, and processing of these digital surrogates, and their importation into a virtual page-turning freeware with basic zooming capabilities. After much thoughtful consideration, the page-turning platform we adopted was provided by www.issuu. com. The selection of partial surrogates of these books was made by the instructors' estimation of their particular relevance to central concepts and themes we wished to bring out in classroom reading and discussion, as outlined in our syllabus: (1) the histories of reading and writing, and the intellectual, cultural, and economic impact of the advent of printing technology; (2) conditions of literacy, education, and access to books; (3) the organization and use of private and institutional libraries; (4) the biblical text as history; (5) encyclopedism and "information overload;" (6) prevailing, and competing, philosophical traditions surrounding Scholastic and Renaissance humanistic discourses; (7) intellectual claims to the relative authority of the institutions of the Church and the secular state, both real and imagined/forged; (8) scholarly investigation and the "romanticizing" of the distant past; and (9) the imaginative literary imitation, and appropriation, of ancient sources. Student consultations of both these virtual materials, and the original books themselves, were specifically integrated into most of our weekly meetings over the course of the semester, requiring students to continue throughout the semester to conceive of the humanistic content of these works in the context of the material circumstances surrounding their production, reproduction, circulation, and consumption as physical objects, alongside related considerations of conditions on the ground: literacy and education, economy, the transforming technologies of book production, censorship, and the like.

Figure 4.1. St. Luke writing his gospel, from the emblem book of Arius Montanus, Humanae Salutis Monumenta (Antwerp: Ex prototypographia regia Christopher Plantin, 1571), Sheridan Libraries, Johns Hopkins University.

TEXT AND CONTEXT: HUMANISTIC QUESTIONS ASKED AND ANSWERED BY THE SCHOLAR'S BOOKSHELF

The core content of this course concentrated on revolutionary changes in the development and conduct of European scholarship amid the monumental transition from the scribal medium to the rapid production and proliferation of material texts printed by moveable type, and the sustained continuity of both media within the early era of print. The revolution in scholarship that accompanied the production of both handwritten and printed texts materially transformed prevailing attitudes toward classical Greco-Roman as well as biblical antiquity, particularly through the Renaissance "recovery" of lost, obscure, forged, and otherwise neglected texts that bore an overwhelming aura of authority due to the very fact of their antiquity. Other influential aspects of this revolution included the formation of secular private libraries, the advent of new philological methods and scholarly approaches to the study of ancient handwriting and writing materials, and the history and philosophy of language more generally.

We also challenged students throughout the semester to understand and interrogate an accompanying novel sense of "wonder" and renewed admiration for this distant ancient world that had suddenly begun to be "recovered" and "revived" by the earliest generation of Renaissance humanists, and a renewed conviction of the importance of "saving" that intellectual inheritance from long-prevailing conditions of neglect, corruption, and ignorance. In this way, we endeavored to illustrate in both physical and intellectual terms that this period of cultural revival subsisted, in many ways, in the veneration and celebration of physical books and manuscripts. Books could function concomitantly as sources of endless fascination and inspiration on the one hand, and as essential physical tools of preservation, unprecedented textual duplication, and the far-flung dissemination of ancient knowledge on the other—each went hand in hand.

Over time, these same sensibilities were mirrored in our students' own processes of exploration within the dual contexts of the Renaissance printing revolution and their own latter-day position within the digital revolution of the 21st century, through a complimentary interaction with these texts as physical objects and versatile digital surrogates. This was manifested in two primary activities: (1) in a range of imaginative exercises assigned outside of class meetings with the purpose of manifesting a variety of interactive and interpretive experiences through direct and creative encounters with the original materials, on-line and in person within the rare book reading room; and (2) live classroom lectures and discussions that moved between assigned readings and physical specimens of books relating to the themes addressed in those readings.

For exercises pursued outside the classroom, early on in the semester students worked at a granular level, considering, alongside their instructors, variations in letterforms, orthography, abbreviations and the employment of ligatures, punctuation, and related physical attributes of the arrangement and pre-

sentation of the text across the page. In an effort to encourage students to think as Renaissance humanists may have thought—recognizing the inherent instability of texts and the need to determine textual authority, as described above—students were given the choice either: (1) to compare an edition of Desiderius Erasmus' famous essay on the *Sileni of Alcibaides* in his bestselling *Adages*, to an expurgated version produced according to instructions stipulated in the ever-expanding *Index of Prohibited Books* issued by the Roman Catholic Church; or (2) invite them to forge an allegedly "ancient" text based on one of the texts or topics covered during the semester. In another example, toward the end of the semester we encouraged our students to think about the nature of textual appropriation and the imitation of ancient authors during the Renaissance. When our students were assigned to read Machiavelli's *Mandragola*, they were also asked to draft an alternative ending to the play to achieve different purposes and effects, whether moral, immoral, satirical, or otherwise, according to prevailing cultural expectations within the author's lifetime.

In actual lectures and discussions in the presence of the physical objects themselves, we remained equally pragmatic and creative at the same time. In a presentation I gave on traditional medieval principles regarding the proper hierarchical organization of human knowledge within the context of a library space, students were encouraged to think about how they might "shelve" the particular contents of the Scholar's Bookshelf in keeping with those norms. It emerged that the inherent interdisciplinarity of many ancient texts defied those norms. In discussing forged or otherwise mythic texts from antiquity we examined a particular "ancient" source as it was quoted—with varying degrees of credulity—by a range of other ancient, medieval, and Renaissance authors who had recontextualized specific passages for purposes far beyond the original author's. We also compared the medieval Scholastic "encyclopedic" tradition of compiling ever-more comprehensive biblical glosses surrounding snippets of St. Jerome's authorized Latin Vulgate with Christian humanist efforts to interrogate a range of original textual sources that long preceded Jerome, particularly through their production of polyglot bibles that seamlessly aligned ancient Hebrew, Greek, and Chaldean sources alongside Jerome's translation. This activity visually transformed the very structure and function of the physical book while also stretching the art and science of composing moveable type to its upper limits. Similarly, when talking about the physical production of books and their own unique processes of material transformation over time, we carefully studied an original binding of an incunabulum (i.e., a book printed before January 1501) that was itself a palimpsest. The book's boards were both covered with parchment leaves that had originally been used to record in manuscript fourteenth-cen-

tury Catholic text, which was subsequently scraped away and reused to print in the fifteenth century a portion of St. Thomas Aquinas' *Summa Theologica*. These very same pages were then finally repurposed in a purely physical application, serving as sturdy covers for an otherwise flimsy pasteboard binding for a handsome edition of Nicholas Jenson's totally unrelated 1476 *Naturalis Historia* of the Elder, whose own margins were heavily glossed in manuscript by a later, ca. seventeenth-century reader. (Figure 4.2)

In each instance, these books did not simply exemplify dynamic textual histories and intellectual traditions. The students' interaction with them physically and visually reified a full range of cultural, political, and philosophical questions rooted in material book production and consumption that, together, shaped and transformed the imaginations, preoccupations, and prejudices of Renaissance scholars.

Figure 4.2. Medieval manuscript and incunabulum palimpsest binding, Pliny the Elder, Naturalis Historia (Venice: Nicholas Jenson, 1472), Sheridan Libraries, Johns Hopkins University.

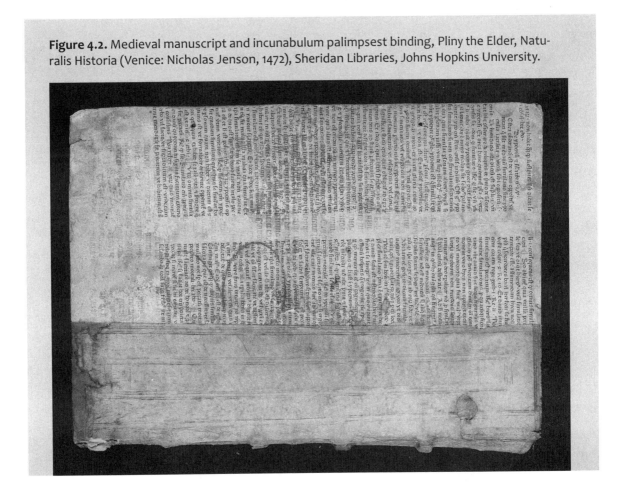

ASSESSMENT

Student reviews of the course were generally very positive, and quite effusive about the opportunity the class sessions afforded to work so intensively with original rare materials that many of them professed never to have encountered before. Graduating seniors, in particular, noted a feeling of gratitude that this course enabled them to become exposed to a universe of rare books and manuscripts that they had never known, and just in the nick of time as they prepared to move on to professional degree programs and careers unrelated to the distant past. As instructors we felt the class has been particularly robust, though we also remarked that the final papers written by the students tended far more to consist of close readings of texts and subjects not treated squarely within in the class, or through the rare book materials themselves. We concluded that, in future, such a course might have a far greater and substantive impact on assigned written work if it were taught at the graduate level, to students with some advanced knowledge of Latin and other modern European languages that were germane to so many of the texts in question.

It would also seem that the large majority of research libraries in the United States will not likely have as full a range of early materials—medieval manuscript codices, incunabula, and sixteenth-century imprints—at their immediate disposal within their respective colleges and universities. This could be overcome, however, through collaborative efforts with larger-scale collections within one's municipality or region, or through repair to the wider universe of digital surrogates available through any number of on-line digital libraries, whether freely available on the Internet or through library subscription. In the latter connection, those digital libraries that specifically digitize the full physical object including bindings, endpapers, &c., and not simply the text pages of a manuscript or printed book would be especially useful. Our own digital surrogates within our virtual Scholar's

Bookshelf did just that, albeit in a limited and necessarily selective way that assumed subsequent access to the original books themselves. In short, we felt that there really was no sufficient substitute for the physical books themselves, even if only in a small number of exemplars, should such a course be duplicated elsewhere.

We could not have even contemplated the on-line resource that we developed without the technical assistance of Johns Hopkins University's Center for Educational Resources (CER). Their expertise in facilitating the construction of creative electronic pedagogical applications suited to particular classes was immensely helpful and, without such support, this classroom experience would not have been possible. The added fact that three faculty members were involved in the project, along with two graduate students and a further two staff members within the CER did complicate our work as much as it enriched it. With so many moveable parts we were able to engage in many especially dynamic content-based discussions, but coordinating and leavening those ideas in the context of a host of practical and technical concerns was especially challenging, even to the point of simply getting everyone into the same room at the same time. The more the merrier, in one sense, but we would strongly recommend keeping this factor well in mind long before preparing for such a course—and in our case we began our work a full two semesters before the course was actually taught.[1]

All of us who were involved considered this course, from the outset, to be something of an experiment within a kind of "laboratory for the humanities" that was technological and physical at the same time. As with any experiment, our methods and findings were complex, and not always consistent with the hypotheses that inspired the initial enterprise. In the interest of economy, we digitally photographed rare books as double-page spreads, which required a great deal of post-photographic processing time splicing and then rearranging hundreds of surrogates, and then systematically realigning them within the page-turning platform we elected to use. That work was made all the more challenging as we had to begin tagging each resulting image with unique bibliographic data. The resulting interface was imperfect as well, in part because we did not have sufficient time to fully align the spliced surrogates in order to make the page-turning experience precisely what we had envisioned. In the end, however, nearly half of our students' experiences were based on active, thoughtful, and critical engagement within the classroom in discussions around original and unique materials, strengthened all the more by further solitary explorations outside of the classroom, in the reading room and on the computer. That opportunity, and indeed the privilege, to undertake such a hands-on engagement with the premodern past also drew the attention of the wider Johns Hopkins University community in the form of a feature, illustrated article in university's *Krieger School of Arts & Sciences Magazine*, now available on-line at http://krieger.jhu.edu/magazine/sp10/f2.html.

NOTES

1. Thanks are owed here to Professors Walter Stephens and Christopher Celenza of the Department of German and Romance Languages and Literatures, and to their graduate students Denis Robichaud and Tania Zampini, as well as to our project colleagues, Macie Hall and Reid Sczerba, in the Center for Educational Resources of the Sheridan Libraries, for their invaluable contributions to the conception and execution of this dynamic undergraduate seminar. Additional thanks are owed to the many members of the staff of the Department of Rare Books and Manuscripts—in particular Amy Kimball, Paul Espinosa, and Heidi Herr—who helped to facilitate with many others this new approach to collections use, increased reading room monitoring and coverage, and the transportation, and management of the collection from across the three different rare book libraries within the Sheridan Libraries system, including the historic George Peabody Library, the John Work Garrett Library at Evergreen Museum & Library, and the rare book and manuscript collections of the Milton S. Eisenhower Library on the main Homewood campus of the Johns Hopkins University.

Oxford University: 'Speed-dating' in Special Collections: A Case Study

Julia Walworth

"you need information to make sense of what you see"

"my chief impression was simply that being an actual historian was very different from what I was doing at the time"

THE ORIGINAL CASE STUDY

Every autumn for the past nine years, a small group of first-year undergraduates studying medieval history at Merton College are invited to report to the library for a morning class.[1] When they arrive they are handed a pencil and a recording sheet and told to take a seat at a large table on which are a number of documents and bound volumes: parchment documents, some with seals attached, account rolls partially unrolled, a manuscript book with decorative initials and script, a handwritten notebook and several printed books. Each item is open, unfolded and ready for consultation, and each is numbered but not otherwise labelled. The students' record sheets have spaces for noting the object number and their observations, with columns labelled: 1) date; 2) language; 3) content or document type; 4) name of persons or places mentioned in the document. After the librarian explains reading room etiquette and rules, including which items may be touched and which not, the students are told that they will be given five minutes with each item, doing their best to determine the information requested on the record sheet. Every five minutes they will be asked to move to another station, until each student has had a chance to examine every displayed item.

It is assumed that the students will have no prior familiarity with Latin or medieval scripts. As the students study the documents, the course tutor, the librarian and the archivist circulate among them, providing encouragement and offering suggestions on where to start to begin to make sense of a document that might be written in an unknown language or in a script that is difficult to decipher. (Figure 5.1) English personal names and place names may stand out in a Latin document; or perhaps the layout or decoration may provide a clue to the type of document even if the student cannot read the text. Available on the table are magnifying glasses and handbooks to abbreviations and dating systems etc, so that students can be shown how to decipher the medieval forms of Arabic numerals.

In the second half of the class each item is discussed in turn. The students reveal what they were able to extract from the documents, and the session leaders have an opportunity to explain more fully the significance of the items. The documents were selected from the college's archives and special collections in order to demonstrate a variety of aspects of the English historical record of the middle ages: royal and papal documents, account rolls recording institutional expenditure, and historical narratives. They were written in Latin, French and Hebrew for institutions and for men and women, aristocrats and townspeople, Christians and Jews. There are thus plenty of avenues for discussion, and the end of the session seems to come very quickly.

The aim of the session is not to teach students to read medieval scripts, to date a manuscript or to dis-

Figure 5.1. Students study documents for five minutes at a time before moving to next document.

tinguish different types of land deeds, but to bring them face to face with original documents at a very early stage in their studies. This is why the session on medieval documents—potentially the most alien items easily to hand—is held quite early on in the first year, while similar sessions with more recent or more familiar items are held for more advanced students. The exercise is helpful for demonstrating how much one's observations are influenced by expectations. The 13th-century Hebrew document is a good case in point, since the Hebrew script is very similar to modern Hebrew scripts, but many students fail to identify the language because they are not expecting to see it in this context. On the other hand, most students are surprised by how much information they can glean, with patience, from a document they cannot really read and by how much information is contained in the non-written elements of a document or book. All

students find that by the end of the session they can begin to decipher at least some words in some scripts.

STUDENT RESPONSES

Two students have recorded their impressions of their first-year special collections session:

Elizabeth Biggs (2009, currently an undergraduate majoring in History)

Medieval documents are usually encountered by students in museums behind glass cases with explanatory notes, so it was unusual and very fun to get to handle real documents from Merton's archives. Moving carefully around each of the documents, allowed to touch and come close as long as we took great care, allowed us to see a range of things which were important enough to Merton over the years to be kept and preserved. A papal letter from the 13th century probably gave the college bragging rights but why other things survived—accounts for long lost expenses, for example—is more of a mystery. The document handling session reminded me of the problems of survival, of the gaps that inevitably remain in the information that we use to answer our essay question for the week. It is because of the gaps and openings that leave room for interpretation that these documents, even the most mundane, make history so interesting.

As well as being exciting, the session was also a reminder that their worth consists of so much more than the words written on paper. But even figuring out what a document is saying is difficult, not even what it means, but just the letters on the page. It was surprisingly satisfying to decipher faded ink and old handwriting, trickier than I would have thought. It also showed me that reading is simply the first step, even if you think you have the words right. In addition to the text itself, it was interesting to look at the other aspects of the document such as the decoration or lack of decoration. However, you need information to make sense of what you see. I managed to confuse the dates on one document with names because the way they were written looked like first names to me, and it was thus the only way I could make sense of them. The experience of handling these papers made me want to do more with original documents, because I enjoy having the building blocks and trying to solve a puzzle.

Ingrid Rembold (*participated in 2006, now a graduate student studying medieval history*)
As a first year, my reading lists were filled with secondary materials; many of the introductory materials were framed in such broad terms

that they ended up being quite far removed from the original sources. And so, it came as a bit of a surprise to see a sample of original manuscripts. They were both more impressive than I was expecting—with their large, wax seals and wholly different style of penmanship, not to mention such alluring names as Richard, King of the Romans—and, at the same time, less so—they chiefly pertained to issues of property and privileges, which at the time I found somewhat unappealing. With a faint recollection of Latin—and crucially without palaeographical training or any knowledge of Medieval Latin abbreviations—looking through the documents seemed a very exciting puzzle, and gradually, with some help, I was able to stumble through a few words.

I wasn't able to do very much with the documents—they were fascinating, but a bit beyond my grasp at the time. I think my chief impression was simply that being an actual historian was very different from what I was doing at the time, and that it seemed very exciting. I still haven't gotten up the courage to do original research that was entirely dependent on archive sources. But I have become more source-based in my approach to my work, and my dissertation this year—much to the surprise of my first-year self—centred around issues of property and privileges.

VARIATIONS
The basic structure of these sessions is simple and can be adapted for almost any subject and for the strengths of different special collections. What all versions have in common is that a small group of students spend a very short period of time with a series of original materials that they haven't seen or studied previously; they are given a short set of questions or categories to direct their observations; and they share observations in discussion in the second

part of the session. For practical reasons, the students move from station to station around a table.

Two facets that have been successfully varied at Merton for different subjects and groups more academically advanced are the selection of items chosen for the sessions and the questions or headings on the record sheets. When the students are more experienced, the questions on the record sheet can be more specific, presupposing prior knowledge through reading and, depending on the condition of the items, participants can be encouraged to examine the items more fully. More importantly, the exercise can be more open-ended, requiring students to think beyond the session and consider approaches to research and further work. For an upper-level class on medieval literature, the record sheet asked the students to look at four aspects of a selection of manuscripts and printed books: the binding; whether the leaves were paper or parchment; evidence for ownership and use; and lay-out and decoration. In this session the students worked in pairs and were encouraged to discuss their observations with each other as they examined each item.

Each student was additionally asked, after they had seen all the books, and before the discussion, to choose one book that they would like to know more about and to tell the rest of the group one research question they would like to pursue and what first steps they would take to begin to find an answer to that question. The general discussion at the end of the session then focussed on these directions for notional future work, and incidentally led to the 'speed dating' nickname for the sessions. Even if several students select the same book, they have never, in our experience, posed identical questions.

PRACTICAL CONSIDERATIONS

- **Advance preparation**. Even though these sessions are not lectures, they work best if all the session leaders are familiar with the items (especially if palaeographical, language or analytical bibliographical skill is involved).

- **Group size**. These sessions are time-intensive and work best for groups of no more than fourteen participants. To allow students (even in pairs) time to look at six or seven objects, then to have a brief discussion of each object and possibly a final discussion of research directions, can easily take two hours. A kitchen timer is a bit crude but can be helpful.

- **Preservation concerns**. Physical contact with the objects is an essential part of the value of the session, yet few libraries are lucky enough to have a dedicated teaching collection, and the excitement of seeing special items can make a lasting impression on students. One or two 'treasures' which can be viewed but not handled can be included in each session. Other objects can be varied from year to year and their use recorded as one would record exhibition exposure, to ensure that a few items do not suffer undue wear and tear. The sessions provide a good opportunity for instruction and supervised practice in safe handling of documents and bound volumes. Decide in advance whether and to what extent participants will be allowed or encouraged to handle the items, turn pages, or open folded plates. Single-leaf documents and photographs can be presented in polyester sleeves, with gloves provided if necessary.

One of the challenges and strengths of these sessions is that students individually examine unfamiliar materials **before** explanation and discussion. Such encounters with original documents greatly enrich their engagement with what can be an alien past and stimulate their desire to understand it. The model can be used effectively with a wide range of materials and can be adjusted for different subjects and for groups of different levels of ability. Although Merton is fortunate in having relatively rich collections for a small library, the model could work equally well in almost any special collections environment.

NOTES

1. These classes have been developed over the years by librarians, archivists and teaching faculty. The basic structure was introduced by Dr Michael Stansfield, College Archivist, and Dr Steven Gunn, Tutor in History and further developed by Mr Julian Reid, College Archivist and the present writer.

THE OHIO STATE UNIVERSITY

Seeing through the 'Priest's Eye': Teaching Medieval Codicology and Book History through William of Pagula's *Oculus sacerdotis*

Eric J. Johnson

In 1281, John Pecham, Archbishop of Canterbury, promulgated his *Ignorantia sacerdotum* (*On the Ignorance of Priests*). A clarion cry to all clergy under his authority, the *Ignorantia* condemned the woeful state of priestly education and training in England during the late-thirteenth century, asserting that the ignorance of priests leads people into doctrinal and moral error and cheats them of a true understanding of God. Pecham's decree did more than just condemn his subordinates' ignorance, however. It also set forth the framework for the systematic teaching of priests—and by extension the people to whom they ministered—in the basic literacy of Christianity. Over the course of the following century, a number of learned priests put quill to parchment in an effort to provide their less knowledgeable brethren with books explaining these fundamental principles of the Christian faith. Chief among these texts was the *Oculus sacerdotis*, or *The Eye of the Priest*, written in the 1320s by an English clergyman named William of Pagula, vicar of Winkfield, a small parish in Berkshire in south-central England.[1]

The above paragraph encapsulates the basic background information I give to my students when introducing them to Ohio State's manuscript copy of Pagula's influential fourteenth-century text. But as significant and interesting as its historical context and textual content may be, in most cases in which I might use this manuscript to teach, the substance of its text actually counts for very little. Written entirely in Latin and never before edited or

fully translated into English, the manuscript's textual contents remain inaccessible to most students; and even if they are fluent in medieval Latin, they would still have to contend with the manuscript's paleographical idiosyncrasies, the absence of modern punctuation, and the complex system of lexical abbreviations used by the scribes who penned the text. On first glance, then, it would seem that for general teaching purposes OSU's copy of the *Oculus sacerdotis* is nothing more than an inert esoteric object, a historical curiosity, an "empty" text. If this is the case, a fundamental question arises: What is the point of using a manuscript like this in the classroom?

As a curator who frequently teaches with medieval books in upper level courses such as "Medieval Manuscript Studies," as well as in course-integrated sessions across the university's humanities curriculum and in occasional instructional scenarios targeting primary, junior high, and high school audiences, it is my job to find ways to help students see past these linguistic and textual obstacles and teach them to recognize that there is more to read and examine in a book than its textual content alone. Its very physical qualities and appearance, I try to demonstrate, serve as active texts encompassing their own peculiar language of signs and symbols telling us about the circumstances and process of the book's own production, the culture in which it was born, the people who made and read it, and the history of its use and transmission. By using a manuscript copy of the *Oculus* as a lens through which we can examine the complex intellectual, cultural, artistic, and material histories underlying medieval books and their production, we can figuratively and literally see through the *Eye of the Priest* and realize that we do not need to look at or understand a manuscript's textual content in order to make use of it as a powerful and practical pedagogical tool.

The particular copy of the *Oculus* I use in my classes is ideally suited to teaching students about medieval textual culture and codicology. Although my use of and focus upon the manuscript varies depending on the curricular needs of each class, generally speaking I ask my students to "dissect" the manuscript by examining it closely from the outside in. We begin with a simple assessment of its size and format and progress inward to analyze its binding structure, its pagination and foliation, the condition and quality of its parchment, its textual layout and appearance, and any paratextual additions or reader-added comments it contains. By considering such features closely, we can learn much about the manuscript's possible origin and provenance, its process of production, how it was used, and the people who used it. Taken together, all of this evidence opens our eyes to the significance of the *Oculus* as both physical artifact and intellectual text.

So what does the Ohio State *Oculus* tell us about itself? The first things we notice are its size and external appearance. The manuscript can be described as a small- to medium-sized folio, perfectly situated between larger typical academic or reference codices intended for communal or institutional service, and smaller devotional treatises produced for individual or personal use. It is bound in tanned, decoratively-stamped, semi-limp leather covers held together by four laced-in leather thong sewing supports. Beyond providing us with a physical description, what might these features suggest about our manuscript? First of all, its intermediate size is perfect for packaging a large amount of information while at the same time remaining com-

pact enough to facilitate easy transportation and use. Additionally, the qualities of the binding make the manuscript both flexible and durable. Its four closely spaced sewing thongs provide strength and resiliency, and its tanned leather covers have been crafted to withstand the rigors of frequent handling and exposure to the elements. Such bindings were common across Europe in the later-medieval period and were valued as an inexpensive, yet sturdy and reliable, means for constructing and protecting books. In apparent contrast to this rugged functionality, however, the binding also features on both its front and back covers extensive blind-stamped decoration consisting of a small ornamental frame set within a larger frame festooned with decorative medallions. Taken together, the binding's functional and decorative characteristics suggest that while the manuscript was intended for heavy use, its textual contents—the fundamental principles and policies of the Christian religion—were esteemed enough to warrant the modest, but extra, expense necessary to provide a small amount of artistic embellishment. Given the fact that the *Oculus sacerdotis* was a highly regarded and often used sacerdotal reference work, it seems hardly surprising that this copy of it would feature both durability and aesthetic appeal in its external physical construction.

While our external analysis of the manuscript would seem to indicate that it survives in its original fifteenth-century binding, we need to turn to an analysis of its internal structure in order to determine if it has come down to us from its original creators in a complete and intact state. The first step in this internal analysis, I show my students, is an examination of the codex's endpapers and flyleaves, or in other words, the scraps of parchment positioned before and after the main text block that are used to solidify the binding and protect the manuscript's primary textual contents. At the front of the book we have a bifolium of clean parchment, half of which is pasted down to the inside front cover with the other half left unglued as a free leaf. Immediately following this appears a large parchment sheet of a disused manuscript service book that has been turned sideways and folded in half to create an additional bifolium of two flyleaves (figure 6.1). The same basic structure occurs inside the rear cover. I ask my students to look closely at the bifolium of flyleaves at the front of the codex, paying particular attention to the gutter, or fold, in the sheet. They quickly discover that at some point in this manuscript's long history, these flyleaves either were re-set, or possibly removed from another manuscript's binding and inserted in this copy of the *Oculus*. Two things make this conclusion apparent: the presence of parallel stress lines running the length of both of the bifolium's leaves on either side of the gutter and the survival of earlier, now superfluous, sewing holes.

Although this evidence concretely shows that the manuscript's front-matter has been meddled with, it only suggests that the *Oculus* itself may have been rebound sometime in its past. To prove this, I lead my students further into the manuscript to examine the individual gatherings of bifolia within the main text block where we quickly determine that the entire manuscript, indeed, once had been rebound. A quick look into the gutters of each bifolium's centerfold reveals the same superfluous sewing holes apparent in the bifolium of flyleaves at the front of the book. But, I show my students, additional, more specific evidence confirming this rebinding emerges if we carefully collate the manuscript to search for clues the original scribe(s) would have left to help guide the binder as he constructed this book.

The basic physical constituents of any medieval manuscript book are its gatherings, or quires, of several bifolia nested inside each other and "tacketed" (stitched) together to form a short booklet. Medi-

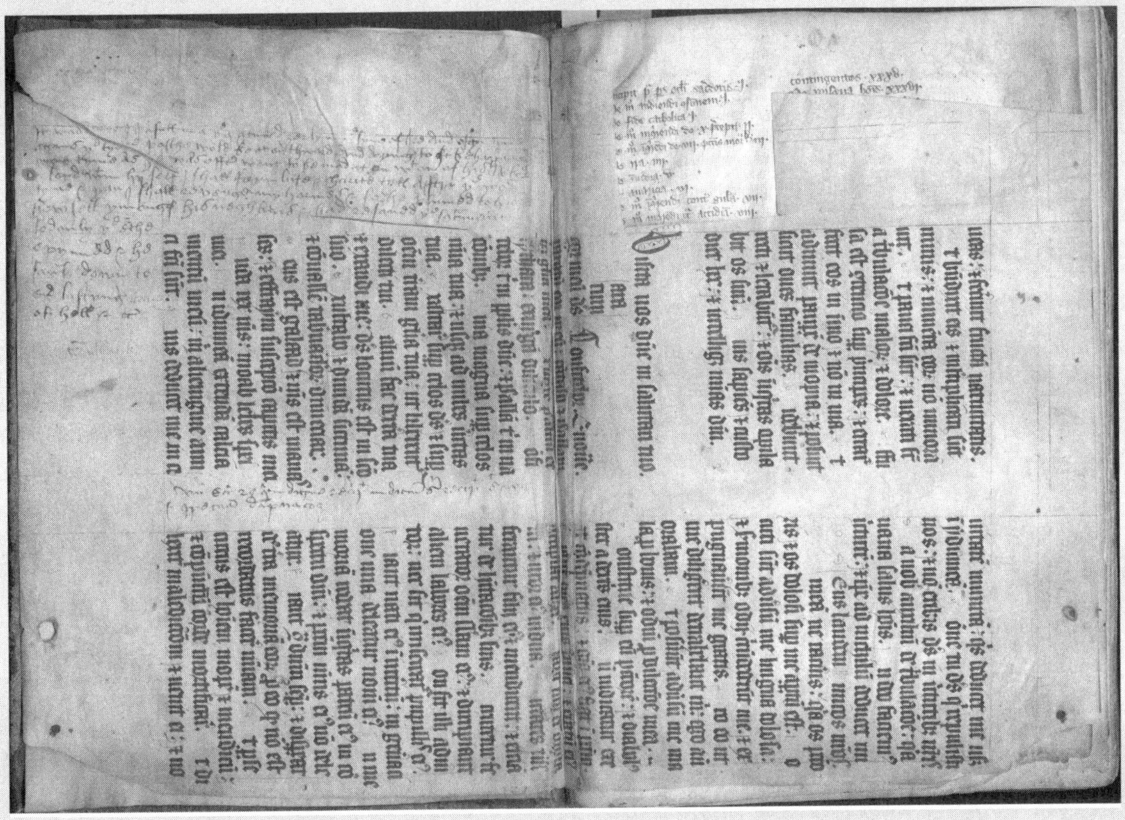

Figure 6.1. Rare Books & Manuscripts Library of the Ohio State University Libraries. MS.Lat.1, front flyleaves

eval codices consisted of any number of these quires assembled collectively, arranged one after the other, and sewn consecutively into a common binding. In order to facilitate the organization and sewing of these gatherings in proper sequence, scribes employed a variety of textual tools, including numbering each individual quire, inserting signature marks on leaves within numbered quires, and writing catchwords at the bottom of the last page of a quire that matched up with the first words at the top of the first page of the following gathering. Upon examining our copy of the *Oculus*, I show my students that its original makers used all three of these tools when preparing their text. At first glance, the manuscript looks complete and intact. Its binding is solid and tight; there are no gaps indicating the absence of large portions of text; and it consists of ten individual quires, including a preliminary gathering of four leaves followed by eight gatherings of twelve and what looks to be a single gathering of ten leaves lacking its final leaf. A careful review of scribal and binding evidence, however, reveals a few substantial problems with this picture. First of all, the first gathering of twelve leaves is bound out of order. While its first three bifolia are nested correctly, the fourth has been bound in reverse order and the sixth has accidentally been nested prior to the fifth bifolium. This muddled arrangement results in the following leaf order: 1, 2, 3, 9, 6, 5, 8, 7, 4, 10, 11, 12. A second problem with the binding becomes apparent when we analyze the surviving catchwords and quire numbering in each gathering. Gatherings 2, 3, 5, 6, and 10 clearly retain their original quire markings at the bottom of the first leaf of each quire, while portions of the quire markings for the seventh and ninth gatherings are still visible. Coupling these marks with the catchwords present at the end of each gathering, we can quickly see that the catchwords at the end of the seventh quire do not match the text at the start of the quire immediately following it. This successive quire's catchwords, however, match the first words of the clearly marked tenth

gathering. This codicological evidence, then, proves that the codex is missing what would have been its eighth quire—a full twelve leaves of the manuscript are absent.[2] Finally, a closer look at the tenth quire reveals that rather than being a simple gathering of ten leaves lacking its final leaf, it is actually a gathering of eight leaves lacking its final leaf, but with two single leaves inserted between the quire's fifth and sixth leaves.

But what does all this tell us? Our close analysis of the *Oculus's* binding structure reveals an incomplete manuscript that was likely rebound somewhat carelessly in the later-fifteenth, or perhaps early-sixteenth, century. While none of the evidence we have uncovered provides exact information identifying the book's original creators or readers, our observations do tell us that this copy of the *Oculus* was likely used heavily from the moment of its completion and was reckoned to be an extremely valuable resource worthy of rebinding and continued use, in spite of the fact that it lacks a full quire's worth of text.

While our investigation of the manuscript's binding configuration tells us much about how it was constructed, a close examination of its parchment leaves, the writing on each leaf, and the codex's overall *mise-en-page* reveals a great deal of useful information about book production, scribal practice, and reading activities in the later Middle Ages. For instance, the quality of the parchment is rough and uneven at best. While age has definitely contributed to some of the artifact's wear—it is 600 years old, after all—it is clear that the parchment used to make this book was of an exceedingly low standard to begin with. Parchment preparation was a very time- and labor-intensive activity that necessitated converting the skin of a living animal, complete with all its own unique flaws and blemishes, into a smooth, clean, supple surface that could easily be written upon. Parchment intended for high-quality manuscripts required painstaking preparation and precluded the use of skins with significant imperfections. The parchment used in the *Oculus*, in contrast, is full of flaws (figure 6.2). Many leaves are wrinkled and yellowish in tone; hair follicles and vein patterning are prominent throughout the book; rough, uneven scar tissue from insect bites, cuts, and scrapes mar the pages; individual leaves are uneven, bearing the marks of untrimmed shoulder and neck contours and the hasty, imprecise cutting of the parchment-maker; and many holes—the result of torn scar tissue or careless knife-work during the skinning of the animal or later preparation of the parchment—are rife throughout the codex. In many instances, there is evidence showing how the book's creators attempted to repair such faults, including small skin patches over holes and stitches in long gashes and tears. The overall condition of the parchment indicates that functionality, utility, and economy were the main factors considered in the production of this book. This copy of the *Oculus* was a simple working priest's text, not a lavish art-piece intended for idle display.

The text written upon these imperfect leaves also reveals much about how the book was produced and for whom it was written. Pricking and ruling, the process of piercing the margins of a leaf with regularly spaced holes that guided the ruling of the page, is apparent on each leaf and illustrates for students a fundamental step in medieval scribal practice. The heavily abbreviated Latin text tells us that the manuscript was created for a specialist audience of educated clerics. Its writing is arranged in two columns, a typical layout for scholarly texts like the *Oculus*, and is pep-

Figure 6.2. Rare Books & Manuscripts Library of the Ohio State University Libraries. MS.Lat.1, fol. 47v.

pered with rubricated characters that help punctuate the text and set off different sections of the treatise. These colored letters and symbols work alongside the thematic headings at the top of each leaf, the chapter summaries and short sectional titles written in the margins, and the topical index inserted at the beginning of the book to help readers better navigate the *Oculus*'s complex text.

In addition to these scribal contributions pointing out how the book's creators intended it to be used, reader-added marginal annotations and homemade bookmarks show us how its audience actually used the book. For instance, a note on folio 2ᵛ points out where a discussion of the sacrament of confession occurs, while on folio 72 a series of parallel slits into which is threaded a folded parchment fragment serves as a simple homemade bookmark. Tangible, unique marks of use like these (and there are many more to be found in the manuscript) bring to our attention small sections of text that were of particular interest to one of the manuscript's readers and reveal valuable details about contemporary private reading practices. While students may not be able to read and understand the *Oculus*'s actual text, a close assessment of physical and visible evidence such as the features described above can still teach them much about medieval book production, reading processes, and textual culture.

As well as providing us with information about the creation and reception of medieval manuscripts and its own place within those processes of production and use, the Ohio State *Oculus* also contains evidence that can help shed light on its particular origins and provenance. When considering the text's origins, we know that William of Pagula wrote the text known as the *Oculus sacerdotis*, although he did not personally write the copy owned by Ohio State. Occasionally medieval manuscripts will provide us with direct testimony in prefatory or colophonic statements explaining who penned the text, where it was written, and who commissioned it. Unfortunately, our copy of the manuscript includes no such information. Instead, I tell my students, we are left to hazard a guess about its origin based on a variety of physical and textual clues. First of all, we can determine the manuscript is of English origin by identifying its paleographical style as a form of *Anglicana cursiva*, a type of cursive handwriting that first developed in England in the thirteenth century and continued to evolve throughout the remainder of the Middle Ages. Peculiar morphological details of the script help us date the script to sometime in the early fifteenth century.

Other features that might help date and localize the manuscript can be found in its binding. Although its semi-limp binding structure was a common feature of many books in the Middle Ages, the blind-stamped patterns decorating its front and back covers offer clues about its origins if we compare them with other contemporary bindings featuring similar structures and decorative patterns. For instance, a comparison of the *Oculus*'s decorative tooling with rubbings of known and recorded binding stamps and tooled marks provides a match with a decorative scheme known to have been used on other English bindings as early as 1495 and as late as the second quarter of the sixteenth century.[3] While it is possible that our manuscript was rebound earlier or later than these dates, the binding's decorative scheme does give us a relatively firm *terminus ante quem* and *terminus post quem* for its rebinding.

Additionally, the manuscript fragments used as flyleaves suggest further avenues for exploration. By identifying the texts included in these scraps—a Psalter, in the case of the front endleaves, and a Missal for the rear endleaf—we might be able to tease out details about the evolution of liturgical or devotional rituals and practices specific to particular geographical areas and how these rites changed over time. These recycled fragments also potentially can tell us much about the milieu in which the manuscript was rebound. Other odd details, such as the illustration of a grinning man sticking out his tongue in the gutter of the rear manuscript fragment endleaf (figure 6.3), when compared to other sources, might also shed light on the book's history. When considered together, the fragmentary service book endleaves and the illustration of the grinning man could suggest a connection with Worcester Cathedral and its medieval library, where a fourteenth-century monk named Richard Bromwych was known to have decorated a number of manuscripts with humorous profiles of monks' heads.[4] This possible conclusion, it should be noted, is highly speculative, but it illustrates to students ways in which we can use a manuscript's physical evidence—no mat-

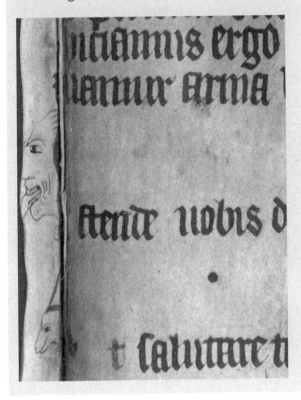

Figure 6.3. Rare Books & Manuscripts Library of the Ohio State University Libraries. MS.Lat.1, detail of gutter of rear flyleaf

lesson used by preachers to enliven their sermons and instruct their listeners. This particular passage concludes with a description of how a man was presumably saved from sin by partaking of the Eucharistic sacrament, after which the earth opened up before him and he was able to witness hell and its punishments. The presence of such a text here is appropriate supplemental information for a priest's handbook concerned with teaching its readers about the sacraments and offering advice on how to deliver sermons. And the fact that it appears in the vernacular reveals that this particular nameless fifteenth-century owner was likely a priest literate in both English and Latin who probably employed the material discussed in the *Oculus* in his work with the lay folk under his spiritual care. Our picture of the *Oculus*'s provenance might be incomplete, but the bookplates, dealer descriptions, and inscriptions it contains can still tell us much about who owned it, how it has been used, and how it has passed from owner to owner over the past 600 years to finally settle in central Ohio.

Although the comprehensive codicological exploration of a source like the *Oculus sacerdotis* might de-emphasize the manuscript's textual contents, such an analysis makes visible to even the most inexperienced student a medieval manuscript's potential to teach us about how books were produced and consumed during the Middle Ages. This approach need not be limited to a study of this one particular manuscript, however. Rather, this overview of how I approach the *Oculus* not as a literary text, but as a physical artifact charged with historical significance communicating itself to us through its own particular language of signs and symbols, serves as a model for how other curators, librarians, and teachers can use the medieval books in their own care to help students see manuscripts not just as historical curiosities or texts accessible only to an initiated few, but as valuable artifacts of cultural memory that offer a clear and vibrant picture of medieval life.

ter how seemingly insignificant—to help us see into its own past with greater clarity.

A variety of clues offering clearer insight into the manuscript's provenance, or history of ownership, is also apparent when we analyze it. Laid into the book is an old return address label identifying the book dealer from whom Ohio State acquired the *Oculus* decades ago. A pair of bookplates affixed to the front pastedown testifies to the manuscript's current and previous ownership, while between them lies a brief, printed description of the codex taken from a dealer's catalogue. Supplementing this evidence of the manuscript's more recent ownership history is an intriguing anonymous inscription found on the verso of the first flyleaf at the front of the book (figure 6.1). Written in fifteenth-century Middle English, the inscription could possibly be an *exemplum*, or short story with a moral or salutary

NOTES

1. The first, and still most complete, look at William of Pagula and his influential text, including a handy list of over sixty manuscripts of the *Oculus* housed in British and American collections, is L.E. Boyle's "The *Oculus sacerdotis* and Some Other Works of William of Pagula," *Transactions of the Royal Historical Society*, ser. 5, 5 (1955): 81-110.

2. The full collational formula reflecting the manuscript's existing structure reads: π^4 1-7^{12} 8^{12} (-8^{12}) 9^{12} 10^8 (10 canc.; + 2 singletons between 5 and 6). I have incorporated the "pi" symbol in accordance with standard bibliographic collational practice for early printed books to represent the addition of "unsigned" preliminary leaves to the main text block.

3. See J. Basil Oldham, *English Blind-Stamped Bindings* (Cambridge, UK: Cambridge University Press, 1952). Roll HM.a (17), pictured in plate XLVII, matches the larger external decorative frame, while roll FP.a (8) matches the inner frame. Oldham cites examples of this combination from 1495, 1519, and 1530-51 (p. 52). Based on this evidence, it seems likely that the binding was executed in London or Oxford. For discussions of Oxford as a center of production for blind-stamped bindings, see Strickland Gibson, *Early Oxford Bindings* (Oxford: Printed for the Bibliographical Society at the Oxford University Press, 1903), and G.D. Hobson, *English Binding Before 1500*, (Cambridge, UK: Cambridge University Press, 1929).

4. R. M. Thomson, *A Descriptive Catalogue of the Medieval Manuscripts in Worcester Cathedral Library* (Cambridge, UK: D.S. Brewer, 2001), xxvii.

"A Special Collection": A Fine Arts-Library Collaborative Project

Claudia Sbrissa and Blythe E. Roveland-Brenton

INTRODUCTION

The Special Collections department, in the main library of St. John's University, New York, has evolved from an eclectic "treasure room" established in the 1960s into a repository of more focused collections of books, manuscripts, and artwork. The University has an enrollment of about 20,000. It is primarily a teaching rather than a research institution, and student engagement is one of its top priorities, especially in recent years. The main library chiefly serves to support the curricula and the research activities of undergraduate and graduate students. Sine 2002, the administration of the Special Collections department has fallen within the responsibilities of the University Archives, which employs one archivist, a staff member and graduate library science student assistants. A library redesign in 2008 resulted in the consolidation of the physical collections from Special Collections and Archives into one much-reduced storage area, with no dedicated classroom or exhibition space. Despite the challenges presented by the lack of staffing and space, we have found ways for Special Collections to be relevant in our institution.

Over a number of years, Special Collections has had moderate success in partnering with teaching faculty, particularly in theology, history and fine arts, to offer class sessions showcasing material from the collection. The most successful collaboration has been with the fine arts department for classes on the history of visual communication, typography, and book arts. The authors (Sbrissa, a fine arts faculty member, and Roveland-Brenton, the archivist and Special Collections librarian) have developed a sustained partnership since 2005 for an undergraduate project in Book Arts. We have found that Special Collections provides important material to expand classroom teaching and offers students hands-on experience with books with which they may not otherwise have the opportunity to engage.

THE ART CLASS AND THE PROJECT

One of the classes Sbrissa offers is an undergraduate course entitled *Book Arts*. It is a mandatory class for all fine art majors offered once a year in the fall semester. Class size averages approximately fifteen students per session. The focus of the class is on creating works of art realized in the form of a book. Students learn how to create hand-made books that explore their conceptual space. They study meaning and object through the examination of historical, theoretical, and technical aspects of artists' books. Working through these methodologies allows for a more comprehensive investigation of ideas and directions as students begin to develop their own artwork.

The students complete six major projects and a series of smaller exercises by the end of the semester. In order for them to negotiate the complex demands of the class, technical and conceptual skills are introduced and built upon project by project. An important component of the student's initial investigation involves researching and analyzing their preliminary thoughts. The research component helps to contextualize their views and provides them with a framework from which they can advance their ideas more fully.

A key assignment developed for this class is a semester-long project entitled *A Special Collection*. This project utilizes the library's Special Collections as a source of inspiration and information. *A Special Collection* is a unique assignment in that it employs skills, both technical and critical, that the students have learned throughout the semester, while drawing inspiration from an outside source. The project begins with a class visit to Special Collections.

VISITS TO SPECIAL COLLECTIONS

The initial class visit to Special Collections provides the students with the opportunity to view and learn about a wide range of pre-selected books—from *incunabula* to art exhibition catalogs, from late 19th-century Japanese crepe-paper fairy tales to true artist books, and from early 20th-century Roycroft books to Barry Moser's Pennyroyal Caxton Bible published at the end of the same century. Many of the most interesting books for this project come from the collection named the "Reference Art File," art exhibition catalogs that were acquired in the 1960s and 1970s through a subscription service from Worldwide Books. A number of these feature novel cover material, multimedia inserts, and a variety of binding styles. We group the selections into assorted categories to highlight certain qualities and characteristics: unusual covers and materials, unique interiors, type, or edges, and form that mirrors content (for example, the catalog of Stephen Antonakos' artwork entitled *"Pillows"* is covered in striped pillow ticking). We have changed some of the books and groupings each time, as we discover new inspiration pieces and rethink the connections between the books in each group. Prior to their first view of these books, students are provided with a bibliography of the works on display with annotations on some of the salient attributes of each book.

On the day of the visit to the library classroom, the books are grouped on tables with labels for each category. In preparation, the students put their backpacks and other items in one corner of the classroom and wash their hands. They are given pencils for note taking and they remain standing throughout the class session. We give a brief introduction to Special Collections and some guidelines about the use and handling of materials from that department. We then move systematically from one category to another pointing out significant facets of the books from the librarian's and the artist's perspective. After this "tour" of the material, the students are free to examine books that intrigue them and take further notes. Most books may be handled by the students, while a few others which are more rare or fragile are shown by the librarian, library assistant or art professor. The class visit lasts for one and a half to two hours.

Following the class session, each student makes individual appointments with Special Collections to examine one or more of the books more closely. They are required to visit at least twice. Usually little intermediation is required by the library staff except for the delivery of the books to the research room and their return to closed stacks at the end of the appointment.

OUTCOME

After the library visits, the students begin to create their actual books, which they work on for the remainder of the semester. The assignment is broken down into several stages involving researching and figuratively deconstructing a book, which includes investigating the genre of the book, its content and concept, form, function and maker/publisher. These preliminary investigations provide a necessary context to assist the students in understanding their impulses and intentions in the process of creating their own work. The students spend a great deal of time working through ideas, both technical and theoretical, with the help of in-class critiques and individual sessions with Sbrissa. They produce several *maquettes* or models of their books throughout the semester, reworking and revising formal and conceptual concerns before the actual piece is completed.

The end result is a unique hand-made book inspired by an in-depth analysis of their selected books from Special Collections, which reflects the students' understanding of the course and highlights their accomplishments. The assignment has led to an impressive body of student work. We offer two detailed examples to demonstrate that work. Clearly, such a brief discussion cannot do justice to the wide-ranging artist books that have been produced for this assignment.

The first example is a book created by Kathleen Hanna (figure 7.1). Hanna's book was inspired by a miniature, limited edition, *Prose and Prophecy: Selections from the Prose and Prophetic Books of William Blake*. The Special Collections book is housed in a custom-made, protective clamshell box produced for it by the preservation department. The seemingly unintentional relationship between the custom-made box and the book imparts a certain emblematic reading of the book as both object and meaning. The book's scale denotes fragility and preciousness, further enhanced by its position in the protective box. The subject matter of the book—Blake's lifelong concern with the struggle of the soul—seems also to be augmented by the physical container in which it is housed. In responding to this book, Hanna utilizes both the formal and conceptual content to inspire her own piece. It consists of a bright red container, reminiscent of a Valentine's Day candy box, which opens to display in its center a tiny coverless book whose fragile white pages have been burned through the core of the entire book. The impact of Hanna's piece is an evocative, rather than exacting, "read" into Hanna's own personal narrative.

The second example features the work of Gabriella D'Abreau (figure 7.2). D'Abreau's book, *Mariana*, was inspired by Antonio Frasconi's *Kaleidoscope in Woodcuts*. Frasconi, one of the foremost woodcut and book artists since the 1940s, combines realist and symbolic imagery to address poetic and socio-political issues. Attracted by his use of lyrical imagery, color and playful yet powerful content, D'Abreau set about creating a book whose format was modeled after Franconi but the content of which dealt with her own personal worldview. The result is a book of fifty-two individually handdrawn and colored illustrations that reveal her unique interpretation.

FUTURE DIRECTIONS

Going forward, we plan to continue to make adjustments to the library visit portion of the assignment.

Figure 7.1. *Left,* Student Kathleen Hanna's book created for *A Special Collection,* 2009. *Right,* A miniature book from Special Collections, *Prose and Prophecy: Selections from the Prose and Prophetic Books of William Blake,* in its custom-made clamshell box. Photo credit: Brian Mikesell

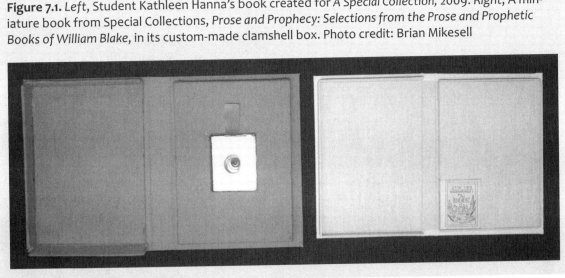

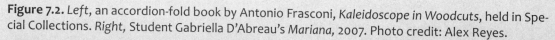

Figure 7.2. *Left*, an accordion-fold book by Antonio Frasconi, *Kaleidoscope in Woodcuts*, held in Special Collections. *Right*, Student Gabriella D'Abreau's *Mariana*, 2007. Photo credit: Alex Reyes.

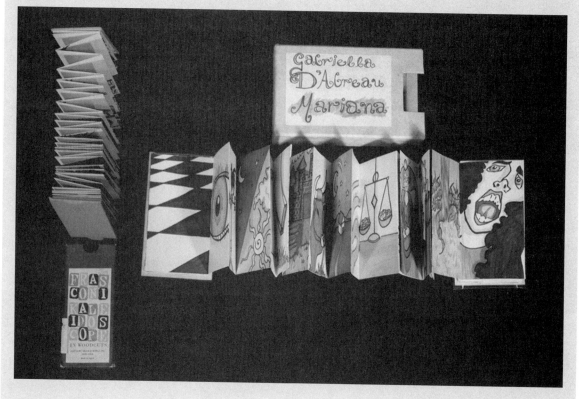

Many of the students are drawn to a small number of books that we have selected for display. Therefore, there is quite a bit of repetition in the use of certain inspiration pieces. On one hand, this can be provocative—demonstrating the multiplicity of artistic visions derived from one book in Special Collections. On the other hand, few of the library's holdings are highlighted and explored. We are still weighing alternative strategies. We could cycle the popular books in and out each semester, but some of them are such wonderful examples of special books, that it would deprive certain classes of the experience of viewing and thinking about them.

We have also have begun paring down the number of books that are shown during the library visit. We have displayed up to fifty books to give students an idea of the range of possibilities. That has proven to be simply too overwhelming for both students

and staff, especially for a visit of two hours. Additionally, we are reconsidering whether the books should be presented in the groupings we have defined or more randomly. Our categorization may discourage the student's own observations about the books.

Part of the project has proven challenging to the library staff. With only two full-time staff in the department, the individual appointments for fifteen to twenty students in a short period of time can be difficult. Special Collections does not have its own classroom space where the books can remain on view for a number of weeks. There are two small research rooms where we can accommodate two to four students for closer study of a small handful of books at one time. Instead of individual appointments, we have begun to schedule blocks of times, during which all the items will be out on library classroom tables for further examination. We believe that this might also prove helpful to the students by giving them a chance to look at the entire range of books again, rather than making a hasty decision about his or her inspiration book during the initial class visit.

We have observed that these art students come to the library for assistance in various aspects of their book arts projects. In particular, they have come to the library preservation department for guidance from the staff in developing their skill in constructing clamshell boxes or other enclosures. Aside from these *ad hoc* observations, we have not yet carried out formal assessments to more fully understand the impact of the assignment on the student experience and their perceptions of the library as a resource. Assessment will be built into future iterations of our joint endeavor.

Importantly, we are planning to extend the project by presenting this work outside the context of the classroom. We will install an exhibition in the library to showcase the best student work alongside the books that inspired them. Although there is a university gallery in another building, we believe that an exhibition within the main library will provide the necessary context for the books on display, attract a broader student audience, and, therefore, call attention to the rich holdings of Special Collections. We are also investigating the possibility of offering the show to other universities as an exchange exhibition, to inspire others to use their own Special Collections and to understand how other schools may be utilizing their collections. As an extension to the exhibition, we will host an interdisciplinary panel to address how Special Collections might be utilized more fully by various departments within a university setting. We will schedule the show to correspond with other book arts events in the New York metropolitan area.

An exciting prospect on the horizon is to begin a collection of student-produced books that will be purchased by the library from individual students. It will be of mutual benefit to the students and the library. The works will be judged by fine arts faculty and librarians. Those selected will receive an offer to be purchased for inclusion in Special Collections. The library will be able to build a teaching and research collection that brings "student engagement" to a new level. Certainly, while we wish to offer a fair price, the costs for the library will be considerably lower than if we were to begin acquiring work by established artists. The students will be able to point to the catalog records of their work in the holdings of a university's Special Collections, helping them as they launch their careers. With those future aspirations in mind, we eagerly look forward to many more years of collaboration and inspiration.

BIBLIOGRAPHY

Antonakos, Stephen, Sebastian J. Adler, and Meredith Long Gallery. 1971. *"Pillows" (1962-1963)*. Houston, Tex.: Fidelity Print. Co.

Blake, William. 1964. *Prose and prophecy: Selections from the prose and prophetic books of William Blake*. Franklin, N.H.: Hillside Press.

Frasconi, Antonio. 1968. *Kaleidoscope in woodcuts*. New York: Harcourt, Brace & World.

Artists' Books: Esthetics, Media, Communication

Ruth Copans and John Anzalone

In 2006, Skidmore College redesigned its introductory core curriculum for first year students. The "First Year Experience" (FYE) program consists of some 40 Scribner Seminars,[1] designed by individual faculty members to explore the interdisciplinary ramifications of their own special academic interests. Scribner Seminar teaching faculty members also serve as mentors and advisors to the 16 first year students who enroll in their seminars. In the second year of the FYE, the College devised an innovative option for the instantly successful program. In their second semester, first year students could elect a one credit Interdisciplinary (ID) course from among some fifteen subjects that were, once again, proposed by faculty who wished to share with them interests that no existing courses satisfied. The Scribner Colloquia are intended to build on the excitement and momentum of the Scribner Seminars by offering an intimate connection to provocative topics designed by self-selecting faculty members, and delivered at a time in the student's academic life that research has identified as potentially vulnerable in contexts as diverse as adaptation to college, motivation, and retention.[2]

As Special Collections Librarian, Ruth Copans had worked extensively to build and promote The Lucy Scribner Library's Artists' Book collection. Although these books have been used regularly by several members of the Studio Art faculty, in 2007 there was no formal course with the Artists' Books at its core. Ruth thus decided to team teach a colloquium with John Anzalone, a French Professor, a fellow enthusiast of bibliophilic history. Team

teaching enabled the diverse emphases we represent to combine in a playful, pedagogically rich experience for our youngest students. We designed the course specifically to encourage a vibrant use of Special Collections, and to include as topics of conversation and inquiry the complexity of the texts and the conditions of their material production; the book as object in terms of structure and illustration. We were aiming, through the Artist's Book, to generate conversations not simply about the history and significance of a special area in the history of printing, but about the continuing evolution of the object of the book in the information age.

In describing the course, we presented a context: "Born in post WWI France of the fertile interplay of painting, poetry and literary innovation, the *livre d'artiste* or Artist's Book has evolved over nearly a century of change into a crossroads for media, communications and esthetics." Eight curious, alert students enrolled for a weekly meeting in the Pohndorf Room, Skidmore's Special Collections sanctum, to delve into the complex, multiple ways of "reading" the Artist's Book. Readings involved essays on the history of the book, on book design and illustration as acts of critical thinking, and on the postmodern and ludic dimensions of the book as object. Class exercises included opportunities for students to dissect a book, and to make a book, so as to emphasize the actual physical presence of books, and the architecture involved in construction of so commonplace an object. We began our course by giving each student a discarded library book to dissect. Although many found this a stressful exercise, they still marveled over the elegant construction of such a simple but durable mechanism. This examination of the interrelationship of structure and function carried over two classes while they read Robert Darnton's "What is the History of Books?" (*The Book History Reader*, pp. 9–18).

We started our examination of illustrated books specifically by looking at William Blake and William Morris. This allowed us to introduce esthetic considerations, and to question the relationship of text to image, even as it initiated our students to the work of two seminal figures in the history of the book. We challenged their analytic skills by assigning them Joanna Drucker's "Conceptualizing the Book" (*The Century of Artists' Books*) to provide an explicitly theoretical context for what they were seeing.

We next presented our students with a unit on the *livre d'artiste* in France and its important precedents for the modern book arts movement. Understanding the rich inheritance from the great French traditions of printing, bookmaking, and bookbinding was an important base from which to evaluate the more modern incarnations of the Artists' Books. Thanks to a sizable collection of sample plates from these books, we were able to allow them close examination of mise en page, typography and illustrations. In parallel with the French connection, we interrogated fine press books, examining the Dove's Press *Bible*, important productions of the Gehenna Press, and some of the other more traditional finely printed books. Readings included Judd and Renee Riese Hubert's introduction to *The Cutting Edge of Reading: Artists' Books*, Stefan Klina's "Definition" (from *Artists Books: A Critical Survey of the Literature*), and Karen Wirth's "Re-Reading the Boundless Book" (from *Talking the Boundless Book*).

Working from the resources our small but select Special Collections allowed, we were able to access a number of important, elegant books produced by Barry Moser and Michael Kuch, one primarily a wood engraver, the other a poet, designer, and engraver. They live and work in close proximity to each other yet because their work has evolved in unique and different directions, they provided us with striking contrasts with Barry Moser, primarily an illustrator, Michael Kuch a sort of inventor. Moser's work emphasizes history, allusion and craftsmanship; Kuch's books brought to the conversation questions of innovative design and structure, and emphasized the role of play and imagination in the creative process.

Two sessions were specifically devoted to women book artists. These enabled the students to examine and assess works by Claire Van Vliet, Carol Blinn, Robin Price, Shirley Jones, Harriet Bart, Julie Chen, and the Women's Studio Workshop. Simultaneously, we read Cathy Courtney's "Julie Chen" (from *Speaking of Book Arts*) and used it as a springboard to conversations concerning the role women have played historically in the production of books, and the issues contemporary women book artists face in the making and promotion of their work. Several women have chosen to use the platform of the book to examine questions of domesticity, historical and political issues in the context of the politics of gender. Here inventive structures combine with biting political commentary, making these books particularly apt objects for close scrutiny and discussion for first year students.

Students were now prepared for a more thorough consideration of the idea of an *oeuvre*. Late in the course we thus devoted individual sessions to two exemplary figures, Walter Hamady and Maureen Cummins. The former was a long time teacher of book arts at the University of Wisconsin. His Perishable Press[3] has inspired a generation of devotees, not to mention apprentices of his style and work. A self-described curmudgeon, Walter Hamady often executed every aspect of the making of a Perishable Press book, from its paper to binding. His colophons often include ludic/parodic descriptions of the clothes pulped to make paper, the prevailing weather conditions during the production, and personal tidbits about his family. His books run the gamut from simple to complex objects and are often idiosyncratic examples of the myriad and at times incomprehensible symbols of his life. Students appreciated Buzz Spector's "Biblioselfconsciousness: Walter Hamady's Gabberjabs" (in **The Book Maker's Desire**) in which the author speaks of Hamady's **Gabberjabs** as erotic objects of desire. It was a significant advantage for the students to be able to consult the complete run of the notoriously scarce Gabberjabs precisely in the context of on-going discussions of the postmodern and playful elements of the artist's book.

Maureen Cummins' books, in contrast, seem the humble objects of everyday family or business life: a ledger, a photo album, a checkbook, a crazy quilt. Upon close reading however, her deeply subversive intentions are revealed. She forces the reader to be an active participant in interpreting her art, to see simultaneously something new and something old, and something new *in* something old. Beyond the aesthetic experience the object provides with its plastic qualities, Cummins also aims at an ideological and political experience of the book as catalyst of awareness; herein lie the power and beauty of her work.

The penultimate class session was devoted to themed books: alphabets, religious, political, erotic, humorous, and grotesque titles graced the book trucks that day, and the quality of student commentary was a gratifying demonstration of the distance they had come since the beginning of term. They saw immediately that we had presented them with another way of analyzing the collection. The shift from artist/creator to theme-based works opened the door to an opportunity to consider how collections can be and have been organized, and what that says about both artists and libraries.

Our final assignment, of which a fuller description appears below, asked the students to propose designs for their own, individual Artist's Book. We did not expect them to make a book, but rather to describe to us what an Artist's Book of their own devising would look like. We encouraged the students to take all the liberties they liked in thinking about their books. We promoted imitation and stressed the need to use only mundane supplies in the making of the mock-up. We urged them to be as imaginative as the many works they had assessed and enjoyed over the semester. The last session of the course was devoted to their musings, and we asked that they be prepared to explain the reasons behind their choices of subject matter and materials when they shared their ideas with their classmates and with us.

We were hardly expecting actual material books but in fact all but one of the students came with elaborate mock-ups in addition to the description. Although the imitations of some of what they had seen and studied were, of course, apparent, what was especially striking was how clearly they had understood and internalized the fundamental idea that an Artist's Book is often a translation, a material rendering of serious ideas that arise at the crossroads of social and personal concerns. We were thus treated to authentic works with personal, political, environmental and psychological dimensions. The discrimination in the selection of materials used was also testimony to the close observations that had taken place. When we consider that this course met for only one hour per week, over a thirteen week term, and that none of the students came with any more than their intellectual curiosity about the subject, their final projects speak eloquently of the power of the special collections/artist's book to engage, to provoke and to stimulate.

The success of the class was measurable in not only the students' excitement and engagement with the books as demonstrated by their projects, but also in the commitment over the longer term to further study. One of our students was accepted into Skidmore's competitive summer collaborative research program for a project on Artists' Books. This involved her working closely as a researcher for several months with Ruth, and then accompanying her to Minneapolis to a conference with a panel on Artists' Books where Ruth gave a paper on her research. This student has just graduated and will in September 2010 begin doctoral study in English at the University of Wisconsin. We find it delightful that she is heading Walter Hamady's way. She also worked in Special Collections throughout her time at Skidmore, curating exhibitions that drew on our Artists' Books collection and serving as a resource to what is now a growing number of students who seem to have gotten the message.

Another student did her senior Honors project on "the tensions between the visual and linguistic power of words." The result was an exhibition called *Text Messages* held at Skidmore's Tang Museum, whose web site describes it as follows:

In *Text Messages* the word is the image. Featuring pieces from the Tang's collection and on extended loan, the show presents a wide range of contemporary works, including prints, drawings, and sculpture. The artists on view approach language through such strategies as the imperative voice, creating "written readymades," and self-reflexivity... Installed in the Kettlewell Print Study Room, *Text Messages* includes work by Nayland Blake, Nancy Dwyer, Angus Fairhust, Matthew Higgs, Jenny Holzer, Christian Marclay, Jane Masters, Marlene McCarty, Erika Rothenberg, and Ed Ruscha (see http:// tang.skidmore.edu/index.php/calendars/ view/306/tag:1/year:all)

The enduring impact of our one credit ID colloquium on at least two of our eight students was measurable. And if the others, some art majors, some humanities majors, melted back into their own academic concentrations, our occasional conversations on campus when we met up with them never failed to evoke the interest the course had generated, the success of the team-teaching/collaborative model, and the abiding appeal of the focused analysis of the book as object of communication and vehicle for artistic creation.

APPENDIX 8.1

ID 151 010 Artists' Books
Final Project Instructions

The final project is to be a design of an Artist's Book of your own, accompanied by a 2-3 page essay explaining the rationale for your choices of text, image, paper, binding, construction, structure, etc.

A mock up of the actual book should be included even though you are not expected to actually create the book.

Please, however, make sure there is a

title page

and

colophon!

You can use computer generated text and image (or just cut out pictures from magazines or whatever) and be as creative (or not) as you'd like

but

by all means

have a GOOD time doing it.

And, make it something that will be fun for us to look at.

We will share these on the last day of class. All of you will get an opportunity to present your book and talk about your choices.

If you've any questions, please don't hesitate to ask us.

John and Ruth

NOTES

1. The seminars bear the name of the College founder, Lucy Scribner. Classes are capped at 16 students, and the teaching faculty also serve as mentors/advisors to the students who enroll in their seminars.

2. ID colloquia are limited to 10 students per section and may be team taught without any increase in the enrollment ceiling. In addition to The Artist's Book, topics have included, among many others, Comic Books and Graphic Novels; Hunger in America; Italian Cinema; Perception; and "Dead Serious," a course on the music and sociology of the Grateful Dead.

3. The Roger Trienens gift of a virtually complete run of the Perishable Press books to the Scribner Library's Special Collections allowed students a privileged look at the sequential output of one of the emblematic book artists' presses in the United States over the last generation. Similarly, the library boasts a complete run of the books Maureen Cummins has created. In choosing these two book artists we were especially mindful of the advantages having these full sets in the collection provided us and the students.

UNIVERSITY OF PENNSYLVANIA

Crazy for Pamela in the Rare Books Library: Undergraduates Reflect on Doing Original Research in Special Collections

Sarah Arkebauer, Toni Bowers, Lauren Corallo, Eoin Ennis, Rivka Fogel, Jessica Kim, Michael Masciandaro, John Pollack, Tatum Regan, Tyler Russell, Sandra Sohn, Marykate Stopa, Jessica Sutro, and Valeria Tsygankova.

INTRODUCTORY NOTE

For more than ten years now, I have regularly led an undergraduate research seminar in the Rare Book and Manuscript Library at the University of Pennsylvania. Over the years, "The *Pamela* Craze: A Research Seminar" has turned into the most exciting and rewarding undergraduate course I teach at Penn; it has a competitive enrollment (currently limited to students in our Ben Franklin Scholars Society) and students in the class produce some astonishingly mature research. Twice-weekly meetings are held in a seminar room in the rare books library, where each student is responsible for original research over a 16-week semester. A course syllabus appears as an Appendix at the end of this article.

Most of the students who enroll in "The *Pamela* Craze" have never used rare books or manuscripts before, and they launch into their research with enthusiasm, even wonder. I am in the fortunate position of hearing students report their delight in making their own discoveries and in developing new skills. They have the chance to work closely with our extraordinarily welcoming and supportive rare books librarians and in the process become familiar with the collection, which over the course of the semester students come to recognize as one of Penn's most valuable resources.

The structure of the course, and the central role of the rare books library in making it possible, origi-nally suggested itself to me when I was lecturing on Samuel Richardson's immensely influential first novel *Pamela* (1740) in a survey course in British novel history. I mentioned the fact that *Pamela* generated a small universe of responses, critiques, parodies, spurious continuations and back-stories, operas, burlesques and farces, poetry and songs, fashion, and pornography, and that only a small fraction of that lively group of texts remains in print or is even known to scholars. Students were interested in this fact and were delighted with Henry Fielding's *Shamela*, one of the only texts from the large number of Pamela-derived items then available to them in a modern edition. (Those were the days of print resources only). It occurred to me that with such a rich rare books library right on campus, I could encourage students to discover some of these texts for themselves.

Anyone who has worked at rare books libraries knows that not all welcome heavy traffic and non-specialized users. At a different institution, the main obstacle to teaching my course in the sacred precincts of the rare book library might have been the librarians themselves. I was already well acquainted with Penn's rare books staff and knew them to be remarkably accommodating toward my own research. But at that time they were not used to having undergraduates around. So it was with some trepidation that I broached the idea of my course with my library colleagues. My concern was entirely needless. It would be impossible to imagine a rare books staff more ready to welcome and assist undergraduate researchers. From the beginning, distinguished librarians came into my classes repeatedly over the semester and worked one-on-one with each of my students. Their commitment to pedagogy and the joy they took in watching undergraduates successfully negotiate the specialized library was more than I could have hoped. It is the library's commitment to undergraduate teaching, fully as much as my own, that has made this course so successful for many years now. In its earliest days, "The *Pamela* Craze" benefited greatly from the generosity and expertise of Daniel Traister, Curator of Research Services; in recent years, my students and I have had the pleasure of working closely with Library Specialist John Pollack.

"The *Pamela* Craze," as our course is called, ends with a roundtable discussion. This chance to look back on the opportunities and challenges posed by research into special collections has become a tradition at the end of each offering of the course: students bring to class the rare materials that they have discovered over the course of the semester, review their work in the Rare Book and Manuscript Library, discuss their ongoing research projects, and talk about the structure of the syllabus and their experience over the semester. In recent years, they have explicitly addressed the relation of electronic databases to the material texts in the rare books library, and they have described their strategies for integrating both into their own learning. This final meeting has proven immensely enlightening to me when it comes to the question of how undergraduates can best use and learn from Penn's collection of rare books and manuscripts, and it has led me to make specific adjustments in the course over the years.

What follows is a transcript of the Spring 2010 semester's final class meeting in "The *Pamela* Craze," the roundtable discussion. We offer it here as a means of demonstrating and celebrating the breadth and maturity of research that undergraduates are capable of when they are welcomed into rare books libraries. Readers are invited to listen to thoughtful undergraduates talk about their experiences in the library in their own voices—what they learned during their semester of research into rare books; how they learned it; what has been surprising or particularly valuable; what might be revised; and what they expect to take from the course into their future work.[1] We are grateful for this chance for *undergraduates themselves* to speak about their experiences as researchers and to gain some experience with scholarly publishing.

The transcript came about in this way: toward the end of the semester, in response to the call for papers by the editors of *Past or Portal? Enhancing Undergraduate Learning Through Special Collections and Archives*, I consulted with the members of the seminar and drafted an abstract that the seminar as a whole subsequently workshopped together. As joint authors, we submitted our abstract to the editors of the volume. Within several weeks, my students and I were excited to learn that our proposal had been accepted for publication. The roundtable transcribed here took place on the seminar's final day of class, April 27, 2010. Jessica Sutro (a member of the seminar) worked with me to produce and edit the transcript from a video of the final class session made by Media Coordinator Sean Zamechek of Penn's School of Arts and Sciences Computing Services. IT Support Specialist Brian J. Kirk assisted Sean, Jessica, John Pollack, and me in producing a YouTube video to accompany this transcript; it can be accessed through the English Department website or the University of Pennsylvania Libraries homepage.

A final note. Readers will notice that many students refer to "my text." They are framing their comments around the semester-long research project described in the appended Syllabus. Each student was assigned to find in the rare books library a *Pamela*-related work published before 1800 and not already included on the course reading list. Students found works from the British Isles, North America, France, and Germany. Some stretched the assignment in the agreeable direction of finding works derived from or indebted to Richardson's second novel, *Clarissa* (1747-48), and some found works of visual art. One found her text not at Penn but at the Library Company of Pennsylvania, a well-known local repository with its own rich collections. As readers will discover, every student developed a strong attachment to the work on which his or her own research focused, and which they had discovered for themselves in the rare books library.

~ Toni Bowers

CRAZY FOR *PAMELA* IN THE RARE BOOKS LIBRARY
Transcript of Roundtable Discussion : "THE PAMELA CRAZE"

Roundtable Participants—
Professor Toni Bowers (TB)
John Pollack, Library Specialist (JP)
Sarah Arkebauer (SA)
Lauren Corallo (LC)
Eoin Ennis (EE)
Rivka Fogel (RF)
Jessica Kim (JK)
Michael Masciandaro (MM)
Tatum Regan (TAR)
Tyler Russel (TYR)
Sandra Sohn (SS)
Marykate Stopa (MS)
Jessica Sutro (JS)
Valeria Tsygankova (VT)

Transcript
Toni Bowers: …. Let's turn now to talking about our course in a more global way. I was very impressed with your comments on the email exchange. Eoin suggested that we think about whether reading the actual text in the rare books library added to your ability to interpret the text or changed the questions

you might ask about it. Remember that posting from Eoin: "For me, seeing the typeface of the words and phrases added a new layer of meaning." And I think it was you, Jessica, who wrote about combining reading the text online and reading the physical text. And then Sandra asked a very interesting question about what she called "the environment of discourse." Trying to put our texts in relation to one another on an historical timeline was what you suggested, Sandra, right? With the goal to piece together a coherent sense of "the *Pamela* craze," or at least our own small version of it—remember this is all still just the tip of the iceberg.

Jessica Sutro: I asked the question about Eighteenth-Century Collections Online (ECCO) versus the regular book. A lot of people, when they talk about online versus the original, talk about the typeface, as Eoin said, the little things that you notice when you have the actual book in your hands versus the online version. But I think it's not just that. I found I was more enthusiastic about the assignment when I was provided with the opportunity to see the actual text. I used both [formats] when I was doing my report, but when I was using ECCO it was just not as exciting. I think that a lot of the enthusiasm in this class came from the fact that we were actually able to go to the rare books library and pick up and see the original text. You feel actually connected to when it was written. That is something that you can't get when you use ECCO.

Eoin Ennis: I'm using a facsimile for this [class session] right now. The typeface is still the same, but that memory of using the actual book—especially the binding, handling it—it's definitely not the same [having a facsimile]. I'm more enthusiastic about the original work.

Marykate Stopa: I think also the original book can give you some clues about the use of the book and the history of it. I know my book[2] and a lot of people's books had three hole punches in the middle, which signified that it was part of a pamphlet, so from that you were able to see into the history of the book. (Bowers_001) Mine was a play, and from the three hole punches we could determine that this might have been sold as a pamphlet [at the theater] as a kind of souvenir.

Tyler Russell: Valeria, yours had the handwriting in the back?

Valeria Tsygankova: Yeah, mine was Richardson's letter/lifestyle manual [known as] *Familiar Letters*, and it was really interesting to see how an early reader had used it. We weren't really able to say *when* the person had used it, but they made notations of certain words or phrases and placed them at the very back of the book. It was interesting to see evidence of someone actually going through and using the book for their own writing.

JS: I think it also inspires you to get more into the research. Valeria investigated whether the pencil that was used indicated that [the writing in the back of the book] was from a particular time. Things like that you wouldn't have researched if you had been looking at it only on ECCO.

I [also] did research on pricing because ECCO had multiple [editions of my text[3]] with various prices and mine had a different price, and that interested me. So there are research questions that you probably wouldn't have asked if you hadn't had the original.

VT: Right now, when we all physically have our books together here, we get a sense of all the writings that come out of *Pamela*, are influenced by it, all together in this one space. It would have been harder to get a feel for that grouping on the internet.

TYR: In mine, there's this great prefatory dedication that was missing from the version on ECCO. ECCO has the entire text, *The Maid of the Mill*, but there's this really long dedication [only in the printed text] which is by the author. It gave an insight into the tone of the whole piece, even though it wasn't a part of the text on ECCO.

TB: That kind of observation allow us insights into the purposes of publication. It also raises questions that we've talked about before concerning what counts as the text. How much *is* the text? At this time, the mid- eighteenth century, what counts as the text often depends on which edition you happen to read, who owned it, how they treated it. Which is sort of very destabilizing, isn't it, to those of us who think we can just go buy our Penguin edition and say, there we have the text. It turns out that the work itself can be something very different.

EE: It seems too, in this period, the printers were very much in on the discussion—it wasn't just the author. Sometimes it was an author-printer, as in the case of Richardson, and the physical book ends up having a lot to do with the text.

Lauren Corallo: Speaking of the construction of the book and what Jessica was saying about researching unexpected questions, there's something that I wouldn't have researched if I hadn't had this physical text.[4] I found the impression of the copper plates used on the page; you can feel on the back of my pages where the printing machine made indentations. Things like that that made me feel closer to the text and caught my eye. Then I went and researched copper plate printing.

Michael Masciandaro: Another thing you get from looking at the actual texts themselves is a sense for the printing, that process, in addition to the words you're reading. When you go online you look at the text as material for [certain kinds of] scholarship, whereas if you look at the original you get a sense of the material text. Mine was Charles Povey's *The Virgin in Eden*,[5] a response to *Pamela* that really vilified the hot scenes [in Richardson's original version]. In the back it had advertisements for all of Povey's other works. The list starts out in normal sized font and then the print gets smaller as you go down, which suggests that the printer just didn't want to print another page. He tried to fit it all on one [page]. Unless you knew something about the printing, you wouldn't have deduced that from ECCO. So it was interesting to see the process of printing as well as the text.

TB: Right—so we have a lot of [what we might call] sociological information we've been able to pick up. Do you feel that you have pushed that toward, or combined that with, textual interpretation [traditionally defined]? Do we understand *Pamela* any differently for having done this work with original publications?

Jessica Kim: Definitely it helps place the text. For example, when I was reading my piece, *A Present for a Servant-Maid*,[6] I thought it was awesome that I was holding a book that somebody else might have been reading in a different century. I thought, this book is as old as America, and I get to hold it. It definitely made me realize how *real* the novel *Pamela* was in the context where it was first published. Sometimes it's easy to just look at the text and forget about the history behind it and the context in which it was published; but because you have an actual artifact of that time, it makes the history much more real.

SA: And you're forced to think about *Pamela*, or whatever book it is, in the [specific] era when it was published, and not in light of everything which has come *after* it. You know, you have your modern copy of a book with a hundred introductions and all these afterwords with timelines. In comparison [the original book is] like a little piece of history.

TB: I'm glad to hear you say that. I wanted to structure this course as a place where students would pause in their syllabi or curricula and look at just one thing for an extended period of time. Because when you encounter most novels on a syllabus, they're in a line. One title leads to another and each text is just a moment precursing the next text. I thought that being able to arrest that process might have interpretive or pedagogical value.

EE: Even with Richardson's own writing, with the four volumes of *Pamela*, you got a sense of what he would have been responding to. Even though I did see the volumes in many ways as a unified whole, you also get a sense of what was prodding him to go on, to answer questions [raised] by some of the other works that were coming out at the same time.

TB: Right—Kelly so bothered him, and Fielding

so bothered him, that he went back and altered his own novel.

VT: I think we get a really strong sense of Richardson responding to readers and readers responding to him in the texts we read. We can see him influencing the parodies, and the other authors influencing him to change his work or to continue his work. And then also all those anecdotes, like that little farm boy who was so influenced by *Pamela* that he would cry and he wanted to be her—things like that. Holding the physical text you get a sense of the readers that it would have been directed towards and the people who would have been using it, and how that changes [over time].

JS: I think that what Michael said was particularly relevant for Richardson because he was a printer and had an active hand in publishing his own works. I have advertisements at the back of mine as well, and it made me think that it's not just the author, it's also the person behind the [author, who matters]. I think this was particularly relevant for our discussions about Richardson. The way he dealt with his text and readers' responses to it is so integral to understanding him and the revisions he made to *Pamela*.

TB: The text kept changing.

Sarah Arkebauer: In the same vein, I think the physicality of the text, and thinking about who's publishing it, helped us to understand why some people reading it at the time might not even have known Richardson wrote it. All of these questions now have obvious answers—of course Richardson wrote this text. But for thinking about how readers understood *Pamela* at the time, having our own time-sensitive documents helped us get into the mindset of those people.

TB: Yes. If readers are told it's a work of fiction, or if they're not told that in the beginning, it's a different book for each of those readers.

MK: When I came into the class I thought of *Pamela* and similar older literature from a very modern perspective—that these were great works of literature. But after seeing the parodies and plays it's kind of taken *Pamela* down and put it more into the context of pop culture at the time, and I think that's really interesting. For example, I really like this set of [eleven] engravings of *Pamela*.[7]

VT: And people would hang them up! The way people interacted with these things is so different from the way that we do now, but having them in front of us makes us realize the way readers would have interacted with these texts.

Rivka Fogel: I usually focus more on contemporary literature; for me "The *Pamela* Craze" was just a class for a requirement that I had to fill. But then we start actually dealing with the texts, and dealing with the history, the pop culture context of the eighteenth century, and the culture of book. I wouldn't have gotten that from a different class—I would not have focused so much on what we focused on.

TYR: I think one habitual thing for me was always to look at the quality of the text, like how good do I think it is. A lot of these pieces work in conjunction with Richardson and they don't make sense without having *Pamela*. And there's a reason they're out of print. But looking at them as responses kind of removed the critic in me. I wasn't really thinking, "am I enjoying this?" It was making sense as an historical response to Richardson. I was thinking about how it responded in its own time, and not just "do I think this play is funny now?"

TB: Right, so you're thinking about the *function* of the text—the text is something that plays a role, rather than just something to be evaluated, admired or not.

JS: [I want to build] off of what Rivka said about the responses [of eighteenth century readers of *Pamela*]. *Pamela* sets up the problems they faced with passive obedience, but then you saw how some people didn't agree with [Pamela's treatment of that issue], or treated it differently; I thought that was really interesting. I also remember that when Rivka presented on her book[8] she said "I can't believe they wrote these things for children"—the book seemed

not fit for children. And Professor Bowers said "actually, during this time, it wouldn't have been seen as scandalous to write this way for children." That kind of feel for a time period I don't usually get as much of, even when I take a class based in historical literature.

John Pollack: So a different interpretative question can be generated—a whole lens that you might not have thought of looking through.

MM: It's not even just in this class that I get a sense of the *Pamela* craze. [I also saw it when] looking at texts from the French Enlightenment. I'm doing my paper on Denis Diderot's *The Nun* which is sort of a response to *Pamela* and *Clarissa*. It's actually quite extraordinary: reading these other works, you see flashes of *Pamela*, or they'll even mention *Pamela*, and it's like, "man, I can't escape this text!" It's really quite extraordinary the impact it had. We can only get a small sense of that with our syllabus here. I feel like I'm going to see *Pamela* referenced in books from now until the end of my schooling; maybe even after that!

JS: Funny you say that because last night I was watching *Jane Eyre* with my roommate. And they had the whole master-servant thing going on and I was watching it and thought—oh my god it's *Pamela*!…

TB: I used to teach this class so that we went into the twentieth century. We read a very interesting book by Upton Sinclair actually called *Another Pamela*. It retells the *Pamela* story in Hollywood. Pamela is a Seventh-day Adventist who gets swept up with the kinds of people that hung around Hearst Castle in the 1930s—it's absolutely hilarious. And we used to end the course with *Pretty Woman*, the Julia Roberts movie, which is a *Pamela* story.

Of course *Pamela* itself has debts; the largest plot of *Pamela* goes way back. What might be some antecedents of *Pamela*?

JK: Shakespeare wrote a play called *Pericles* and in that play there's a character who's taken to a brothel and she converts everybody.

TYR: I just read that a few weeks ago for a class, and I thought the same thing. She works in a brothel and all the men who go in to visit her—you see them go in the door, the scene cuts, and they all come out saying "I will never come back to a brothel—it changed my life!"

SA: I think this speaks to how this class was organized. We were focusing on *Pamela* not just for its [isolated] literary merits, like Ty was talking about earlier. The literary merit of *Pamela* can be enhanced by looking at the greater context. Usually when we read something in a class it's because it's a "great work of literature." Not to say that this isn't great literature, but to think about its impact is interesting.

Sandra Sohn: I think we're definitely more skeptical about each author's merits as a writer and also we consider them more as people. What I thought was really interesting in this course was the whole Fielding-Richardson dynamic. I thought that was really very multi-layered. When I was reading Richardson I recognized parts that I thought were a response to something else, and Fielding was definitely a response to Richardson. I think we tend to put writers of really old texts—we etch them in stone. We don't really consider them as people who are affected by other authors, who are affected by a more general discourse.

JS: I think Richardson's easier to do that with [than other authors]. I took a Jane Austen class last semester and it was often said, "don't try to interpret what she's doing because we don't really know her life." We don't get a really good sense [of Austen] in the way that we do of Richardson through the letters that he wrote. He had such an active dialogue with readers. With other authors, we don't usually have the opportunity, the insight into the dynamic relationship authors have with their own texts. I think Richardson is kind of a unique case in that [way]. A lot of authors we can't do that with, and if you try our teachers often say, "no, don't guess the author's intentions." Intention seems to be off limits.

TB: We've talked about that [the issue of the author's intention], and about trying to balance out

our approach in Richardson's case. Richardson is an author who in several places, within or external to his novels, says "this is what I was attempting to do." We might not believe that straight on—he's going to have rhetorical or other reasons for saying it at that point or to that person—but we can take it on board. It's not that we have to bracket out everything the author says, [as if] the last person who knows anything is the author. But we [do] try to perform a more nuanced analysis of that kind of information. And you're right, for such an early author, we really have a lot from Richardson. By now we all know how coy he was, how aware of shaping his self-representation, and how aware he was of audience. We can never just simply believe Richardson, but what he says does matter.

One thing I'm very encouraged to hear is the way several of you have described your experience in this course as a chance to step up as an interpreter and say, "I can ask questions of this text that maybe haven't been default questions in my education so far." As an undergraduate, you tend to approach the text, [as] several of you have said, [taking it] for granted that "this is a Great Work of Art. That's why it's still in print and I am reading it." We've been confronted this semester with works that may or may not be works of art. Certainly our considerations of the second half of *Pamela* [speak to and] complicate the issue here. We have the rest of the very same book, by the [same] canonical author, and yet what's happened to "Part II" in literary history? I hope [that recognizing such paradoxes] has forced you to think more like mature critics.

Tatum Regan: One of the most interesting parts of Richardson was how reflective of the anxieties of the time [his works were].

TYR: Well, like Sarah said, a lot of what we read didn't have [modern editorial] introductions. In introductions you invariably have a sentence like "the hugely influential work of—" and then you never really explore that; you say, "oh, it shaped these other books later." But here we are actually looking at books published later that same year, holding and seeing real books that were a direct result [of *Pamela*]. There's no doubt that *Pamela* was influential—it [directly] influenced all the other authors that we read.

TB: We have evidence for that before our eyes.

TYR: There's something very different about actually exploring and finding evidence of influence. Rather than just saying "two hundred years ago this was an influence."

SS: I think Ty definitely has a point. When I was reading *Pamela Censured*,[9] for instance, I never forgot the timeline in which it was published. It was released within ten days of the fourth edition of *Pamela* and it was also published a little bit after *Shamela*. I definitely considered that timeline when reading the text; the text reflects the discourse at that moment.

TYR: And with all these pieces we were also looking at a timeline in a matter of months, not decades or centuries. We were saying "this came out at the end of 1740, this at the beginning of 1741."

TB: We needed to know that. For some works, [we needed to know] which *volume* came out when.

JP: I think there's something important about that. An old professor of mine used to point out that we live in a timescale of days and weeks and months, not decades and generations, but it's very hard to reconstruct that in a literary history. But you guys are doing precisely that. It does give you a completely different timeline in a way that often, as you point out, just gets swept away while thinking of a much longer period. That's a terrific point.

TB: I hope that helps everyone to *not* make generalizations like "in the eighteenth century, people thought…." Because we now know that in March of 1741 people thought many different things and quarreled with each other about them all. It's really important not to collapse the past in a way that we wouldn't accept for the present.

VT: It was interesting to learn about the timeline of Richardson's composition and [the development

of] his own thinking. It was especially interesting to learn about *Familiar Letters*[10] and the set of letters in it that stages the beginning of *Pamela*. There's a servant writing to her father and saying, "I'm in this situation, I don't know what to do," and the father says "you should leave." And then she writes that she has left. The entirety of *Pamela* just [doesn't happen]. It's so interesting to learn about that text being the stepping stone for Richardson, how everything came out of that beginning point.

TB: Another of these shibboleths that we're always told—like "don't think of intention"—is the notion that characters have no life outside of the text. After starting *Familiar Letters*, Richardson asked, "Well, what if she had stayed?" and he writes another story. And clearly the people of his time thought of Pamela as having a life that far exceeded Richardson's text. Everybody felt authorized to write *Pamela in High Life*[11] or whatever, just as if Pamela did have, or could have had, an existence outside Richardson's text. For many good reasons, I discourage students from thinking that way habitually. But it is important to realize that in Richardson's time, they didn't have our critical superegos putting a ceiling on what they could ask or imagine. That's part of the reason why we have this phenomenon that's so interesting, "the *Pamela* craze," because people's imaginations were in some ways more free.

JP: And that might not be untrue of pop culture today. There are people who take characters in fiction or television extremely seriously and think of them outside those situations.

TYR: It's like Star Trek fan fiction.

TB: Or Detective Munch from *Law and Order SVU*—skinny guy with gray hair. That *character*, Detective Munch, has had roles in maybe twelve other TV shows, and he's always Detective Munch. He enters other shows as if there were a Detective Munch who could be detached from *SVU*. So in effect he's a sort of Pamela figure in that structural way.

MM: It's really interesting to me that he tried to

pass the letters off as an actual event that happened and himself as an editor. He honestly tried to do that. It makes the preface to the second edition really interesting—he had someone renowned write these phrases about Pamela as if she were an actual person. It's tough to talk about Richardson's intentions, but it's clear that he did intend Pamela to be seen as an actual person. Now the repercussions of that—everybody could take Pamela [into their own stories]—he probably didn't foresee. But I think it is quite interesting that he honestly tried to pass it off as an actual event that happened [to a real person].

TB: Right, he sort of created a Frankenstein. It's a fascinating detachability.

JS: [The course] gave me a better understanding of why people become obsessed with certain works. Why were they so interested in *this* part of *Pamela*, or why did *this* scene inspire so much writing? I think Mike [pointed to] that one scene in his text, and asked why were they so obsessed with one [particular] scene? It made me think back to last semester—we asked why Jane Austen is so popular today; there were a lot of proposals, but no one could really come up with an answer. This course makes me think a lot more deeply about a person's interaction with a text and why they respond to parts of it the way they do, why it resonates now.

Why, for example, when we read Fielding was everyone like "oh I love this"—because he uses the same style of humor, of satire, that we see on the Daily Show—it's all around us today. Certain things resonate during our time period again, even though they were written a long time ago. That was interesting for me.

SA: I think it speaks to the detachability you were talking about. When I talked about this class to my friends outside of it, I said, "I don't know about this *Pamela* itself, but talking about it is a lot of fun." [Laughter] I think that's what's great about *Pamela*—the way that it sparked this whole entire dynamic world so that we can step away from the text itself and look at all of its repercussions.

SS: I think it also helps us to look at literature in general [differently]. When I read modern books, I also tend to consider a book as a finished work of art, and I consider it as a piece that the author basically handed me. But looking at *Pamela* we can see the whole idea of literary discourse magnified. Back then there weren't as many works published and the literary community was relatively small, so *Pamela* created a large reverberation. A lot of people responded to it. We can actually trace those responses, whereas maybe today it wouldn't be as visible because there are so many different modes of media and there are so many different writers responding that you can't really isolate [the discourse] as you can for the *Pamela* craze.

TAR: I completely agree. [This course] forced me to realize texts aren't produced in a vacuum; it's not just the work itself. Often I sit down and I'll read a book and it's about the words on the page and really nothing else, but this course put works within a context and forced me to think in a different way about texts in general.

TYR: But also not putting them into a [quick] context like, "this was written during the Cold War." We're [often] trying to put texts in context, but with the minimal amount of effort and time.

JP: It's hard to put things into real or deep context.

TYR: Yes. We have to contextualize, you know, nine other novels over the course of sixteen weeks, and there just isn't the time to actually explore what each context means.

TB: Even now, we're just sampling the best-known works of the *Pamela* craze. But you're right, there is a kind of scholarly responsibility that you've been learning. If you're going to make statements about voices from the past who can no longer speak back and explain themselves, you're going to have to educate yourself.

JK: Looking back at the past [in comparison with] today, I think another big difference is copyright. Today there are all these regulations that prevent people from creating a *Pamela* craze, but back then copyright wasn't as [developed a concept]. That's another important thing to remember when we look back at the *Pamela* craze.

JP: So we'd have Harry Potters running around in a million different directions if things weren't completely under the control of a publication syndicate now.

JK: There are spin-off books. J.K. Rowling wrote *Quidditch Through the Ages*. But it all comes from the same author, because copyright protects that. That's the difference.

JS: I'm researching copyright history for my paper for this class. I was going through the MLA [bibliographical database]. If you just type in "copyright," you get a lot of things, because copyright is always going to be a big issue.

But it's funny. Someone mentioned fan-fiction. For popular works today, you can find someone online rewriting their own version, [replicating] the *Pamela* craze. Online there are not really many restrictions on that. [Internet] fan-fiction is almost the same thing as the *Pamela* craze, except it's not officially published and you don't sell it. But it's online and there's a huge community reading it.

TYR: I brought it up as a joke, but there's a huge body of Star Wars and Star Trek—

JS: And Harry Potter—

SS: I think Star Wars is different, though, because it's from further back, whereas the *Pamela* responses were relatively contemporary [to the original text]. People are more into Star Wars now because it's a [longstanding] pop culture phenomenon that everyone's familiar with.

JP: But presumably you could do something similar; you could look at Star Wars in its context. When was it?—thirty years ago? There was a Star Wars response at the time, too. You could look at it today, or you could study it in multiple moments.

TYR: The reason people feel entitled to do this is they think George Lucas created a universe he didn't fully explore. And that's also what [Richard-son's contemporaries thought] he did—Richardson created all these characters and all these scenarios which he didn't fully populate, fully flesh out.

MM: One thing that distinguishes *Pamela*, though, is that it was so divisive. It was almost a war. The back of our book talks about the Pamelists and the anti-Pamelists. It's different from something like Star Wars, which either you write off as fantasy entertainment or you just love it. There's nobody who actually hates it—well, there might be some people who hate Star Wars but it's not really divisive like *Pamela* was. [*Pamela*] really divides people. You have Aaron Hill on one side and you have Henry Fielding on the other. I think that's an extraordinary dynamic [surrounding] *Pamela*.

TB: [The existence of] "Pamelists" and "anti-Pamelists" was the burden of the introduction we all read to the *Pamela Controversy* multi-volume set, remember?[12] The editors argued that very few people seem to feel neutral about *Pamela*. Michael is pointing out that people [do feel neutral about Star Wars;] those who don't love Star Wars just don't care about it much at all. They don't move beyond just not caring to that place of [the very angry] anti-Pamelists.

SA: I was thinking about how this might occur today. The example I thought of was *The Da Vinci Code* and how that spawned all these other books about what was going on there. Maybe this is in light of the copyright situation, but [I noticed that] all the books that surrounded *The Da Vinci Code* weren't about the characters or what was going on in the novel but more about, "is this historically accurate?" I think that maybe what Pamela offers isn't, thanks to copyright, as possible today. You wouldn't be able to have as many literary responses to it. You can't produce another *Harry Potter* of your own.

TB: You can't produce responses that claim the same [imaginative] territory.

SA: Exactly. It has to be more ancillary.

VT: Also, responses can be literary while at the same time [raising] bigger questions, like "what is virtue" and "is Pamela performing or is she essentially good." Bigger questions like that can be explored through a fan-fiction type of medium.

TYR: There were essays and letters attached to *Pamela*, but a lot of the criticisms we found were in the form of entertainment.

TB: *Pamela* generated more *Pamela*. That's right. Really even in Richardson's own case that was true. To the extent that he wanted to discuss his novelistic purposes, much more than in the letters we looked at he [simply] wrote more novels, and he just kept rewriting *Pamela*. His response to criticism was to do the same thing again, but differently.

That's what Fielding did in *Shamela* and *Joseph Andrews*, too. Think about how in *Joseph Andrews* Fielding has those introductory chapters that talk in a critical voice about what novelists should be doing and what they should not be doing. And now, he says, here's my next chapter where I do the right thing. That's very different from today. We're content now (and here's the pot calling the kettle black) to just be somebody who talks about other people's primary works. I don't feel at all obligated to produce novels of my own in order to be a novel critic. [Laughter.] In the eighteenth century they took a perhaps more creditable approach.

RF: When it comes to copyright—Sarah and I are actually in a different class that looked a little bit at this certain poet whose son reigns over anything that the father ever published—there are only three things that this poet ever wrote that are published right now. And to [the son] it's because even going so far as to comment on the text tarnishes the totality or perfection of it. Here we're talking about detaching a character from the text and taking it forward [into another text] and about how Richardson kept on rewriting in response. That was his way of keeping control of his intentions for the text. Interpretation and rewriting overlap.

TB: Yes, Richardson kept inserting himself back into the conversation. He didn't just leave the text there for people to do what they wanted with it, he kept coming back and correcting everybody and redoing it. That's an important fact about Richardson.

I mentioned before this book I'd been reading by David Brewer, *The Afterlife of Character*.[13] It has a very interesting chapter on Pamela as a character who basically had a life of her own. Brewer's claim is that *Pamela* is in a line of characters who were pursued by subsequent writers, beyond their original text, but that Pamela is the first of such characters where the author himself continued to be a pest to the people who wanted to claim the character. Brewer compares earlier examples, like Shakespeare's Falstaff. Falstaff appears in lots of places, but Shakespeare [is dead, he] isn't there to say, "oh, Falstaff wouldn't say that," or "please don't use Falstaff for that purpose." Writers just nodded to Shakespeare and then did whatever they wanted with Falstaff. In the case of *Pamela*...the author is constantly throwing his oar back in. That changes the phenomenon—the fact that the author continues for quite a while to be part of the mix. It changes what happens, and it changes the tone.

I wondered whether you felt any differences in *tone* [across the works of the *Pamela* craze] as the decades passed. We've been talking as if every work we looked at was written in 1741, but some of your works were quite a bit later, right? We might think about differences over time and the ways our various texts work together to create not just a moment in time, really, but three decades or whatever it is. I wonder if some people whose works were not from 1741 or 42 noticed anything about the tone or the presentation that suggests that what could be taken for granted (or what couldn't be taken for granted) changed as time passed.

TYR: Mine was *The Maid of the Mill* from 1765.[14] Other texts were embedded in it, a lot of them. I felt that the further away we got from 1740, the authors seemed to have more of the feeling that they had a right to interpret the text. Characters weren't necessarily Pamela any more, they were characters *based on* Pamela. With different names. And the setting [of *The Maid of the Mill*] was entirely different. As time went on, authors were more able to "make the text their own," and not just write *Pamela* again, or some version of it, in a different setting.

TB: *Pamela* becomes more of a pretext than a subject of discourse in itself.

SA: My text was *A Collection of Moral and Instructive Sentiments*,[15] from 1755. It's Richardson himself retrenching his ideas and distilling his moral messages—like "look here's what I was trying to say" or "look here are the lessons"—as if rewriting the text again and again wasn't enough to tell these people, "this is how it needs to be interpreted."

RF: Mine was from 1773,[16] and it's like "this is *Pamela* but for children." It's him distilling even further, "these are the lessons I want you to learn for future generations so that you [can] be virtuous and I am telling you what virtue is." Some of the thought-points [from the novel are there], he picks very specific ones.

TB: So it's a form of abridgment by that point.

TAR: I was going to say that with *Nanine*,[17] which was my text, the debt to *Pamela* was implicit rather than explicit. Voltaire never even said, "Richardson's *Pamela*." *Pamela* was more a pretext rather than something to work off [directly] and try to get financial benefit from [as many of the earlier writers did].

EE: For my text, *The Power of Sympathy* from 1789,[18] [*Pamela*] had been absorbed already. The whole set-up of the maid and the master was hardened into convention so that he only had to suggest it, and then he could go on from there. He didn't really go into it in detail—*Pamela* was so well known that you could just echo the set-up and then move on.

TB: So your text comes at a point when *Pamela* has become part of the furniture of the culture and doesn't even have to be addressed directly. That's an important shift.

VT: It's also interesting to see how Richardson's image changed over time. My work [*Familiar Let-*

ters][19] was published in the early 1740s, but this particular edition I read is the seventh, so it came out after Richardson's death. On the title page he's referred to as "the late Mr. Richardson, author of *Clarissa* and *Sir Charles Grandison*." There's an eliding of *Pamela* as a less mature or earlier part of his career that the publishers of this book didn't necessarily want readers to remember.

TB: That's important. Perhaps the biggest loss in our one-semester course is that we couldn't read the other two novels. It is important to see how Richardson revised *Pamela* in his later novels. Also, how his work was understood over time, what his reputation was like [and how it mutated], and how his career and his work were managed by others after his death.

LC: Despite the [later] applications or uses of *Pamela*, whether they were explicitly uses of *Pamela* or not, Richardson's original works still remained very important. These drawings of scenes from *Clarissa* [from Chodowiecki's *Clarissens Schiksale dargestellt in Vier und zwanzig Kupferblättern*][20] were produced fifty years after *Clarissa* and yet they still include the page numbers and the chapter numbers that the scenes correspond with. It's obvious that the artist meant for them to be used alongside reading *Clarissa*. So the original works were still very important.

TB: Yes—very good point.

JP: You can have both tracks. You can have the textual survival and re-readings, in some form or another, but you can also have this completely implicit debt, works that are vaguely connected and taking something for granted.

TB: Yes. So [*Pamela* is], in a sense, diluted, yet seems to get more and more reified at the same time.

MM: I have a question. We talked about what happened to Pamela later on, what parts of Pamela slipped into the popular consciousness rather than being addressed directly. My book [(Povey, *Virgin in Eden*)] actually did directly address the moralizing issue. I guess it was [published] around the time of the Great Awakening, as well. It seems interesting to me that Richardson wanted a moralizing tone in *Pamela* and that's what the [usual] interpretation was at first, whereas later on that sort of was dropped. What is commented on, what [aspects] of *Pamela* we tend to see now, are not so much the morality but different aspects. It's interesting. Perhaps the [emphasis on Pamela's] moralizing tone or [its status as] a moral conduct book is specific to Richardson's time, and what grew out of that is different from what he even could have imagined.

TB: So perhaps the moral lessons were originally more important than the political questions or the class questions, at least for some readers.

MM: I don't see *Pamela* as a function of the Great Awakening, but [I mention the Great Awakening] as a way of suggesting that what was important to Richardson's first readers became less important later. The aspects of the text people chose to be influenced by changed over time.

TB: So we're seeing, from a different angle what Jessica Kim noticed when she pointed out that Franklin was so invested in publishing *Pamela* at great expense for particular reasons specific to his position *here*, not necessarily for Richardson's reasons.

JP: It also makes the problem of context—well, you just tripled everybody's work, because it becomes multiply complicated. You have to look at the context in the 1770s which may be very different than the 1740s and so you want to know both those contexts and everything around [them] to get your story [right].

TB: Maybe we could talk for a moment about your experience as undergraduates in the rare books library. What is easy or not easy about it, what worked well? How accessible is the library to your lives and schedules? I'm asking about this particularly for the transcript that we will make, which will be for rare books librarians who perhaps have not gotten used to doing what John Pollack does— working with undergraduates.

JS: I was surprised by the amount of trust that was placed in us.

JP: Crazy! [Laughter]

JS: I think that amount of faith in us to handle these texts—I was expecting that we would have to wear gloves—just being able to interact with them on such an intimate level was something I was surprised by. We were given access and I think without that it wouldn't have been the same experience.

When I first went into the rare books library, this girl came in and I think she might have been a graduate student. (Going in there makes me feel really scholarly! [Laughter]) She brought out this huge manuscript that she proceeded to start unrolling and I just thought "this is so cool." Even being in the same room as that makes you feel like you're being more of a scholar than you usually are in your normal daily life. Just to be in that environment where everyone in that room is very focused on their text and looking for little details, that is something you don't get sitting on the third floor reading a secondary source.

JP: So it's solitary but it's also collective—I completely agree. It's a shared space in an interesting way.

SS: I think it makes your research a lot less alone. I remember when I was reading *Pamela Censured*,[21] John walked in and I started talking to him about the book and then Professor Stallybrass walked in and he was one of the secondary sources that I was quoting in my report! I told him what I was quoting him on. It's interesting because it creates a forum. Everyone's really available to you. Whereas when I'm reading more modern works or reading something that's not in the rare books library—well, the main library is huge and it's easy to get lost in it and get buried in books and forget that there are other *people* who are resources for you as well.

JS: Even if you don't know *Pamela* or you don't know the manuscript that graduate student is researching, you can interact with people on the level of having the experience of working with early texts. We don't know each other's texts as intimately as we'd like, but we still have the common shared experience of working in the rare books library. Everyone in the room can share and relate to that, even if we're not studying the same thing.

SA: I found the staff of the rare books library very helpful. It was my first time and they were all very friendly and helped me get my book and everything. There's sort of this implicit trust I guess, like Jessica was saying. You're there, so you're part of the dialogue.

TB: You must be a serious person.

SA: Yes. It's a welcoming environment.

JP: Dialogue is an important point. There is a dialogue with these materials, you are having a dialogue with them, and that's really exciting.

JK: I was obsessed with the work called *A Present for a Servant Maid*,[22] and John helped me find it at the Library Company of Philadelphia, because I really wanted to report on it, but we couldn't find a copy here. So I thought that was remarkable as well, that he would have taken the time to search for it with me.

JP: Well, you know, no library is an island, that's the way it is—we're all part of a larger world. Nobody's got all the books.

Your comments earlier about the connections between the electronic world and the physical world are fascinating and the kinds of things that not just librarians, but scholars too, are obsessed with. I mean, how is our reading experience different now that we have all this online access? And what's the point of the books themselves now?

TB: Why maintain this rare books library at all, administrators might ask? It's important to have answers, I think.

JP: Absolutely. And there are some interesting answers here.

RF: I'm used to dealing with things online, but the physical world of books just makes the experience so much more personal. I mean we all love books, we're all dorks, we like smelling them, [Laughter]. But when you're reading something and it's falling apart or it's brown and there's marginalia inside it—you can't replicate that experience online.

JP: I think that's true. And it's not to necessarily privilege one over the other..

RF: They're just totally different. There's a community that spreads out around reading books and manuscripts that are rolled up and tucked away.

TB: A community of tremendous privilege, which I hope everybody has felt this semester. The privilege of being welcomed as undergraduates, and for me as a teacher with an undergraduate class, to be permitted to teach my class in the rare books library—that's unheard of in most places. Our privilege to sit around this table with our rare books in front of us from our own university library—I really still can't get over it, how terrific it is, and how underused.

JP: Well, you're opening things up. It's easier to say, "here are the questions and the answers." But in fact, when you open the door in this way there are lot more questions than answers, and that's actually brilliant.

APPENDIX 9.1
Syllabus: English 341-301 | Spring 2010

Professor Toni Bowers
Office: Fisher Bennett Hall 239

"THE PAMELA CRAZE: A RESEARCH SEMINAR"

In 1740 Samuel Richardson, a London printer, published what turned out to be one of the most influential and controversial novels ever written, *Pamela: or, Virtue Rewarded*. It tells the story of a servant girl who repeatedly resists the sexual overtures of her powerful "master," Mr. B., and of the supposedly happy ending that her virtuous behavior eventually earns.

The questions about power, class, gender, virtue, and meaning that *Pamela* made visible sparked an enormous amount of writing in its day and ever since. Was Pamela really virtuous, or did she manipulate Mr. B's desire for her in order to gain wealth and social position? Who is the agent of the seduction in *Pamela*, and who its object? What is the nature of Pamela's "virtue," and what is the quality of her "reward?" Is women's virtue different from men's? Is marriage necessarily a form of economic exchange, even of prostitution for women? These are some of the questions that *Pamela* raised for readers of the eighteenth century, and that continue to this day to be debated in writing surrounding this controversial work.

In this advanced seminar, we will examine the universe of writings that have emerged since 1740 in response to *Pamela*, concentrating on the years immediately after the novel's first publication. Starting with *Pamela* itself and with Richardson's own defenses of it, we'll look at the multitude of "Pamelas" that crowded eighteenth-century publication lists. Emphasis will be placed on independent library research and on the recovery and interpretation of eighteenth-century texts. Students will learn to use sophisticated research tools—electronic databases, microfilm collections, and rare book libraries, for example—efficiently and critically. Because the primary material is demanding and voluminous, we will be engaging very little with secondary writing or literary theory *per se*.

This class is intended for Ben Franklin Honors students. With extra space, it will first accommodate advanced English majors. It will be most useful to those intending soon to go on to graduate school in a humanistic research field.

Requirements

The **reading** for this seminar will be extensive and demanding. We will be reading real eighteenth-century texts, few of them masterpieces, most of them long, and often in their original format and typeface. The most important requirement is that you carefully read each assigned selection before attending class, take notes, and be prepared to discuss particular language as well as general plots and characterizations.

Over the course of the semester, each student will find one *Pamela*-related work that is not included in the assigned reading. This will probably take the form of a microfilmed text or a rare book. You might select a particular edition of *Pamela*, or an eighteenth-century pamphlet, sermon, or letter about the novel, or a set of visual works, or a parody, or an adaptation (e.g., play, opera, children's book, sermon; abridgement, translation). Study the work you select, bring it to class (in photocopied form, if necessary; original form preferred), and give a **pre-**

sentation of not more than 30 minutes where you talk about the text, its possible audience, its relation to *Pamela*, its materiality and its place in literary history.

Final essays will be submitted in two stages:

1. an **abstract** of 3-5 paragraphs (not more), to be presented in class on either April 15, April 20, or April 22, and

2. a **final essay** of 10-12 pages due under the door of my office (FBH 339) at 4 pm on the day scheduled for the final exam. (There will be no final exam.)

The paper assignment is intended to give you a chance to do truly original research into eighteenth-century literature. Your goal is to address a worthwhile question. In response to your question, argue a thesis using evidence gathered from careful, close reading of the primary text(s) that you select. Your essay might enter an ongoing critical debate, reinterpret particular episodes or charac-

terizations, or consider the relation between materiality and meaning, for example. It might deal with Richardson's *Pamela* or with later response(s) to it, or combine the two. It *can* make use of secondary literature, but secondary citation is not required of everyone: it depends on the topic and materials you select.

In general, as long as you write about a *Pamela*-related text or texts, offer a sound and interesting argument, and use textual evidence, the specific problem or question you address and the texts you use are up to you.

Please feel free to consult with the instructor during office hours as your ideas begin to take shape.

Required Texts

1. Bulkpack for sale, Campus Copy Center.
2. *Pamela* for sale at Penn Book Center, 34th and Sansom St.
3. Handouts distributed in class

Course Schedule

Finish reading by the date listed. Always bring the text and your reading notes to class with you.

* = in Bulkpack or handout.

Week	Date	Tuesday	Thursday
1	1/14	—	Course Introduction
2	1/19, 20	*Pamela* (Vol I)	*Pamela* (entire)
3	1/26, 28	*Pamela*	*Pamela*
4	2/2, 4	*2nd Edition Prefaces, etc	Keymer and Sabor, *Pamela Controversy* Intro. (at Rosengarten Reserve)
5	2/9, 11	*Pamela*, "Part 2"	*Pamela*, "Part 2"
6	2/16, 18	*Pamela*, "Part 2"	Henry Fielding, *Shamela*
7	2/23, 25	Eliza Haywood, *Anti-Pamela*	*Anti-Pamela*
8	3/2, 4	*'Pamela the Second' in *Universal Spectator*, or *Weekly Journal* (24 April, 1 May, 8 May 1742)	*Pamela; or, The Fair Imposter…A poem, in five cantos.*
9	3/9, 11	— Spring Break —	
10	3/16, 18	* *Pamela censured : in a letter to the editor…*	*Henry Fielding, *Joseph Andrews* (selections)
11	3/23, 25	*Joseph Andrews*	*Memoirs of the life of Lady H—the celebrated Pamela.*

Week	Date	Tuesday	Thursday
12	3/30, 4/1	*Memoirs of the life of Lady H...the Celebrated Pamela/ *Pamela's conduct in high life, to the time of her death...	* Pamela's conduct in high life, to the time of her death. Publish'd from her original papers.
13	4/6, 8	*A Dramatic Burlesque Of Two Acts, call'd Mock-Pamela: or, a Kind Caution ot Country Coxcombs, Interspers'd with Ballads...	John Cleland, Memoirs of a Woman of Pleasure [Fanny Hill]
14	4/13,15	Fanny Hill/ Review	Presentation of Abstracts
15	4/20, 22	Presentation of Abstracts	Presentation of Abstracts
16	4/27	Last Day of Class: Roundtable	

NOTES

1. I have lightly edited roundtable comments, with help from seminar member Jessica Sutro, to facilitate reading.

2. Samuel Arnold, *The Maid of the Mill. A Comic Opera. As it is Performed at the Theatre Royal in Covent Garden. The music compiled, and the words written by the author of Love in a village* (London: J. Newberry [etc.], 1765).

3. James Love, *Pamela: A Comedy: as it is Perform'd Gratis, at the late theatre in Goodman's-fields* (London: Printed for J. Robinson, 1742).

4. Daniel Chodowiecki and LK Kosegarten. *Clarissens Schiksale dargestellt in Vier und zwanzig Kupferblättern* (Leipzig: Bey Heinrich Graff, 1796).

5. Charles Povey, *The Virgin in Eden, or The State of Innocency : deliver'd by way of image and description...* (London: Printed by J. Roberts ; and sold by such as sell pamphlets and news-papers; and at the author's house, 1741).

6. *A Present for A Servant-Maid: or, the sure means of gaining love and esteem. Under the following heads. Observance. Avoiding sloth. Sluttishness...* (London: Printed and publish'd by T. Gardner; and sold by the booksellers of town and country, 1743).

7. *Twelve Prints of Pamela : Representing the Principle Actions of her Life,* (London: Printed for Carington Bowles..., 1774).

8. Samuel Richardson, also attrib. Oliver Goldsmith, *The Paths of Virtue Delineated, or, The History in Miniature of the celebrated Pamela, Clarissa Harlowe, and Sir Charles Grandison,* (London: Printed for S. Crowder, T. Lowndes, S. Bladon and R. Baldwin, 1773).

9. *Pamela Censured : in a Letter to the Editor...* (London: Printed for J. Roberts..., 1741).

10. Samuel Richardson, *One Hundred and Seventy-three Letters Written for Particular Friends: on the Most Important Occasions...* [*Familiar Letters*], (London: Printed for C. Hitch and L. Hawes [and 7 others], 1764).

11. John Kelly, *Pamela's Conduct in High Life, to The Time of her Death. Publish'd from her Original Papers...* 2 vols. (London, 1741).

12. Thomas Keymer and Peter Sabor, eds, *The Pamela Controversy: Criticisms and Adaptations of Samuel Richardson's Pamela, 1740-1750.* (London: Pickering & Chatto, 2001) xiii-xx.

13. David A. Brewer, *The Afterlife of Character, 1726-1825* (Philadelphia: University of Pennsylvania Press, 2005).

14. Samuel Arnold, *The Maid of the Mill. A Comic Opera. As it is Performed at the Theatre Royal in Covent Garden. The music compiled, and the words written by the author of Love in a village,* (London: J. Newberry [etc.], 1765).

15. Samuel Richardson, *A Collection of the Moral and*

Instructive Sentiments, Maxims, Cautions, and Reflexions, Contained in the Histories of Pamela, Clarissa, and Sir Charles Grandison...., (London: Printed for S. Richardson, 1755).

16.   Richardson, Samuel, also attrib. Oliver Goldsmith, *The Paths of Virtue Delineated, or, The History in Miniature of the celebrated Pamela, Clarissa Harlowe, and Sir Charles Grandison*, (London: Printed for S. Crowder, T. Lowndes, S. Bladon and R. Baldwin, 1773).

17.   Voltaire, *Nanine: Comédie en Trois Actes, et en vers de dix syllabes...* (Paris: Chez Barba, libraire..., 1819).

18.   Charles Brockden Brown, *The Power of Sympathy: or, The Triumph of Nature. Founded in Truth*, (Boston: Printed by Isaiah Thomas and company, 1789).

19.   Samuel Richardson, *One Hundred and Seventy-three Letters Written for Particular Friends: on the Most Important Occasions...* [*Familiar Letters*], (London: Printed for C. Hitch and L. Hawes [and 7 others], 1764).

20.   See n. 4.

21.   *Pamela Censured: in a Letter to the Editor...* , (London: Printed for J. Roberts..., 1741).

22.   *A Present for A Servant-Maid: or, the sure means of gaining love and esteem. Under the following heads. Observance. Avoiding sloth. Sluttishness...*, (London: Printed and publish'd by T. Gardner, 1743).

Putting the Material in Materiality: The Embedded Special Collections Librarian

Megan Mulder and Carolyn Jones

In the fall of 2008, Special Collections Librarian Megan Mulder was an "embedded librarian" in an undergraduate seminar class offered by the Wake Forest University English Department. Carolyn Jones was an English major and a student in the class. Both here offer their thoughts and perspectives on the experience.

THE PROJECT

In 2008 Dr. Miriam Jacobson of Wake Forest's English department was preparing to teach a class called "Writing and Materiality in Renaissance English Poetry." An upper-level undergraduate seminar on Renaissance poetry had been offered before, but this time Dr. Jacobson was proposing to, in her words, "refocus the class around a new central idea, the relationship of the Renaissance practices of writing and printing to the selves expressed in the poems."[1] In order to bring materiality to the forefront Dr. Jacobson wanted to make the material itself—16th and 17th-century poetry in print and manuscript—an integral part of the class.

Renaissance poets were themselves acutely aware of the materiality of their texts. The transition from a manuscript to a print culture was still underway in the 16th century, and authors often alluded either directly or symbolically to aspects of writing, printing, and publishing. Examining books from the library's special collections would help students understand how and why the material texts were created, copied, and disseminated—which would in turn illuminate aspects of the poetry. Dr. Jacobson's hope was that "rather than pretending that these texts are modern and transparent, by incorporating the study of book history into our analysis of poems, we can reveal how different sixteenth-century culture was from our own."[2]

LIBRARIAN'S PERSPECTIVE

When Miriam Jacobson approached me about the possibility of my taking an active and ongoing role in her Renaissance Poetry seminar, I eagerly agreed. Increasing undergraduate use of special collections materials is a priority for our department, so there was strong administrative support for my taking on the project. Relevant holdings in Wake Forest's Rare Books Collection were not extensive—approximately 500 titles from the 15th-17th centuries—but included enough books to make a collaboration worthwhile. Dr. Jacobson and I first thought that the class might hold its meetings in the special collections reading room so that materials from the collection would be available on a daily basis. However, the enrollment grew too large for the room to hold the class comfortably, and our Director of Special Collections was reluctant to commit our only study space for an entire semester to a thrice-weekly class.

As an alternative, I offered to be an "embedded librarian" in the class. Undergraduate instruction and engagement is a primary focus for Wake Forest's library in general, and librarians in other departments had successfully embedded in classes and programs in the university.[3] The embedded librarian concept originated with corporate librarians, who borrowed the term from embedded war journalists. Their idea was that librarians would leave the library and locate themselves wherever their users were, to provide information and services on the spot. As adopted by academic libraries the embedded model has generally meant that librarians attach themselves to particular classes, in person or online, to provide bibliographic instruction and/or technical support throughout the term.[4]

As an embedded special collections librarian in "Writing and Materiality and Renaissance Poetry" I attended all class sessions, participated in lectures and discussions, and assisted students in using special collections materials for research. But my primary role over the course of the semester was not to teach research methods, but to provide and interpret the material objects which illustrated central concepts presented in class. What this meant, from a practical standpoint, was that I tried for each class session to make available some type of material relevant to the topic on the syllabus. Analyzing Renaissance texts as material objects generated in the context of a broader culture was a new methodology for many of the students. Most were enthusiastic about the new approach; a few were skeptical. But all of the students needed concrete examples to understand how and why materiality could be important in the study of poetry.

A very simple exercise early in the semester provided one example. Edmund Spenser is well represented in our collection, so I was able to show the class editions of *The Faerie Queene* from five different centuries. Students examined the various editions, ranging from a 1590 first edition to a modern scholarly reprint, and began to think about and discuss how the physical features changed and how these changes might affect readers' experience of the poem.

Dr. Jacobson also felt strongly that the students needed to gain an understanding of the broader culture of Renaissance England, and in particular to understand the ways that it differed significantly from our own. Ideas about authorship and copyright, symbolism and allegory, and even the ap-

propriateness of marginalia were all very different in the 16th century, and these differences had major implications for the students' understanding of the poetry.

For students to understand this Renaissance print culture they needed first of all to grasp that the technology of the printing press was still quite new, and that the implications for authorship, dissemination of texts, and ideas about intellectual property were very much in flux. Discussion of 16th century printing practices and examination of a large number of Renaissance imprints over the entire semester proved vital in reinforcing this concept. In each class period students held, examined, and read aloud from books printed in the era they were studying. Direct experience with 16th century books helped students begin to move beyond their own historical assumptions. Margreta de Grazia and Peter Stallybrass, in a seminal article on materiality in Shakespeare studies that was one of the class's secondary readings, observe that "When the materiality of the early texts confronts modern practices and theories, it casts those modern practices and theories into doubt, revealing that they, too, possess a specific—and equally contingent—history. It makes us face our own historical situatedness."[5]

Students began to understand their historical situatedness as they confronted and discussed unfamiliar features of Renaissance books. For example: a class assignment early in the semester had each student choose a single word from any of the works under study and use the OED and other sources to trace the word's origins and development. Encountering the lack of standardization in spelling, typesetting, layout, and attribution of authorship in 16th century texts was an important part of this etymological study. As students became aware of the malleability of Renaissance texts, they could see how this applied to words themselves—how poets could deliberately use variant spellings to achieve shades of meaning or double meanings in their works; or conversely, how errors and random edits in the printing shop could obscure an author's intended meaning.

THE EMBEDDED EXPERIENCE

In retrospect I believe that the most important aspect of my role as embedded librarian in this class was the embeddedness itself—the fact that I attended and participated in nearly every class session, and that I brought books into the classroom, as opposed to students coming into the separate space of special collections.

In some ways my embedded experience was a longer-term version of the librarian-faculty collaborations that occur regularly in special collections with class visits or assignments. But my having an *ongoing* role in the class had unique benefits. As Pablo Alvarez observes, special collections instruction often requires that the librarian assume "the challenging and critical roles as both teacher and interpreter of the collection, which may deal with topics beyond his or her area of expertise."[6] Collaborating with a faculty subject specialist meant that I could benefit from her expertise in an area that was not my particular specialty. And being present for class lectures and discussions gave me a first-hand understanding of student interests and questions. I was able to use special collections materials to follow different themes (e.g., *memento mori* symbolism, or the tension between our poets' desire for public recognition and their distrust of the new print media) throughout the semester, providing different examples of the same concept or using the same book more than once to illustrate different ideas. If a class discussion went off on an unforeseen but interesting tangent, I could bring relevant books to the next session. As the students saw special collections materials integrated into their literary studies in a variety of ways, they too became more confident about using the material as part of their research process.

The physical act of bringing the books out of the library and into the classroom also proved more important than I had anticipated. Dr. Jacobson scheduled three class sessions in the Rare Books reading room, during which we examined materials that were too large or fragile to be transported. But for the rest of the class sessions I carried selected books with me into the classroom. This had the happy effect of helping to "demystify" the Renaissance books. Out of the rarefied atmosphere of Special Collections, students were more willing to treat the books as objects to be read, handled (carefully), and analyzed.

At the end of the semester, most students commented favorably on the integration of special collections materials into the class, with many singling it out as one of the most valuable aspects of the course. Not all feedback was positive, however. Some students felt that too much time was spent on examining books and that just one visit to the Special Collections Department would have been enough. If we teach the class again, Dr. Jacobson and I plan to strengthen the focus on book history to help the students understand the theoretical underpinnings of a new historicist approach to literary studies. We also hope to give students more direct (if possible, hands-on) experience with Renaissance printing and writing methods.

STUDENT'S PERSPECTIVE

From the student perspective, Megan Mulder's presence as an embedded librarian in Dr. Jacobson's class was the initial hook that captured my attention. I did not have any familiarity with the literary period and entered the class with, at best, ambivalent feelings toward poetry. Admittedly, I joined the class simply because it met a requirement for my English major. From the start, I was surprised that undergraduate students were not only allowed to handle the rare books which Megan brought from the special collections, but were also encouraged to engage with the material on both a physical and intellectual level.

As I became more familiar with the intricacies of Renaissance printing including varying paper qualities, ink, typeface, and marginalia, I made connections between the material culture of writing and printing and the poetic text. Entire passages of poetry gained new meaning. For example, the lens of material culture further illuminates Sir Philip Sidney's sonnet sequence, *Astrophil and Stella*, especially the difficulties that the lover, Astrophil, is willing to face to prove his devotion to Stella. Throughout the course of the poems, the speaker, Astrophil, attempts to gain his beloved's favor not only for the emotional pains he suffers but for actual physical effort—the arduous task of sharpening quills, making ink, and so forth that must occur before he commits his thoughts to paper. Astrophil then goes one step further in his admiration by using the recent innovation of printing to announce his devotion on a public level rather than just circulating manuscripts of his work. By understanding the printing process, I was able to better appreciate the effort and dedication involved with producing a new publication. Also, unfamiliar aspects of Renaissance printing, for example the long S, were demystified and became almost commonplace after a semester of reading texts as they were originally printed.

After examining how the printing process of the time shaped the meaning of Sidney's poetry, the class then considered what had an impact on the literary culture of the period, including author's rights to his work, mass publication, and circulation. The consumer culture of books affected who was writing and what was being published. Megan's explanation of how poetry was printed and presented to the public in the world of Renaissance England combined with Dr. Jacobson's knowledge of the texts and authors provided me with a solid foundation from which I then could form a more complete understanding of life at the turn of the seventeenth century.

In my experience as an undergraduate, and now graduate English student, this synthesis and application of text for increased understanding rarely occurred even in classes taught by the best professors. Professors usually limit themselves, and as a result

their students, to that which is present within the modern version of the text. This limitation excludes valuable information present solely in originals or facsimiles, especially regarding the visual formatting of the text and how that affects reader reaction. This original information often also clarifies language and references in the text that would have been common knowledge during the Renaissance.

Having Megan in the classroom also helped to tailor the class to students' needs and interests. The pertinence of the original books to the discussions, which showed how these unique materials can supplement each poem, garnered interest in visiting the Special Collections department outside of class time, either to browse for additional material related to 16th and 17th century poetry or to discover what hidden gems the library has to offer. In addition to becoming comfortable handling the rare books, I came to regard Megan as a resource outside of class, who could make that initial solo visit to the Special Collections department less intimidating.

CONCLUSIONS

Our successful embedded special collections librarian experience required a certain amount of effort from all concerned. The teaching faculty member needed to be flexible and willing to incorporate special collections materials into the daily curriculum. The librarian had to be prepared to invest a great deal of time and effort over the course of the semester. And the students had to be open to learning new ways of approaching the study of literature. But in our experience, all this effort was worth it. As Dr. Jacobson observed at the end of the class, "by addressing books and texts as fashioned objects, we were able to shift students' perspectives on literature, giving them new and different analytical tools and providing them with fresh ways of looking at poetry."

NOTES

1. Miriam Jacobson, email message to author, February 11, 2010.

2. Miriam Jacobson, email message to author, February 11, 2010.

3. Susan Sharpless Smith and Lynn Sutton, "Embedded Librarians: On the Road in the Deep South," *College & Research Libraries News* 69: 2 (2008): 71-4, 85.

4. Sara J. Beutter Manus, "Librarian in the Classroom: An Embedded Approach to Music Information Literacy for First-Year Undergraduates," *Notes*, 66 (2009): 249-61; Russell A. Hall, "The "Embedded" Librarian in a Freshman Speech Class: Information Literacy Instruc-tion in Action," *College & Research Libraries News*, 69 (2008): 28-30.

5. Margreta de Grazia and Peter Stallybrass, "The Materiality of the Shakespearean Text," *Shakespeare Quarterly*,. 44: 3 (1993): 257.

6. Pablo Alvarez, "Introducing Rare Books into the Undergraduate Curriculum," *RBM: A Journal of Rare Books, Manuscripts, and Cultural Heritage 7: 2 (2006): 94-104.*

What is Primary: Teaching Archival Epistemology and the Sources Continuum

Michael J. Paulus, Jr.

In his short story "Tlön, Uqbar, Orbis Tertius," the Argentine writer Jorge Luis Borges narrates the discovery of a world that initially exists in an encyclopedia fabricated by a secret society. But over time, through books and artifacts, the imaginary Tlön begins to break into the material world of the story. Borges, who both labored and luxuriated in libraries, here and elsewhere "persistently returned to the archive as his primary metaphor."[1] Through his explorations of the relationship between representation and reality, Borges reminds us that the archive, broadly defined as the repository of human time, is not inviolable. Those of us who work in concrete archives are aware of the evidential and epistemological issues that pertain to the materials that are in our repositories. Because of our specific knowledge about the potential utility of these materials for research and our general knowledge about the sources of knowledge, archives and special collections are ideal laboratories for teaching and learning about the complexities of accessing and analyzing "the raw material of history," or what we commonly refer to as primary sources.[2] Using examples drawn from a variety of undergraduate courses in which archival and special collections have been used, this chapter explores the complex concept of primary sources and introduces a model that can be used to help determine the primacy of sources of knowledge.

AN EPISTEMOLOGY OF THE ARCHIVE[3]

Primary sources are typically explained by differentiating them from secondary or derived sources.[4] But once such a distinction is made, it must be qualified immediately: definitions vary across disciplines; most sources are mixed; and the answers sources present depend on the questions being asked of them. An early twentieth-century book about teaching history in primary and secondary schools offered this helpful example: "John Fiske's account of what happened at Lexington, April 19, 1775, is a primary source for determining John Fiske's conception of the events at Lexington; it is a derived source for obtaining information about the events themselves."[5] The definition of what is primary ultimately will be determined by research questions, disciplinary methodologies, and course and peer expectations.

All of this may be obvious to an experienced researcher. A professor of religion once told me that a primary source was like pornography—he knew it when he saw it. But how clearly is the contingent nature of sources grasped by undergraduate students? And how consistent are we when we teach students about them? A recent study of "primary source literacy" revealed that while undergraduate students "exhibited a basic understanding of the distinction between primary and secondary sources, they generally failed to grasp that some sources could not be so easily defined." This study's authors concluded that students need "a more nuanced understanding of primary sources."[6] Students would also be helped by a more nuanced articulation of a concept that is taught inconsistently, if not incoherently.[7] But rather than obtaining a competency that enables an artificial bifurcation between abstract notions of primary and secondary sources, the real capability that students need to cultivate concerns understanding the nature of the sources of knowledge. This involves an understanding of evidence (what we know) as well as of epistemology (how we know what we know). These issues can be explored by introducing students to unique and rare materials that may function as primary sources and by providing students with a framework that enables them to understand the affordance of primariness or primacy.

THE SOURCES CONTINUUM

After a number of years teaching undergraduate students about archives and special collections at a small liberal arts college—through basic presentations about materials and how to access them as well as through in-depth assignments and research projects that involved using them—I abandoned attempts to ask and answer the question about what a primary source is and instead began discussing the interrelationship between research questions and sources. With a question in mind, one can begin to think about the sources of knowledge that may exist and about which of these, based on certain qualities, may be primary. Whatever sources are extant and

available will then shape the research process. Out of a number of discussions and exercises, a model emerged that provided a framework for exploring and conceptualizing the primacy of sources (see figure 10.1). This model, the sources continuum, is a two-dimensional continuum that extends out from an event, text, or phenomenon—from whatever the object of study is. The X axis represents temporal and spatial proximity; the Y axis represents transformation of either content or form.[8] Within this continuum, sources can be plotted and analyzed within the context of time, distance, and change. The sources continuum can be used at the beginning of the research process, to conceptualize the sources of knowledge that may exist, and it can be used when one has sources in hand, to organize and analyze the evidential value or accuracy of sources.

Manifestations of ancient texts provide excellent examples of how this continuum can be used to represent the transmission and transformation of texts and information from antiquity into the present. First-year students at Whitman College often read, as part of a core curriculum, modern editions of ancient texts such as *The Epic of Gilgamesh* and the Bible. In an effort to supplement the close read-

Figure 10.1. The Sources Continuum

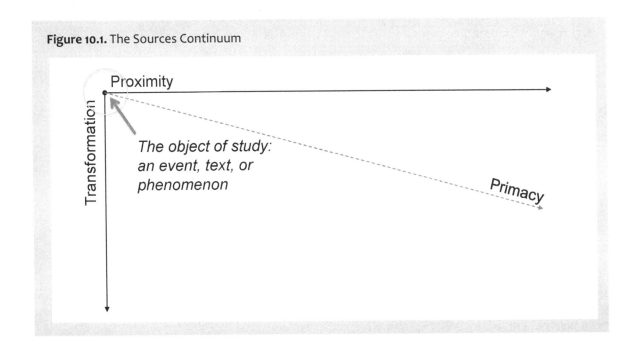

ing of texts with an introduction to the history of books, I presented materials—cuneiform tablets, manuscript codices, early printed books—and lectured about the transition from orality to literacy, the transition from manuscript to print culture, and textual criticism. Assuming an event, historical or performed, behind an ancient text, one moves across the horizontal axis of the continuum as the event is represented and re-represented over time. At the same time, one moves down the vertical axis of the continuum as that event is transformed through representation and interpretation. The quality of primacy usually weakens with time and distance from the event; it weakens even more rapidly as communications about the event are transformed. Figure 10.2 represents how an ancient event could be chronologically succeeded by a series of manifestations—an oral tradition, a manuscript tradition, an unreliable commentary, a vernacular translation, a manuscript forgery, a critical edition, a dynamic or non-literal translation, a good commentary, and a digitized manuscript—and how these could vary in terms of transformation and, consequently, primacy. Judgments have to made about the extent to which each manifestation has been transformed,

but as one goes through this evaluative process one begins to get a sense of what may function as primary and the limitations of accessible sources due to lack, loss, or language. For an undergraduate course, a good translation based on a critical edition may suffice as a primary source (and such texts are described as such in the Whitman College *Catalog*[9]), but students should be aware of their dependence on translators, editors, and others. To illustrate further how the sources continuum can be used for teaching undergraduate students, I will provide examples from a variety of disciplines under three broad topics: the relationship between meaning and materiality; the relationship between events and evidence; and the difficulties of digital documents.

FROM TEXTS TO BOOKS

Humanities scholarship may be concerned primarily with texts, but, as Jonathan Rose points out, "The problem with focusing on texts is that no one can read a text—not until it is incarnated in the material form of a book."[10] In an attempt to connect artifactual literacy with information literacy, I incorporated into the introductory library class at Whitman an exercise

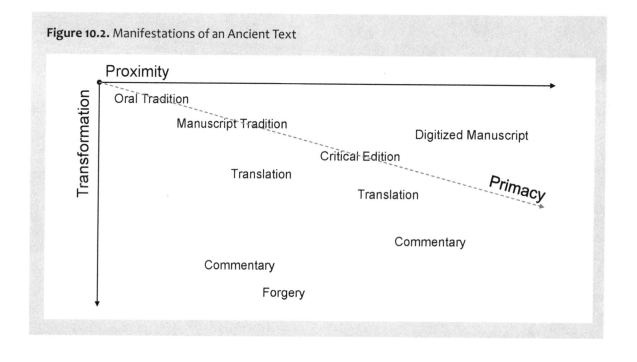

Figure 10.2. Manifestations of an Ancient Text

that had students study the material aspects of rare books.[11] I introduced Robert Darnton's communications circuit, to illustrate how books are produced and disseminated, and then I had each student spend time with a book (with an interesting publishing history) and answer questions about the book's who (creators), what (genre and subject), where (location), when (date), why (function), and for whom (audience).[12] The students then shared some of their answers and I explained how books have a dual nature—a body and soul, container and contents—and how each book and our knowledge of it is shaped by processes from publication through reception. Situated within the sources continuum, these material artifacts can be seen as products of transformative processes that unfold through time, as written manuscripts become printed books, which may then be reedited and republished. This exercise was useful in literature classes, too, and both models were helpful when I was simply exhibiting single books from Whitman's collection, such as a first edition of Darwin's *On the Origin of Species* (for a biology class) or the *Nuremberg Chronicle* (for an art history class).

Another example of how materiality shapes meaning involves an exercise and assignment that I used in an English class on Restoration and eighteenth-century drama. Students were asked to compare the texts of plays in their textbooks with printed plays from the eighteenth century. Since the textbook consisted of composite "modernized" editions without dedications, prefaces, lists of actors and actresses, and ("in the main") prologues and epilogues, the students discovered many things about the performances and early publications of plays that they were studying.[13] The sources continuum provides a framework for showing the progression from performance to publication, and from contemporaneous printings to modern(ized) editions that nobody in the past had even heard or read.

FROM EVENTS TO EVIDENCE

Connected with the relationship between materiality and meaning is the relationship between evidence and events. When an event is the object of inquiry, the sources continuum can be used to imagine, organize, and analyze potential sources. In a general studies class at Whitman called Critical Voices, which examined "the historical and ideological roles played by 'others'," students attended an archival orientation session to explore regional history through historical manuscripts.[14] Each student was given a different type of document (certificate, photograph, map, scrapbook, etcetera) to study and was asked to share something interesting about it. Collectively, the documents provided a chronology of historical events, many of which are unevenly documented, and through discussions about each document students became aware of the region's history, related material that is extant (and not) in the archives, and how such sources could be used in their class research projects. Using the sources continuum, events and related sources could be represented in a manner that facilitated discussions about the lack of certain sources, such as oral traditions, and the absence or asymmetry of evidence surrounding many activities.

Historical manuscripts were also part of the introductory library class at Whitman. In an exercise similar to the rare book exercise described above, I had each student study a different type of document and answer questions about its who (creators), what (form and subject), where (location), when (date), why (function), and for whom (audience). As the students shared what they had discovered, I drew their attention to the distinctive material formats of what they were seeing and touching and we discussed how messages and media are related. I would also explain how the authenticity and accuracy of sources can be assessed by looking at both the intrinsic and extrinsic qualities of records, and by considering the processes that created and preserved them. In addition to information and artifactual literacies, I attempted to incorporate a broad historical sensibility into the session, and I used this exercise in history and religion classes as well.

The sources continuum brings these content, container, and context literacies together. A particularly rich example involves the killing of the missionaries after whom Whitman College is named. On November 29, 1847, Marcus and Narcissa Whitman and a number of others were killed by a group of Cayuse Indians at their mission site near present-day Walla Walla, Washington. The historiography surrounding this event is complicated and contentious, and the variety of sources related to it presents numerous challenges for anyone seeking to understand what happened. One historian cataloged twenty-four eyewitness and contemporary accounts of the attack and the subsequent month-long captivity. Some of these were reduced to writing within a few days of the events, others were recorded many years later, and many of these latter records were the memories of those who had been children at the time of the events. Additionally, some early records were created by individuals who were not present but were in the area and connected with the events in some way. And then there are the Cayuse accounts and traditions of what happened, some of which were recorded at a trial in 1850 and others that were transmitted orally.[15] The sources continuum provides a way of arranging these accounts and other sources—in the form of letters, reports, depositions, memoirs, and interviews inscribed and reinscribed on various media—chronologically, and it reveals the interpretive moves involved in determining degrees of transformation. Deciding what is primary is a matter of many such moves.

DIGITAL DOCUMENTS

When I teach students to attend to the dualistic nature of books and records, I point out that such analysis is applicable to digital documents as well. As individuals and institutions increasingly make useful digital materials publicly available, such un-vetted sources require sophisticated levels of analysis. Online, the authority once bestowed on physical libraries and archives is often transferred to

a discovery system.[16] While neither physical repositories nor discovery tools are, in the context of this discussion, sources, the materials found in physical libraries and archives are often self-authenticating or documented in such a way that authenticity can be validated or investigated. In a virtual environment, however, where we have "archives in the wild," authenticity and accuracy are harder to establish.[17] In a primary sources seminar at Whitman, a colleague and I used the sources continuum to illustrate how digital data sets precede research articles and also to explore transmission issues related to documents disseminated by WikiLeaks.[18]

Even in a curated environment, since we can only preserve *access* to digital documents and not the documents themselves, there is only access to simulacra.[19] What, for example, is the original inscription of an email? The completed copy residing in the sender's computing system or the recipient's (not to mention the copies stored at intermediate locations)?[20] All of these copies may be distinguishable chronologically, on a very precise timescale, but the email may not undergo any traceable transformation. If, however, the email is converted or migrated to a different format, some of the original characteristics of the email (e.g., metadata, formatting, attachments) may be lost. As with physical books and records, the sources continuum can be used to conceptualize how digital documents move and are transformed through time. As the availability of supplementary research data—in the form of data sets, raw records, and gray literature—increases in all disciplines, and as new cross-disciplinary methodologies emerge, opportunities for teaching students to work with digital documents as sources will increase.

CONCLUSION

In our so-called digital age, when we must increasingly contend with the "inherent instability of texts," the ability to "think like an archivist or special collections librarian" is a valuable critical skill.[21] Teaching students to differentiate between abstract qualities of primary and secondary sources—or, worse, holding up archetypical forms of primary sources such as newspapers[22]—is an inadequate competency. Archives and special collections, as repositories of unique and rare materials that are curious and complex, sometimes correct and sometimes corrupt, can function as sites of learning about the nature and use of primary materials and their role in the construction and transmission of knowledge. The sources continuum provides a productive framework for teachers and students working with artifacts and representations from and about the past. Once students have a sense of what types of primary sources are and are not available and an appreciation of the evidential and epistemological issues associated with them, they will be better prepared to identify, select, and interpret appropriate sources for their research. And their research, in turn, will be shaped by a deeper understanding of what can be known and how it can be known. Teaching students a sophisticated understanding of primary sources is a unique contribution that archives and special collections can make to undergraduate education.

NOTES

1. Jane Taylor, "Holdings: Refiguring the Archive," in *Refiguring the Archive*, ed. Carolyn Hamilton et al. (Boston: Kluwer Academic Publishers, 2002), 244.

2. Jill Lepore, *Encounters in the New World: A History in Documents* (New York: Oxford University Press, 2000), 6.

3. This phrase comes from Matthew P. Brown, *The Pilgrim and the Bee: Reading Rituals and Book Culture in Early New England* (Philadelphia: University of Pennsylvania Press, 2007), 203: "I mean a study of not only what we know from the evidential record … but also how we know what we know."

4. For the relevant information literacy standard, Standard One, see *Information Literacy Competency Standards for Higher Education* (Chicago, Ill.: American Library Association, 2000), 8.

5. Henry Johnson, *Teaching of History in Elementary and Secondary Schools* (New York: The Macmillan Company, 1922), 4.

6. Joanne Archer et al., "Investigating Primary Source Literacy," *The Journal of Academic Librarianship* 35 (2009): 414, 419.

7. Emmett Lombard, "Primary and Secondary Sources," *The Journal of Academic Librarianship* 36 (2010): 251-53.

8. The use of "transformation" here is comparable to the use of the word in copyright law, when "raw material [is] transformed in the creation of new information, new aesthetics, new insights and understandings." Pierre N. Leval, "Toward a Fair Use Standard," *Harvard Law Review* 103 (1990): 1111.

9. *The Catalog: 2010-2011* (Walla Walla, Wash.: Whitman College, 2010), 38.

10. Jonathan Rose, "From Book History to Book Studies," http://www.printinghistory.org/programs/awards/awards_2001; David Beard, "From Work to Text to Document," *Archival Science* 8 (2008): 217-26.

11. This class, Library 100, is an elective, one-credit course that teaches information literacy skills to first- and second-year students. See *The Catalog*, 117.

12. Robert Darnton, "What Is the History of Books," in *The Case for Books: Past, Present, and Future* (New York: PublicAffairs, 2009), 182.

13. "Procedures," in *The Broadview Anthology of Restoration & Early Eighteenth-Century Drama*, ed. J. Douglas Canfield and Maja-Lisa Von Sneidern (Peterborough, Ont.: Broadview Press, 2001), xx.

14. *The Catalog*, 38.

15. Clifford M. Drury, *Marcus and Narcissa Whitman and the Opening of Old Oregon*, Vol. 2 (Glendale, Calif.: A. H. Clark Co., 1973), 224, 387-89.

16. A recent study revealed that many young adults perceive search engines as credible sources. Eszter Hargittai et al., "Trust Online: Young Adults' Evaluation of Web Content," *International Journal of Communication* 4 (2010), 483, http://ijoc.org/ojs/index.php/ijoc/article/view/636/423.

17. Jeremy L. John et al., *Digital Lives: Personal Digital*

Archives for the 21st Century: An Initial Synthesis, Version 0.2 (2010), vii, http://britishlibrary.typepad.co.uk/files/digital-lives-synthesis02-1.pdf.

18.   This class, Library 300, is an elective, one-credit course that "uses archival materials to help [third-year] students prepare to undertake significant primary source research as part of their senior thesis." *The Catalog*, 117.

19.   "[A] digital document, because its perceptible form is always being manufactured just-in-time, on the spot, can't ever sever its relationship to a set of manufacturing technologies. It requires an elaborate set of technological conditions—hardware and software—in order to maintain a visible and useful presence." David M. Levy, *Scrolling Forward: Making Sense of Documents in the Digital Age* (Arcade Publishing, 2001), 152.

20.   Geoffrey Yeo, "'Nothing is the Same As Something Else': Significant Properties and Notions of Identity and Originality," *Archival Science* 10 (2010): 106.

21.   Robert Darnton, "The Information Landscape," in *The Case for Books*, 23; Magia G. Krause, "'It Makes History Alive for Them': The Role of Archivists and Special Collections Librarians in Instructing Undergraduates," *The Journal of Academic Librarianship* 36 (2010): 409-10.

22.   Darnton warns, "[N]ewspapers should be read for information about how contemporaries construed events, rather than for reliable knowledge of events themselves." "The Information Landscape," 27.

Archival Sound Recordings in Undergraduate Education: The Rubén Cobos Collection of Indo-Hispanic Folklore

Victoria Lindsay Levine

Archival sound recordings preserved in academic library special collections provide exciting opportunities for undergraduate education.[1] Among these recordings are ethnographic field tapes of singers from specific ethnic communities, times, and places, performing a wide variety of musical styles, repertories and genres. Field recordings are made by ethnographic researchers from disciplines such as music, dance, linguistics, folklore, and anthropology. In many cases, once the collector has archived the field tapes, the materials are rarely used. This is because most ethnographers make their own field recordings as a method of collecting primary source material, and consult archival recordings only for purposes of comparison and historical study. Yet these materials can be a rich source for teaching undergraduate students basic research skills, including musical transcription, textual transcription and translation, comparison of variant versions of tunes and texts, concordance searches, analysis, and interpretation.

For better or worse, archival collections of field recordings may require considerable attention before they can be used in undergraduate education. Collections must be inventoried in order to survey the scope and content of the recordings, and the recordings must be catalogued and indexed to facilitate the retrieval of individual entries. The original recordings must be transferred to contemporary media, and preferably digitized, for purposes of preservation and accessibility.[2] The potential benefits to undergraduate students and to the host institution as a whole warrant the laborious process, which creates opportunities for collaborative research uniting archivists, students, staff, and faculty. This chapter provides a case in point through a description of the Rubén Cobos Collection of Indo-Hispanic Folklore, a set of field tapes archived in Colorado College's Tutt Library.

Spanish New Mexican music in the twentieth century was documented in several important collections, including the John Donald Robb Archive of Southwestern Music (University of New Mexico), the Juan B. Rael Collections (American Folklife Center, Library of Congress),[3] and the Arthur L. Campa Collection (Library of Congress), among others.[4] The Rubén Cobos Collection is less well-known, but equally significant.[5] Cobos taught Spanish at the University of New Mexico from 1944 until 1977. His research focused on the documentation and analysis of the way Spanish was spoken in New Mexico during the mid-twentieth century, and his recordings provided primary source material for his scholarly publications. His interest in what was happening on the ground during his lifetime may help to explain the unusual scope and content of the Cobos Collection.

No direct evidence explains the criteria Cobos used to select the materials he collected. However, the materials themselves suggest that he was uncritical; he was extraordinarily eclectic in whom, what, where, and when he recorded. He taped men, women, and children from all over northern New

Mexico and southern Colorado, as long as they were speaking or singing in Spanish; he even recorded himself reading the texts of *alabados* that had been written down in Penitente *cuadernos* (notebooks).[6] Cobos recorded in the context of interviews, family events, and public lecture-performances. He did not privilege genres considered representative of Spanish colonial forms, nor did he apply any particular aesthetic criteria to the performances or performers he recorded. As a collector, therefore, Cobos broke with what the folklorist Américo Paredes called the "Hispanophile" approach of earlier scholars, who tended to emphasize New Mexico's cultural and physical isolation from Greater Mexico (Paredes 1993:130). This eclecticism is also the collection's great strength for scholars who wish to understand the full range of Spanish New Mexican verbal and musical expression in the mid-twentieth century. Upon his retirement in 1974, Cobos deposited 358 seven-inch reels of tape in the Special Collections department of Colorado College's Tutt Library, in the hope that the materials would enhance, and be used in, our Southwest Studies program.[7] The collection includes more than 2,000 separate entries, about 950 of which are songs or performances of instrumental music.

By the time I arrived at Colorado College, the recordings had been gathering dust for fourteen years and our staff was eager to develop the collection. I began working with it in 1992, quickly realizing that the recordings could be useful in both music and Southwest Studies courses. I catalogued and indexed the musical entries in the collection, working intermittently for seven years in collaboration with students and staff, finally publishing a co-edited catalog (Levine and Chace 1999). As we prepared the catalog, Amanda Chace dubbed the musical performances from the reel-to-reel tapes onto cassettes to enhance preservation and accessibility. Our Archivist and Curator of Special Collections, Jessica Randall, later had the cassettes digitized.[8] The catalog, which is indexed by song title

and genre, facilitates use of the Cobos Collection in teaching. In addition, it makes the collection's music entries accessible to other patrons, including scholars, community members, and perhaps most importantly, descendants of the performers Cobos recorded.

I use the Cobos Collection in two courses. One is an upper-division course on comparative music theory, which explores concepts of musical thought, process, and musicianship in various cultures. It includes aural skills practica focused on formal analysis of recorded performances and transcription of songs from the Cobos Collection. Musical transcription, or music dictation, involves writing out actual musical sounds in staff notation while listening to a piece of music as it is being performed. Learning to transcribe music strengthens students' aural and analytical skills and their understanding of staff notation. It challenges them to think about differences in aural perception and interpretation among various listeners, decision-making processes that effect visual representations of musical sound, and the role of transcription in the analysis of musical form and design. Finally, it introduces students to related methods in music scholarship, including the use of primary sources and concordance searches. Songs in the Cobos Collection are ideal for teaching transcription because they feature stylistic components that are familiar to the students while still offering enough ambiguities in meter, rhythm, pitch, melodic contour, and phrasing to present sufficient challenge. The assignment sheet in Appendix 1.1 provides details on the transcription projects.

I also use the Cobos Collection in an interdisciplinary Southwest Studies course, which introduces students to methods of analyzing and interpreting Southwestern expressive media (music, written and oral literature, drama, visual arts, and material culture) and addresses theoretical issues in Southwest Studies (collecting, intellectual property rights, repatriation, decolonization, consumerism, tourism, authenticity, representation, and appropriation). In order to apply interdisciplinary analytical methods and theoretical concepts in an original case study, each student researches an archive in Tutt Library's Special Collections. Students may use any of the college's archives, so long as it involves expressive media and is relevant to Colorado or the Southwest. The most successful projects have featured the letters, sermons, and diaries of late eighteenth-century religious leaders in Colorado Springs; the diaries of early residents of Colorado Springs, including memoirs of the westward journey; the scrapbooks of Colorado College students from the first decade of the twentieth century; and the collections relevant to Helen Hunt Jackson, William Jackson Palmer, and the Sand Creek massacre. Students who work with the Cobos Collection transcribe and translate the lyrics of particular songs and analyze them within their cultural and historical contexts. The assignment sheet in Appendix 1.2 provides details on the interdisciplinary archival research projects.

Using the Cobos Collection in undergraduate courses accomplishes several educational goals. It familiarizes students with archival materials that are unique to Colorado College, highlighting the special resources that define the character of our institution. It engages students with materials that represent an important ethnic group of the Southwestern United States, the geographic region we celebrate through our flagship interdisciplinary program. Most importantly, it teaches students basic skills that provide a foundation for more advanced research. Initially, some students are uncertain as to what they can accomplish with these materials or are uncomfortable using them because the format, procedures, and technology are unfamiliar. But by the end of the course, virtually every student feels a sense of achievement and many derive pleasure in working with archival materials. Each year a few students become inspired to continue working with archival materials through independent or senior capstone projects. Some—as undergraduates—present papers based on their research at professional conferences. Others decide to pursue graduate degrees in musicology, library science, or translation on the basis of this work. It may seem remarkable that archival sound recordings could play such a defining role, at least for certain students, in undergraduate education. Yet these materials give students in the humanities and fine arts the opportunity to experience what draws many of us to academic life: the fascination of scholarly detective work, the friendships that develop through collaborative research, and the satisfaction of contributing to the production of knowledge.

BIBLIOGRAPHY

Averill, Gage. 2011. "A (Copy)Right to Sing the Blues." *Society for EthnomusicologyNewsletter* 45(1):9-10.

Koegel, John. 1997. "Village Musical Life Along the Rio Grande: Tomé, New Mexico Since 1739." *Latin American Music Review* 18(2):173-251.

Lamadrid, Enrique R. 2000. "Cielos del Norte, Alma del Rio Arriba: Nuevo Mexicano Folk Music Revivals, Recordings 1943-98." *The Journal of American Folklore* 113:314-22.

Levine, Victoria Lindsay. 1993. "Two Colorado Sources of Spanish New Mexican Music." *American Music Research Center Journal* 3:65-77.

Levine, Victoria Lindsay and Amanda Chace, editors. 1999. *Music in the Rubén Cobos Collection of Spanish New Mexican Folklore: A Descriptive Catalogue.* Colorado Springs: The Hulbert Center Press of the Colorado College.

Paredes, Américo. 1993. *Folklore and Culture on the Texas-Mexican Border.* Austin: University of Texas Press.

Robb, John Donald. 1980. *Hispanic Folk Music of New Mexico: A Self-Portrait of a People.* Norman: University of Oklahoma Press.

Weigle, Marta. 1976. *Brothers of Light, Brothers of Blood: The Penitentes of the Southwest.* Santa Fe: Ancient City Press.

APPENDIX 1.1: Transcription Project

Each student will complete at least three transcriptions of Spanish New Mexican songs from the Rubén Cobos Collection, an archive of recorded sound housed at Colorado College. Copies of the cassette tapes are on reserve in the Albert Seay Library of Music and Art. Expect to spend at least one hour per day on transcriptions. Your transcriptions should include one song from each of the following genres, completed in the order given:

1. *Indita* or *Corrido*
2. *Romance*
3. *Alabado* or *Alabanza*

Search for concordances in published sources (such as Robb 1980) and attach copies of published transcriptions to your transcription; describe the differences between your representation of the song and transcriptions by other scholars.

In selecting a song to transcribe, use the index of the catalogue to find multiple versions of the song; then listen to several different versions before deciding which one to transcribe (some are more audible than others). If you do not know Spanish, do not attempt to transcribe the song text at this time; focus on melody, meter, rhythm, and form. If you do know Spanish, you may provide a text underlay. You need only transcribe one verse (or verse and chorus pair) of the song, but provide a written description indicating how subsequent verses differ from what you have transcribed. For the transcription workshop that concludes each week of class, bring a photocopy of your transcription for each member of the class to enable collaborative editing. Your final version of each transcription should incorporate the results of collaborative editing and should be neatly copied in ink (or prepared using Finale software). Transcription will be easy for some of you, more difficult for others. If you find it easy, increase your level of individual challenge by completing additional transcriptions in each genre. Hint: the *alabados* are the most difficult for many students because of highly melismatic text settings and ambiguities in meter and rhythm.

Transcriptions will be assessed on the basis of clarity, aural skill, difficulty of the song chosen, effort, and completeness. For the project to be considered complete, you must include a final, corrected copy of the transcription, written in ink; a brief description of the process you used to choose the recording; and a copy of published concordances with a brief description of how your transcription differs.

APPENDIX 1.2: Interdisciplinary Archival Research Project

Working individually, each student will conduct original research on a piece of expressive culture using archival materials found in Colorado College's Special Collections. The purpose of this project is to enhance research, analysis, and interpretation skills, to improve academic writing through editing and revising multiple drafts of a substantial research paper, and to prepare students to undertake major research projects, such as senior theses. On the second day of class, we will meet in Tutt Library for an introduction to the Colorado College archives provided by Jessica Randall, Archivist and Curator of Special Collections. Each student will choose a topic and begin archival research during this session. The project as a whole is carried out in four phases.

PHASE 1: ARCHIVAL COLLECTIONS

Prepare a report on one of the archives in Tutt Library's Special Collections that contains materials relevant to Colorado or the Southwest. First, choose the archive you wish to study. Next, obtain biographical information on the collector/s including his or her motivations, goals, and approaches in assembling the archive. Then discuss the history of the archive; its size, scope, focus, and content; media included; how scholars gain access to the archive; how it is organized; and how to use it in research. Conclude with a discussion of the kinds of projects in which this archive would be useful. Include a bibliography of sources consulted for biographical information on the collector/s. Expect to spend about 8-10 hours on this phase of the project (not including writing time).

Write a paper about 5 pages in length based on your research. The paper must be typed (size 12 font), double spaced, paginated, and stapled prior to submission. Papers will be assessed on the basis of completeness and accuracy of information, writing style, organization, and effort. Do not use on-line internet sources, except for collection guides.

PHASE 2: DETAILED STUDY

Complete a detailed analysis of the archive you studied in Phase 1. First, choose the piece of expressive culture you wish to study in detail (song, story, letter, poem, diary, sermon, piece of visual art). Next, provide a detailed description and analysis of the style, form, and content of the piece. Illustrate your description with visual representations of the piece. Conclude with a comparison of the piece you analyzed to other archival examples of the same medium. Include a bibliography of sources consulted for descriptive and analytical criteria. Expect to spend about 8-10 hours on this phase of the project (not including writing time).

For a photograph or piece of visual art

Include information on who made the piece; the materials used to make the piece; where these materials are found or how the artist acquired them; the cultural tradition from which the materials derived; how the materials were worked; special techniques or processes used to produce the piece; the age of the piece; its shape and size; the relation of shape to function; the use or function of the item among the people who produced it; color symbolism; surface designs or patterns; the use of repetition or complementarity as design elements; texture; and other visual features.

For a piece of music

Include information on who composed and/or performed the piece; the instrumental and vocal resources used in performance; where the genre originated; the cultural tradition from which the instruments derived; special vocal timbres and/or instrumental techniques used in the performance; the age of the piece; the length of the piece; the relationship between length and function; the use or function of the piece among the people who produced it; stylistic characteristics such as timbre, melodic contour, time elements (tempo, meter, and rhythm), melodic texture, form and design; the language, content, structure, and meaning of song lyrics; the use of repetition or complementarity as design elements; and other aural features.

For a verbal performance, written or audio

Include information on who wrote or performed the piece; the literary or oral resources used in creating the piece; where the genre originated; the cultural tradition from which the genre derived; special literary or performance techniques used in the piece; the age of the piece; the length of the piece; the relationship between length and function; the use or function of the piece among the people who produced it; stylistic characteristics such as narrative voice, meter, rhyme scheme, form and design; the language, content, structure, and meaning of the text; the use of repetition or complementarity as design elements; and other literary or oral features.

Write a paper about 5 pages in length based on your description and analysis. Follow the same guidelines provided for the first paper.

PHASE 3: EXPRESSIVE CULTURE IN CONTEXT

Write a paper that incorporates your first two projects into a complete case study of one particular piece of expressive culture, as found in an archive collection, placed within a broader cultural and historical context. Interpret the significance and meaning of the piece as it relates to one of the issues we have discussed this block (collection, ownership, representation, appropriation, decolonization, tourism, hobbyism, authenticity, tradition). Conclude with suggestions for further research. Provide a bibliography of all sources consulted. Expect to spend about

8-10 hours on the interpretive phase of the project (background reading and research, not including writing time).

Write a paper about 15 pages in length based on your research (about 10 pages of the paper will come from your first two papers). Follow the same guidelines provided for the first two papers.

PHASE 4: FINAL PAPER AND PRESENTATION

Incorporate all of the editorial revisions I provided on the first three drafts of your paper into this final copy. This paper will form the basis of your class presentation. Practice your presentation and provide handouts as well as audio or visual aids as appropriate. Time your presentation so that it lasts no more than 15 minutes (you will not be able to read your entire paper).

NOTES

1. I am grateful to Jessica Randall, Colorado College Archivist and Curator of Special Collections, for her foresight and initiative in digitizing the Cobos Collection. I thank Jessica Randall and Amy Brooks of Tutt Library Special Collections, along with Daryll Stevens, David Dymek, and Anette Megneys of the Albert Seay Library of Music and Art, for their generous guidance of our students as they work with the Cobos Collection and other archives. I thank the staff of the Hulbert Center for Southwestern Studies—Judith Pickle, Jim Diers, Kathy Kaylan, and Suzi Nishida—along with former students Amanda Chace, Tamara Roberts, and Rudy Sánchez for their tireless assistance with this project. I appreciate the funding I have received to support this project from the Colorado College Faculty/Student Collaborative Research Grants, Humanities Division Research and Development Grants, and Hulbert Center Jackson Fellowships.

2. The status of archival recordings under federal copyright law, and the legality of preserving them and making them accessible through digitization, is a major concern for archivists, scholars, students, and

community members alike. The Historical Recording Coalition for Access and Preservation, with the support of the American Library Association and eight other national professional organizations, is seeking an amendment in copyright law that will clarify this situation (Averill 2011:10).

3. A superb website, titled "Hispano Music and Culture of the Northern Rio Grande: The Juan B. Rael Collection," is available at http://memory.loc.gov/ammem/rghtml/rghome.html.

4. These collections, along with the copious print sources and commercial recordings of Spanish New Mexican music that are available, have been thoroughly described by John Koegel (1997) and Enrique Lamadrid (2000).

5. Detailed information on Rubén Cobos and the his-

tory, structure and content of his collection appears in Levine 1993 and Levine and Chace 1999.

6. The Penitentes are members of a lay Catholic organization for Hispanic men in northern New Mexico and southern Colorado; the organization is properly known as La Fraternidad Piadosa de Nuestro Padre Jesús Nazareno (The Pious Fraternity of Our Father Jesus the Nazarite). For additional information, see Weigle 1976.

7. Cobos also deposited 61 reels of tape in the John Donald Robb Archive of Southwestern Music at the University of New Mexico, but these recordings were removed from the collection in 2002 and are no longer available.

8. See http://www.coloradocollege.edu/library/Special-Collections/Cobos.html.

Building a New Model: Faculty-Archivist Collaboration in Architectural Studies

Nova M. Seals

Many special collections and archives departments encourage use of their materials to illustrate a lesson or lessons in course curricula in various subject areas. The access that most professors usually seek for their students amounts to a special collections and archives visit for one discrete assignment. This type of assignment developed by faculty to simply expose students to primary sources is not unusual but it offers no opportunity to develop any user expertise with, or understanding of, how primary sources, particularly archival materials, are organized and how one conducts archival research in a strategic way.[1] While it is common for students to receive rudimentary assignments to interact with primary sources, it is rare to have an entire course planned around primary sources found in a special collections and archives department, particularly with faculty members and special collections librarians and archivists working in close collaboration. Arguably, archival education is best practiced and learned when faculty members and archivists can successfully work together as partners to develop courses utilizing primary sources as the primary texts. This allows undergraduate students an opportunity to gain unfettered exposure to primary sources, to strategically conduct original research, and to understand how their experiences using primary sources relates to their greater depth of knowledge.

In an effort to offer undergraduate students at Connecticut College studying architectural history a richer experience in learning about the development of their campus and its architecture, a faculty member and the college archivist collaborated in planning and developing a seminar course using materials from the college archives as the primary texts. Planning an entire course around these primary source materials offered the students an opportunity to take ownership of their learning experience in a unique way.[2] Students also gained a deeper appreciation for the institutional history of their college.

ARCHIVES OVERVIEW

The college archives at Connecticut College was established in 1989 in a seminar room in the Charles E. Shain Library, the main library on the Connecticut College campus. Although the college archives and special collections are part of the same unit the two entities were separated physically until fall 2008, when a renovation allowed special collections and archives to be joined in one space, now referred to as the Linda Lear Center for Special Collections and Archives. The archives portion houses approximately 1,130 linear feet of archival material, primarily primary sources. The mission of the archives is to collect and preserve the permanent record of the college. While the archives is charged with encouraging use of the materials by administrative offices, faculty and scholarly researchers, it is also committed to "encouraging the use of the archives by Connecticut College students, thereby providing them with research experience involving primary source materials."[3] As the repository for documentation of the college's history, the archive's strongest institutional collections are the documents of the Connecticut College Arboretum and the records and photographs documenting the evolution of campus architecture. In addition to preserving the institutional history of Connecticut College, the archives also manages the documents of the American Dance Festival from 1947 to 1977, when the Festival called the campus home. There is one archivist who also provides oversight of the college's records management program and assists with special collections as needed.

ARCHIVAL INSTRUCTION

Information about Connecticut College's archives and its holdings is distributed through library literature, the college website and library instruction sessions. When course listings are released, the college archivist contacts professors whose classes may benefit from materials found in the college archives and proposes collections that may be of interest. Professors who desire to pursue projects with an archival component for the classes work with the archivist to select materials for the class and schedule a time to bring the class in. When the class comes to the archives, the archivist provides an overview of the institutional archival collections as well as the materials pre-selected by the professor (and in some cases the archivist). This type of visit involves some level of collaboration and thoughtful discussion between the faculty member and archivist. If particular pieces of a collection have been selected, the archivist discusses the collection from which materials have been pulled as well as other collections that could complement or supplement the students' research. This model has been used successfully for classes in architectural studies, landscape architecture, theater studies, gender and women's studies, and sociological methods.

DEVELOPING A DIFFERENT MODEL

During the summer of 2007 an architectural stud-

ies professor, Professor Abigail Van Slyck, asked the college archivist about the possibility of teaching a course using materials from the college archives to highlight the college's institutional history. The class was scheduled for the spring of 2008. During the initial planning stages of course development, Professor Van Slyck refined the goals of the course during repeated visits to the archives and after many conversations with the college archivist. In these early discussions, the archivist acted as a consultant, offering information about the content of collections that might be of possible interest for the course while leaving the selection of collections and materials for class use to the professor.[4] The end result was a seminar course on the architectural history of the college for nine students (primarily juniors and seniors) using archival materials found in the college archives as the primary texts for the course.

As the professor planned her syllabus for the course, she discussed the themes and topics for each class and the archivist worked with her to select archival materials that fit within the theme. For each class, secondary reading materials were assigned to provide the students with a framework for assessing and evaluating the primary sources that they would be studying in class. Because the archivist did not have a subject specialization in architecture, the archivist read the secondary course readings for the course to attain subject knowledge, to better inform supplemental selection of materials for the classes, and to prepare to meet the research needs of the students in the course.

The archivist provided an overview during the first meeting of the seminar class. During the meeting, the class was given an introduction to archives in general, common practices and procedures for use, the types of information (and their formats) found in archives, archives etiquette and an introduction of the materials in the Connecticut College Archives that would be of primary interest to the students over the course of the semester. The initial class meeting in the archives offered the students an opportunity to experience the archival setting informally. It also allowed the archivist to meet new researchers who would be spending a great deal of time in the archives.

The seminar class met once a week. In addition to the normal class meeting time, each student was required to sign up for a weekly time (one hour) to conduct their own research in the college archives. In order to accommodate each student and his or her research needs, the archivist scheduled these appointments so that none overlapped. Each appointment was, essentially, one-on-one. These individualized sessions were driven by the students, with each student making decisions about materials that they wanted pulled (the archivist would offer options in tangential collections as appropriate). With the onus upon the students to make their own selections for further study, they were more engaged with the entire process of primary source discovery and research.[5] During the beginning of the semester these individual study appointments required prior preparation and planning by the archivist because each appointment served as a workshop with the archivist giving some amount of instruction (archival, bibliographic, etcetera) during each visit.[6] The planning and preparation for all of the student appointments took approximately four hours each week.

Because the course was taught prior to the special collections and archives renovation, there was insufficient space in the original archives facility to accommodate an entire class. The architectural seminar class met in a classroom in the library. Prior to each class meeting, the archivist pulled pre-selected materials and delivered them to the classroom, and returned to retrieve the materials from the room at the end of the class meeting. Procedures for handling materials were discussed with the faculty member before each class. Class preparation amounted to approximately one hour each week.

Prior to each class, students were required to post a journal entry on the course website. The students were expected to comment on the secondary readings in a thoughtful way and discuss how the readings related to the primary sources from the college archives. The students' journal entries not only drove their discussion during their regular class meetings, but the journal assignments gave the archivist a starting point for working with the students upon their weekly visits to the college archives.[7] Reading the students' journals required an additional one hour each week.

COURSE ASSIGNMENTS

In addition to the journal entries, the students were given three major assignments. Each student was assigned two essays on the architectural and social history of individual buildings on the Connecticut College campus and a final narrative essay or thematic project exploring the campus history in a creative way. Similar to the course itself, the assignments for the course were heavily dependent upon primary sources in the college archives.

In order to complete their assignments, the students needed to have access to current working architectural records (primarily architectural plans) as well as archival records. Providing access to current records, housed in a small room which serves as a technical library, involved making arrangements with the college's facilities management personnel. Each student was required to be supervised by either the professor or archivist, during two individual appointments. These appointments were scheduled in addition to the students' self-scheduled individual study hour in the archives, which obligated an additional eight hours of the archivist's time to the seminar course.

All assignments produced by the students in the seminar course were deposited in the college archives. Through the students' efforts, the archives was able to build a subject file of campus architecture by building. Each file contains a history of a particular building as well as photocopies of primary sources used to write the history; while redundant in many cases, the photocopies have proven quite useful for information students found outside of the institutional archives at Connecticut College.

The work products produced by the seminar students have aided the efforts of other researchers, particularly administrators and architects interested in building renovations on campus. In an effort to showcase student work in the archives, the archivist has used the student essays and projects to develop lectures and presentations. Other students have built upon the work of the architectural seminar students as well.

Aside from developing a course that enriched student learning, there were other accomplishments. This course allowed the archivist to build relationships with other administrative offices on campus, particularly facilities management, in regard to communication and transfer of materials to the archives. Also, the new model of faculty-archivist collaboration was repeated, with success, when the architectural studies seminar class was taught the following term. The faculty-archivist collaborative model was again used, successfully, for a long term oral history project which was a major component for a seminar course in gender and women's studies.

If success is measured by numbers, the development and implementation of this collaborative model has proven successful for the archives at Connecticut College. The number of scholarly visitors to the archives during the following academic year increased 78%, while use of archival services (measured by number of archival reference requests) increased 115% from the period before the seminar course occurred. Additionally, the course and its use of primary sources served as a catalyst for driving discussions about the archives, its role, and the importance of the college's primary sources on campus. These discussions continue to garner program support, attention, and use, which is critical for any archives program.[8]

FINAL THOUGHTS

Collaborative projects such as a faculty-archives partnership of this scale are not to be entered into blindly. The level of responsibility accepted by the archivist made necessary additional effort that fell outside of the archivist's job description; but, taking on the responsibility of archival education is important, particularly when relating it to academic curricula.[9] The additional class and appointment preparation time was considerable, and the hours spent reading secondary materials to acquire knowledge of an unfamiliar area of study was not miniscule. The archivist's other professional duties still had to be fulfilled which required working more hours. But the overall success of the course justified the effort.

Every program or institution may not think the commitment worth the effort (especially when staff is limited), each program must assess its priorities. At Connecticut College, the goal was to, ultimately, get archival materials into the hands of the students and generate interest in exploring the knowledge available through the research and use of primary sources. By creatively and thoughtfully collaborating with a faculty member who had a common objective, this humble goal of enriching student learning with primary sources was attained.

BIBLIOGRAPHY

Connecticut College Archives Program Manual (2008). Linda Lear Center for Special Collections and Archives, Connecticut College. New London, CT.

Dearstyne, Bruce W., "What is the Use of Archives? A Challenge to the Profession," American Archivist 50 (Winter 1987): 76-87

Falbo, Bianca. "Teaching from the Archives," RBM: A Journal of Rare Books, Manuscripts, and Cultural Heritage vol. 1, no. 1 (2000): 33-35.

Greene, Mark A. "Using College and University Archives as Instructional Materials: A Case Study and an Exhortation," The Midwestern Archivist, vol 14, no.1 (1989): 31-38.

Malkmus, Doris J. "Primary Source Research and the Undergraduate: A Transforming Landscape," Journal of Archival Organization 6 (2008): 47-70

Matyn, Marian J. "Getting Undergraduates to Seek Primary Sources in Archives," The History Teacher vol. 33, no. 3 (May 2000): 349-355.

Meo, Susan Leighow. ""In Their Own Eyes": Using Journals with Primary Sources with College Students," The History Teacher vol. 33, no. 3 (May 2000): 335-341.

Schmiesing, Ann, and Deborah R. Hollis. "The Role of Special Collections Departments in Humanities Undergraduate and Graduate Teaching: A Cast Study," Libraries and the Academy (2002): 465-480.

Yakel, Elizabeth, and Deborah A. Torres. " AI: Archival Intelligence and User Expertise" American Archivist 66 (Spring/Summer 2003): 51-78

NOTES

1. Yakel, Elizabeth, and Deborah Torres, "AI: Archival Intelligence and User Expertise," *American Archivist* 66 (Spring/Summer 2003): 52.

2. Falbo, Bianca, "Teaching from the Archives," *RBM: A Journal of Rare Books, Manuscripts, and Cultural Heritage* 1, no. 1 (2000): 34.

3. Connecticut College Archives Program Manual, Linda Lear Center for Special Collections and Archives, Connecticut College, New London, CT (2008), 3.

4. Malkmus, Doris J., "Primary Source Research and the Undergraduate: A Transforming Landscape," *Journal of Archival Organization* 6 (2008): 48.

5. Schmiesing, Ann, and Deborah R. Hollis, "The Role of Special Collections Departments in Humanities Undergraduate and Graduate Teaching: A Cast Study," *Libraries and the Academy* (2002): 473.

6. Matyn, Marian J., "Getting Undergraduates to Seek Primary Sources in Archives," *The History Teacher* 33, no. 3 (May 2000): 355.

7. Meo, Susan Leighow, ""In Their Own Eyes": Using Journals with Primary Sources with College Students," *The History Teacher* 33, no. 3 (May 2000): 336.

8. Dearstyne, Bruce W., "What is the *Use* of Archives? A Challenge to the Profession," *American Archivist* 50 (Winter 1987): 77.

9. Greene, Mark A. "Using College and University Archives as Instructional Materials: A Case Study and an Exhortation," *The Midwestern Archivist* 14, no.1 (1989): 36.

A Novel Approach: Teaching Research through Narrative

Stephanie Boone and Jay Satterfield

INTRODUCTION

For many first-year students the prospect of writing a 15- to 20-page research paper is daunting. They have written few if any documented essays in high school. Those who have written a research paper think that they must see how many sources can dance on the head of a pin: stacks of quotations and engorged bibliographies equal a research paper. Often they are either unschooled or unpracticed in evaluating the academic credibility of their sources and in judging their suitability. Even fewer students have used primary sources in original research. While most students bring some research experience and knowledge of citation conventions to college, they have yet to become part of the scholarly conversation.

Helping students to enter that conversation is one of the goals in the first-year writing courses at Dartmouth College. Besides learning effective strategies for generating ideas, structuring papers, and revising their work for their audience, students must understand how research as process and product informs their writing, deepens their understanding of their topics, and hones their critical thinking. Assignments and exercises that reveal research as a way to unravel a mystery help de-mystify (and valorize) the research process and make the student the primary investigator in search of a story: two outcomes that have extraordinary power in shaping their habits of mind.

In a writing course that features a novel that defies students' expectations of the genre (it is not linear *and* incorporates primary sources), such outcomes pose two challenges for the instructor: help-ing students to not only decode the novel, but also to appreciate the virtuosity of its narrative structure, one reliant on primary sources; and helping them understand how to address and work with primary sources in their own work.

Those challenges arise when teaching Michael Ondaatje's *The English Patient,* a novel that relies on primary sources (historical and geographical records) to plot the multi-layered narrative, create characters, and color and historicize its settings. The novel incorporates such disparate texts as records from the Royal Geographical Society, passages from texts on desert exploration written by several early-twentieth-century explorers, including Hussein Bey and Count Laszlo de Almàsy, and quotations from Herodotus' *Histories.* The novel is a nexus of many histories including, but not limited to, geography, exploration, politics, archaeology, art and music, and the personal mnemonic records of the characters and real persons, that collide and reside in the planes of the text and in the memories of the characters.

Moreover, *The English Patient* does not offer the reader the whole narrative: it is neither continuous nor laid bare. The reader has to fill in the gaps and pay close attention to the multiple histories at play. The novel's *play* is mimetic in that it imitates the real gaps and holes left by betrayals in love and war, which are but two of the novel's themes. These gaps arise from shifts in time to *perform* as narrative sandstorms: each narrative break reveals and conceals other narratives at work. Dealing with the gaps becomes rather like Pelmanism, a reference in Ondaatje's novel, where the reader comes across a scene or a line that matches a previous scene or some future scene.[1] Think of the old television game show *Concentration,* which is rather like the experience of reading this novel. The time shifts, gaps, and discontinuities attenuate, frustrate, and challenge the reader's understanding (or immediate comprehension) of the historical and personal events in the story. For some students, the properties of Ondaatje's narrative disorient and confuse. The shifts between present and past, the random musings of the characters, the interjections of histories seemingly unrelated to the plot, leave many students drowning in mysteries. Unable to navigate the shifting sands of the narrative, at first some students dismiss the novel as *just a love story.* Like most primary source research, the novel does not dispense all the answers, or plug all the gaps, and it leaves a raft of questions at the end. Rather it bestirs the imagination to consider what is not resolved.

To help students appreciate the novel and inoculate them against frustration with the structure, it is useful to have them perform the kind of investigatory work central to the production of *The English Patient:* examine primary sources in order to find (construct) a history, or narrative, and to autopsy the body narrative. Actively constructing a narrative from un-bundled, un-ordered documents parallels in many ways the Ondaatje project. Even more, such an exercise approximates the original research the students will be expected to conduct in their academic careers.

To achieve those ends, we created for students an experience wrapped around an exercise wrapped around an enigma that we hoped would inspire them to consider a new paradigm for writing and research. We wanted them to experience reading, writing, and research as an exploration that requires them *to act*—specifically, to observe, to interrogate, to decode, to analyze, to synthesize, to hypothesize, to theorize. We wanted them to experience research as narrative, and narrative as research, or, as Ondaatje would have it: "The Sand Sea."[2]

PREPARATION

We began by selecting a compelling story from the College Archives about a Dartmouth student who had served in the Second World War (the setting for Ondaatje's novel): Charles "Stubbie" Pearson, valedictorian of the class of 1942, captain of the football and basketball teams, poet, scholar, and social leader on campus. Along with dozens of his classmates, he joined the U.S. Navy upon graduation to become a pilot. In 1944, he was killed in action in the Pacific while dive-bombing a Japanese ship.

Because Pearson was an accomplished student and athlete, we have solid documentation of his college years and his life in the Navy, but the collections yield almost nothing about his childhood. We embraced this incomplete record: we used documents from Pearson's adult life to show the value of primary sources while still exposing the gaps that nearly

Figure 3.1. Charles Pearson, valedictorian of the class of 1942, captain of the football and basketball teams, poet, scholar, and social leader on campus

always frustrate users of archival materials. From a wealth of information, we selected eight small groupings of key documents that marked signal moments in Pearson's academic and military careers. To maximize the pedagogical potential, we chose documents representing different types of sources: published/unpublished, official documents/informal letters, images/texts. In addition, it was essential for the assignment that none of the groupings told too much of the story. Each grouping documented some fragment of Pearson's life, but no more.

MATERIALS

1. 1942 Dartmouth yearbook, the *Aegis*; an undated Dartmouth College Press release about Pearson as first captain of both the football and basketball teams; a glossy photo of Pearson in letter sweater from 1942 (see figure 3.1).

2. Pearson Valedictory Address, *The Dartmouth*, May 10, 1942; the cover to August 1942 *Dartmouth Alumni Magazine* showing photos of all of the Dartmouth members of the Class of 1942 who joined the Naval flight unit together.

3. Letter from Dartmouth President Ernest Hopkins to Pearson, May 5, 1943; letter from Pearson to Hopkins, [April 1943].

4. Two letters from Pearson to Sally Neidlinger, February 8, 1943 (see figure 3.2), and March 10, 1943.

5. U. S. Department of Defense Distinguished Flying Cross citation for Charles Pearson, 1942.

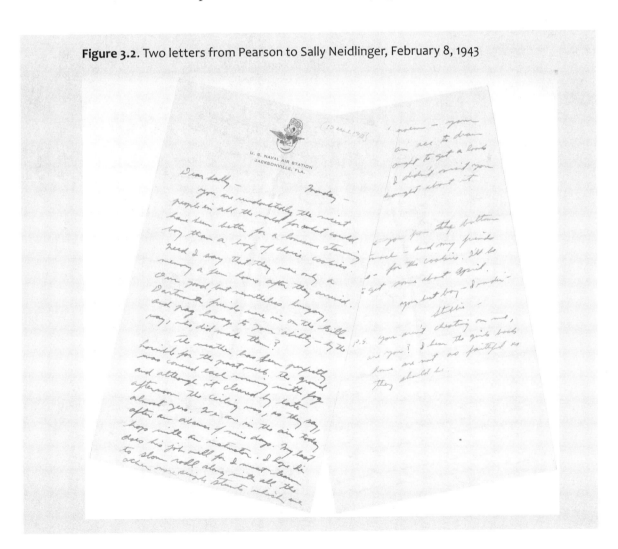

Figure 3.2. Two letters from Pearson to Sally Neidlinger, February 8, 1943

6. Dartmouth College, "Dartmouth Alumni Who have Died in the Service," 1946 (see figure 3.3).
7. Letter from Dartmouth President Ernest Hopkins to Ernest H. Giusti, May 1, 1944; letter from Ernest H. Giusti to Ernest Hopkins, April 8, 1944. Giusti was a member of the Dartmouth class of 1942 who witnessed Pearson's death.
8. James Idema. "To Pearson." *Poetry: A Magazine of Verse* 70 (August 1947): 242. Idema was a member of the class of 1942 who knew Pearson as a poet.

The materials came from several collections: Pearson's alumni file contained many of the pieces, but the Neidlinger letters were part of a manuscript collection given to Dartmouth by Sally Neidlinger; the correspondence with President Hopkins came from the President's Papers; *Poetry* from the general stacks; and the yearbook and student newspaper from the Archival serials collections.

CLASS SESSION

The class began with a brief introduction to the concept of research and writing as narrative, and to the idea of telling a story through fragmentary documentation: this provided a clear link to Ondaatje's text (so, made it of immediate interest to the students) and tied it to the overall course goals.

Once the students had paired up, we asked them to think about their sources and examine them for fifteen minutes. Because we arranged the materi-

Figure 3.3. Dartmouth College, "Dartmouth Alumni Who have Died in the Service," 1946

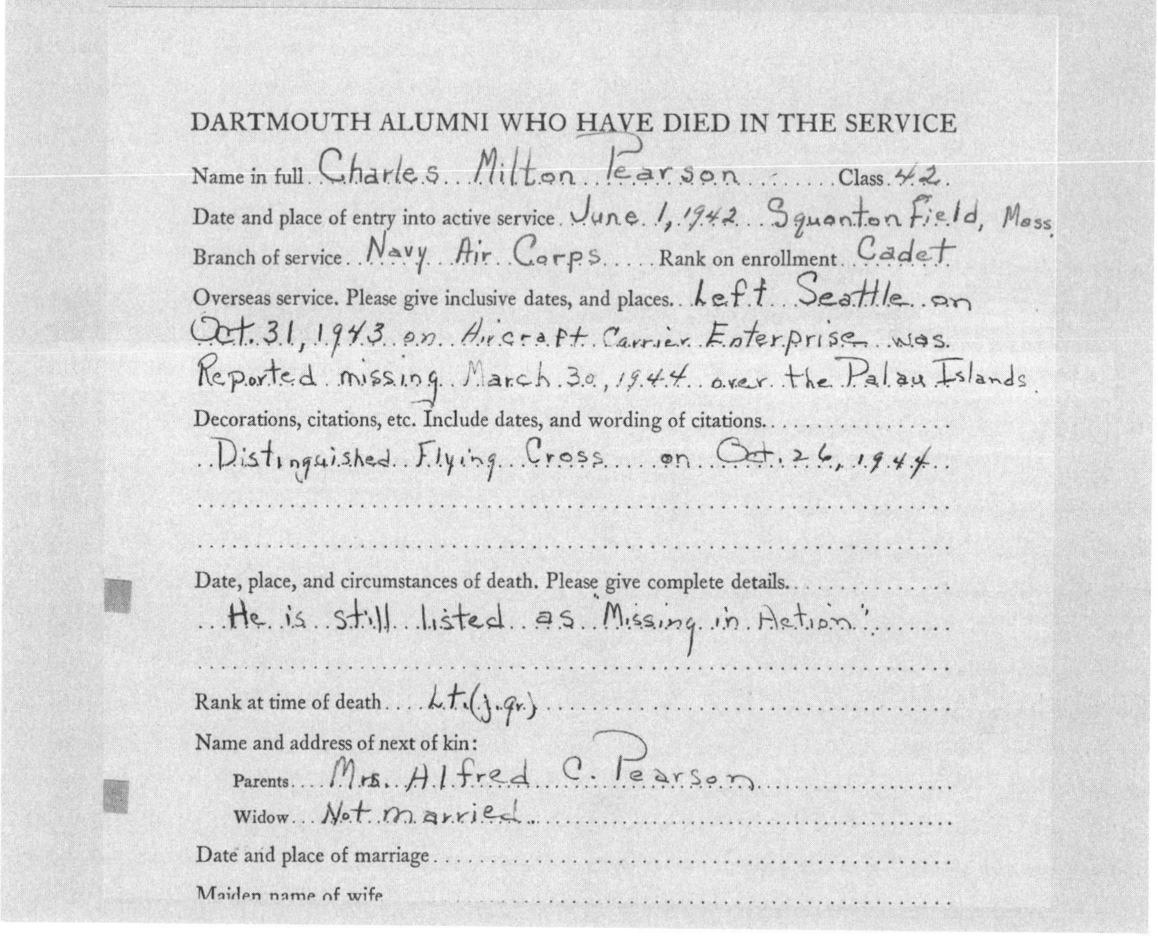

DARTMOUTH ALUMNI WHO HAVE DIED IN THE SERVICE

Name in full Charles Milton Pearson Class 42

Date and place of entry into active service June 1, 1942 Squantum Field, Mass.

Branch of service Navy Air Corps Rank on enrollment Cadet

Overseas service. Please give inclusive dates, and places. Left Seattle on Oct. 31, 1943 on Aircraft Carrier Enterprise. was Reported missing March 30, 1944 over the Palau Islands.

Decorations, citations, etc. Include dates, and wording of citations. Distinguished Flying Cross on Oct. 26, 1944.

Date, place, and circumstances of death. Please give complete details. He is still listed as "Missing in Action".

Rank at time of death Lt. (j.g.)

Name and address of next of kin:

Parents Mrs. Alfred C. Pearson

Widow Not married

Date and place of marriage

Maiden name of wife

als chronologically, a story of "Stubbie" emerged as each group reported their findings. The first group saw the charismatic and highly successful student athlete, and the second group told of his articulate and patriotic valedictory speech. A little eye rolling accompanied those first few images and documents from Pearson's college years: he seemed the "big man on campus"—more stereotype than individual. But, as the next two groups witnessed both his struggles and doubts in flight school, the class came to appreciate that they were no longer dealing with an abstraction, but rather a real person. As the next three groups revealed the details of his death, the students' perceptions of their subject shifted dramatically. Pearson finally became one of them, particularly at the moment when they read James Idema's poem, "To Pearson," published in the prestigious *Poetry*. This and other documents in the second half of the exercise told a different story than the students had imagined at the beginning of the exercise: Pearson became a tragic figure, a sensitive poet, seemingly at odds with the gung-ho, patriotic athlete the first group saw.

As the groups reported, the students made connections among the documents: they created new meaning from their materials as fresh information explained and contextualized other fragments. After hearing the reports, we asked for a volunteer to "tell the whole story." Even though it was based on real research in primary sources, the students saw that the narrative was replete with gaps and assumptions. The holes in the narrative, and some of the assumptions the volunteer made to tell the story, opened the discussion. How does the process of archival research (how we go about it and what we can and cannot find) shape the narratives we tell? Further, how do researchers cope with gaps that may arise and imperil the reading of complex narratives? The students made the assumption that "Sally" was Pearson's girlfriend. Nothing in the selected materials indicated her age or that she was the daughter of the dean of the College. All that the

students could see was Pearson's flirtatious letters, thanking her for sending cookies and chiding her for going to a dance: "You are not cheating on me are you?" What the documents did not show was that Sally was only 13 years old. Further research after the class revealed that Sally was an adolescent with a terrible crush on this good-looking college boy, a frequent guest in her father's house. So the question arises: Do the letters have to be read differently depending on the relationship of writer and audience? Yes, because people pitch their rhetorical strategies based on their relationship to their audiences. Dartmouth President Hopkins maintained a close connection with many students and his correspondence reflects his friendship with Pearson. When we asked the students to imagine carrying on a correspondence with a College administrator, they quickly understood that they could not rely on their own experiences to evaluate documents from the past or interpret all relationships.

THE OUTCOMES

The close collaboration between an instructor and a librarian combined with some very compelling archival materials generated a productive dialogue. Neither of us had a preconceived notion of how to conduct the session. We discussed the book's challenges and then worked through several different strategies before settling on our method, rejecting any sort of "show and tell." We wanted to create an active learning environment where the students would enact the very thing we sought to teach. It worked because we framed every aspect of the exercise to support the course's goals by expanding the students' range of intellectual inquiry. Unexpectedly, we created a teaching strategy that translates well into other settings. All archives have a trove of rich stories for this kind of exercise: we mined the collections for materials on a 1778 smallpox outbreak on Dartmouth campus that we used similarly in a biology course on epidemiology.

In retrospect, we need to adjust our methodology in two ways. Initially, in order to make sure the students grasped the core objectives, we arranged the materials in chronological order. We now realize the students could have handled a non-linear approach, more closely related to the structure of the novel. In subsequent sessions, we will have the pairs report in a random order. More problematic, we tried to create each document grouping so it offered the students a substantial and interesting fragment of Pearson's life. But, while each grouping offered roughly equal evidentiary value, the students did not experience them as equally difficult to read and interpret. While some pairs were unsettled by what appeared to be cryptic documents, others breezed through documents that seemed easy to decode. We understand now that we need to help students overcome their tendency to read only at a literal level, to really interrogate their sources. For example, a seemingly simple document from 1946 is headed "Dartmouth Alumni Who have Died in the Service" (see figure 3.3) yet states Pearson was "still listed as 'Missing in action.'" None of the students questioned the disparity or wondered what that may have meant in 1946 after the war?

We achieved our two main objectives: a better understanding of the novel and a guided foray into the process of primary source research. The exercise mirrored the novel in structure and mystery and set the students up to pose new, more sophisticated questions about the novel and the characters. Further, Pearson's identity as a Dartmouth student made him a character the students could relate to more immediately than the characters in the novel. This increased their interest, and, consequently, their willingness to engage in and learn from the exercise. They really wanted to know what happened to him. The collaborative nature of the exercise (first working in pairs, then as a class) created a safe environment to interrogate primary sources. Beyond the session, the exercise gave the class a

"special" shared experience that helped them bond as a group, thus fostering better discussions in class sessions that followed.

Just as Ondaatje asserts his novel is "a mirror walking down a road," the class session signified a critical marker on the students' academic paths.[3] The exercise primed them to engage actively, rather than sit passively, in a broader scholarly conversation. We did not set out to teach them to do research or evaluate primary sources, rather we wanted them to understand the research process as the construction of narrative and that varying sources have very different effects on that "story." They emerged from the class with a new notion of how history is constructed as an *assemblage*, a clearer notion of how to frame research questions and how to interrogate their sources. Despite the cultural and temporal distance between the students and the documents, they could still personally relate to the story—at its base, it was the story of a Dartmouth student. That familiarity combined with the aura of the original (for most students, their first encounter with "real stuff") helped to transform their notions about research and its constitutive power. The students shed some of their jaded "just-look-it-up" mentality toward research and became actively engaged in a dialogue with the object of study. The exercise transformed them from consumers of known information to producers of new knowledge. It elided the distance between the student and the texts, and consequently, invited them into the scholarly conversation.

NOTES

1. Michael Ondaatje, *The English Patient* (New York: Knopf, 1992; Vintage Books, 1993): 20. Citations are to the Vintage edition.
2. Ibid. 5
3. Ibid. 91

EMORY UNIVERSITY

Teaching First-Year Writing with "All The Detritus, Debris And Ephemera" of Literary Manuscripts

Elizabeth A. Chase

In "Excavating the Imagination," Ronald Schuchard calls for "a revolution in special collections ... that says special collections libraries have a vital teaching mission in the university."[1] He encourages archives to reach out to both graduate and advanced undergraduate students, and many special collections have done so, extending their teaching programs and opening their reading rooms to student researchers. However, few programs focus explicitly on beginning students. First-year students comprise a significant potential user group for archival instruction programs; while these students require structured assignments that differ from those presented to advanced undergraduate majors, they stand to gain significant skills that will benefit them as advanced students. This chapter specifically explores the pedagogy of teaching first-year composition students at Emory University, using the literature collections housed in the Manuscript, Archives, and Rare Book Library (MARBL). By putting first-year composition students quite literally in touch with the materials of literary creation, instructors open new avenues for students to engage with and understand the writing process.

Based on my experience as a graduate student instructor in Emory University's Department of English, and as Coordinator for Research Services managing MARBL's instruction program, I designed the syllabus for a course fulfilling Emory's first-year writing requirement. The course description reads:

ENG181: Writing about Literature—Writers on Writing

What can we learn about writing from writers? How does our understanding of the relationship between reader and writer, reading and writing, or writer and writing change when we look at what authors themselves have to say about their craft? This class focuses on writing about literature by looking at writing as work: a process of thought, imagination, dead-ends, and fresh starts, even for the most gifted of poets or novelists. In order to see the work that goes into writing, we will focus on authors whose collections are found in Emory's Manuscripts, Archives, and Rare Books Library. A significant portion of our classes will take place in MARBL so that we can closely examine manuscripts of poems or short stories, as well as the essays, notes, letters, and other materials that provide insights into each author's relationship to his or her work. Throughout the course, we will also devote attention to students' own writing. In order to develop the ability to think analytically about literature and to construct persuasive and well-written arguments based on that analysis, we will develop a vocabulary of literary terms, and all students will be required to participate in a number of in-class writing workshops.

The syllabus I created is for a course based wholly in MARBL utilizing numerous collections, including the Flannery O'Connor-Betty Hester letters, Langston Hughes materials, the Seamus Heaney collection, the Alice Walker collection, and others. These collections were selected to highlight writers who talk about the writing process in their work, while also providing rich material for literary analysis. After selecting relevant collections, I created the assignments described below, using the guidelines suggested in "Utilizing [MARBL] for Class Assignments."[2] An instructor working with a smaller special collections repository could focus on a single author or modify the number of visits to the archive accordingly. It is the structure and sequence of assignments in a first-year archives-based course that is vital, while the subject area, number, or range of collections used could be easily varied.

SYLLABUS PLANNING

Prior to planning assignments, however, an important first step in designing any archives-based course is to meet with the archivist(s) who will assist your class. Ideally, the archivist should be a part of the syllabus and assignment planning process, as he or she will be familiar with those collections best-suited to undergraduate research. The archivist will also know when the reading room may be busiest and can suggest scheduling due dates for periods when Research Services staff will have more time to work with beginning researchers. Ultimately, taking the time to work with staff prior to finalizing your syllabus or assignments will help to ensure a productive experience for your students. Last but not least, be sure to keep the archivist informed of your students' research experience and their projected needs.

SHAPING STUDENTS' FIRST IMPRESSIONS

Prior to distributing any archival assignments, I advocate scheduling an introductory visit for your students; this allows them to enjoy the discovery of rare and significant materials and to experience the archive without the distraction of specific assignments or due dates. During the introductory visit, ask the archivist to show items related to the course topic as well as his or her favorite items and to highlight the archives' collecting strengths. Showing a mix of artifacts gives students a sense not only of the materials they will use during the semester, but also allows them to see the archivist's excitement about the collections and to understand the wide range of materials and topics represented in the archive. In these initial sessions, students are often excited, engaged, and in some cases, in awe of the materials presented. They gain a sense of the unique materials on offer in the archive and this prepares them, and hopefully instills them with excitement when they return for their first assignment.

In drafting my syllabus, I provided students with an opportunity to talk about what they saw and ask any questions they may have during the class meeting immediately following their first archives visit. For the same class, students read a handout on MARBL's policies and rules for researchers, as well as Lynee Lewis Gaillet's "Archival Survival: Navigating Historical Research"; class discussion centers on the unique challenges and opportunities of archival research and how it can shape our view of literary texts. Gaillet's is one of numerous articles published in recent years that can help to prepare students to undertake archival research. She provides researchers with a detailed list of eleven questions they should ask about archival data, including:

- "When approaching the archive, what do you think or hope you will find? Remember, you may have to refine, redefine, and sometimes abandon hypotheses ... depending on the content of the archive."

- "Ask yourself how best to corroborate your assumptions and claims."
- "Ascertain the motives inherent in the materials studied. What is their nature, and who commissioned their creation?"[3]

Her tips and methodological considerations assist the new researcher in better understanding the requirements, limitations, and possibilities of archival material. Used as a precursor to assignments that build students' research skills, her article enables students to understand the special challenges, considerations, and fun of working in the archives.

"SCAFFOLDING" ASSIGNMENTS

After reading about archival research, and then reading two short texts by authors whose collections they will use in their first assignment, students return to MARBL for the first in a series of progressively intensive research experiences. These assignments are based on the concept of scaffolded student learning. In "Fostering Historical Thinking with Digitized Primary Sources," Bill Tally and Lauren B. Goldenberg suggest that "when students have structured opportunities to construct meaning from primary materials, and critically examine those meanings, they feel more invested in the results."[4] The authors advocate breaking down students' approach to documents into steps that instructors can tie to specific critical thinking skills. This scaffolded approach urges teachers to view "historical thinking" as a six step process, including:

Observation: Scanning and parsing the document, observing details
Sourcing: Considering who made the document and what their motives are
Inferencing: Making inferences, speculating, guessing about meaning
Evidence: Citing evidence when making inferences or drawing conclusions
Question posing: Cultivating puzzlement, keeping track of one's questions

Corroboration: Comparing what is found to what one already knows, other documents, etc.[5]

Assignments, Tally and Goldenberg argue, should focus on progressively building students' skills through manageable tasks, to make primary document research approachable, interesting, and comprehensible. For my syllabus, I translated this approach into a series of five assignments, described below.

Assignment 1: MARBL Blog

After each visit to MARBL during the semester, students are required to write a blog post reflecting on what they've seen and observed. The first blog assignment is due in response to the general, introductory visit to the archive. Here, students are asked to write about what they saw, what surprised them, and what they hope to learn over the course of the semester. After reading Gaillet's article, the class then returns for a show-and-tell related to a specific author on the syllabus. Following this second visit, students are asked to more detailed observations about a few of the items on display. This second reflection asks students to begin the process of observation: thinking about both the intellectual and physical contents of archival documents. Over the course of the semester, students are asked to be increasingly detailed and critical in their observations as their research skills grow. The blog thus gives students a place to practice the skills used in their papers and final project in a less formal setting.

Assignment 2: MARBL Lab

After completing and receiving feedback on two blog posts, students return to MARBL for a lab day, building on the observations skills practiced in their posts through interaction with a specific document. This assignment requires research on the instructor's part to select specific documents to assign to each student in the course. While archivists can often provide instructors with a list of appropriate collections, instructors must be prepared to visit the archive and conduct item selection themselves. Documents selected should have:

- Legible handwriting
- Significant revisions or significant contextual information
- A direct relationship to a published item on the students' reading list
- Multiple points of entry for analysis
- A few points that clearly suggest to avenues for secondary research or leaves unanswered questions

These requirements are challenging, but documents that meet these criteria will be approachable while still preparing students for later, extended work with archival material.

For the lab itself, students are provided with a document analysis sheet that asks them to answer the following:

1. What type of document is it? (Diary, draft, letter, etc.)
2. Who created or wrote it?
3. When was it created?
4. Why was it created? Who is its intended audience?
5. What do you notice about its physical format and condition? Be as detailed as possible in documenting its appearance: note any tears, tape, crossed out lines, or other information that might be a clue as to the context under which it was created. For instance, if your item is a letter, is it on letter head that tells you where the person was when it was written?
6. What is its relationship to the other documents around it in the folder and/or box? In other words, is your item one of multiple drafts? Is it one of a number of letters to the same individual, and if so, what does this tell you about their relationship?
7. What can you learn from it that you wouldn't learn from a published text? If you are work-

ing with a draft, what differences do you see between the draft and the published work?
8. What questions does it raise for you? What *can't* you learn from this document, that you would need other sources to answer?

Through the lab, students learn the critical questions and observations to bring to each document they analyze. Directed questions focus their attention on learning observation, sourcing, and inferencing. I then suggest to students that they keep a notebook or file documenting each item they view while conducting research for use in their next assignment, a short paper.

Assignments 3 and 4: Short Paper and Presentation

A short, directed research paper and presentation form the next step in building students' archival research skills. This assignment is described in MARBL's guide to student instruction:

Paper assignment based on poem drafts (English)
For this assignment, students are asked to sign up for a particular poem by a poet being read as part of the course syllabus, and pre-selected materials are put on hold in MARBL under the instructor's name. Their paper is based in part on the discoveries made from their examination of the draft material. In the instruction session to prepare students for this assignment, MARBL staff will discuss what to look for in a draft and how seeing a poem-in-process changes how we view or understand the poet's finished work.[6]

The short paper focuses on developing evidence gathering, question posing, and corroboration skills. Students are asked to write 4-5 pages on a topic provided by the instructor. In addition, they present their findings to their classmates in a 10 minute oral presentation. Sharing their work with the class helps students to begin thinking about how best to convey conclusions to an audience, in preparation for their final project: a mock exhibit.

Assignment 5: Mock Exhibit

One advantage to a composition course is that writing takes many forms; depending upon your departmental guidelines, students may not have to write a traditional research paper as a final project. Emory's Department of English requires that an overall amount of writing be completed over the course of the semester. The form and type of that writing is at the discretion of the individual instructor. My final assignment, therefore, asks students to select items and create the text for a small exhibit. Depending on the space, staffing, and other parameters of a specific special collections, instructors may be able to have the students' exhibit placed on display for a period of time, giving students a real audience for whom to write.

Exhibits require multiple levels of argumentation: an overall narrative suitable to a brochure or introductory panel that gives viewers a broad overview of the content and thrust of the exhibit; panels that explain the focus of smaller subdivisions of items within an exhibit; and individual item captions that convey the significance of a specific artifact and its relationship to the exhibit's overarching theme. Asking students to create this text requires them to think about the language, documentation, and levels of evidence appropriate to each type of caption. Furthermore, it requires that students think explicitly about audience and consider the difference between the depth of an argument laid out on paper and that made in the span of an item caption or brochure.

For instructors who choose to have students complete a mock or actual exhibit, Jennifer Brannock's article, "Creating an Exhibit in Special Collections and Using it to Promote Collections and Educate Users" provides a thorough introduction to the steps involved in exhibit design. Brannock walks readers through: determining a topic, researching the topic, selecting materials, arranging the items, and writing labels and explanatory text, discussing each step briefly.[7] Thus, this reading is included in the English 181 syllabus as an introduction to students' final assignment.

In addition, as they begin working on their exhibits, students are assigned to read Linda Bergmann's "The Guilty Pleasure of Working with Archives." In her article, Bergmann notes that "the potential to identify closely and uncritically with selves represented in an archive can be greater than the temptation to identify with authors of published sources."[8] She discusses her own emotional response to collection, and reminds readers that archives often contain items never intended for a public audience. Thus, her article asks students to think about the critical and ethical implications of their research. By placing this reading at the start of the final project, students are asked to consider their own critical stance regarding the materials with which they are working. For instance, how does that stance affect the way he or she has chosen to present materials in an exhibit? How might someone else approach the same documents from a different perspective? Are there questions he or she has not asked about a document, because he or she accepted the author's own perspective? Once student have learned how to make critical observations about a document and support those observations with secondary research, then we can begin asking them to interrogate their own assumptions and those of the authors with whose papers they work. Thus, this final project asks students to bring together the six "habits of mind" described by Tally and Goldenberg, in order to present a coherent argument about their chosen documents.

CONCLUSION

Ultimately, a student should leave this course—or a similar course—with a specific set of research skills they have built incrementally over the semester.

But in addition, the class strives to teach students to inhabit the role of critical thinker and observer, skills that translate beyond archival research. While my goals for a MARBL-centered, archives-driven course are ambitious, using the rich literary materials available in archival collections enables students to expand their understanding of argumentation and composition. Archives provide students with a rich opportunity to learn fully what it means to be a researcher: one who is skilled at both searching for information, bringing his or her critical thinking skills to bear on that information, and synthesizing the results into a coherent argument. However, perhaps what is most important is the excitement and energy such hands-on work can bring to the composition classroom and its students and instructors.

BIBLIOGRAPHY

Bergmann, Linda. "The Guilty Pleasures of Working with Archives." In *Working in the Archives: Practical research methods for rhetoric and composition*, edited by Alexis Ramsey et. al, 220-231. Carbondale, IL: Southern Illinois University Press, 2010.

Brannock, Jennifer. "Creating an Exhibit in Special Collections and Using It to Promote Collections and Educate Users." *Mississippi Libraries* 73.2 (2009): 32-34.

Gaillet, Lynee Lewis. "Archival Survival: Navigating Historical Research." In *Working in the Archives: Practical research methods for rhetoric and composition*, edited by Alexis Ramsey et. al, 28-39. Carbondale, IL: Southern Illinois University Press, 2010.

Manuscript, Archives, and Rare Book Library, 2009. "Utilizing the Manuscript, Archives, and Rare Book Library for Class Assignments." Accessed August 31, 2010. http://marbl.library.emory.edu/sites/marbl.library.emory.edu/files/2009_Guide_to_Class_Instruction.pdf

Schuchard, Ronald. "Excavating the Imagination: Archival Research and the Digital Revolution." *Libraries and the Cultural Record* 31.1 (2002): 57-63. Accessed August 31, 2010, doi: 10.1353/lac.2002.0014.

Tally, Bill, and Lauren B. Goldenberg. "Fostering Historical Thinking With Digitized Primary Sources." *Journal of Research on Technology in Education* 38.1 (2005): 1-21.

NOTES

1. Ronald Schuchard, "Excavating the Imagination: Archival Research and the Digital Revolution," *Libraries and the Cultural Record* 37.1 (2002): 60, accessed August 31, 2010, doi: 10.1353/lac.2002.0014.

2. MARBL. 2009. Utilizing the Manuscript, Archives, and Rare Books Library for Class Assignments. http://marbl.library.emory.edu/sites/marbl.library.emory.edu/files/2009_Guide_to_Class_Instruction.pdf (Accessed August 31, 2010).

3. Lynee Lewis Gaillet, "Archival Survival: Navigating Historical Research," in *Working in the Archives: Practical research methods for rhetoric and composition*, ed. Alexis Ramsay et al. (Carbondale, IL: Southern Illinois University Press, 2010), 35.

4. Bill Tally and Lauren B. Goldenberg, "Fostering Historical Thinking With Digitized Primary Sources," *Journal of Research on Technology in Education* 38.1 (2005): 11.

5. Stearn et al., cited in Tally and Goldenberg, "Fostering Historical Thinking," 6.

6. MARBL, "Utilizing," 2.

7. Jennifer Brannock, "Creating an Exhibit in Special Collections and Using It to Promote Collections and Educate Users," *Mississippi Libraries* 73.2 (2009): 32-34.

8. Linda Bergmann, "The Guilty Pleasure of Working with Archives," in *Working in the Archives: Practical research methods for rhetoric and composition*, ed. Alexis Ramsey et al. (Carbondale, IL: Southern Illinois University Press, 2010): 230.

Common Ground: A Collaboration between the Harvard University Archives and the Harvard Yard Archaeology Project

Barbara S. Meloni

"No smoking, drinking, or glass-breaking—what?" This reference to 17th-century Harvard College laws leads the catalog description for *Archaeology of Harvard Yard (Anthro 1130/31)*, a course that makes extensive use of the Harvard University Archives services and collections as students literally uncover Harvard history. The course is offered by the Department of Anthropology and taught by faculty who are strong advocates for the value of merging archaeological research with archival research. It is the central component of the Harvard Yard Archaeology Project (HYAP), an ongoing, multi-faceted research program run collaboratively by the Department of Anthropology, the Peabody Museum of Archaeology and Ethnology, and the Harvard University Native American Program, which examines "Harvard as a changing multicultural space, the relationship between archaeology and the historical record, and the nature of public archaeology."[1]

Offered every other year since 2005, *Archaeology of Harvard Yard* is a year-long course that typically enrolls about 25 students. The fall semester is devoted to a full-scale archaeological excavation in Harvard Yard on the site of the earliest College buildings. The spring semester focuses on artifact analysis and public presentation of fall discoveries. While each year's dig has turned up an array of items representing four centuries of Harvard and New England history, a goal of the archaeological work has been to locate physical evidence of the Indian College, which was built in 1655 to house Native

American students at Harvard. The Indian College also served as the location of the College printing press, on which was produced the first Bible printed in North America, an Algonquian translation by John Eliot. The most recent (2009) excavation team was elated to discover a building trench filled with bricks and other construction material likely connected to the Indian College, along with pieces of 17th century metal printing type.

The Harvard University Archives collections and staff have served as an integral course resource from the start. The Archives involvement is twofold: we offer instruction and ongoing support for archival research and we provide an Archives presence beyond the reading room at course-related events. The course has had an impact on our archival methods as well, prompting us to change our collection description practices to enhance the discovery of historical content relating to 17th and 18th century Harvard/Cambridge/New England history and material culture.

RESEARCH SUPPORT

Archaeology of Harvard Yard students are primarily interested in our 17th and 18th century collections, including University administrative and financial records (especially records documenting foodways and building construction), maps, plans, rules and regulations, personal papers of presidents and faculty, student diaries, expense books, and other accounts of daily campus life. Students use these resources to develop strategies for the excavation, identify and analyze discoveries, and fulfill course assignments. The direct connection between the artifacts that students uncover and the research they conduct to provide an historical context for those artifacts makes for a dynamic archival experience. The discovery of pipe stems leads to a look at College laws, disciplinary records, and personal expense accounts; the discovery of part of a name etched on a glass shard leads to lists of dormitory residents, class records, and biographical accounts. Students in the course experience the complementary nature of archaeological and archival research—they use archives as an archaeological tool, and incorporate their archeological results into the historical narrative.

Our initial meeting with the class is a one-hour orientation session in the Archives that includes a brief introduction to archival research methodology and the logistics of using the reading room, as well as a demonstration of the care and handling of material. (With students often arriving in the reading room directly from the dig, "wash your hands" is our mantra.) This is the first visit to an archives for many of the students, and it's obvious that they are both overwhelmed and excited by the resources available to them.

The introduction is followed by a "show, tell, and touch" display of items from our collections, selected with input from course instructors both for the "wow" factor (old and/or related to the Indian College) and to demonstrate archival research methods. The nature of the course allows us to use a "digging through layers" metaphor as we introduce the students to a variety of records and provide examples of how to connect an archaeological discovery to an historical document. The hands-on opportunity helps to demystify the archival experience by promoting the document as another artifact to investigate. For example, students are encouraged to turn the pages of 18th century president Benjamin Wadsworth's original diary to read entries describing the construction of a building in Harvard Yard,

evidence of which they may encounter in their fieldwork. Although the published transcription is more legible and a digital facsimile of the diary is available online, the original has the immediacy of President Wadsworth's touch. We use items on display to demonstrate how to build accounts of 17th and 18th century daily life from a variety of sources—College laws, lists of kitchen utensils, or even a plot plan that delineates a privy trench. One of the most significant display items is Harvard's Charter of 1650, under which the University is still governed. The Charter, which includes acknowledgement of the donations of "many devoted persons" to support the "education of the English and Indian youth of this country, in knowledge and godliness," has been espoused by the Harvard Yard Archaeology Project as Harvard's early commitment to Native American education. The words of the Charter paired with the archeological traces of the Indian College form a striking example of the complementary roles of artifacts and documents as historical evidence.

The perspective of course participants has led us to new insights about our collections as well. We typically display College Book I, the earliest volume of University records, at many Archives events because it contains the first (1642) drawing of Harvard's *Veritas* seal. *Archaeology of Harvard Yard* instructors and students, on the other hand, were amazed when they browsed a few pages further to discover that the volume also contains a list of early graduates that includes the name of Caleb Cheeshahteaumuck, an Indian College student.

While this introductory session is certainly not long enough for students to learn all they need to know about archival research, our goal is to familiarize the students with our resources and our reading room and to fervently emphasize "ask for help and don't procrastinate." Students are provided with a checklist of items on display, along with subject and methodology guides produced by Archives staff. These include an extensive online research guide to early Native American resources at Harvard.[2]

At the orientation session we begin to address student expectations about the amount of time needed for archival research, the scarcity of online resources, and the creativity needed to find material. Follow-up one-on-one reference meetings with students centered on their specific interests are time-consuming for public services staff, but are more productive in guiding research, especially for course assignments. Students have commented that the breadth of resources is sometimes too much of a good thing—and that they welcome help in narrowing topics and identifying relevant sources. In order for students to fully utilize archival resources without getting "lost" in the Archives, research paper assignments have evolved since the course was first offered. Students were originally asked to construct research protocols and develop exhibit themes with open-ended topic choices, such as dress, economics, education, environment, ethnicity, foodways, gender, government, landscape/geography, or trades/industry. In contrast, recent assignments emphasize student biography and daily life. For example, the mid-term assignment asks students to interpret the archaeology of the Yard in a new way, from the perspective of a student of the time:

> Research the life of a Harvard student who lived during the 17th or 18th century. Conduct primary and secondary document research and write a description or creative narrative in the form of a letter, diary entry, or whatever else communicates your student's experiences effectively. Write a detailed description of the material life of this student based on excavations, readings, and your knowledge of material culture. "Outfit" this student's life with appropriate objects (at least three of which would be something we might excavate in the Yard) and include reasoning as to how/why these objects would be owned and/or used by the student during his life at Harvard.

It was clear that students made better use of available sources, and seemed more comfortable following trails to related sources, with this assignment. As one student remarked: "I loved looking through the Faculty Records and tracing my student as he was made a 'waiter to the lower table' or as he was cited for staying out at night and 'drinking prohibited liquor'. These brief notes helped me to imagine, however incompletely, who he was and how my experience at Harvard would compare to his."[3]

BEYOND THE READING ROOM

While the most substantive part of the Archives collaboration with *Archaeology of Harvard Yard* is assisting students with research, Archives staff members also travel outside the reading room to attend course-related events. These include the opening and closing ceremonies that bracket each excavation, and "results days" when students present their findings to an enthralled public at the dig site.

We also participate in a seminar during the spring semester for Harvard Yard Archaeology Project partners, including Harvard faculty, students, program directors, and representatives from Native American tribes and state and local historical organizations. During the half-day seminar, *Archaeology of Harvard Yard* students engage participants in lively discussion about the context and public presentation of their fall discoveries. The 2007/08 seminar provided guidance for a student-curated exhibition documenting the technical and historical aspects of the students' work. *Digging Veritas: the Archaeology and History of the Indian College and Student Life at Colonial Harvard* was installed at the Peabody Museum and is available as an online exhibition.[4] The 2009/10 seminar focused on opportunities for long-term public commemoration of the Indian College.

Interacting with students at the excavation site and in the seminar room is a definite advantage when it comes to working with them in the Archives reading room. Students (and faculty) recognize Archives staff as genuinely interested partners and we're better prepared to guide the archival research based on our first-hand look (and on-site conversations) about their work.

ENHANCED DESCRIPTION AND DISCOVERY

The Archives holdings are a great match for the course, but until recently, the brevity or lack of bibliographic records for many of the early collections hindered the discovery of useful documents. The effort to identify historical documentation to satisfy new research interests relating to the material culture of New England, like the topics of this course, has changed the Archives descriptive practices to accommodate a broader perspective, bringing previously hidden content to light through careful examination and ensuing enhanced description of 17th and 18th century material.

Where a perceptive researcher previously *may* have noticed an entry in the Archives print shelflist that read simply "Journal of Eliphalet Pearson," there is now a description in Harvard's online library catalog that reveals a wealth of discoverable information for *Archeology of Harvard Yard* students relying on keyword searches: "Daily entries [in Pearson's journal] describe a wide range of students' rebellious conduct, which included … breaking windows, intoxication, moving and breaking furniture, stealing firewood, firing pistols, building bonfires… filling door locks with stones, drawing on lecture room walls with gravel, and silencing the morning chapel bell by filling it with molten pewter plates stolen from the kitchen."

GOING FORWARD/CONCLUSION

Future plans for the ongoing collaboration between the Harvard University Archives and *Archaeology of Harvard Yard* include making more resources available online, continuing to refine research guides and course assignments, and investigating the use of mobile devices to "ask an archivist" or access Archives resources from the field. The Archives staff greatly appreciates the in-depth opportunity afforded by this partnership to engage with students and the curriculum and to re-evaluate our approaches to access and discovery of our collections. We always look forward to the next excavation and to return visits from students inspired to continue their archival experience.

NOTES

1. For more information on HYAP, see John D. Stubbs, Patricia Capone, Christina J. Hodge, and Diana D. Loren, "Campus Archaeology/Public Archaeology at Harvard University, Cambridge, Massachusetts," in *Beneath the Ivory Tower: The Archaeology of Academia*, ed. Russell K. Skowronek and Kenneth E. Lewis (Gainesville, Florida: University Press of Florida, 2010), 99-120, and *The Harvard Yard Archaeology Project* at http://www.peabody.harvard.edu/harvard_yard.

2. *Harvard University Research Guide to Native American Resources at Harvard*, http://isites.harvard.edu/icb/icb.do?keyword=k18801

3. Rachel Bennett, e-mail message to author, August 20, 2010.

4. *Digging Veritas: the Archaeology and History of the Indian College and Student Life at Colonial Harvard*, http://www.peabody.harvard.edu/DV-online/

Engaging the Text

Carla Mary Rineer and Marilyn McKinley Parrish

Over the past seven years, we have developed an interdisciplinary teaching pedagogy that engages students with primary source texts. We began this collaboration hoping to open the doors of the Archives and to foster creativity and critical thinking in students taking English and Women's Studies classes. We have been rewarded by the imagination our students employ and the interest expressed by other faculty members about our philosophy and practices. We share a philosophical framework that is informed by feminist and critical theory and rooted in constructivist pedagogical practice.

Carla Mary Rineer: Truth is very important to me, and in quest of it, I challenge students to upend the common practice of formulating a thesis statement and then finding evidence to support it. Too often, the familiar process resembles Cinderella's stepsisters' attempting to wear her shoes. Like the sisters in the Grimm version of the tale, force fitting information to prove an assumption requires amputation of toes, the facts that just don't fit the narrow confines of a glass slipper. Instead, why not engage with a primary source, ask a question, read some secondary material, and construct a thesis that more accurately reflects the facts?

Marilyn McKinley Parrish: One of the great strengths of Archives & Special Collections at Millersville University is that the area serves as an excellent teaching archive. Engaging students from across the university with primary source materials creates an opportunity to depict the archives as a laboratory for learning. It is very important to me to create a welcoming environment where students interact with potentially disruptive perspectives from other times and in which they are encouraged to reflect on their own assumptions of what "normal" daily life can be. This case study explores the process of teaching students in English 110 (Composition) to develop creative nonfiction essays based on primary sources.

THE PROBLEM

We were confronted by two perplexing problems born of our fondest professional hopes. Parrish, Special Collections Librarian & University Archivist at Millersville University, had a deep desire to open archival materials to all undergraduate and graduate students. Rineer, long time adjunct, now tenure track, in the English department, a.k.a. inveterate teacher of English Composition, had an equally intense desire to create a plagiarism-proof research paper assignment that would teach students the conventions of MLA citations and yet not bore them, or her, to death. They hoped for an answer that would meld together Parrish's extensive and growing collection, Rineer's long-standing passion for archival research, their shared philosophy of teaching and learning, and the students' perennial longing to write "creatively." Of course, the solution had to, at the same time, be pedagogically sound.

Like all new approaches, the assignment required a hard look at reality. We brainstormed a fresh assessment of who our students are—often first generation college students with varying degrees of preparation and narrow conceptions about how to write that invariably led them to exclude the "self" from the writing process. We embarked on extensive pedagogical soul-searching about how students *really* learn to write research papers. We wondered if working with primary sources could meet the most profound aspects of substantive learning: to develop critical thinking skills and to foster creative expression. Our shared philosophical aims to expose students to uncommon narratives, leading students to challenge assumptions about the past and the present had to be part of the mix.

For her part, Rineer came up with an assignment that summoned students to "chase rabbits," that is to read a primary document and ferret out the ideas mentioned within and to research them. The assignment's major premise was to create a space in which to wonder, to encourage deep reading and thinking, and to base research on each student's own notion of what is interesting. Preparation for the class visit to the archives is minimal so as not to limit each student's approach to primary sources to "what the professor 'wants.'"

LEARNING IN ARCHIVES & SPECIAL COLLECTIONS (MMP)

To envision the scene English 110 students encounter as they enter the Archives & Special Collections reading room at Millersville University, consider that the area is located on the 4th floor of an ugly 1960s brick building currently preparing for a much needed and extensive renovation. This location houses the university archives, as well as rare books, manuscripts, and other primary source materials. Students enter the reading room, pick places to sit and chat with each other. Some examine texts set before them. Sources are distributed on tables by topics and include early Millersville photographs, catalogs, yearbooks, issues of the student newspaper; trial and confession documents recounting local murder trials; home health guides from the late 19th and early 20th centuries; civil war letters and diaries; pro and anti suffrage tracts;

Figure 6.1. Photo of Millersville students engaging with primary sources

19th century text books in history, math, English; and examples of early American children's literature.

When the class begins, Dr. Rineer provides an overview of the primary source assignment. I welcome the students and offer a brief introduction to Archives & Special Collections. We then begin a discussion of primary and secondary sources, the types of resources students can find in our area and online, as well as the care and handling of rare materials, and other information that will make their return research trips more effective.

In our discussion of primary source materials, I ask the students to imagine that it is 30 years in the future and they are asked to write a comprehensive account of Hurricane Katrina or the BP Oil spill. What types of sources, created at the time, are available for them to use for this study? Students generally mention newspaper accounts, diaries, and letters (sometimes they start out thinking traditionally). Yet when I ask who writes letters home on a regular basis, few students raise their hands. Eventually students say they would use local and national TV coverage, interviews with people affected by the disaster (at the time or later through oral histories), websites or blogs. A student suggests that 911 recordings could be a good source of information about the event as it is happening. We talk about the wide variety of sources available and the important, though partial, perspective that each brings. We discuss the differences between memoirs or oral histories in which participants reflect back on events in their lives, and archival documents that are created for a very different purpose, right at the time (such as 911 recordings).

As a way to begin the experience of interacting with texts, I hand out a photocopy of a primary source, along with a list of questions to consider. On this day, students are examining a handwritten letter from the 1860s. Working in groups, they decipher the handwriting while noticing unique features of the letter. They jot down notes relating to date/time period, author, location, and content.

They consider gender, class, and race issues related to the source. They also note what doesn't make sense to them, the issues that they wonder about. A class discussion follows. We begin by discussing basic descriptive elements of the source. Where was the letter written? When? What can we tell about the author of the letter? Was the person well or poorly educated? How do we know? What can we tell about the gender, race, or class of the letter writer? One student insists that the letter was penned by a woman because it was so poorly written, based on her assumption that women were less well educated than men. Does everyone think so?

Some students disagree, noting the remarks within the letter and the date, which indicate that a Civil War soldier wrote this text. Most students conclude that the letter was written by a Confederate soldier, based on remarks about "Old Abe" and "Jeff Davis." In fact, it was written by Joseph Mathews, a Union soldier from Brickerville, Pennsylvania, about 20 miles north of Millersville, in Lancaster County. The facts open up a discussion about the assumptions we can make about texts from other times. Why might Joseph be frustrated with Old Abe? Why does he propose lobbing cannon balls over to the White House, which he can see from his camp, if Old Abe refuses to make "piece" with Jeff Davis? What do his words say about the daily morale and desires of soldiers?

After we discuss the letter, students select one of the sources on their tables to examine in more detail, considering similar questions about context and content. Later students report back to the class, particularly highlighting sections of sources that surprised them. This process provides a template for students to use to examine their own document following the class session and their wonder and surprise becomes the basis for their creative nonfiction essays. The more comfortable students feel, the more they speculate, wonder aloud, and understand perspectives that seem foreign to contemporary sensibilities. Home health guides that describe the importance of sleeping with the head of a bed outside a window (sheltered by an umbrella!), or the value of a dry "friction" bath, or descriptions of typical daily activities for mothers or servants in 19th or early 20th century households disrupt what students consider "normal." Yearbook photographs or listings of student height, weight, and matrimonial prospects from 1915 cause students to laugh out loud and ask questions why this information would be included. Conversely, students are stunned by oral history transcripts of interviews with African American alumni who attended Millersville in the late 1950s and early 1960s which describe professors openly declaring that they will never to give anything above a C to African American English majors or wondering why these students don't go to school with their own kind. Such accounts help students to ask questions about the prevalence and impact of cultural and institutional racism—exactly what we hope they will do.

SELECTING THE SOURCE AND FRAMING THE QUESTION (CMR)

At the end of our day in Archives and Special Collections, I invite students to think of something that interests them, something *they* would like to know more about. I tell them that anything can be investigated in a scholarly way and urge them to brainstorm about possible areas to investigate. Often, students have great interest in war. If the American Civil War tantalizes them, Parrish may suggest diaries from Andersonville prison or the wartime correspondence among the

Figure 6.2. MS. Letter from Joseph Mathews to brother John, date. Courtesy of Millersville University Archives & Special Collections.

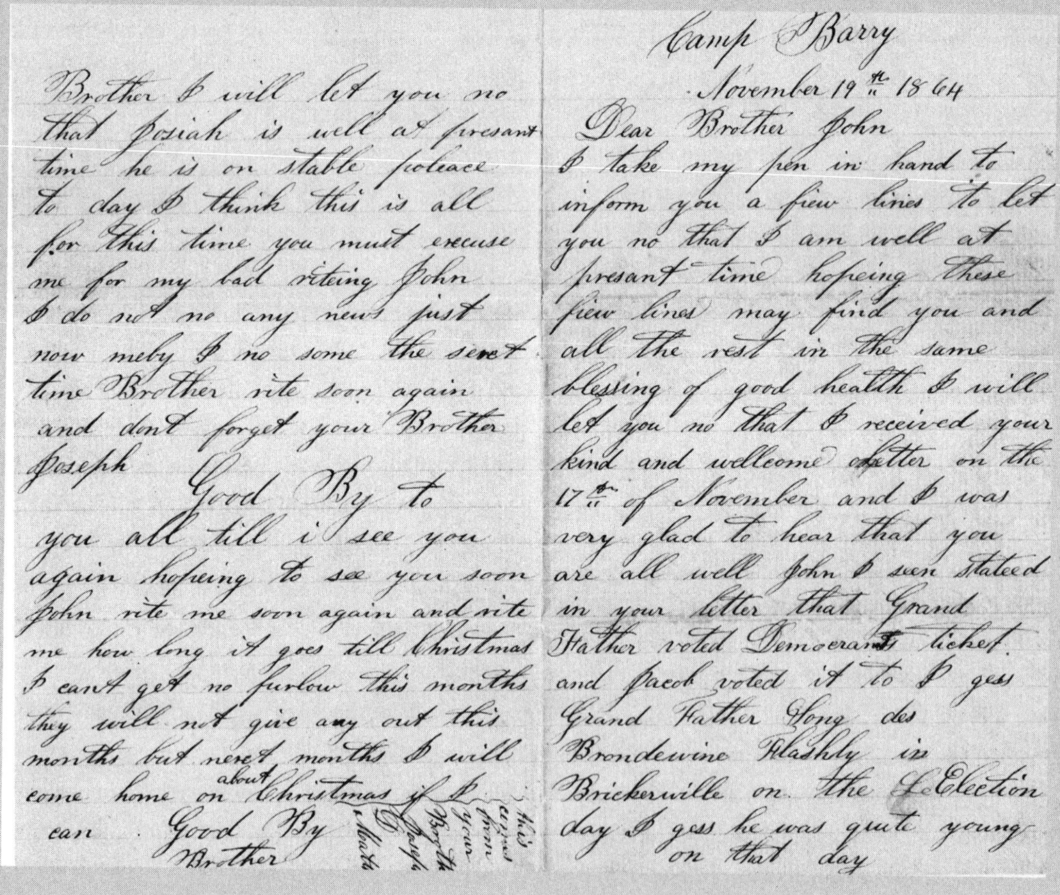

Brother I will let you no
that Josiah is well at presant
time he is on stable police
to day I think this is all
for this time you must excuse
me for my bad riteing John
I do not no any news just
now meby I no some the next
time Brother rite soon again
and dont forget your Brother
Joseph
Good By to
you all till i see you
again hopeing to see you soon
John rite me soon again and rite
me how long it goes till Christmas
I cant get no furlow this months
they will not give any out this
months but next months I will
come home about on Christmas if I
can Good By
Brother

this comes from your Brother Joseph Matths

Camp Barry
November 19th 1864
Dear Brother John
I take my pen in hand to
inform you a few lines to let
you no that I am well at
presant time hopeing these
few lines may find you and
all the rest in the same
blessing of good health I will
let you no that I received your
kind and wellcome letter on the
17th of November and I was
very glad to hear that you
are all well John I seen Stateed
in your letter that Grand
Father voted Democrats ticket
and Jacob voted it to I gess
Grand Father Long des
Brondewine Flashly in
Brickerville on the Election
day I gess he was quite young
on that day

Mathews family. Or students may make use of family correspondence. For example, one student used letters that passed between his grandparents when an ocean separated them during World War II.

Once the source is chosen, students develop their own research questions, which is the most important and daunting step in the process. Framing questions is largely a matter of concretizing the flutter of internal thought into the stability of language. To assist students to focus and express thought, I conference with them individually, asking a series of questions to discover precisely what they find fascinating. The final question may be based on the content of the primary source—How did the North and the South treat POW's, the same or differently? Or, on something tangential to it—since the spelling and syntax in the Mathews letters is often incorrect by our standards, when, how, and by whom were the rules of American grammar codified? Or, what was the general education level in Pennsylvania just before the Civil War? In every case, students frame a question—*not a thesis*—based on their own curiosity and proceed to find an answer using additional primary sources and/or appropriate secondary ones.

INCORPORATING SECONDARY SOURCES (MMP)

Secondary sources provide the essential context to allow students to write creatively about their research questions. If they are wondering about the authors of anti-suffrage publications from the early 20th century, secondary works by scholars in the field can assist their explorations. If they are concerned with issues of creating a healthy home in the late 19th century, journal articles or books that address health and class within North American society can provide valuable clues.

In our second session together, I introduce students to appropriate secondary sources that can help provide background information for their project (math pedagogy in the 1880s, a mob hit as reported in the New York Times during the 1930s,

higher education for women in the mid 19th century, etc.). We discuss the process of finding reliable and authoritative secondary works and students spend the remainder of the class session doing their own searching of the literature, with assistance from both of us.

CREATIVE NONFICTION ESSAYS (CMR)

After reading, absorbing, and doing profound thinking about their sources and their research questions, students formulate a response. Rather than using the standard research paper format, I encourage students to engage in writing creative non-fiction in an inventive format. To whet their imaginations, students read a variety of creative non-fiction essays in periodicals and in textbooks like *The Fourth Genre* (Root & Steinberg, 2006). To draw them out of their stagnant comfort zone and to free them from grade anxiety, I promise to reward risk taking. The results are generally astounding, especially for students who have not excelled in writing the traditional research paper.

In our experience, student responses take many forms. One student chose to write about how math was taught in the nineteenth-century within a dream framework. This soon-to-be secondary math teacher wrote a narrative about falling asleep in an MU math class and dreaming of being a student in a nineteenth-century classroom. Using old math texts from our special collections, she discovered that learning before calculators and "math manipulatives" called for practice, practice, practice, and rote memorization. Another first year student used the letters nineteenth-century MU student Sally Bolton wrote home to construct her own epistolary history of learning across the centuries at our institution.

REFLECTIONS

Ultimately, our work together satisfies both our professional and private consciences: we believe we have constructed a sound pedagogical process that addresses our own, personal philosophy of education: that learning is personal; that choice and creativity are essential; that primary sources provide connections to real people, helping students to honor the times, life situations, and everyday concerns of others; that examining narratives helps students look more deeply to explore the story behind "the story."

We believe that a particular strength of our collaboration is that learners drive the process. Because students are more accustomed to faculty-driven assignments, our approach can at first be frustrating, but as they become comfortable with the role of "makers of meaning," they generally delight in being part of the scholarly conversation. As our collaboration has unfolded, we find that social constructivist perspectives of teaching and learning (Elmborg 2006, Vygotsky, 1962) resonate with and continue to inform our approach.

Each Special Collections area or Archives has fascinating and unique local content that can be made available to first year undergraduate students for their research. What photographs, texts, or objects are unique to your institution? How can you supplement available online primary sources with archival documents specific to your area and institution? What faculty members on your campus might be open to collaboration in the development of creative assignments using primary sources? The collaborations you begin will shape the lives of your students, your colleagues, your collections, and to a great extent your own philosophy and practice.

BIBLIOGRAPHY

Elmborg, J. Libraries in the Contact Zone: On the Creation of Educational Space. *Reference and User Services Quarterly*, 2006, 46 (1) 56-64.

Vygotsky, L. S. *Thought and Language*. Cambridge, Mass: M. I. T. Press, 1962.

Root, R. L., & Steinberg, M. *The Fourth Genre: Contemporary Writers of/on Creative Nonfiction*. White Plains, New York: Longman, 2006.

NEW YORK UNIVERSITY

Computing in the Humanities @ NYU Libraries

Janet Bunde, Deena Engel, and Paula Feid

INTRODUCTION

New York University Libraries hosts a welcome reception each September for freshman Presidential Scholars. The Dean of NYU's College of Arts & Sciences [CAS] and the Dean of Libraries make short presentations at these receptions, each relating their own library experiences as undergraduates and their belief in the primacy of the library as key to academic success. We highlight NYU Libraries' special collections as containing rich and unique raw materials for original research and encourage students to consider them as a resource for their senior theses.

As follow up to this event, each section of scholars (7 sections total) comes to the library with a faculty preceptor for a hands-on introduction to the Libraries' resources and services. The undergraduate librarian tailors each session to the section's specific needs and offers to facilitate connections with any library service. One of the faculty preceptors recognized the opportunity this presented for a humanities computing class she was teaching and contacted the undergraduate librarian to explore ways to integrate the Libraries' special collections into her curriculum.

CLASS DESCRIPTION

Students enrolled in *Computing in the Humanities* have taken at least one semester of web design and implementation as well as at least one semester of computer programming in a high level language. The course is open to students majoring or minoring in Computer Science.

PROJECT REQUIREMENTS

The final project in this course requires students to build a digital archive that centers on a collection of artifacts, documents, pictures and/or other primary source materials. Each student designs his/her site to be accessible both to scholars who are researching source materials and to the general public; in other words, the sites contain both a digital collection (a "catalogue") and an electronic exhibit (a "narrative").

The project is broken down into six assignments. This strategy is designed to meet two pedagogical goals. First, for undergraduate students, breaking down a large project into smaller, more manageable tasks models the process of project management so that students learn to appropriately group, prioritize, and integrate the computing and research tasks. Second, this breakdown follows the steps of a typical software application project in this field. Following are the six assignments:

1. Design Phase: In the first assignment, students prepare project proposals and post them to their websites. The proposals include the subject of the sites along with brief descriptions of the primary source materials; some sources for secondary research on these materials such as books, scholarly journals and other sources; the goals for the sites; and the scholarly criteria they will use for evaluating the sites.

2. Defining and Working with Primary and Secondary Source Materials: Students identify samples of their selected primary and

secondary source materials. They scan, transcribe (where appropriate) and post to their sites at least three examples of the primary source materials. They also create web pages with at least two correctly cited secondary materials. The goals of this assignment are for students to experience working with their source materials before building the sites so they can anticipate and resolve any hardware and/or software problems ahead of time and to identify secondary sources which can be used while they work on the projects.

3. Online Digital Catalogue: Students complete the scanning and photographing of their primary source materials and use XML, XSLT and related technologies to build the catalogues. Students design their own standardized structures for capturing the data on the items in the collections. Both thumbnails and large versions of all images are made available to users, and scans of text documents include links to transcriptions where appropriate. Students meet with the instructor or the Teaching Assistant during this phase in order to assess their progress.

4. Podcast: With the digital catalogue complete, students are ready to create and/or prepare appropriate multi-media objects for their online archives. For example, all students are required to prepare podcasts. Other multi-media objects (e.g. sound files) are optional, depending on the subjects of the projects.

5. Narrative: Students write and post narratives to contextualize their catalogues. They also finish implementing the navigation and other aspects of the websites using xHTML, CSS, PHP and JavaScript. This assignment is the draft of their complete websites, and it is this version that students present to the class.

Figure 7.1. Sample digital archive project

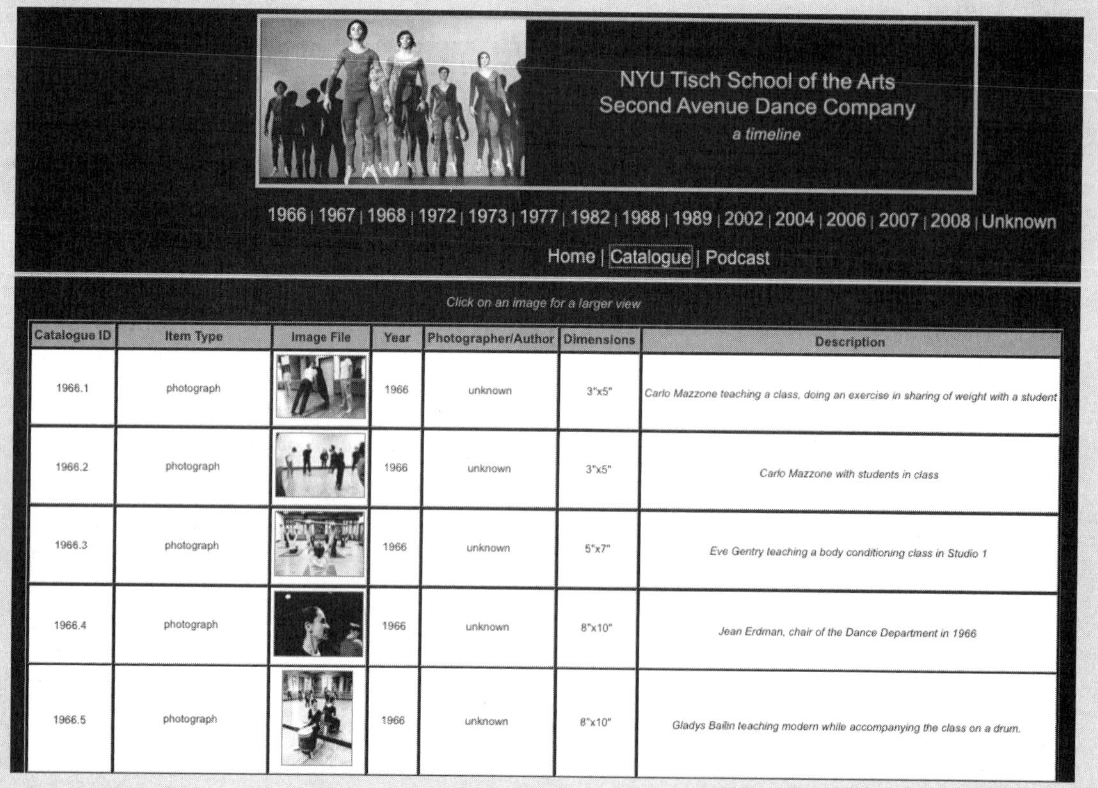

6. Final Project: The final project is due at the end of the semester in lieu of a final exam.

SPECIAL COLLECTIONS INTEGRATION

The assistant University archivist, undergraduate librarian, and instructor met prior to the beginning of the semester to discuss how to integrate archival and research instruction into the course. The librarian and archivist agreed to co-lecture to the students for one class session, explaining how to find and read archival finding aids, how the University Archives encodes finding aids, and how to locate relevant secondary sources for their projects.

FACTORS FOR SUCCESS

We believe several operational factors contributed to the course's success. First, the archivist oriented Archives staff and maintained thorough records for each student, so that staff serving rotating shifts on the front desk were aware of the students' projects. Second, students scheduled meetings with the archivist and the professor to ensure the feasibility of students' projects. Third, it was important to have a librarian who was familiar with the project goals and requirements available to field students' contextual questions, provide assistance with secondary sources, and make referrals to subject librarians.

There were also two significant contextual factors that facilitated and strengthened this collaboration: the Libraries' sustained outreach effort with faculty in the scholars programs; and the close alignment between the instructor's course objectives and ACRL's Information Literacy Competency Standards.[1]

NYU librarians promote their instructional services to teaching faculty in a variety of campus venues, emphasizing their keen interest in collaborations that move beyond the "one-shot" library instruction session. The personal connections that strengthened this project developed as a result of conversations following a library workshop and at a reception attended by faculty and librarians.

Librarians at NYU not only participate in interdisciplinary and inter-institution projects but also discuss their roles in these projects in classroom settings. The instructor invited the classics librarian to talk about NYU Libraries' participation in the Advanced Papyrological Information System (APIS), a virtual library of ancient papyri begun in 1996. Other guest speakers included a professor who serves as the director and editor of the Margaret Sanger Papers Project (http://www.nyu.edu/projects/sanger/) and the digital conversion specialist who is responsible for the Afghanistan Digital Library (http://afghanistandl.nyu.edu/). These and other presentations served as real-world examples of solutions to the challenges of managing information on a large scale, introduced the broader context of current ongoing humanities computing initiatives, and demonstrated the roles played by academic librarians and related professionals.

This project required students to demonstrate more than a dozen outcomes prescribed by the Association of College and Research Libraries' Information Literacy Competency Standards.[2] Most of the performance indicators and outcomes for Standard One, "[T]he information literate student determines the nature and extent of the information needed," were demonstrated in the design phase when students described their primary source materials and identified secondary sources.[3] They worked closely with the instructor and "modifie(d) the information need to achieve a manageable focus," and in asking their own research questions, they arrived at the recognition that "existing information can be combined with original thought, experimentation, and/or analysis to produce new information."[4] Via presentations by librarians and digital publishers, they became familiar with "how information is formally and informally produced, organized and disseminated," "identifie[d] the value and differences of potential resources in a variety of formats," and realized that "information may need to be constructed with raw data from primary sources."[5]

Students demonstrated outcomes delineated in Standards Two, "accesses needed information effectively and efficiently," [6] and Three, "evaluates information and its sources critically and incorporates selected information into his or her knowledge base and value system,"[7] when they developed research plans; scanned, transcribed and posted examples of their selected primary sources to their web sites; and cited their secondary sources after evaluating them carefully. Several of the students went beyond NYU Libraries resources by utilizing interlibrary loan, making appointments at other libraries and archives in New York City, or using letters and interviews to retrieve primary information.[8]

Standard Four calls for students to "use information effectively to accomplish a specific purpose."[9] Students in Computing in the Humanities created their own systems for organizing their information when they produced an on-line catalogue of the primary source materials they used. They also prepared podcasts, wrote narratives, and presented their projects to the class.

Finally, the project introduced students to the economic, legal and social issues surrounding the use of information and information technology that are encompassed by Standard Five.[10] It became clear that students needed more guidance when it came to fair use, privacy, and institutional policies.

AREAS FOR IMPROVEMENT

This course is scheduled to be taught again in Spring 2011, and based on issues raised by student projects from the first two semesters of the course, we plan to change the syllabus in the following ways. The archivist and librarian will emphasize the importance of citing sources when including images or documents from repositories or websites other than the University Archives. Clear citations will allow archives staff to perform rights analyses if the projects are published on the University Archives website.

Figure 7.2. Sample digital archive project.

Home I J.J. Stevenson Collection I Memories of Dr. P.L. Schenck I Catalogue I Contact I Visit the *NYU Archives*

NYU and the Civil War

For my final project for the course Computing in the Humanities, I set out to find a picture of life at New York University during the Civil War. During my research at the NYU archives, however, I discovered very little information on the subject.

What I did find were documents relating to NYU graduates who served as physicians and surgeons during the war. In my research I used two main sources: the J.J. Stevenson Collection and the Memories of Dr. P.L. Schenck. This site serves as both a *catalogue* of the documents from those sources and biographical sketches of the individuals contained therein. I have also included relevant information on the Civil War to put the material from the documents in context.

J.J. Stevenson   Memories of Dr.   Catalogue
Collection   P.L. Schenck

Figure 7.3. Sample digital archive project.

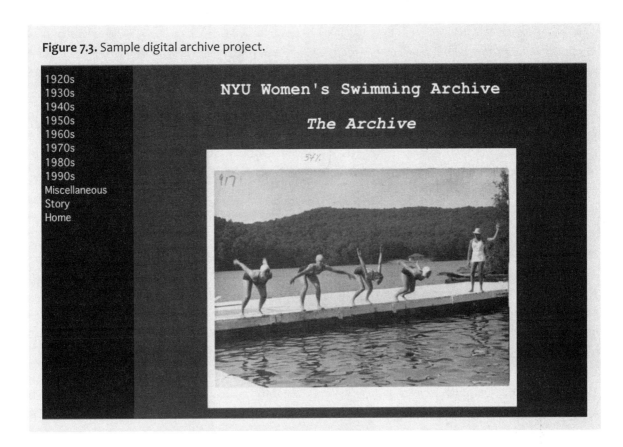

The archivist will discuss privacy issues relating to the publication of University records that mention students. For students who wish to create or include audiovisual interviews or other materials, we will provide release forms for the participants so that these projects may be published online.

HOW THIS PROJECT MAY BE ADAPTED BY OTHERS

We have distilled the following six recommendations for archivists, librarians and teaching faculty who propose courses that involve a significant archival research project. These recommendations may seem obvious, but adhering to them led to the course's success.

First, convene all faculty and staff participants before the course begins to let each person know what will be required of them throughout the semester. To encourage participation and create a space for collaboration, this meeting should include archives and library staff, faculty, and IT staff (if applicable).

Second, maintain clear channels of communication between the instructor and library and archives staff throughout the semester. If the course has a Blackboard page or other resource, the archivist and librarians should be included as instructors to facilitate students' contact with them.

Third, allow students access to archival materials, even if you need to alter standard repository procedures to do so. You might need to extend hours for students who work or take classes during the day. We allowed students to digitize archival materials themselves; in fact, this was a core portion of the final assignment. Proper handling procedures were easily taught, and staff could correct any practices they witnessed that were not appropriate.

Fourth, if student projects will be published, online or in printed form, be aware of copyright and privacy issues that the materials may raise (both for archival materials and those supplied by the students).

Fifth, recognize that novice researchers may take a longer time to adapt to the nuances of archival research than your normal user clientele and build time for instruction and adaptation into the syllabus. Some undergraduates are unfamiliar with the procedures required to conduct even a research project that is narrow in scope. Beginning with online resources helps you to meet students halfway by introducing your resources in a medium that they understand and use frequently.

And sixth, for courses with technological components, it is important to provide adequate T.A. and instructor support from the Computer Science Department to help students avoid frustration in de-bugging their websites during the programming and implementation process.

ADDED BENEFITS

It should be noted that students in the *Computing in the Humanities* course were not required to draw their materials from the University Archives and several students compiled their own primary sources. One student who used her own family photos engaged extensively with librarians in her hunt for secondary materials that would tell her more about the Lithuanian towns in which her relatives had lived. The undergraduate librarian referred her to NYU's Slavic studies librarian who referred her to a colleague at New York Public Library who referred her to a librarian/photo archivist at YIVO, the Institute for Jewish Research. At each one of these meetings, the student found another clue or reference that got her closer to eventually locating a Yourtzeit, or memorial book, for Lithuania; she discovered that all three of her family towns had been destroyed on the same day during World War II. In conversation at the Dean's Undergraduate Research Conference where she won an award for her project, the student attributed her excitement about the course to the shared curiosity and sense of partnership she experienced working with librarians who persisted with her in her search. Rather than being frustrated by the difficulty, she was energized to find that there was a network of librarians and researchers available to help her. This student, and five other students in the *Computing in the Humanities* class, have expressed interest in careers in librarianship as a direct result of their projects. This course also yielded an unexpected benefit for the undergraduate librarian. The instructor recommended her to serve on a panel for the competitive research conference that several students in this class entered with their projects.[11] Since then, the College of Arts & Sciences has invited the librarian back as a jury panelist for the annual conference, a valuable opportunity for understanding and celebrating undergraduate research at NYU.

BIBLIOGRAPHY

Association of College and Research Libraries. *Information Literacy Competency Standards for Higher Education.* http://www.ala.org/ala/mgrps/divs/acrl/standards/informationliteracycompetency.cfm

New York University College of Arts and Sciences. *Inquiry: A Journal of Undergraduate Research.* Volume XII, 2008.

NOTES

1. Association of College and Research Libraries. Information Literacy Competency Standards for Higher Education. http://www.ala.org/acrl/standards/informationliteracycompetency
2. Ibid
3. Ibid., Standard One. Performance Indicator 1.
4. Ibid., Standard One. Performance Indicator 1. Outcomes d and f.
5. Ibid., Standard One. Performance Indicator 2. Outcomes a, c, and f.
6. Ibid., Standard Two.
7. Ibid., Standard Three.
8. Ibid., Standard One. Performance Indicator 3. Outcome b.
9. Ibid., Standard Four.
10. Ibid., Standard Five.
11. The students' abstracts were included in an annual New York University College of Arts and Sciences publication called "Inquiry: A Journal of Undergraduate Research" Volume XII, 2008.

"Pulling on the White Gloves … is Really Sort of Magic:" Report on Engaging History Undergraduates with Primary Sources[1]

Doris Malkmus

New active learning techniques that utilize primary sources to engage students and develop critical thinking skills have become widespread in K-12 classrooms. To determine the degree to which these techniques had infiltrated college teaching and what impact these new methods would have on librarianship was the objective of an online survey of 627 historians (2007-2008) and 25 hour long interviews (2009).[2] This report discusses the advantages and barriers faculty encounter when using primary sources, the differences between support for them in baccalaureate and research institutions, and three distinct ways that primary sources are used in the history—documents analysis in lower division courses, archival search skills in historical methods courses, and one-to-one reference services in upper division courses. This study, while specifically about the field of history, offers insights into how primary sources can be integrated into reference services across the humanities.[3]

REVIEW OF RELATED LITERATURE

Until recently, relevant theory and discussion about active learning techniques using primary sources was found in the literature of educational psychology and history. Library literature included almost none, and what was reported showed that Special Collections materials were underused and poorly integrated into library instruction sessions.[4] In the last five or ten years this has changed and librarians have published case studies of how they include primary sources in outreach and reference services.[5]

The turn toward active learning methods in history began in earnest in the 1990s, when educational psychologists like Samuel Wineburg re-conceptualized how history is taught. He emphasized that teaching students to "think historically" meant teaching them to use the tools of the discipline (criticizing sources, corroborating evidence, interrogating the context of creation). "Learning" required active engagement, rather than passive memorization.[6] Roused by these theories, academic historians developed a variety of new, active, teaching methods, which often began with a thought-provoking set of primary sources—photographs, letters, graphics, etc. Teachers then guided students in the use of the tools of the discipline to uncover connections and meaning.[7] Historians coined the phrase, "scholarship of teaching and learning" (SOTL),[8] to signify scholarly attention to teaching. Lendal Calder, a seminal figure in SOTL, exemplified this approach when he reconfigured his U.S. history survey, omitting the textbook and instead asking students to discuss original documents and later providing divergent scholarly interpretations of that evidence. He then guided students to question sources, make connections, and evaluate alternative perspectives.[9]

Recent case studies in archival and library literature illustrate how these theories influenced user education sessions to focus on *thinking* as well as *research* skills. Archivists Jim Gerencser and Malinda Triller describe specific active teaching methods used in a history methods course.[10] Peter Carini's

2009 workshop on teaching with primary sources focused on the competencies and critical thinking skills that students should develop while learning with primary sources.[11] In reference library literature, case studies about library instruction sessions demonstrate how instructors used documents to stimulate student questions and curiosity before showing them how to search in library resources for the answers to their questions.[12]

METHODOLOGY

This study was based on an online survey sent to 4,002 historians listed as teaching American history on the Web sites of history departments, complemented by 25 hour-long interviews with volunteers from the survey.[13] The 627 respondents to the online survey represented a statistically valid sample for the broad swath of historians teaching undergraduate history.[14] All respondents were invited to contribute open-ended comments. One hundred and ninety-one left comments and will be referred to as "responders" in this paper. In addition, 25 randomly-selected volunteers from the survey were interviewed. Each participant was asked to give details about his or her teaching load and practices, as well as an assessment of student reactions to using primary sources. Survey findings provide broad quantitative data (see published survey results),[15] while comments and interviews provide the rich contextual details that shed light on the context and significance of the survey statistics.[16]

FINDINGS

The vast majority of history faculty consider primary sources an essential part of teaching history. Responders noted that "using primary sources…helps develop analytical and critical thinking skills,"[17] and "enables students to learn what professional historians do and teaches them to think historically."[18] Faculty also agreed that teaching with primary sources is more rewarding for faculty and students. Another responder noted, "Well-structured assignments incorporating substantial use of primary sources

stimulate greater student interest, greater intellectual involvement in the work, better understanding and retention of the subject matter of the course."[19] Only three out of 25 interviewees did not consider primary sources essential to teaching history.

Primary sources, however, also present a greater challenge to students. Almost all interviewees mentioned the difficulty of teaching students to think independently. One responder wrote that students had "enormous resistance"[20] to drawing their own conclusions. Others called undergraduates "daunted,"[21] and one wrote, "even history majors are very intimidated."[22] While educational psychologists consider the ability to form independent opinions in the face of conflicting evidence a distinct phase of cognitive development,[23] some faculty interpreted student resistance as evidence that students were underprepared or apathetic.[24] This convinced a small proportion of responders to rely on lectures, textbooks, and standardized tests.[25] The range of opinions suggests that librarians and archivists should assess faculty attitudes and ambivalence and begin outreach with faculty members already inclined to teach with primary sources.

BARRIERS AND SUPPORT

All faculty indicated that the highest hurdle for them in teaching with primary sources was the difficulty of striking a balance between conveying subject content and teaching critical thinking skills. One interviewee noted that lectures are "still considered the gold standard"[26] and another remarked, "When I'm teaching a broad survey course, I feel responsible to cover certain topics."[27] Despite this constraint, an interviewee stated, "I don't think [lecturing is] the best pedagogy. …You get much more engagement from students and much more critical thinking if they are reading."[28] Teaching faculty who have already created many "gold standard" lectures have to retool to implement new methods.

Class size, course load, and departmental support also had an impact on the use of primary sources with new active learning methods. Liberal arts institutions were significantly more supportive than research universities. Liberal arts colleges often have small classes as well a cultures that reinforce the values of a critical and independent thinking. Faculty at these colleges tend to weigh teaching skills at least as highly as publication in tenure review. Research universities, on the other hand, place a premium on research and training graduate students.[29] In both institutions, heavy course loads make it difficult for faculty to teach with primary sources and active learning techniques. One faculty member with less than 10 years of experience noted, "If you have 200 students a semester, can you even once ask all 200 of them to write a six- to 10-page paper?"[30] Lecture hall seating also inhibits student discussion—faculty responded by modelling how a historian interrogates a primary source,[31] leading discussions of the whole class in the lecture hall ("Never quite as interactive as one would like"),[32] or assigning students to discuss primary sources as dyads.[33] An area with some promise for expanding the use of primary sources is the discussion sections often taught by graduate students. This is a much needed area for outreach, study, innovation, and collaboration.[34] All these factors—large classes, heavy teaching loads, discouraged faculty, and underprepared students—compound each other and affect outcomes when teaching with primary sources.

ONLINE PRIMARY SOURCES— CHANGING PRACTICES

Ninety percent of faculty use published primary source materials to teach, with interviewees citing the high cost as a problem, and their convenience as the principle incentive.[35] Seventy-eight percent used online primary sources and 87 percent agreed they would benefit from knowing more about the online primary sources in their field. However, discovery of digital sources was a significant barrier; one interviewee reported, "I spend a lot of time; some-

times I'm still up at 2:00 in the morning, searching online for illustrative images that I can put [online] that will enhance a lecture.[36] Of 25 interviewees, 14 used Google to find primary sources, 11 checked the Library of Congress or National Archives Records Administration sites, and 11 found new information from colleagues. Not one of the interviewees searched the digital collections of universities or historical societies,[37] and more faculty mentioned getting information about online primary sources from their students (7) and conferences (7) than from librarians (5). When asked if a gateway site or search platform for digitized primary source collections would be valuable to their students and themselves, their answers were an immediate and emphatic, "Absolutely,"[38] Oh, absolutely,"[39] "Absolutely. Yes! A big yes!,"[40] Fabulous of course. Absolutely fabulous!"[41] Numerous responders wrote that they had "a pressing need"[42] for "a clearinghouse of online archives that registers updates and makes clear the extent of holdings."[43] Learning to navigate the abundant, but poorly structured, deluge of online primary sources presents challenges for faculty and opportunities for archivists and librarians to improve discovery systems.[44]

HANDS-ON LEARNING IN THE ARCHIVES

Archival sources, by their very materiality, engage students in a way that complements the accessibility of "virtual" primary sources. A responder commented, "Students are bowled over by the actual documents,"[45] while interviewees were even more emphatic, saying "There is something kind of magical and phenomenological about being confronted with a document that's 350 years old."[46] "My impression is that it's energizing for them to actually put their hands on the physical documents."[47] One faculty member noted, "I have seen over the years all kinds of students from exceedingly good to very mediocre get turned on by actually picking up a letter written by a soldier in the Civil War or written by a frontier woman here in Illinois."[48]

Despite this advantage, only 39 percent of survey respondents assigned sources from an archives in half or more of classes—25 percentage points below faculty who agree their students have access to an archives with relevant materials. Faculty noted the limited hours, small reading rooms, and minimal staffing that make it difficult to take classes to archives or assign archival resources. One interviewee noted that the world class archives on her campus was not a resource for her classes since she "couldn't haul 168 people over there, even in batches."[49] Constructing functional class spaces in or near archives would send a strong signal to faculty that Special Collections is serious about undergraduate use of materials..

Coordination of assignments by teachers and archivists is indispensable. One faculty asserted, "Instructors cannot send students to archives ... without providing a lot of support, first in class, in precise assignment material, in samples and run-throughs, and in repeat trips... Archival visits must be built into the syllabus and structured with follow-up activities and discussion."[50] This voice of experience contrasts with familiar anecdotes about teachers who assign archival research to large classes without notifying the archivist, preparing students by explaining the nature of archival research, or checking to see if the archives has materials related to the course. These frustrating episodes probably contribute to the 6 percent of survey respondents who strongly disagreed that students enjoy or benefit from archival research.[51] Another responder noted that a successful assignment "requires teamwork between the archivist and historian."[52] Archival assignments, like any new endeavor, requires [sic] significant time and effort, but faculty assert they are rewarded when students sense something "magical" or decide to become history majors.[53]

TEACHING HISTORY WITH PRIMARY SOURCES

The undergraduate history curriculum utilizes primary sources in distinct ways in the freshman survey course, historical methods course, and upper division sub-field courses. Freshmen need to learn to evaluate evidence, read closely, compare points of view, consider purpose and audience, and judge truth claims in the light of other evidence. Online primary sources are most convenient for in class use, while archival materials were reported to be more meaningful for students.

In an example from a Yale freshman seminar, the archivist and instructor pre-selected sets of documents illuminating the theme of the course, the faculty modelled close reading of primary source documents, and then had students analyze their pre-assigned set of documents in small groups.[54] Assignments using this approach can be matched to the level of the students—from simple description of their documents, developing provisional narratives to connect the documents, or assigning secondary research and papers. Freshman seminars like this can lay a foundation for habits of critical thinking as well as build the student's knowledge of history.

The second point in the history curriculum that introduces primary sources is the historical methods course for majors. Five of 25 interviewees reported that the methods class was the only class that they brought to the archives, and three of those brought them "just to show them what's available" and "to get a sense of what earlier documents look like."[55] Three interviewees arranged class trips to other archives in the region.[56] Eight of 25 interviewees never took classes to archives, which when extrapolated to education majors who minor in history, suggests that a quarter of K-12 history teachers will never visit an archives or do any research in primary sources before graduation.

Research papers for upper division classes constitute the most traditional use of primary sources in the undergraduate curriculum, and the one at which archivists were most appreciated. One responder spoke for many when he or she remarked "librarians and archivists are quite effective in one-on-one sessions with students after they have defined a topic."[57] Reference and outreach to classes, required a different skill set. Another responder reported "I am always disappointed in the presentations that the archivists make. I typically know far more about how to make [the material] accessible and meaningful to the students."[58] Another reported that some archivists "act as gatekeepers and do not like students. As younger and more newly trained archivists take over, I have noticed a positive difference."[59] These generalizations most likely reflect the transition in the archival profession from an emphasis on stewardship to an emphasis on access. In this transition, archivists must learn something of new teaching practices and collaborate with subject librarians.

CONCLUSION

Faculty in a wide variety of fields—rhetoric, communication, and English, as well as cultural, environmental, women's, ethnic, gender, and religious studies have found primary sources effective in engaging students in the adventure of discovering and learning. Archival sources that engage students are complemented by ever-accessible online sources. Local records—documenting water quality to council minutes and local news—are particularly useful in helping students see the impact of national and international events in familiar contexts. Creative uses of primary sources in new teaching methods engage students, develop their critical thinking skills and increase subject retention. This study highlighted the "magic in pulling on the white gloves,[60]" but also identified barriers such as the need to cover content, high faculty course loads, large class sizes, departmental culture, and inadequate archival facilities. Underuse of libraries online and in house primary resources present research libraries with the motivation to support active learning methods in undergraduate courses. Libraries committed to excellence should not only adapt their services to new teaching methods, but encourage their subject librarians to coordinate their outreach efforts with special collections librarians and archivists to actively promote the use of their unique resources.

NOTES

1. Interview 320025, p 21.

2. For a copy of the survey tool, and analysis of results, see appendices in Doris Malkmus, "Teaching History to Undergraduates with Primary Sources: Survey of Current Practices," *Archival Issues: Journal of the Midwest Archives Conference*, 31(1)(2007), 25-45.

3. The growing emphasis on promoting special collections holdings is evidenced, for example, in the Special Collections Task Force 2001–2006, "Special Collections Task Force Final Status Report, 2006," Association of Research Libraries, http://www.arl.org/rtl/speccoll/spcolltf/status0706.shtml (accessed July 15, 2010).

4. O'Donnell found only 34 citations in the library literature related to archival reference between 1984 and 1998. Frances O'Donnell, "Reference Service in an Academic Archives," *Journal of Academic Librarianship* 26, 2 (March 2000): 110. Shan Sutton and Lorrie Knight reported that 125 students annually took part in special collections instruction sessions at the University of Colorado, compared to 1,500 who attended the general library workshops. Shan Sutton and Lorrie Knight, "Beyond the Reading Room: Integrating Primary and Secondary Sources in the Library Classroom," *Journal of Academic Librarianship* 32, 3 (May 2006): 320–5; 321. Schmiesing and Hollis found only 23 percent of visits to special collections were course related, suggesting underutilization of primary sources by undergraduates. Ann Schmiesing and Deborah R. Hollis, "The Role of Special Collections Departments in Humanities Undergraduate and Graduate Teaching: A Case Study," *portal: Libraries and the Academy* 2, 3 (2002), 468.

5. For more a complete literature review see "Doris Malkmus, ""Old Stuff" for New Teaching Methods: Outreach to History Faculty Teaching with Primary Sources," (accepted for publication) *portal: Libraries*

and the Academy(2010): . Information guiding K–12 teachers in the use of primary sources is well developed and often useful for teaching non-majors. The following are suggested readings: the Teacher page on the Library of Congress site for using primary sources. Library of Congress, "Teachers: Bringing the power of primary sources into the classroom," Library of Congress, http://www.loc.gov/teachers (accessed July 19, 2010); the National Archives Records Administration Web page, Educators and Students, offers the greatest number of sources of information about teaching with primary sources, although they are focused on online primary sources. National Archives and Records Administration, "Educators and Students," National Archives and Records Administration, http://www.archives.gov/education/ (accessed July 14, 2010). The best-known site devoted to college-level teaching is located at the Center for History and New Media at George Mason University. This site organizes online primary sources by theme and offers teaching ideas related to the topic. Center for History and New Media, "About," Department of History and Art History, George Mason University, http://chnm.gmu.edu/about (accessed July 15, 2009). These three sites were "first stops" for many of the interviewed faculty. The new California Digital Library, Calisphere, http://www.calisphere.universityofcalifornia.edu/ (accessed July 14, 2010) is the premier example of a search site for digital sources designed with teachers in mind and completely unknown to academic faculty at the time of the interviews.

Articles related specifically to K–12 in archival literature include: Katharine T. Corbett, "From File Folder to the Classroom: Recent Primary Source Curriculum Projects," *American Archivist* 54 (Spring 1991): 296–300; Sharon Anne Cook, "Connecting Archives and the Classroom," *Archivaria* 44 (Fall 1997): 102–17; Michael Eamon, "A 'Genuine Relationship with the Actual': New Perspectives on Primary Sources, History and the Internet in the Classroom," *The History Teacher* 39, 3 (May 2006): 297–314; Julia Hendry, "Primary Sources in K–12 Education: Opportunities for Archives," *American Archivist* 70 (Spring/Summer 2007): 114–29; Anne J. Gilliland-Swetland, "An Exploration of K–12 User Needs for Digital Primary Source Materials," *American Archivist* 61, 1 (1998): 136–57; and Anne J. Gilliland-Swetland, Yasmin B. Kafai, and William E. Landis, "Integrating Primary Sources into the Elementary School Classroom: A Case Study of Teachers' Perspectives," *Archivaria* 49 (Fall 1999): 89–116.

6. Sam Wineberg, *Historical Thinking and Other Unnatural Acts: Charting the Future of Teaching the Past* (Philadelphia: Temple University Press, 2001), 77.

7. Kathleen McCarthy Young and Gaea Leinhardt, "Writing from Primary Documents: A Way of Knowing in History," *Written Communication* 15 (January 1998): 25–68, see review of practices, especially p. 26–8. See also Gaea Leinhardt, Isabel L. Beck, and Catherine Stainton, eds., *Teaching and Learning in History* (Hillsdale, NJ: Lawrence Erlbaum Associates, Publishers, 1994).

8. Indiana University, Bloomington, Libraries, SOTL, Selected Library Resources on the Scholarship of Teaching and Learning, Indiana University, Bloomington, Libraries, http://www.libraries.iub.edu/index.php?pageId=3208 (accessed July 14, 2010).

9. Lendal Calder, "Uncoverage: Toward a Signature Pedagogy for the History Survey," *Journal of American History* 92, 4 (March 2006): 1358–70. As SOTL developed, the principal professional historical organizations devoted more articles and resources to teaching, giving rise to the Organization of American Historian's *Teaching the Journal of American History* and the American Historical Association's online magazine, *Perspectives on History*.

10. James Gerencser and Malinda Triller, "Hands-on Instruction in the Archives: Using Group Activities as an Engaging Way to Teach Undergraduates about Primary Sources," *Journal for the Society of North Carolina Archivists* 6, 2 (Winter 2009): 55–66.

11. Peter Carini, "Archivists as Educators: Integrating Primary Sources into the Curriculum," *Journal of Archival*

Organization 7, 1/2 (January–June 2009): 41–50.

12. Shan Sutton and Lorrie Knight, "Beyond the Reading Room: Integrating Primary and Secondary Sources in the Library Classroom," *Journal of Academic Librarianship* 32, 3 (May 2006): 320–5. Susan E. Cooperstein and Elisabeth Kocevar-Weidinger, "Beyond Active Learning: A Constructivist Approach to Learning," *Reference Services Review* 32, 2 (2004): 141.

13. For detailed information about the survey design, survey tool, and analysis, see Doris Malkmus, "Teaching History to Undergraduates with Primary Sources: Survey of Current Practices," *Archival Issues: Journal of the Midwest Archives Conference,* 31(1)(2007), 25-45.

14. The number of respondents included 415 tenured faculty, 100 tenure-track faculty, 66 instructor/adjunct, and 10 other. The category of instructor/adjunct included a wide variety of new Ph.D.'s and emeritus that did not constitute a coherent group. Associate degree institutions were so severely underrepresented that they are not included in this report. This article will use the term "faculty" to refer to all respondents, and the terms "tenure track" and "tenured" to refer to those groups specifically. The number of tenured faculty exceeded their proportion in the profession by 14 percent, while tenure–track faculty were underrepresented by 31 percent. Nationally, doctorate-granting institutions comprise 31 percent of the total; in this survey they comprised 48 percent. "Instructor/adjunct/lecturers" and "Others" included a wide mix of emeritus professors, long-term adjuncts at community colleges, and new graduates that did not clearly represent any single group for purposes of analysis. In respect to institutional categories, universities were slightly overrepresented compared to national statistics; associate-level colleges comprise 30 percent of the national total, while in this survey they comprised only 1.2 percent—so severely underrepresented that they were not included in the analysis. Research about teaching with primary sources at community colleges is urgently needed.

15. See full survey results in Doris Malkmus, "Teaching History to Undergraduates with Primary Sources:

Survey of Current Practices," *Archival Issues: Journal of the Midwest Archives Conference,* 31(1)(2007), 25-45

16. Footnotes for comments also note the faculty status, type of institution, years of experience, and access to an archives. Footnotes for interviews do not include identifying information to protect the privacy of interviewees.

17. Comment 81, tenured, baccalaureate, 11–15 years, no archives.

18. Comment 34, instructor, university, 11–15 years, yes archives.

19. Comment 167, tenured, university, 15+ years, yes archives.

20. Comment 148, tenured, masters, 15+ years, yes archives.

21. Comment 65, tenure-track, university, 11–15 years, yes archives.

22. Comment 56, tenure-track, university, 11–15, no archives.

23. William G. Perry, Jr., *Forms of Intellectual and Ethical Development in the College Years: A Scheme* (New York: Holt, Rinehart and Winston, 1970).

24. One interviewee wrote that local high schools had crushed any budding historical curiosity through a regime of textbooks, fill-in-the-blank worksheets, and multiple choice tests. He felt they were underprepared for work with primary source work. Interview 320026, p. 8.

25. One responder from an institution with low admission standards wrote students "have never been taught how to [analyze a] document or find any primary source, let alone understand what is primary versus secondary" and "a 60 percent failure rate is typical in a survey course here." Comment 174, tenured, masters, 11–15 years, yes archives.

26. Interview 320014, p. 30.

27. Interview 320018, p. 31.

28. Interview 320014, p. 9; p. 8. For insight and an enjoyable read about the history profession's conservatism regarding new teaching methods, see Len Caldol, " Uncoverage: Toward a Signature Pedagogy for the History Survey," *Journal of American History* 92, 4 (March

2006): 1358–70.

29. A strong proponent of using primary sources counseled "younger faculty in…[his] institution to adopt [teaching with primary sources] with caution since it may draw substantial time away from publication, which is the primary consideration for tenure here." Comment 167, tenured, university, 15+ years, yes archives.

30. Some faculty asked students to keep journals or portfolios documenting their reactions to assigned primary sources. Interview 320033, p. 11; 320007, p. 3.

31. Interview 320026, p. 6; interview 320013, p. 2

32. Interview 320011, p. 5.

33. Interview 320016, p. 13

34. This survey and interviews did not include graduate students; in light of the fact that they are learning to be teachers, more research into opportunities and barriers to using primary sources is indicated.

35. On responder reported, "I've stopped using a print document reader and am trying to use only primary sources available on the Web in my survey classes this semester. This is, in part, a reaction to the high cost of the readers." Comment 130; tenured, masters, 6–10 years experience, yes archives.

36. Interview 320035, p. 24.

37 The exception to this generalization is that several faculty mentioned the well-known Civil War website, "Valley of the Shadow," at the University of Virginia, http://valley.lib.virginia.edu/. (accessed July 15, 2010.)

38. Interview 320016, p. 21.

39. Interview 320013, p. 21.

40. Interview 320012, p. 24.

41. Interview 320035, p. 28.

42. Comment 95, tenured, baccalaureate, 15+ years, yes archives.

43. Comment 178, tenured, university, 11–15 years, yes archives.

44. For example, one responder wrote, "It is very time consuming to explain to a large class how to interpret sources." Comment 21, instructor, Master's, 15+, yes archives.

45. Comment 45, tenure track, university, 6–10 years, no archives.

46. Interview 320030, p. 30.

47. Interview 320032, p. 8.

48. Interview, 320012, p. 25.

49. Interview 320035, p. 35.

50. Comment 20, instructor, university, 0–5 years, yes archives.

51. The percentage of those who strongly disagreed was highest for those with 0–5 years of experience, but those who moderately disagreed were evenly distributed among all years of experience

52. Comment 23, instructor, baccalaureate, 6–10 years, yes archives.

53. Comment 40, tenure-track, university, 11-15 years, yes archives.

54. Bill Landis, "A Primary Source Case Study: Getting Stuff into First-Year Undergraduates' Hands at the Yale University Library" (presentation, Society of American Archivists 2008 Annual Conference, August 24–31, 2008, San Francisco, CA). See the Society of American Archivists Annual conference site, http://saa.archivists.org/Scripts/4Disapi.dll/4DCGI/events/82.html?Action=Conference_Detail&ConfID_W=82#schedule (accessed July 21, 2010). To access the Landis paper, scroll to session 605.

55. Interview 320036, p. 9.

56. Other interviewees took methods classes on day-long trips to find resources in different repositories. Interview 320012, p. 17; 320039, p. 7.

57. Comment 173, tenured, university, 15+, yes archives.

58. Comment 153, tenured, university, 11-15 years, yes archives.

59. Comment 106, tenured, baccalaureate, 15+ years, yes archives.

60. Interview 320025, p. 20–21.

Lighting Fires in Creative Minds: Teaching Creative Writing in Special Collections

David Pavelich

THE RISE OF CREATIVE WRITING

In his 2009 book *The Program Era: Fiction and the Rise of Creative Writing*, UCLA professor Mark McGurl argues that, "the rise of the creative writing program stands as the most important event in postwar American literary history."[2] McGurl's claim is controversial, but the fact at its heart is well documented: the rise of creative writing as an academic discipline in the United States has been meteoric. The University of Iowa Writers' Workshop, for instance, began only in 1936. Seminal and still influential, it was the first creative writing degree program in the United States. Other institutions such as Cornell University and the University of Houston quickly followed Iowa's lead and developed well-known creative writing programs.

As testament to the growth of these programs, the Association of Writers and Writing Programs (AWP) currently reports nearly 500 member institutions, and there are many other post-secondary institutions that offer creative writing courses but are not members of the AWP.[3]

Growth in the number of students earning creative writing degrees is, not surprisingly, proportionate to growth in programs. According to statistics provided by the National Center for Education Statistics, U.S. degree-granting institutions awarded 2,333 creative writing degrees in the 1997-98 academic year (1,013 bachelor's degrees; 1,314 master's degrees; and 6 PhD degrees). 10 years later, the total number of creative writing degrees granted annually had more than doubled to 4,895 in 2007-08 (2,265 bachelor's degrees; 2,618 master's

degrees; and 12 PhD degrees).[4] What's more, many students not majoring in creative writing often enroll in one or more creative writing class during their academic careers. Cornell University's *Chronicle Online* reported in 2007 that, "[m]ore than 500 Cornell undergraduates enroll in campus creative writing courses annually."[5]

Creative writing programs offer special collections librarians unique outreach and instruction opportunities. It is commonly assumed that literature derives purely from inspiration—novels, poems, and creative essays flow effortlessly from their authors' hands directly onto paper or screen. Because of this, creative writing students (as well as students in the visual and performing arts) rarely receive direct outreach from libraries. This assumption, however, is blind to the importance of research, craft, and publication in the creation of new literature. Special collections librarians are poised to provide important lessons in primary research, writing and editing processes, and modes of publication.

Special collections instruction for creative writing classes offers a fresh opportunity to merge traditional special collections instruction methods (such as the "show-and-tell"), the workshop approaches found in writing programs, and the bibliographic instruction goals of our general reference peers—to teach how to find, how to assess, and how to make use of information. Special collections instruction should be designed to provide the three types of participant in the room—faculty, student, and librarian—equal opportunities to participate in the activity. In order to meet a variety of learning styles, special collections librarians need to develop a student-centered approach to leading sessions, and should encourage active learning by integrating sessions into the goals and flow of the syllabus; stressing discussion over presentation; provoking critical thinking; and selecting the most provocative/evocative materials available to them.

What follows are five examples of creative writing sessions held in the Special Collections Research Center at the University of Chicago Library. Each suggests a different approach to instruction, but all are unified by their emphasis on collaborative teaching and class discussion. Such examples are always local and tied to the strengths of unique collections, but the approaches are extendable in many settings.

HISTORICAL FICTION

"[T]here is generally no substitute for knowing what you are talking about," quipped Wallace Stegner, novelist and founder of the Creative Writing Program at Stanford University. "Many fictions, whether they involve history or some aspect of contemporary life not in the common experience… represent more knowledge, both from experience and from research, than shows on the surface."[6] In other words, writing historical fiction requires advanced research skills, which libraries are prepared to provide. A tale set in the 1920s, for instance, elicits countless research questions: *What clothes does my character wear? What cigarettes does she smoke? What buses or trains does she ride?*

Teaching in the University of Chicago's Graham School of General Studies Writer's Studio, novelist Achy Obejas visits the Special Collections Research Center annually with her students to discuss research for fiction writing. These visits have demonstrated that, for creative writing classes, it is crucial for the instructor to participate in the discussion. As a living and published author, the instructor carries an important artistic authority. Obejas narrates her own experiences with research; she may stress the importance of food in fictional scenes and pro-

vide literary examples, while the librarian provides instruction on how to research food from different cultures or time periods.

In a presentation designed by librarians, Obejas' students are guided through formats such as historical newspapers, magazines, maps, and printed ephemera. They are also instructed in searching for narrative elements like food, costume, and transportation. As always, instruction sessions for historical fiction stress "format agnosticism" and include introductions to searching and using manuscripts, printed books, and electronic resources.

EDITORIAL INTERVENTIONS

In 2008, University of Chicago poet Garin Cycholl asked his poetry students to read Michael O'Brien's acclaimed *Sleeping and Waking*, a volume of poetry published by Chicago publisher Flood Editions. The Special Collections Research Center holds the editorial files for Flood Editions, and Cycholl and his students visited the library to investigate the development of *Sleeping and Waking* from manuscript to published book. As a group, we examined O'Brien's original manuscript, read aloud from recommendations for changes found in the editor's correspondence, discovered poems cut from the published version, and discussed whether we agreed or disagreed with the editor's suggestions.

The session was an exercise in critical thinking. Differences of opinion were voiced, and the young poets assumed the role of editor and witnessed the value of the editorial process. "The students really enjoyed working with the poets' papers," commented Cycholl. "I tried to impress on them an understanding of poetry as a way of being in the world, not simply work carried on alone, but a conversation with other poets, editors, and readers. The poets' letters and exchanges developed students' sense of this conversation…. These exchanges also influenced the workshop's larger dynamic in that writers began to see the influence of workshop conversations on their own work."[7]

DRAFTS

Poet Leila Wilson brought her students from the creative writing program at the School of the Art Institute in Chicago to the Special Collections Research Center to discuss the concept of revision. Wilson wanted her students to see poems by well-known poets in various drafts, which are found in the records of *Poetry: A Magazine of Verse*, and to discern the improvements made to poems over multiple iterations.

The session was designed around drafts of poems written by poets on the class's syllabus. A sustained discussion, however, centered on two versions of Roethke's poem "Reply to Censure," which appeared in *Poetry* magazine in November 1937. Accompanying the two versions of the poem is a brief letter from Roethke to *Poetry* editor Morton Dauwen Zabel, in which Roethke says, "Thank you for… the suggestions, which I have tried to follow. I believe the piece is much stronger, for I have eliminated most of the abstract words."[8] The class discussed how the second version of the poem was possibly less "abstract," adding to students' understanding of both Roethke's work and the more general concepts of concrete and abstract language.

The manuscripts served as evidence of the labor of craftsmanship. Successive drafts by eminent poets like Roethke make clear that the processes of writing—most specifically revision—apply not just to student writers, but to all poets, including canonical modernists.

VERSIONS

"Literature, and the making of literature, is usefully approached from the angle of its material productions," suggested University of Chicago poet Peter O'Leary after a class session in special collections. "I like bringing young poets to the archives to show them that even the greatest works of literature have undergone changes at the hands of printers, publishers, and even poets themselves, sometimes long after the works themselves have initially appeared."[9] O'Leary visited the Special Collections Research Center with his beginning poetry writing class to answer three stated questions: *What is it like to publish poetry? Who publishes poetry? And when something is published, does that mean it can't ever be changed?*

To answer these questions, Walt Whitman's idiosyncratic approach to composition was the session's focus. Whitman famously changed the text of *Leaves of Grass* between 1855 and his death in 1892, revising and adding to his long poem, creating a poem by accretion. To demonstrate the changes, students, instructor, and librarian read aloud from, and discussed, several editions of the poem published during Whitman's lifetime. The class also examined samples of Whitman's manuscripts in both facsimile and holograph forms. The students were challenged to consider not just the "material production" of various editions, but the quality of the poem as it grew through the years.

SELF-PUBLISHING AND ALTERNATIVE BOOK FORMS

At many institutions, little magazines, artists' books, and small press publications live in special collections. University of Chicago poet and assistant professor Jennifer Scappettone has drawn on the Special Collections Research Center for an assignment for her intermediate poetry students: "I want each of the students… to make a chapbook at quarter's end," Scappettone wrote. "[T]he idea is to expose them to small-press journal editions and chapbooks of differing proportions, materials, and scope."[10]

Scappettone has two stated goals, to get her students' "imaginations going," and to "reacquaint their generation with the *book* as medium." These sessions are broadly historical, with an emphasis on recent poetry and handmade books. One session with Scappettone and her students began with a discussion on the history of the pamphlet and chapbook as forms, beginning with German Reformation *flugschriften*, working through 17th century English chapbooks, and ending with contemporary avant-garde publications. The group then talked about the tradition of self-publication, from Walt Whitman's *Leaves of Grass* and Gertrude Stein's Plain Editions to the present. In the end, students examined how chapbooks and pamphlets were made and identified ways for the students to make quick, handmade books of their own. Important literary works are often originally published modestly, so the session stressed inexpensive printing methods, such as photocopying, and easy hand-binding, like stapling or sewing. Students were empowered to present their own work in an expressive and DIY (do-it-yourself) medium.

CONCLUSION

While this chapter focuses on strategies for the use of manuscripts and rare books in creative writing instruction, it has a second, broader message. Within colleges and universities, academic departments and areas of emphasis are born, change, and occasionally disappear. For special collections libraries to remain vibrant and relevant presences on these dynamic campuses, librarians need to identify, reach out to, and evolve innovative ways to provide services to developing user groups; the creative writing phenomenon is only one example among many (African or African American Studies, Latin American Studies, and Middle Eastern Studies stand out among them).

And finally, there is at least one value to bringing young writers to our collections that cannot be easily described: inspiration. "Though it is always helpful to the young to be steered and guided toward what may catch their interest," reflected Stegner, "I would be inclined, also, to throw open the library and let them find many things for themselves. The delight of discovery is a major pleasure of reading; and discovery is one of the best ways to light a fire in a creative mind."

NOTES

1. The author is now at Duke University.
2. McGurl, Mark. *The Program Era: Postwar Fiction and the Rise of Creative Writing*. Cambridge, Ma: Harvard University Press, 2009.
3. The Association of Writers & Writing Programs http://www.awpwriter.org/membership/index.htm (Accessed August 31, 2010).
4. U.S. Department of Education, National Center for Education Statistics. Integrated Postsecondary Education Data System (IPEDS), "Table 275. Bachelor's, master's, and doctor's degrees conferred by degree-granting institutions, by sex of student and discipline division: 2007-08." (This table was prepared July 2009.) http://nces.ed.gov/programs/digest/d07/tables/dt07_265.asp?referrer=list (Accessed August 31, 2010).
5. George Lowery. "Cornell's Creative Writing Program ranked among the nation's best." *ChronicleOnline*. August, 2007. http://www.news.cornell.edu/stories/Aug07/creativeWriting.gl.html (Accessed August 31, 2009).
6. Wallace Stegner. "On the teaching of creative writing." *On teaching and writing fiction*. Edited by Lynn Stegner. New York: Penguin, 2002.
7. Email with Cycholl, July 16, 2009.
8. Theodore Roethke to Morton Dauwen Zabel. *Poetry: A Magazine of Verse Records*, Box 40, Folder 15, Special Collections Research Center, University of Chicago Library.
9. Email with O'Leary, July 10, 2009.
10. Email with Scappettone, January 3, 2008.

Special Collections Instruction in the Sciences: A Collaborative Model

Barbara Losoff, Caroline Sinkinson, and Elizabeth Newsom

Science undergraduates seldom have the opportunity to interact with historical primary sources that are the foundation of scientific thought and scholarship. At the University of Colorado, Boulder (CU), collaboration between librarians and faculty resulted in the development of an active learning model for undergraduate biology students and other science classes. This project arose in response to a request for hands-on, experiential learning to engage students on the history and the relevancy of science through books, manuscripts, and realia. This chapter presents a model for using special collections to augment student learning in the life sciences, tracing the steps from the initial collaboration, to the hands-on session, and finally to the design of an active learning module.

The richness of CU's Special Collections Department spans numerous disciplines and includes literary manuscripts and realia. Two prominent donations, the Sam Tour Collection and the Charles DePuy Collection, provide the basis for the department's scientific materials. These collections include first editions of Franklin's *New Experiments*, Hooke's *Micrographia*, and Beilstein's *Handbuch*. Sadly, many students may not uncover these treasures because approximately 45 percent of the department's holdings are accessible only via card catalog. As a result, class visits are a primary source of student exposure to the collections. Since its inception in 1963, special collections instruction was handled by a mix of librarians and/or paraprofessionals all of whom had other duties (cataloging, acquisitions, exhibit construction, etc.) limiting

the ability to offer classes. From 2000-2004, and following the hire of an instruction librarian in 2001, the department saw a 75 percent increase in the number of CU classes receiving instruction in Special Collections.[1] Although arts and humanities students have been the primary users of special collections, the department does have a history of teaching science classes and actively encourages the science faculty to take advantage of instruction opportunities.

Several libraries have recognized the potential for special collections to inspire students' learning and have provided various models of class integration. Schmiesing and Hollis (2002) describe a humanities-based model for enhancing undergraduate and graduate learning through a collaborative effort between a special collections librarian and a German professor.[2] Visser (2003) presents a hands-on undergraduate session for a microbiology course with an accompanying bibliography.[3] Alvarez (2006) describes an undergraduate History of Science class where students address "censorship in the first two-centuries of printing."[4] In each experience the authors note positive outcomes including students' awareness of historical context and the humanizing of course content through physical objects. In Alvarez's model students learn the historical context of censorship by physically interacting with Copernicus' *De Revolutionibus* of 1566. Gardner and Pavelich (2006) ask students to relate materials to themselves and their lives which connects students to course content and "provides an important humanizing perspective."[5] The central theme of each of these models is the collaboration between librarians and faculty. Through collaboration, the potential of transforming special collections departments into "learning laboratories where students work hands-on with primary documents, and incorporate them into original research projects" may be realized.[6]

COLLABORATION

In 2002, a CU science librarian and a biochemistry faculty member, Professor Shelley Copley, began discussions which provided the impetus for extended collaboration with the Special Collections department. Professor Copley expressed an interest in exploring ways to engage both biology majors and non-majors in a course on infectious diseases. The science librarian suggested introducing the undergraduates to related primary materials in special collections as a means for enhancing the course content and collaborated with the special collections librarian to identify materials that would engage the students. With the assistance of the special collections staff, the science librarian created an annotated bibliography which included an account of the plague at Aleppo in 1756, illustrations of rat-catchers and corpse bearers from 1839 (see figure 10.2), Redi's work from 1668 that

Figure 10.2. Image from The cries of London (London: John Bowyer Nichols and Son, 1839) showing a rat catcher during the plague years.

disproved the theory of spontaneous generation, and a working Culpepper-type microscope from 1770 (See Appendix 10.1). All participants considered this collaboration a success, but several years went by before Professor Copley taught the class again and could make time for visiting special collections.

In the winter of 2009, Professor Copley informed the science librarian that she was teaching a course in the spring on the history of microbiology, including infectious diseases. The two began preparations for another special collections visit. For this session, the science librarian wanted to incorporate teaching methods to enhance student learning and contacted the instruction librarian as well as the special collections librarian. Once this team was established, the librarians began identifying potential primary materials and were assisted by Professor Copley, who provided the content knowledge for the class session. The librarians drafted an annotated bibliography and developed an enhanced website for the course, which included color photographs, a slide show of materials, and secondary source databases.[7] In spring 2010, students attended a session in the Special Collections Reading Room where the librarians provided historical context and physical description of each piece, while answering student questions.

Feedback was uniformly positive, with several students indicating an eagerness to further investigate the collections and to explore the mysteries therein. Professor Copley, impressed by the level of student engagement, invited the special collec-

Figure 10.1. Image from Micrographia: Or, some physiological descriptions of minute bodies made by magnifying glasses (London: J. Martyn, 1665), showing drawing of a flea.

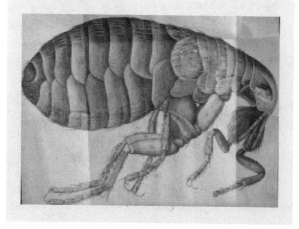

tions librarian to attend a biochemistry department meeting to present on the class experience of visiting the library and to display the associated website. The librarian answered questions about the materials held in special collections and explained the procedure for class visits. The faculty response was enthusiastic with many questions and positive comments.

With this positive feedback, the librarians were poised to continue outreach and to promote the incorporation of special collections into the science curriculum. However, the librarians also realized that the awe stimulated by special collections materials could be channeled to encourage self-directed student-researchers. The lecture based format of the initial session appeared necessary given time constraints; however, the design restricted the cooperative and active learning potential inherent in special collections instruction. With that in mind, the librarians planned an assignment and class to reposition students and librarians as co-investigators, working collaboratively to inspire learning. The librarians intend to test the assignment in 2012.

FUTURE GOALS AND ASSIGNMENT

The assignment, as the librarians conceptualized it, is founded on cooperative instructional strategies that encourage active student participation. According to the *Encyclopedia of Educational Psychology*, cooperative learning processes "significantly restructure classrooms from passive learning environments, with the teacher dominating instructional conversation, into engaging environments where students actively participate."[8] As in previous sessions, the librarians and teaching faculty will compile a bibliography of special collection materials related to class content. The materials will be available in the reading room for close examination, but the students, rather than librarians, will be responsible for describing and researching the materials. Students will pair with a classmate and will select a resource from the bibliography to examine, research, and evaluate. Student pairs will share their findings in a summary and presentation given to the entire class in the Special Collections Department at a later date. Librarians will provide support for inquiry through consultations as well as a list of library reference sources, historical databases, and related resources.

In order to guide the evaluation, students will respond to a series of questions which prompt investigation of the source's historical context, relatedness to current information sources, physicality, and creator. Students will also be asked to reflect on their motivation for choosing the source and continued curiosity about the source. Similar questions were used in the special collections assignments de-

---

Table 10.1. Evaluation Questions

1. Title/ Description:
2. Creation date:
3. Printer or Scriptorium:
4. Who created or authored the source? Provide information about them.
5. Who was the intended audience? Who would have used this? Describe user characteristics.
6. What was the intended function of the source? Describe.
7. Describe the format, physical material, and typography or handwriting. What does the physical appearance tell you?
8. Does the piece remind you of any modern information source? Why or why not?
9. Why or why isn't the source relevant today?
10. Is it considered canon in the sciences? Why or why not?
11. Why did you choose this source?
12. What other questions do you have about the source?

signed by Gardner and Pavelich and by Gerencser and Triller.[9] (See table 10.1).

These questions and assignment aim to meet four main objectives: (1) Provide exposure to the rich materials available in special collections, (2) Provide an active and collaborative learning environment, (3) Facilitate critical evaluation of information sources, (4) Introduce students to additional library information sources.

The librarians identified 'exposure to the rich materials available in Special Collections' as a core objective because of the potential for these materials to inspire students. Students are given an authentic learning experience with physical objects in order to interact with course content, in which, as Gardner and Pavelich identify; students acquire "information about historical context and gain a broader understanding of the topic under discussion."[10] Furthermore, special collection libraries are an ideal setting for active learning instructional design where tactile representations of the subject are available.[11]

Cooperative and active learning were essential to the assignment design. Student-centeredness and the recognition of students' prior knowledge are two core aspects of active learning environments, which the assignment meets by allowing student self-selection of the studied material. Students' interest and curiosity drive the research and presentation, creating ownership of their own learning. Librarians and teaching faculty may contribute and join in the dialog, but they do *not monopolize* the session. By presenting findings and impressions, students share their knowledge with peers and in so doing increase their learning.

The third assignment objective, critical evaluation of information sources, is united with the information literacy goals of the Library's mission. The assignment asks students to investigate and pose questions about sources, in order to evaluate information critically and to reflect on the process of information creation, distribution, and

scholarly discourse. In terms of content, students may explore scientific theories and beliefs which have since been disproven, perhaps theories about disease contraction or apothecary remedies that were once commonly accepted (See figure 10.3). By comparing historical texts with modern scientific thought, students will uncover stark contrasts which reveal the importance of being critical consumers of information.[12] Students will also observe how knowledge and information evolve through discourse and communication. While these goals are further reaching than special collections, the intriguing nature of rare materials offers an engaging lesson in critical evaluation.

The final objective of the assignment was to expose students to additional library resources by asking them to consult secondary sources. Librarians will provide a digital course guide to assist students in these efforts including significant reference sources in the sciences, biography, and history. The guide responds to the students' desire to explore awe-inspiring materials while simultaneously widening their resource awareness. The librarians themselves are another library resource highlighted by the assignment. Students are invited to meet librarians for individual consultations and coaching, which may help them with the assignment but are services available for future information needs as well.

The structure of this assignment may be easily revised to meet the needs of other disciplines or courses. Librarians and faculty could tailor the bibliogra-

Figure 10.3. Image from Cheap and good husbandry (London: W. Wilson, 1648) showing title page.

phy and sources to match the course focus or subject matter; students could also contribute to this stage of the assignment.[13] Similarly, the evaluation questions, to which students respond, could be readily revised to meet class objectives whether those are critical evaluation, contrast of primary and secondary sources, disciplinary history, production history, or physicality of the source. And finally, the outcome of the assignment need not be a presentation. Other possibilities are a multimedia project, a collaborative online wiki or bibliography, or even a traditional research paper.

CONCLUSION

Drawing on the expertise of all the collaborators, this active learning model was designed to engage undergraduates in both the history and relevance of science through the use of realia. Special collections' have the ability to humanize science, to inspire awe, and to bring history to life. By exploring the connections from past to present, the librarians are poised to continue collaboration in the sciences and to encourage the incorporation of special collections into the science curriculum.

APPENDIX 10.1
Bibliography—MCDB 1030 Plagues and People

Barbara Losoff
Science Library
4/7/2003

PLAGUE

Boccaccio, John. *The Decameron.* Philadelphia: J.P. Horn, 1928.

- Kredel's 1620 English translation; detailed description of the plague and conditions in the streets.

Russell, Alex. *The Natural History of Aleppo and Parts Adjacent.* London: A. Millar, 1756.

- Contains account of the plague at Aleppo.

Manuscript Bible leaf. Paris: early 13th century.

- Shows Job covered with boils and lying on a dung heap

Defoe, Daniel. *A Journal of the Plague Year.* 1665. Bloomfield, Conn.: Limited Editions Club, 1968.

- Fictional account of the plague in London told first hand; contains statistical information.

Smith, John Thomas. *The Cries of London: Exhibiting Several of the Itinerant Traders of the Ancient and Modern Times.* London: John Bowyer Nichols and Son, 1839.

- Illustrations of rat catchers and corpse bearers.

Chamberlayne, John. "Remarks upon the Plague at Copenhagen in the Year 1711." *Philosophical Transactions of the Royal Society,* v. 28 (1713), pgs. 279-281.

- Provides theories as to why the poor are more likely to die of plague (i.e. their "nasty manner of Living."

Schedel, Hartmann. *Nuremberg Chronicle.* Nuremberg: Anton Koberger, 1493.

- Illustrations of physical abnormalities and death.

Microscope

Hooke, Robert. Micrographia: or, Some physiological descriptions of minute bodies made by magnifying glasses. With observations and inquiries thereupon, 1665.

Gentleman's Magazine. London: Edw. Cave, vol. 13 (1743).

- Provides descriptions and preventative measures for a variety of ailments: influenza, plague, and consumption

Wall, J. "A Letter…concerning the Use of the Peruvian Bark in the Small Pox." *Philosophical Transactions of the Royal Society* v. 44 (1747), pgs. 583-595.

- Case studies of particular persons struck with small pox and treated with Peruvian Bark

Sahagun, Bernardino de. *Codice Florentino.* Mexico: Secretaria de Governacion, 1979. Facsimile edition of the Florentine Codex (16th century)

- contains drawings of people dying of small pox.

CONSUMPTION, INOCULATION AND SMALL POX:

Willich, A.F.M. *The Domestic Encyclopedia: or a Dictionary of Facts & Useful Knowledge.* Philadelphia:

Abraham Small, 1821. v. 1 & 2
- Includes entries for consumption and inoculation

Cole, Mary. *The Lady's Complete Guide; or Cookery in all it's Branches.* London: G. Kearsley, 1788.
- Information on consumption.

Cheap and Good Husbandry, 1648.

Cullen, William. *First Lines of the Practice of Physic for the Use of Students in the University of Edinburgh.* Philadelphia: Steiner and Cist, 1781.
- Accounts of plague and small pox, their prevention and cure.

Allen, John. *Synopsis Medicine, or, a Summary View of the Whole Practice of Physick.* 1749.
- Inoculation of small pox.

Montagu, Mary Wortley. *Letters of the Right Honourable Lady Mary Wortley Montagu.* London: T. Becket and P.A. De Hondt, 1763.
- Describes small pox inoculation practices in Turkey which Montagu later helped introduce in England.

French, John. *The Art of Distillation or a Treatise of the Choicest Spagriricall Preparations Performed by Way of Distillation.* London: E. Cotes, 1653.
- Describes distillation of plants, animals in an effort to combat plague, consumption.

Smith, Elisha. *The Botanic Physician, being a Compendium of the Practice of Medicine.* New York: Daniel Adee, 1844.
- Symptoms, diagnosis, and care of patients with small-pox and pulmonary consumption. Early medical illustrations.

Webster, Noah, et al. "Epidemics of Influenza in 1647, 1789-90 and 1807" *Contributions to Medical and Biological Research,* v.2, 1919.

Encyclopedia Britannica, 9th Ed. Philadelphia: J.M. Stoddart Co., 1875. v. 21, p. 415-424

Schizomycetes/Pasteur and anthrax

Term proposed by Nageli in 1857 to include all those minute organisms know as Bacteria, microbes, etc. Robert Koch 1870 proves that microorganisms cause infectious diseases by injecting anthrax spores into mice. Pasteur and Anthrax—1882 develops the first successful vaccine to prevent anthrax in animals.

Encyclopedia Britannica, 9th Ed. Philadelphia: J.M. Stoddart Co., 1875. v. 15, p. 315

Malaria

Marsh miasma or paludal poison, hill fever, jungle fever. The term malaria was introduced into English medical literature in 1827 by Macculloch. Deadly fevers have been recorded since the beginning of the written word. Quinine made from the bark of Cinohona tree in S. Am. Used more than 350 years ago to treat malaria.

Encyclopedia Britannica, 9th Ed. Philadelphia: J.M. Stoddart Co., 1875. v. 17, p. 63-68.

Anthrax

Records of anthrax go back to ancient times, supposedly the murrain of Exodus. Virgil mentions it, but alludes to anthrax as only a disease of cattle. Murrain is a term applied to extensive outbreaks of disease in cattle. One of the symptoms is boils, also known as woolsorter's disease.

Redi, Francesco. *Esperienze Intorno Alla Generazione Degl'Insetti Fatte da Francesco Redi.* Firenze: All'Insegna della Stella, 1668.
- Redi disproves the theory of spontaneous generation and introduces the scientific method.

NOTES

1. Deborah Hollis, "Special Collections Department Annual Report for Fiscal Year 2003-2004," University of Colorado, (2004):1.

2. Ann Schmiesing and Deborah Hollis, "The Role of Special Collections Departments in Humanities Undergraduate and Graduate Teaching: A Case Study," *portal: Libraries and the Academy* 2, no. 3 (2002): 465-480.

3. Michelle Visser, "Inviting the Rabble: Changing Approaches to Public Service and Access in Special Collections," *Public Services Quarterly* 1, no. 4 (10, 2003): 29-41.

4. Pablo Alvarez, "Introducing Rare Books into the Undergraduate Curriculum," *RBM: A Journal of Rare Books, Manuscripts, & Cultural Heritage* 7, no. 2 (2006): 99.

5. Julia Gardner and David Pavelich, "Teaching with Ephemera," *RBM: A Journal of Rare Books, Manuscripts, & Cultural Heritage* 9, no. 1 (Spring 2008): 88.

6. Jennifer Howard, "Special Collections as Laboratories," *The Chronicle of Higher Education The Wired Campus,* http://chronicle.com/blogPost/Special-Collections-as/8490/?sid=at&utm_source

7. See http://ucblibraries.colorado.edu/services/instruction/courses/mcdb.htm for more information.

8. Robert J. Stevens, "Cooperative Learning," in *Encyclopedia of Educational Psychology,* ed. Neil Salkind and Kristin Rasmussen (Los Angeles: Sage Publications, 2008): 1: 187.

9. See Julia Gardner and David Pavelich, "Teaching with Ephemera," *RBM: A Journal of Rare Books, Manuscripts, & Cultural Heritage* 9, no. 1 (Spring 2008): 86-92; and James Gerencser and Malinda Triller, "Hands-on Instruction in the Archives: Using Group Activities as an Engaging Way to Teach Undergraduates about Primary Sources," *Journal for the Society of North Carolina Archivists* 6, no. 2 (2009): 55-66.

10. Gardner and Pavelich, p. 92.

11. Schmiesing and Hollis, p. 466.

12. Shan Sutton and Lorrie Knight, "Beyond the Reading Room: Integrating Primary and Secondary Sources in the Library Classroom," *Journal of Academic Librarianship* 32, no. 3 (2006): 321.

13. Schmiesing and Hollis, p. 473.

More than Gold Leaf: Teaching Undergraduates in Capstone Courses about the Scholarly Use of Medieval Manuscripts

Julie Grob

As the University of Houston has embraced a more research-based curriculum in recent years, the needs of undergraduate students in upper level history courses have changed. Rather than viewing medieval manuscripts solely as examples of material culture that contextualize their study of the Middle Ages, our history students need to understand how scholars actively use medieval manuscripts in their research. However, in a field where primary sources are both fragile and extremely valuable, how does a special collections librarian convey to students the unique nature of research with original manuscripts? In this case study, I share the approach I used when redesigning the special collections visit for a medieval history capstone course, an approach which I believe would translate well to other research-oriented courses.

In 1998, the Boyer Commission on Educating Undergraduates in the Research University published the highly influential report "Reinventing Undergraduate Education: A Blueprint for America's Research Universities." One of its ten recommendations for undergraduate study is that "The final semester(s) should focus on a major project and utilize to the fullest the research and communication skills learned in the previous semesters..." in a course "that corresponds to the capstone of a building or the keystone of an arch."[1] The capstone course, now a common feature at universities, is a culminating course for the student's major and prepares her for graduate or professional work.

In 2007, the University of Houston History Department began requiring that their majors com-plete such a course prior to graduation. The development of seminars that would introduce students to the skills used by professional historians[2] reflected a broader movement that was occurring at the university. In 2008, UH unveiled a five-year campus-wide Quality Enhancement Plan (QEP) related to undergraduate research. The QEP is a required component of the reaffirmation of accreditation process for the Southern Association of Colleges and Schools.[3]

The adoption of capstone courses and the QEP-driven focus on research has helped to increase the number of faculty who are interested in exposing their students to special collections materials. In courses such as the English Department's "Introduction to Literary Studies" and "1771: Four Cities in One Year", students visit the Evans Room (our dedicated classroom) and conduct hands-on research with literary manuscripts and eighteenth century books. Other classes require students to come to Special Collections and work with original documents in archival collections, using primary sources to develop their research papers. However, these approaches are not feasible for students studying medieval history, art, or literature, as the Library's primary source materials are limited in number and too fragile to withstand extended handling.

Special Collections at the UH Libraries holds the largest collection of manuscripts in Houston—12 books and 8 individual leaves. Items in the Medieval and Renaissance Manuscripts Collection range from a 13th-century Paris Bible filled with historiated, zoomorphic, and decorated initials to a 15th-century Italian choral service book speculatively attributed to a seminary in Rome. Because the collection leans heavily towards devotional and theological works of the 14th and 15th centuries, Special Collections has supplemented these originals with high quality facsimiles that represent earlier centuries and secular topics. This collection is a popular teaching resource for faculty in the departments of Art, Art History, English, History, Modern and Classical Languages, and Music.

In 2007, Dr. Sally Vaughn, a scholar of medieval history, began redesigning several of her upper level courses as capstones. These courses included The Normans, The Crusades, and The Early Middle Ages. The latter course will be used as a representative example for this case study. Vaughn's 2009 syllabus opens by stating, "This class is a Capstone Seminar, which seeks to teach you both the substance of the class subject, The Early Middle Ages, and the professional methodology of historical research and writing." The major project for the course is the preparation and presentation to fellow students of a 10 page paper during a mock conference at the end of the semester. In addition to reading and discussing monographs about the early middle ages, students also read and discuss a book on performing research. They visit the Library twice for instruction sessions, one with the History Librarian on finding and evaluating database and web resources, and one with the Digital Projects and Instruction Librarian for Special Collections on original primary sources.

Dr. Vaughn had previously contacted me by e-mail in the spring of 2009 and asked if I would give a presentation to students in her Crusades course on "manuscript sources and their uses."[4] In my prior teaching with manuscripts, I had focused almost exclusively on showing students the physical aspects of the books in our collection and explaining how the books were produced. However, for a capstone course I needed to better align the special collections visit with her pedagogical goal of training students about the research methodologies of the professional historian. I decided to provide an abbreviated version of the traditional manuscript book "tour," while adding a discussion about where original manuscripts can be found, how print and digital facsimiles can supplement original manuscripts, and what a manuscript book can reveal about its origin and use to the scholar. The focus of the capstone course encouraged me to adapt my typical medieval manuscript class session to one that introduced information literacy skills for using manuscript sources.

By the time Vaughn brought her Early Middle Ages class to Special Collections in the fall of 2010, a new structure for the Special Collections class visit was fully established. Each three-hour visit now comprises three parts: a "tour" in which students view original medieval manuscripts and learn how they were produced, an unstructured period during which students can independently explore relevant facsimiles, and a group discussion about how scholars conduct research with manuscripts. An assessment quiz at the end of class helps to gauge how much the students learned about manuscript book production and the research methodology of the medieval studies scholar.

For the "tour" part of the class, I invite students to gather around two tables, one of which displays manuscripts and materials related to parchment and writing (e.g., animal skins, quills), and the other which displays manuscripts and materials related to illumination, decoration, and binding (gold leaf, a burnisher). As I go over the basics of manuscript production with the students, I point out as many marks of production as I can—prickings, guide letters, and the missed passage of a psalm that has been added in by the corrector. I make sure that every student has a chance to see the marks up close because they so powerfully convey not only the techniques used, but the human reality of manuscript production. I pepper my talk with questions such as "Who knows what parchment is made from?" and "Do you think that if you were a scribe you would ever make a mistake?" in order to engage students and encourage interactive discussion. I emphasize several overarching themes—that manuscript production happened in both monastic and secular environments, and that manuscripts were designed according to a set of conventions rather than created as imaginative works as art.

Following the "tour", students spend some time looking at facsimiles spread out on other tables, divided into Early Medieval and High Medieval groups. The facsimiles provide access to one-of-a-kind books such as the *Book of Kells* and the *Bury Bible*, and books that cover secular themes such as the amusements depicted in Alfonso X's *Book of Chess, Dice, and Draughts*. This unstructured time also gives students the chance to experience the books one on one as they were intended to be experienced. Additionally, I use this time to offer students a look at the decorations and miniatures in our Bible and Books of Hours, as only the professor and I handle the books directly during class. For most of my class visits in which students work with facsimiles of medieval books, I give them a worksheet to fill out that requires them to interact with and evaluate one particular facsimile. However, with the capstone courses, I prefer to give them a more unstructured time that segues into a short break, so they will be fresh for our discussion.

During the discussion, I lead students through five questions about how scholars use medieval manuscripts for research. I also encourage Dr. Vaughn to share tales of her own experiences doing research, which often involve trips to European libraries. These stories add a lively dimension to the discussion, and help students connect the rather generic research skills they are learning about to the reality of their professor's experiences.

For the first question, "what kinds of scholars use medieval manuscripts for their research?" I ask students to identify various disciplines in which scholars may consult manuscripts for research, and they usually respond energetically by calling out fields like history, religion, science, art history, and music. For the second question, "where can scholars find medieval manuscripts?" we discuss the dispersal of manuscripts around the world. Students are usually quick to understand that they would be more likely to find manuscripts in Europe than Texas! I also explain that some manuscripts are inaccessible because they remain in private hands. Because most manuscripts that would be referred to by undergraduate in their papers can be found through online search engines, I only touch briefly on the availability of printed bibliographies and union catalogs like WorldCat.

Following an explanation of how to find manuscripts in the UH Libraries catalog, we look at several catalogs of national libraries such as the British Library, *Bibliothèque Nationale de France,* and the Koninklijke Bibliotheek in the Netherlands. We also look at the websites of a few private libraries and museums, such as the Morgan Library, Getty Library, and Walters Art Gallery. Viewing these catalogs and websites with their specific access points teaches students how manuscripts are located and used by scholars. For example, the Manuscript search page on the British Library's website uses homegrown manuscript numbers, leading to a discussion of shelfmarks and how manuscripts are often classified differently than other books in a library.

When the discussion moves to the next question, which asks about alternatives to original manuscripts, we talk about print facsimiles, like those they looked at during the unstructured part of the class, and microfilm libraries like the Vatican Film Library at St. Louis University and the Hill Museum and Manuscript Library at St. John's University.

I read students a short excerpt from a 2000 article published in *Chronica,* the newsletter of the Medieval Association of the Pacific:

"Just a few years ago, medieval manuscripts, the most important source of our knowledge of the Middle Ages, were mostly inaccessible to the public and even to scholars. Fragile, unique, they were jealously kept protected by institutions and made available only to a few selected scholars. Today libraries around the world are working on complex digitization projects to make available their original manuscripts... expanding the breadth of scholarly research opportunities in what can only be called a revolution."[5]

This quote gives students a good understanding of what the digitization of manuscripts has meant for medieval scholars. I also show students several digital resources that are geared towards unadorned historical documents, rather than works like Books of Hours. The first is the Anglo-American Legal Tradition website, and the second is the Domesday Book.

For the fourth question I ask students what qualities make manuscripts different from other resources. Students are usually quick to point out that they are one of a kind, and expensive. I also share with them stories about manuscripts that have been split up, and how some manuscripts exist only as fragments or bindings for other books.

The final question of the discussion considers how researchers approach manuscripts for scholarly use. I open this up by asking students what skills scholars might need in order to study manuscripts. This leads them to do some critical analysis of manuscripts as sources. They invariably mention the need to read Latin or Western European languages, which gives me the opportunity to explain that medieval Latin is different from classical Latin, and that many words in medieval texts were abbreviated to save space. We also talk about the need for scholars to know paleography, codicology, and iconography in order to interpret medieval books. Familiarity with the standard parts of a book such as a Book

of Hours or the history of transmission of texts may also be important for medievalists. Finally we discuss provenance, or the history of ownership, and its importance in studying medieval manuscripts.

Because the Early Middle Ages capstone course contains an information literacy component, I felt that it was especially important to measure student learning after the class visit. Otherwise how could I know if students were really taking away an understanding of how scholars conduct research with medieval sources? To measure comprehension I developed an assessment quiz that I handed out at the end of class. (See Appendix 11.1). I have experimented with creating and refining assessment tools for several years, using SurveyMonkey surveys either delivered online or printed off and filled out at the end of class.

The Early Middle Ages assessment quiz includes a mix of multiple choice questions about manuscript production and open-ended questions about the resources and skills that scholars might need to study medieval manuscripts. Students' answers to the former demonstrated to me that not all were clear that both monks and secular scribes made manuscripts. Answers to the latter highlighted the points that students remembered most clearly, such as that scholars might need to know medieval Latin. As the class continues to be taught and assessed over multiple semesters, this data will become more useful.

The redesigned History capstone class visits with medieval manuscripts have led to more lively class sessions in which students engaged critically with the idea of not just enjoying the beauty of these objects, but using them as resources for understanding the Middle Ages. I believe the third part of the class visit, in particular—the discussion about where scholars find rare materials and how they work with them—could be adapted successfully for other capstone or research-intensive courses. Students studying the American women's movement might consider the fugitive nature of sources that were not collected by institutions focused on traditional male-dominated politics and history. Students studying a country like Cuba might learn about the difficulties scholars encounter attempting to travel there to conduct research in the National Archives, and how university libraries, particularly in Florida, are making digital collections available.

The medieval history instruction sessions were redesigned partly to address the limitations of teaching with fragile manuscripts. However, the new structure helps students think through the types of issues that researchers encounter in a way that could easily transfer to primary sources in other formats. By encouraging students to put themselves in the places of scholars working with rare and archival materials, special collections librarians can successfully introduce them to the skills employed by professional historians and academics across a variety of disciplines. [6]

APPENDIX 11.1
HIST 4395 Assessment

1. Manuscript books were made out of which of the following? (Choose one correct answer).
- ❑ Paper
- ❑ Papyrus
- ❑ Parchment

2. Manuscript books from the early middle ages (before 1000 A.D.) would have been made by which of the following? (Select all that apply).
- ❑ Monks
- ❑ Secular scribes
- ❑ Printers

3. Scholars from which of the following disciplines would be likely to study medieval manuscripts? (Select all that apply).
- ❑ History
- ❑ Art history
- ❑ History of science
- ❑ Religious studies
- ❑ Music
- ❑ Other (please specify)

4. What other resources might a scholar use to study medieval manuscripts, other than the original manuscripts?

5. What skill(s) might a scholar need in order to successfully conduct research with medieval manuscripts?

6. Is there anything related to manuscripts that you would have liked to learn more about during the class visit?

NOTES

1. Boyer Commission on Educating Undergraduates in the Research University. *Reinventing Undergraduate Education: A Blueprint for America's Research Universities*: 27-28. Boyer Commission on Educating Undergraduates in the Research University, Room 310, Administration Bldg., State University of New York, Stony Brook, NY 11794-0701,1998. http://naples.cc.sunysb.edu/Pres/boyer.nsf/

2. "Capstone Courses and the Honors Thesis," Department of History, University of Houston, accessed August 16, 2010, http://www.class.uh.edu/hist/undergrad_honorsthesis.asp

3. University of Houston. *Discovery-Based Learning: Transforming the Undergraduate Experience through Research: the University of Houston Quality Enhancement Plan.* Houston, Tex.: University of Houston, [2008].

4. Sally Vaughn, e-mail message to author, January 9, 2009.

5. Medieval Association of the Pacific. "Electronic Resources for Medieval Studies," *Chronica* 59 (2000): 1. http://www.cmrs.ucla.edu/map/Chronica/Chronica2000.pdf

6. The author would like to thank her colleague Valerie Prilop and former colleague Rebecca Russell for their invaluable reading of an earlier draft of this chapter.

Making It Personal: Engaging Students with Their University

Ellen D. Swain

National higher education associations in recent years have emphasized the value of "original research" in undergraduate pedagogy, which in turn has positioned university archives' efforts to promote the use of primary sources in the classroom. At the University of Illinois at Urbana-Champaign (UIUC), this focus on undergraduates and primary sources has translated into rich and imaginative research using materials at the University Archives' Student Life and Culture Archival Program (SLC Archives). By partnering with two campus initiatives, the Ethnography of the University Initiative (EUI) and the undergraduate rhetoric E-book project, the SLC Archives has introduced Illinois students to archival research in powerful ways.

A primary goal of any academic archives is to support the teaching mission of the university. Anna Allison, in her 2005 study of undergraduate instruction at ARL member special collections departments, found that ninety-six per cent of her survey participants were involved in some form of archival instruction.[1] The SLC Archives too has worked to position itself as a relevant and useful resource for undergraduate education on campus. It has not been easy. Staff vacancies, the absence of a target user group, and the remote location of the SLC Archives were initial barriers to use in the late 1990s. With the advent of a unique, investigative initiative on "the University" and new opportunities to work creatively with the undergraduate rhetoric program, the SLC Archives has become a valued partner in teaching. This essay will discuss its role in these campus projects and outline some

of its struggles, solutions and successes in inspiring and enabling students to conduct primary research in meaningful ways.

THE STUDENT LIFE AND CULTURE ARCHIVAL PROGRAM (SLC ARCHIVES)

Established in 1989 with an endowment from the Stewart S. Howe Foundation, the SLC Archives is a nationally unique program, administered under the University Archives, with a two-fold mission: to document fraternity and sorority life in the United States and student life and experience with a particular emphasis on Illinois. Stewart S. Howe, UI alumnus '28 and founder of a national fraternity public relations service, not only provided the endowment which supports a full-time archivist, two graduate assistants, and all programming activities, but also donated his massive collection of fraternity histories, journals, publication files and other student life historical materials, now at the center of what has become a renowned repository for the study of national fraternity and sorority umbrella organizations, publishers' personal papers, and social and honor societies.

Of equal importance is the SLC Archives' mandate to document student experience at Illinois, including activities of individual students and alumni, student organizations, student related campus departments, and administrators. Diaries, scrapbooks, letters home, oral histories, photographs, ephemera, course work, publications, as well as official reports, correspondence and files from administrative and academic departments bring student culture to life from the early years of the university in the 1860s to the digital culture of the 2010s.

These rich and diverse resources had a limited campus audience in the 1990s. For two years prior to the author's arrival in 1999, the SLC archivist position was vacant or was filled by temporary staff and the Program had lost contact with campus units, faculty and student organizations. Through word of mouth and networking efforts, the SLC Archives slowly began to rebuild a campus user base. Two programs were most responsible for this resurgence in use: the Ethnography of the University Initiative (EUI) and the undergraduate rhetoric program.

ETHNOGRAPHY OF THE UNIVERSITY INITIATIVE (EUI)

Most university archives document student life and culture as part of their mission. The fact that the SLC Archives is a one-of-a-kind research center devoted specifically to the study of student experience made it a perfect collaborator with a newly established campus initiative called the EUI. Founded in 2002 by UIUC Anthropology professors Nancy Abelmann and William Kelleher as a year-long study initiative through the University's Center for Advanced Study, the EUI has developed into an interdisciplinary, multi-campus endeavor in which classes from a wide array of disciplines use ethnographic methodology to explore and question issues relating to the local University community and environment.[2]

Each semester (starting in 2003), six to eight EUI affiliated courses offer students the opportunity to explore the university in disciplines as diverse as anthropology, English, kinesiology, and urban planning."[3] At its foundation is the idea that students ought to be both learners and producers of knowledge and that, regardless of major or discipline, undergraduates can and should take an active role in the research mission of the university. EUI student projects reflect a wide array of student inquiry which investigates student culture, the institutional

impact of the university on the local community, and the university's social structure in terms of race, ethnicity, class and gender.[4]

Utilizing qualitative methods, students in EUI-affiliated courses also create web-based ethnographic inquiry pages with links to their field notes, interviews, maps and other critical documents which, with the student's permission, are deposited in the University's digital repository IDEALS (Illinois Digital Environment for Access to Learning and Scholarship) for future students, and others, to build upon or contest.[5] Because "IDEALS preserves student created documents related to the process of their research, the EUI IDEALS archive serves as a unique and publically accessible documentation of student learning."[6] This "online archives" is a critical component of EUI and an exciting resource for the SLC Archives researchers.

ARCHIVES WORK WITH EUI

The SLC Archives has had an early role in EUI. The author served on the initial study group for the project and currently serves on the internal advisory board. She works closely with EUI faculty to map out resources for individual classes, provide instruction on archival use and research, and assist with planning class assignments and papers. In addition, she hosts instruction sessions with classes (both in the Archives and in the classroom) and works one on one with individual students. Each spring, she gives a presentation at the annual EUI faculty development seminar about Archives' holdings and suggests possible archival sources for each individual EUI class proposal.

Some inquiries are well suited for archives holdings. For example, using archival sources, students in an EUI anthropology class chose a past student with whom the EUI student had something in common (similar background or interests) and compared and contrasted his/her student experience with that of the alumnus/a. Other examples include an EUI English class studying current students' extracurricular writing practices that examined past student diaries and correspondence, and EUI Natural Resources students investigated student use of the Quad over time.

THE UNDERGRADUATE RHETORIC PROGRAM AND E-BOOK PROJECT

The undergraduate rhetoric program and EUI have a close relationship. Two directors of undergraduate rhetoric have served as EUI directors and English and rhetoric courses heavily participate in the EUI program. The SLC Archives' involvement with rhetoric began shortly before EUI's establishment in 2002. The program invited the author to present at its instructor workshops, and through word of mouth and some networking, the SLC Archives soon became a popular resource and class destination. Archives use statistics began to climb and by 2003 undergraduate use had tripled in only three years. By the end of the decade, use statistics had broken all records as part of a general trend strongly supported by rhetoric and EUI class instruction sessions and student research visits.

As with EUI classes, the author meets with instructors who contact her to identify sources for the specific assignment and tailors the instruction session accordingly. Sessions include logistical information, instruction on search strategies using the archives' online database and digital resources, and on primary source research methods. All instruction sessions, whether in the SLC Archives or the classroom, include time for students to ask questions and examine an array of primary sources related to the assignment.[7] Course assignments include traditional research papers, short essays analyzing primary sources, and onsite exercises in which students evaluate a primary source during the class visit. One instructor routinely asks students to create a time capsule composed of items that best represent their college experiences. Her classes explore materials that past students have saved and later students deposit their essays in the SLC Archives.[8]

In 2008-2009, inspired by her experiences with EUI as both co-director and participating faculty member, undergraduate rhetoric director Catherine Prendergast revolutionized the rhetoric curriculum by authoring and instituting an electronic textbook which, like EUI, focuses on the UI as student laboratory and subject of investigation. Prendergast explains that the rhetoric program needed a book "sculpted" to its particular student body; one that assumed students had a high degree of formal knowledge about writing but little research and analytical skills.[9] Instituted in fall semester 2009, Ebook writing assignments focus on students' experience and exploration of their surrounding environment. Features include embedded video clips of faculty speaking on writing from a number of perspectives which are integrated into chapters on writing, critical analysis and research, primary sources, and citation methods.

Prendergast believes that EUI started her "interest in mining the archives as a treasure trove." The Ebook chapter on primary sources includes writing exercises which draw on several SLC Archives items embedded in the text and assignments requiring students to conduct research in the archives. Since all newly hired instructors are required to use the Ebook in their first year of teaching and nearly 1,000 students use the book each fall, the SLC Archives has been overwhelmed with use—a good problem to have but a problem no less.[10]

SUCCESSES, STRUGGLES AND SOLUTIONS

Both EUI and the freshman rhetoric program have provided the Archives with wonderful opportunities to connect with students from a wide range of majors and disciplines and to engage first year students in archival research early in their college careers. Certainly, there have been struggles. Students can be intimidated by archival research which requires a different set of skills than other types of inquiry. Staff members try to relieve student reservations by explaining procedures in detail and describing how the search room operates. A less flexible issue is the remote location of the Archives Research Center (ARC), where the SLC Archives is housed, and the fact that ARC and the University Archives are in separate locations and have limited hours.

However, two of the biggest obstacles facing the Archives' instruction efforts have been managing the large number of students that visit the Archives and working with unprepared students who have had little instruction on using archives. Issues associated with heavy use are well-documented by others, including wear and tear on archival materials, misplacement of materials, and high demands on limited staff time.[11] Students whose classes did not attend an instruction session and are clueless about primary source research are another problem. The SLC Archives has addressed these issues by creating resources to assist instructors with primary source instruction prior to class visits or in some cases in place of them. In addition, the Archives' primary source tutorial, created using materials from its holdings, defines a primary source, provides information about using the Archives' online database, and walks the student through an exercise on analyzing a primary source.[12] Instructors are encouraged to assign the tutorial to students before their class visit or in place of it if necessary. The SLC Archives also continues to digitize heavily used resources including oral histories and has created an elaborate set of research guides on UIUC in the Cold War era in response to strong interest in subjects during this period such as Illinois' pioneering 1968 affirmative action program.[13]

Communication among archives and rhetoric program and EUI staff has been key to serving the needs of all involved. For instance, in a spring 2010 meeting with rhetoric program, library, and archives staff, archivists expressed concerns that students were not coming to the archives prepared with "researchable" questions and weren't knowledgeable about how to search for materials. Rhetoric staff listened and two substantial discoveries came from this meeting. Rhetoric and archives staff discovered that inquiries that archives staff considered answerable (sources existed that supported the question) were not necessarily the questions rhetoric instructors wanted students to ask. Rhetoric staff wanted students to run into dead-ends, reformulate questions, and think about how to find new answers. Secondly, many instructors were not preparing students effectively to use the archives. They needed to spend more time in class working on search strategies and primary source instruction with their students.

Impressively, rhetoric staff has crafted solutions to these problems by "building in" an information literacy component to the Ebook's primary source chapter that provides information about primary sources and the archives and requires all instructors to dedicate class time to doing practice searches on the archives online database. The quality of instructors' engagement with students will determine in large part how well students understand and feel comfortable with archival research. In addition, the rhetoric program successfully requested funding from campus to outfit four rhetoric classrooms with multiple LCD screens, projectors, and computers that will enable students as a class and individually to do multiple searches on the archives' database simultaneously. Prendergast says that the need to partner with librarians and archivists drove the development of this information literacy component of their teaching. This adaption has meant that students are more prepared when they come to the archives and feel comfortable using our sources.

Through our partnerships with the EUI and the rhetoric program, the SLC Archives has connected students to the history of *their* university in personal and meaningful ways. We look forward to continuing and building on these important collaborations which are enabling students to critically analyze their surroundings through past and present lens.

NOTES

1. Anna Elise Allison, *Connecting Undergraduates with Primary Sources: A Study of Undergraduate Instruction in Archives, Manuscripts, and Special Collections* (master's thesis, School of Information and Library Science of the University of North Carolina at Chapel Hill, 2005): 26. Available online at: http://etd.ils.unc.edu/dspace/bitstream/1901/158/1/annaallison.pdf [Accessed by the author, March 6, 2011].

2. See EUI web site at: http://www.eui.illinois.edu/ [Accessed by the author , March 7, 2011]

3. EUI website, "EUI Story,": http://www.eui.illinois.edu/ ADD ADDRESS[Accessed by the author , March 7, 2011]

4. See EUI web site: http://www.eui.illinois.edu/ [Accessed by the author on March 7, 2011]; Ellen D. Swain, "Ethnography of the University Initiative (EUI): A New Approach to University History and Archival Research," paper given at the International Council on Archives, Section on University and Research Institution Archives Conference 2007: 13-17 August, Dundee Scotland.; Students also present their research at a bi-annual EUI student research conference which includes poster sessions and panel presentations and discussion.

5. Gina Hunter, Nancy Adelman, Timothy Reese Cain, Tim McDonough, and Catherine Prendergast, Interrogating the University, One Archival Entry at a Time," *Change* 40, no. 5 (September/October 2008): 42. IDEALS website: https://www.ideals.illinois.edu/handle/2142/755 [Accessed by the author on March 7, 2011]

6. EUI web site, "Quick Facts":http://www.eui.illinois. edu/about_quick_facts.html [Accessed by the author, March 7, 2011; See also Sarah L. Shreeves, "Student Research on the University, in the Archives, and in the IR." An Age of Discovery: Distinctive Collections in the Digital Age–ARL-CNI Fall Forum. Washington, D.C. October 16, 2009.

7. For classroom instruction sessions, the author uses copies or duplicates of primary sources as examples.

8. Another instructor, whose EUI rhetoric class explored 1960s student protests on campus, re-enacted a protest march to the UI president's house (which is next door to the archives) as part of the class visit to the archives to examine materials concerning the topic.

9. The Ebook was attractive also because the technology was available and the text could be easily changed from year to year and students' writing assignments and space can be shared and discussed, similar to a social network setting. Furthermore, using local source material was not only more meaningful but permissions for use were much cheaper than other materials. Interview with Catherine L. Prendergast, March 8, 2011.

10. 965 students used the book in fall 2010. Interview with Catherine L. Prendergast, March 8, 2011.

11. See Anna Elise Allison, *Connecting Undergraduates with Primary Sources*, 42.

12. See: http://www.library.illinois.edu/village/primarysource/index.htm [Accessed by the author, March 7, 2011.]

13. See: http://www.library.illinois.edu/archives/slc/researchguides/coldwar/ and http://www.library.illinois.edu/archives/slc/researchguides/ [Accessed by the author, March 7, 2011.]

Teaching Research and Learning Skills with Primary Sources: Three Modules

Ryan Bean and Linnea M. Anderson

The Archives and Special Collections (ASC) department of the University of Minnesota Libraries uses primary sources to teach research skills and learning strategies for finding, evaluating, and using information. The department's collective experience teaching college students about archives and research over the years reveals a key lesson on what resonates with them: experiencing history and historical research "up close" through working with actual primary sources, letting the documents speak for themselves, is much more effective than listening to staff presentations *about* archival materials. Increasing demand for class sessions posed the challenge of continuing to create a meaningful educational experience with primary sources that was based on this strategy but worked for much larger groups of students. ASC leveraged the opportunity created by developments in instructional and information literacy goals at the university to revise existing teaching methods and develop new tools, while maintaining an authentic and engaging experience with primary sources. Staff collaborated to develop three class modules in which students engage in a hands-on exploration and analysis of a set of primary sources, take part in demonstration/discussion sessions with curators, and attend an orientation. These are designed to make history immediate and personal, spark students' interest in primary sources and build critical thinking skills that they can apply to all sources. The modules are flexible enough to work for a variety of disciplines and skill levels and can be used alone or in combination with each other to form a "tool kit" for teaching with primary sources.

Between 2005-2008, campus-wide, University Libraries and departmental initiatives emphasized information literacy, student learning outcomes, instructional support, interdisciplinary projects, and awareness of learning styles. This created an ideal environment for promoting the use of primary sources for instruction and fulfilling a long-standing departmental goal to better integrate collections into the curriculum. In addition, these initiatives made available training and resources that helped ASC identify the need to more consistently and intentionally *deliver key messages and develop skills* and to think more deliberately about pedagogy and outcomes.

Concurrently, a rapid rise in the enrollment of a core undergraduate history course, "How to do History," created increased demand for teaching with primary sources. ASC had been using archival material to prepare small sessions of the class to write their required senior paper by developing archival research skills and exposing the students to primary sources. When the course became a requirement for all undergraduate history majors, enrollment more than doubled. This challenged ASC to revise existing instructional methods for the class and to be more systematic about teaching, while at the same time maintaining the ability to expose students to primary sources in a meaningful way. It was also viewed as a chance to fill a long-recognized need for reusable tools to make teaching and working with faculty more effective and efficient. Staff analyzed and refined existing teaching methods, with learning styles, learning outcomes and information literacy in mind. They also sought input from faculty teaching the course and incorporated ideas gathered from staff training and other resources. The result was a program of three related instructional modules designed to attract interest, convey key ideas about primary sources, introduce archival theory and practice, and develop learning and research skills.

MODULE ONE, ARCHIVAL CASE STUDY

The Archival Case Study is a short discussion and demonstration session with a curator. The two most common topics are acquisition and the physical characteristics of primary sources. These prepare students to think critically about primary sources and to understand how the perspectives and resources of record creators and collectors influence the form and content of sources.

Conversations about acquisition demystify a topic that most students had not previously considered. A curator shares stories of how collections are donated, purchased, discovered, and even rescued or hidden. He or she describes efforts to secure donations by working with individuals, organizations, and communities to earn their trust (particularly when working with historically disenfranchised groups) and to become the caretaker of their heritage. Through these stories of how primary sources come to the archives, students discover how personal, political, social, and economic issues affect collecting and learn that a collection may provide just one perspective on a topic or may not contain all the information they need. The session also introduces the issues of how collecting and the availability of documentation affect research.

The other topic used for the Archival Case Study is the physical characteristics of primary sources. Students look beyond the information on the page to uncover meaning in the materials and processes used to create a document, its condition, and its annotations or markings. The learning objective of

this session is the importance of understanding the historical context of primary sources and how that can be revealed through their physical characteristics as well as their informational content.

In one version of the case study, students explore a variety of document formats and are encouraged to speculate about the meaning of physical characteristics. Discussion includes such topics as: why a particular paper was chosen for printing a poster, the design of letterhead or printed forms, deciphering annotations and marginalia, comparing communication technologies, and the implications of obsolete formats. Another physical characteristics case study focuses on forgeries, forgers, and their affect on the historical narrative. In this session, a curator shares stories about forgeries and students learn about the printing process, make sample prints, and then examine the difference between their forgeries and originals under a digital microscope or loupe.

Module one uses experimentation, visual analysis, and an informal, conversational style to introduce concepts and issues about primary sources. If understanding the nature of archives is the teaching goal, it is able to stand on its own. It also introduces many of the concepts that are addressed in modules two and three creating familiarity with the variety of terms, concepts, and procedures found when doing archival research. Both case studies are designed to get students to realize that primary sources have meaning beyond their informational content. They also learn that that research involves understanding the historical context of a source and that evaluation and authentication are part of the research process.

MODULE TWO, ARCHIVES ORIENTATION

Module two is an orientation that uses a building tour combined with a question and answer session to introduce students to a number of key points about the ASC department, archival practices, and primary source research. They find out about procedures that are often very different from what they are used to in a regular library setting or when doing research online. The walking tour helps to break down some of the barriers students may experience when navigating the facility and using unfamiliar procedures. Presenting policies and procedures through a tour also engages the students so that they ask more questions and acquire more information.

By viewing everything from loading docks, to processing workrooms, and storage areas, they also learn that preserving primary sources takes resources, effort, and specialized knowledge. This tempers expectations and builds understanding concerning policies and procedures. When the students go eight stories underground and walk through the climate-controlled storage facility, lovingly called "the caverns," which is two football fields in length, they see the large volume of primary sources in ASC available for research. The tour visually teaches students that using primary sources can be time-intensive and that making an appointment with an archivist to discuss their project and doing some background research on their topic will save time and makes their research more manageable. It is also a visual reminder for 21st century college students that not all information is online.

Module two builds familiarity and logistical competencies needed to overcome a major barrier preventing students from using primary sources: namely, unease with and ignorance of archival policies and procedures, collections and facilities. The orientation enables students to begin to visualize themselves as researchers who will use primary sources.

MODULE THREE, HANDS-ON EXERCISE WITH PRIMARY SOURCE DOCUMENTS

Module three, a hands-on exploration of a set of primary source documents and small group discussion, is the core of the "How to do History" experience in the archives. This module is designed to develop critical thinking skills for analyzing, interpreting, and connecting information.

The presentation style, topics and documents used, discussion questions, and varied learning activities help to make the hands-on exercise interpersonal, relevant, and appealing. They also create enthusiasm about using primary sources for research. When developing the class, staff chose primary sources that reflect an accessible or timely topic, have a "hook" that will attract the attention of undergraduates, and form part of an interesting or unusual narrative. Using visual sources, such as posters and photographs, also helps attract the students' attention. In addition, documents that are annotated, censored or edited or that reflect the perspectives and prejudices of their creators help get the message to students that they need to critically evaluate their sources.

To save time during class, ASC staff shares a list of topics and related secondary readings with the instructor prior to the visit. The students form groups of 6 to 8, based on interest in a particular topic. The reading—ideally, based on research using the same records that the students will use in class—creates a basic understanding and knowledge base for interpreting the material.

During the hands-on exercise, the students in each small group work in pairs with a pre-selected box. Each pair starts with a flagged item in their box, but browsing is encouraged. They complete a document analysis worksheet (Appendix 13.1) that asks a series of questions intended to promote careful reading and critical thinking. Staff also engages students with questions as needed. Examples of questions asked by the worksheet and staff are:

- Who created the documents and why?
- What do the sources tell you about their creator? (Look for evidence of document creator's, priorities, corporate culture, personal biases, etc)
- What patterns, recurring themes or topics are present?

- Do the records tell the entire story?
- What information is missing and what else might you need to know?
- What research projects can you do with these sources?
- What research questions do they pose?

Next, led by staff, students share their responses from the worksheet and discuss how each item used in the exercise holds a piece of the story, creating a group "a-ha!" moment. This teaches them that the big picture is uncovered through carefully reading and thinking critically about the sources, being open to what they uncover, connecting disparate pieces of information, and even asking what information might be missing. When the group members disagree about which documents are significant or interesting or when they compare their interpretation of the documents to the pre-class reading, it helps them understand that primary sources may be subject to many different interpretations. Staff members also encourage students to use their sometimes strong reactions to documents that reveal a bias to think more deeply about the context of the documents and to form possible research questions based on them.

Modules One and Two are an effective lead-in for Module Three, but it is also effective on its own. Though at least an hour is preferable for the hands-on document exercise, it has been used for everything from a brief exploration and discussion of document types to multi-day research projects. Some classes use it as the launching point of a semester-long group or individual project that culminates in a presentation, paper, or exhibit. It has frequently been used in graduate classes, with documents tailored to the specific focus of the class or research interests of the students and, with more time available, for exploration and conversation with the curator. In addition, a single staff person can present the concepts from the hands-on exercise to a large group by projecting scans of documents that reflect various themes and issues and engaging the group in discussion and analysis.

Module Three uses conversation to expose students to key elements of the archival research process: evaluating and connecting primary sources and developing good research questions. Using unfamiliar and varied resources gets students out of their information "comfort zone" and encourages them to think about sources in new ways. Questions posed by staff and the worksheet encourage the students to dig deeper and ask questions of the sources they encounter. Intellectually linking the items to each other and to the secondary reading builds awareness the role of perspective, interpretation and narrative. These elements of the hands-on exercise foster skills and knowledge to help the students develop their own informed interpretations of history based on evidence.

SUMMARY

The work done to develop the "How to do History" class has created an adaptable model for using primary sources to teach groups that vary in terms of academic discipline, size, age, and skill level. It has also created a set of scalable and re-purposeable teaching modules. The orientation, discussion and demonstration session and hands-on exercise can be used on their own or in combination. The amount of time needed to complete them is flexible. Though an academic setting facilitates this kind of instruction with primary sources, the model also applies to archives at museums, historical societies, historic sites and other institutions. The three modules can also be adjusted (based on the topic, rarity of material, language of material, or forms of material available) for use by younger middle or high school age scholars. They have already been used for classes in a variety of disciplines including sociology, American studies, literature, social work, anthropology, design, the arts, and public history as well as for groups of adult learners. The success of the modules is due to a number of factors, including timely implementation and relevance to institutional goals, varied and engaging activities, adaptable and reusable modules, and skills and concepts that are relevant to what the students need to accomplish.

LESSONS LEARNED AND NEXT STEPS

ASC work with the "How to do History" course presents a model for using primary sources to teach research and learning strategies. Faculty and student responses, including positive, post-class student assessments, indicate the teaching modules' ability to interest students, convey key concepts and develop skills. Over three years, we have consistently refined our approach learning valuable lessons along the way.

First, be responsive to the needs of different learning styles. By using varied and engaging activities we are able to accommodate all learning styles. This ensures that at some point all students have the opportunity to have a meaningful exposure to archival research which helps to demystify the process. Secondly, by taking cues from institutional initiatives, we were able to focus our approach and tap into a large amount of expert content. Furthermore, by tying many of our efforts to the revamped Student Learning Outcomes we were freed from having to justify using a particular approach. We identified that the three modules develop the student's ability to *"locate and critically evaluate information" and "master a body of knowledge and mode of inquiry" and "understand diverse philosophies and cultures."* Using this language can be a tool when communicating the objectives of the modules to faculty.

The third lesson learned was the need to be flexible. The reality of accommodating 60 to 80 students while maintaining our standards in regards to content covered seemed nearly impossible. However, once we analyzed what we wanted to cover, and the limitations of time and space, the module idea became apparent. Now, ASC is better able to mix and match our content, honoring the goals of the instructor while not having to compromise on the content we felt was key to preparing the students to use archives.

The fourth lesson was to be intentional. This lesson encompasses all other lessons. We intentionally set out to discover a win-win situation where we could meet the goals of the faculty, students and archives staff. We were immersed in an environment emphasizing learning styles, student learning outcomes and information literacy. We intentionally sought to identify areas where our class addressed these themes. Then we incorporated this language both internally and externally as we planned and promoted the class. Additionally as we learned more about these areas, we reflected on the content and found ways to strengthen our teaching modules. For instance, the goal of promoting information literacy informed both the worksheet and the use of a variety of content types in module three.

We already have plans on how to expand our success with "How to do History." We intend to create online versions of our instructional modules, in particular creating more content focusing on the logistical aspects of archival research. By creating this content, we hope to better use the limited amount of "face time" we have with the students as well as integrate the information into the instructor's class web site and library course page for the class. One other area we are investing in is systematic assessment. We know anecdotally that the archives visit is a high point of the class, and that the students are better able to articulate both appropriate research topics and agendas. However, we do not have hard data on what the students gain from the modules. We want to assess students' understanding of primary sources before and immediately after class, as well as long-term outcomes at the end of the senior paper course.

ACKNOWLEDGEMENTS

The authors wish to give thanks to David Klaassen, whose knowledge of and love for archives and special collections nurtured the How to do History *course. His guidance and expertise have helped make the class into the dynamic offering it is today*

APPENDIX 13.1

COLLECTION ANALYSIS WORKSHEET

UNIVERSITY OF MINNESOTA
LIBRARIES

Names

_____

_____

Part I: Thinking Questions

Use this general set of thinking questions to ground group overall discussions.

1. From whose viewpoint are we seeing or reading or hearing? From what angle or perspective?
2. How do we know when we know? What's the evidence, and how reliable is it?
3. How are things, events or people connected to each other? What is the cause and what is the effect? How do they fit?
4. So what? What does it matter? What does it all mean?

-Habits of Mind, adapted from Deborah Meier

Part II: Questions for use with an individual item or items where appropriate.
Complete with your Partner(s)

1.	Item Information:
	1. When and where were these items created? How do you know?
	2. For what audience or purpose do you think these items were created? Is there a bias?
	3. What evidence in the items helps you know why they were created?
	4. List three pieces of information you've learned from the items that you think are important.

APPENDIX 13.1

COLLECTION ANALYSIS WORKSHEET   PAGE 2, CONTINUED

2.	**Unique physical characteristics of the item: (e.g.** Handwritten, typed, stamped, seals, notations, letterhead, material, etc)

Part III: Questions for discussion with all table members and group leader.

3.	**Questions:**
	1. How do the items that you examined relate to selected reading?
	2. What topics or questions might these items help answer?
	3. Can you form a research question from this material? What is your question?
	4. What, if any, information is missing?
	5. Some questions that came up were…………..

*Adapted from National Archives and Records Administration worksheet. 2/2008. L. Hendrickson. (revised 2/2009 R. Bean)   http://www.archives.gov/education/lessons/worksheets/

Teaching Digital History through the University Archives: The Case of *Nebraska U: A Collaborative History*

Peterson Brink, Mary Ellen Ducey, Andrew Jewell, and Douglas Seefeldt

The idea for *Nebraska U: A Collaborative History* emerged in the Archives & Special Collections of the University of Nebraska-Lincoln Libraries (UNL) in response to a desire to expose our collections to a broader audience. We knew, as every archives staff knows, that we held innumerable treasures in our collections that were not fully appreciated by our audience. Simultaneously, we felt that our university's student body was under-exposed to primary research in a professional archive, and we looked for an opportunity to bring more students into active engagement with the materials. A digital project that involved undergraduate students would potentially accomplish both of these goals: students would personally work with collections and learn more about the benefits of archival research through use of the materials in potentially compelling interpretative projects, and the online world would be able to discover our collections digitally.

WHAT IS *NEBRASKA U*?

Nebraska U: A Collaborative History (http://unlhistory.unl.edu) is an effort to help prioritize, digitize, and contextualize materials held within the University Archives in the UNL Libraries. The site is currently imagined as a combination of an access point for digitized University history materials (multimedia and texts) and a series of student-driven research projects with focused presentations on select subjects, which build upon and link to transcribed texts, scanned images, and other digital derivatives

of archival material. Such a site is a unique resource for the many researchers, scholars, and members of the public interested in the history of the University of Nebraska, and it provides excellent visibility for materials in the Archives.

An important part aspect of the project's design is the way it serves as outreach to the campus and, specifically, its use as a pedagogical tool. Kenneth Price, Professor of English, and his students were the first collaborators on the project in his fall 2005 class "Electronic Texts: Theory and Practice." As part of the course, students selected a topic from several suggested to them, did research in the Archives, selected materials for digitization, scanned images and/or encoded texts, and wrote essays contextualizing their material. In the years since this initial collaboration, many students have continued to contribute to the site, both via classrooms and the University's Undergraduate Creative Activities and Research Experiences (UCARE) program.[1] The most significant collaboration in the past few years has been with Douglas Seefeldt's "Digital History" course. Undergraduate students in that course were assigned a *Nebraska U* project, which means they had to select a topic relevant to the history of the University of Nebraska, research that topic in the Archives, prepare or obtain digital surrogates of selected primary materials, and then construct a project analyzing and synthesizing those materials for web publication. At writing, there are 28 student projects from the spring 2008 and fall 2009 semesters published online as part of this program covering a wide range of topics, including the history of the marching band, the University's response to the Ku Klux Klan in the 1920s, the emergence of the Chicano Studies program, and the scandal of the 1912 Yearbook recall.

STRATEGIES

Our experience building *Nebraska U* in the past few years has taught us much about the best way to efficiently and effectively work with student collaborators. One thing we've learned is that a general introduction to the Archives and how to use materials is essential to the success of the project, both for the students and the Archives staff. This initial training session leads to the opportunity for staff to get to know individual students, to become involved in the research, and to provide a wide variety of records

and collections for use. It was very important that the right information is provided during this initial training. We shifted from providing a brief tour of the collections and resources we felt would elicit student interest to explaining to students how to use collections, what they would need to do to use the collections, how we run the department, and what kind of care and handling would be required for the use of the materials. This is what Elizabeth Yakel and Deborah A. Torres define as "archival intelligence: the researcher's knowledge of archival principles, practices, and institutions, such as the reasons underlying archival rules and procedures."[2] This initial training session is followed up by several other interactions with the students once they have identified their topics, including one-on-one reference interviews, training sessions on digitization best practices, and classroom visits to discuss and

Figure 14.1. A screenshot from Jessica Dussault's Nebraska U project "The Pride of All Nebraska: A Band's Growth from the Military Tradition" at http://unlhistory.unl.edu/exhibits/show/nebraskaband.

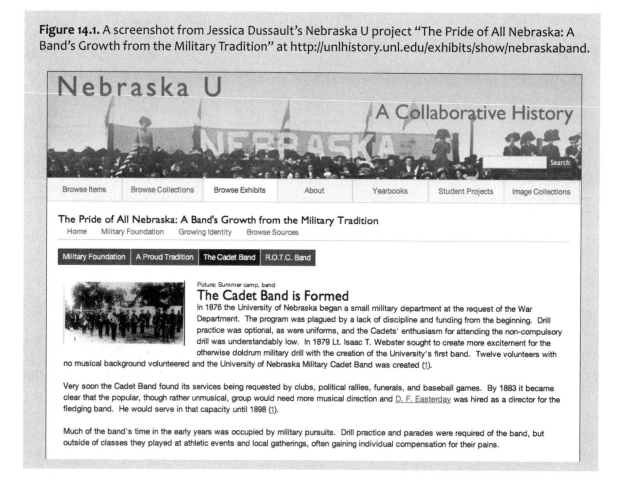

troubleshoot issues the students have during the creation of their online projects.

In the classroom, the students were prepared for building *Nebraska U* projects by studying relevant materials on the history of computing, digital history theory and practice, and university history. Students were charged with the task of exploring the methods of digital history by assessing the value of digital media tools and environments to historical inquiry and communication. Historians Daniel J. Cohen and Roy Rosenzweig identify seven potential contributions of digital media and networks to the historian's task: "capacity, accessibility, flexibility, diversity, manipulability, interactivity, and hypertextuality (nonlinearity)."[3] Students from a variety of majors including, advertising, anthropology, cultural studies, English, film studies, history, marketing, political science, and psychology took up the challenge and read, thought, wrote, and discussed a wide range of new and old facets of the historian's craft to prepare them to design and implement a small thematic digital archive.

On the technical side, our strategies for building *Nebraska U* have altered over the years. Our first attempts at building content for the site were based on experience we had at the Center for Digital Research in the Humanities at UNL (http://cdrh.unl.edu) building thematic research collections (see, for example, the *Walt Whitman Archive* at http://www.whitmanarchive.org or the *Willa Cather Archive* at http://cather.unl.edu). Such digital scholarly publications were designed to follow the established standards of the digital humanities community. With a heavy emphasis on presentation of texts, our thematic research collections had their foundations in Text Encoding Initiative (TEI)-conformant XML files that were transformed for web presentation using Extensible Stylesheet Language for Transformation (XSLT) files. Given our success with this model in the past, and given its fit with best practices established by the digital humanities and libraries communities, we thought it made the

most sense as the structure for *Nebraska U.*

In our first efforts at building content for the new site, the XML/XSLT model seemed to work. We created a few marked-up texts locally, built a stylesheet, and had a basic web design that we felt would work well with the kinds of student projects we imagined. Our first classroom collaboration—with Kenneth Price's course in the UNL English Department—encouraged us further. The students in that course selected largely text-based projects: transcriptions of unique archival documents or essays accompanied by limited illustrations. The students in Price's course also had training in XML markup as part of their curriculum, completing challenging transcriptions and markup of poetry manuscripts. So, since their final project for *Nebraska U* was completed after some markup training, the technology presented only limited challenges to them. We certainly had to train and help individual students, and we had to revise the stylesheet to accommodate all the variations in their specific projects, but the XML/XSLT model seemed reasonably efficient and robust for the needs of the project.

Yet even while we were confidently moving ahead with more content-creation on this model, we detected cracks in the surface, limitations that would need to be addressed. A couple of the students in Price's course clearly wanted to build their arguments around images, not texts. Their evidence for analysis was visual, and they hoped to build a website that would highlight the visual artifacts. Though we were able to include their images on the site, they were integrated into the design in a clumsy way: photographs stacked in a long-scrolling page, interrupted occasionally by analytical text.

When we entered into our next classroom collaboration, with Douglas Seefeldt's "Digital History" course in the spring of 2008, we persisted with the existing XML/XSLT model, reasoning that most projects would be text-based and that we needed to adhere to—and teach—accepted markup standards. Though overall the experience with this class was successful and students created several interesting research projects, it became clear that the XML/XSLT model needed to be reconsidered. Too often, the projects imagined by the students were poorly represented by the text-heavy markup scheme. These students, unsurprisingly, imagined web-based articulations of their historical research that were rich in interactivity, distinctive page layouts, and heavy use of images. This desire to build unique web projects (rather than just write texts accompanied by illustrations) was absolutely appropriate to the readings and discussion of their course, which was focused on the ways historiography is re-imagined using the digital medium. Though we were trapped in our existing infrastructure for that semester, we noted and, frankly, empathized with the frustration of some students who wanted more control over layout and content .[4]

Furthermore, in the context of this history course, which included instruction focused on editorial markup theory but not practice, the XML creation proved frustrating for both students and faculty. After Archives faculty provided the students with in-class training in XML, a template file, and markup guidelines, the students built their projects on multiple computers and various software. When the students delivered their XML for uploading to the project server, a range of mistakes and problems had to be addressed before the files could be transformed by the stylesheets and published online. Though some of the problems were tried-and-true parsing errors (that is, markup that didn't follow the project schema), many of the problems were character encoding issues. The students' insistence on using Microsoft Word and other software not designed for markup editing resulted in XML that was clogged with "smart quotes," control characters, and mysterious, invisible bits of code that required tedious hours of work to find and eliminate. The use of improper software meant that proprietary or incompatible characters migrated with the students' transcriptions as they cut-and-paste into the XML

template that was provided for them, and the presence of those characters prevented the XML from being transformed by the XSLT processor; instead of a lovely webpage, the transformation would spit out a list of character-encoding errors.

Ultimately, the students found the experience to be both challenging and rewarding, as a sampling of their end-of-semester self evaluations reveals. One student reflected, "I spent a lot of time sitting in front of my computer and marking up text. This was really difficult at first, but the more encoding I did, the more confident I felt working with XML." Another confessed, "it took many 'self-pep-talks' to spend the hours upon hours in the library and late nights encoding material, but in the end, it's all worth it." Others found their interaction with archival materials to be the most rewarding part of the project: "the best part of this whole experience…was doing the research. Being able to get my hands on original documents and handle the old yearbooks and look into the past is what draws me to history." Others found the tools and interactive medium to be rewarding: "after multiple semesters of nothing but writing papers the way others want, I was finally able to branch out and do what I wished to do." Overall, the student comments from this class did encourage us that our goal of getting undergraduates to appreciate and be engaged with unique historical materials was being achieved.

As we looked toward future classroom collaborations with the program, however, we knew that we would prefer to find a new technological infrastructure for supporting student projects. We lacked the resources to build something natively, so we began investigating other software options. About that time, Omeka was released by George Mason University's Center for History and New Media. Omeka (http://omeka.org), "a free, flexible, and open source web-publishing platform for the display of library, museum, archives, and scholarly collections and exhibitions,"[5] is designed for our precise needs. It is meant to empower institutions and individuals to build high-quality, standards-compliant web-sites without requiring extensive technological expertise or time investment. In the summer 2009, we began the process of switching from the XML/XSLT model to the Omeka-driven site, and by the fall semester 2009, we were ready to collaborate for a second time with students in Seefeldt's "Digital History" course using the Omeka platform.

In brief, Omeka requires users to create digital "items" and "collections," which are typically digitized objects—texts, photographs, videos, etc.—from the Archives. Once the user has created the "items" and appropriate metadata for each item,[6] the user can then create an "exhibition" from the items. It is this "exhibition" that is the opportunity for the students to provide analysis and synthesis on their topic. The exhibition combines text, selection and arrangement of items, and development of sections and subsections—in short, it provides students with a chance to do history using the highly visual and interlinked rhetorical methods of web publication.

After solving some problems with the Omeka preferences and settings related to linking in Exhibit pages, font size, navigation conventions, and default image size, the students were able to quickly master the interface and build their thematic research archives to present their annotations and interpretations. For some, the entire process was novel, as this student self-evaluation conveys: "Before this class I had not ever been in the archives, used a microfilm reader, scanned documents, or used interlibrary loan." Most of these undergraduates developed a new relationship with the Library in general and the Archives in particular, as did this student: "Special Collections became my home on campus; little did I know that I was succumbing to the lure of pure research." Another student confessed, "I am not afraid of computers the way I was at the beginning of the semester. I see how digitization, unlimited access and collaboration will enhance my work as a historian in the future."

The experiences shared by librarians, archivists, and faculty working with the Nebraska U project have been challenging and rewarding. From simply introducing advanced undergraduates to the rich collections of the Archives and the possibilities of digital media to opening up those collections to the vast and varied audience interested in University history throughout the world, the endeavor is a model for interdisciplinary collaboration. For students, it can be a defining experience of their undergraduate career: "the final project of this semester proved to be one of the most challenging of my academic career... Working with Omeka forced me to be adaptive in my presentation of my research. This challenge to deviate from the typical term paper format might prove to be one of the greatest experiences of my final year as an undergraduate." *Nebraska U* gave them an opportunity to contribute to the University's mission to create knowledge, as this student put it: "I think my biggest motivation in the class has been the idea that my work will actually be on the web. I'm leaving a project to the university that other students can build on, and hopefully, people (especially alumni) will turn to for information. That's pretty cool!"

BIBLIOGRAPHY

Cohen, Daniel J. and Roy Rosenzweig. *Digital History: A Guide to Gathering, Preserving, and Presenting the Past on the Web*. Philadelphia: University of Pennsylvania Press, 2006.

"Omeka: Serious Web Publishing," Center for History and New Media, accessed July 26, 2010, http://omeka.org/about/

Yakel, Elizabeth and Deborah A. Torres. "AI: Archival Intelligence and User Expertise," *The American Archivist*, 66 (Spring/Summer 2003): 51-78.

NOTES

1.   This program is an excellent endeavor of the University of Nebraska-Lincoln to give undergraduate students the opportunity to work with faculty mentors on

distinctive research projects. For more information, please see http://www.unl.edu/ucare.

2.   Elizabeth Yakel and Deborah A. Torres, "AI: Archival Intelligence and User Expertise," *The American Archivist*, 66 (Spring/Summer 2003): 52.

3.   Daniel J. Cohen and Roy Rosenzweig, *Digital History: A Guide to Gathering, Preserving, and Presenting the Past on the Web* (Philadelphia: University of Pennsylvania Press, 2006), 3. This book is also available at http://chnm.gmu.edu/digitalhistory/

4.   The limitations we've indicated above are not necessarily limitations of XML/XSLT, but rather limitations of our own understanding and mastery of those technologies at that time. The process made us consider how to apply these technologies to a capaciously-themed project on University history rather than the exemplar digital humanities archive projects that are more narrowly focused on an author or an event. No one intimately involved in the collaboration was a trained programmer or expert technologist. Instead, we were faculty and staff dedicated to use the tools and expertise we did possess to find ways to improve instruction and build innovative collaborations for Archives and Special Collections.

5.   "Omeka: Serious Web Publishing"

6.   We do not depend upon a sophisticated level of metadata in the Omeka system, as we concluded that the diverse group of people creating the metadata—particularly students—would be unlikely to create uniformly high-quality metadata. Instead, we inform the students (who are being graded on their projects) that part of the evaluation of their projects is the quality and extent of the metadata they create.

Student as Historian/Student as Historical Actor: Documenting the Student Experience at the University of Oregon

Heather Briston[1]

The key to integrating special collections into any course is to begin the faculty collaboration in the development stage of the course. When the focus of the class is student experience and student life, having students involved in the development and evolution of the course provides authenticity to course methods.[2]

STUDENT INVOLVEMENT— COMING OUT OF INFORMATION NEED

The development of the course "Reboot the past, Upload the future," with its "Documenting Freshman Year Experience" project, evolved from an information need. An upper level student in a primary source based research class, Conor Ross, wanted to compare and contrast the experience of University of Oregon (UO) students over time. As the course instructor and university archivist, I explained to him that we had very few papers of students or about their experience beyond the student newspaper and the yearbook, save one 1915 diary of a student in her freshman year. While in the short term Conor had to modify his paper topic, he took on the challenge of solving the problem of students' voices absent from the university archives.

Documenting student life was always a goal of university archives, but one where the records fell short. Students are the largest group on campus and the reason the university exists, but in many archives their voice is proportionally underrepresented, save for official records like transcripts, and more formal records like yearbooks and student newspapers. Compared to campus administration and operations, their time on campus is fleeting; most of the records only document students when they officially come in contact with the university, rather than their personal experience.

UO FRESHMAN INTEREST GROUP ENVIRONMENT

At the University of Oregon, approximately two-thirds of incoming freshman have the opportunity to select from over 60 Freshman Interest Groups (FIGs). Students in these FIGS are co-enrolled in two large-enrollment courses on different but related topics and in College Connections, a small-enrollment, one credit seminar. The seminar, taught by a faculty member and an undergraduate teaching assistant, serves as a discussion section to bring out the common themes of the two larger courses and highlight the interdisciplinary aspects of the subjects, and provides some foundation for introduction and integration into the university community. The intellectual rigor of the classes goes beyond the traditional "study skills" course, and provides the opportunity for freshmen to grapple with discipline specific issues in a smaller environment.

2007-2008: "LIVING AUTOBIOGRAPHY" AND "HIDDEN HISTORY"

Conor's idea was to capture the student experience by having all incoming students write journals about their freshman year and donate them to the university archives. While that suggestion was perhaps too ambitious, it sparked a project to get students involved in documenting their own history. Conor began meeting with an adjunct faculty member in the History department, who was interested in creating a new learning experience and helping students to engage with history in ways other than rote memorization. It was at this point that our three-way collaboration began. The historian was involved in a FIG that combined a history course and a folklore course; Conor became the undergraduate teaching assistant for the FIG. One of the hallmarks of the FIG program is to integrate project-based learning into the College Connections course. Conor's documentation idea became the project, later known as the "Documenting Freshman Year Experience" project.

Students in this FIG were given a summer reading assignment of the freshman year entries from the 1915 diary of Lucille Saunders. Throughout the term, analysis and discussions of the diary paralleled discussions of their own experience as freshmen. The historian used these examples to support a layered exploration of agency, bias, and primary sources, with the goal of helping the students to understand their role as both historians and as historical actors. To support this apprenticeship as historians, the class met in Special Collections and University Archives (SCUA) twice during the term. The first visit was an introduction to working with primary sources; students worked in groups with materials that dated from 1915. The group activity built connections between materials from the past and what today's student creates. The class also visited at the end of the term, in order to donate the journal entries that comprise their projects, and to learn about preservation, the role of the donor through the deed of gift, and issues of privacy and copyright. A group photograph was taken to document their class.

Figure 15.1. "Living Autobiography," 2007, preparing to make Lucile's world of 1915 come alive

Figure 15.2. "Hidden History," 2009 class picture

In that first group in 2007, all but two students participated in the project. Many included printouts of digital photos they had taken or ephemera they had collected like ticket stubs and fliers along with their typed and handwritten journal entries. As a part of the SCUA donor agreement, the students specified when the materials can be open for research; surprisingly, six students designated that their journals could be open immediately, and another one was open by the end of the academic year. The collection of student journals was arranged and described along current archival best practices, with a finding aid available in the Northwest Digital Archives,[3] and a catalog record to improve access to those portions of the collection that were open to research. In its second year, the structure for the class went largely unchanged. There was a new undergraduate teaching assistant, a student who experienced the seminar the year before.

STUDENT INVOLVEMENT: INTRODUCTION OF WEB 2.0 TOOLS

For a class with the student experience literally as its core, and one developed in large part by a student, it is no surprise that the next incarnation of the course came at the instigation of the new undergraduate teaching assistant, Matt Villeneuve, who suggested integrating Web 2.0 tools into the course, providing opportunities for students to express themselves in the media with which they feel most comfortable. His idea was to include multiple new platforms—a wiki for summer reading discussions, introductions, and class discussions; a blog about the course; an assignment using Facebook as a primary source; and the opportunity for students to go beyond the bounds of the typed journal entries and have the option to document the term using a blog, videos, photo montage, or podcasts.

Figure 15.3. Working with the 2009 cohort on their donation day

These opportunities energized us all. They allowed the professor to bring out issues of the impact of technology on historical documentation and primary sources—the change in documented voices—and to explore technology's effect on the teaching and learning of history. As archivist, I was able to expand the discussion of preservation into issues of born digital records, introduce the debate of a digital gap or digital abundance as the future of historical documentation, and explore the issue of the digital divide in the documentation of history, all issues that come alive when students have their own history and their own work on the line. And it helped Matt, the teaching assistant, to start to build a community of students before the beginning of classes, and to promote new ways for us all to engage with the material.

COLLABORATION BETWEEN FACULTY, ARCHIVIST, AND UNDERGRADUATE TEACHING ASSISTANT

The course works, remains popular, and is evolving into its fifth year because of the dynamic collaboration among professor, archivist and, the most unusual element, undergraduate teaching assistants, who provide the prime ingredients for the evolution of the course and insure that the student perspective is addressed throughout. The faculty brings the academic rigor and the history pedagogy to the course. The archivist brings the knowledge of collections and primary source discovery, combined with insights from archives management. The students in the course are able to use this experience as a window into both the documentary process of history providing insight into their role as historical actors, observing, interpreting, and documenting their experience, as well as researchers of history exploring the experience of one of their predecessors. These activities take the students beyond class work that is just an exercise, to an authentic experience where they are contributing knowledge to the community that will have a lifespan beyond the class. At the same time the project serves a pragmatic role and the university archives is able to collect materials on a difficult to document group that is integral to the history of the institution.

One of the desired outcomes from the seminar and the documentation project is to debunk the notion by students that their experience is not "history," and to reinforce that their experiences are as critical a part of the history of the university as the activities of the faculty and administration. Many of the students noted at the end of the term that they did have a better sense of what it meant to be both a historical actor and a student of history. "Yes, I never thought of myself as making history. I am no Cleopatra, but I still made history."[4] The faculty member characterizes the seminar as an apprenticeship in the discipline of history and becoming a historian. They start small, working with one person, Lucille Saunders, and one period, 1915. This serves as a foundation through which "students develop a keen sense of historical concepts including causation, agency, memory, authenticity, bias, perspective, voice, context, and provenance."[5] While hands-on work of students with primary sources is not unusual, and increasingly students are involved in building collections in archives, the donor experience as the final step in this project brings an added dimension to the learning.

With the introduction of Web 2.0 tools into the class, not only were the options expanded, but the impact of technology on history became another dimension for the class to explore. Wiki participation allowed the students to develop a community even before they came to campus, introducing themselves and discussing the readings. The proportion of students to actually use new media for projects in

this class was not large, but it did result in six blogs, three video journals, and one set of podcasts, all of which are being made available through our institutional repository when the students designate they can be opened to the public.[6] In the review of the class, we noted that while students may have been consumers of Web 2.0 content, they had not been producers (beyond Facebook participation); students noted that they had not engaged new social media in a participatory mode previous to this class.[7]

ADAPTING THIS COURSE AND PROJECT TO OTHER UNIVERSITIES

The University of Oregon is not the only university integrating primary sources into undergraduate education, while at the same time finding it challenging to document student life. Any way to regularize the documentation of the student experience is a valuable addition to the history of the university. Journaling and reflective essays are often assigned in introductory writing courses; collaboration with the archives could fulfill two requirements, and build a strong relationship between archives, faculty, and students, as well as model research behavior in special collections for students. For those universities or colleges that have special small enrollment courses for freshmen, the format of this course would be best supported in a seminar that was based in history. It provides an infrastructure for approaching historical questions and unique materials, while at the same time making the process accessible for new students in the form of an apprenticeship. For many students, the class provides their first opportunity to look at history in a way different from memorization of names and dates.

A PLAN FOR CONTINUED IMPROVEMENT OF COURSE

All of those involved with the class are pleased by the student involvement evidenced by the final projects and their understanding of their role in contributing to university history. A challenge for the course is to help students understand the intersections of the two major courses, World History and Introduction to Folklore. This year the course will use the lens of university history to bring the two disciplines together: there is much folklore intermingled with university history, especially as it is found in the realm of student life. The 2010 version of the course will also add a group inquiry project that will involve students selecting a tradition or topic of student life and using as their sources the currently open student journals and selected materials from the university archives.

The "Reboot the past, Upload the future" course and "Documenting Freshman Year Experience" project support many goals for undergraduate teaching and learning. Together they provide a means for project based learning and apprenticeship for freshmen interested in history, and an avenue for their faculty to lead them through larger issues of historical documentation and analysis. They provide an opportunity for students to engage with primary sources early in their university careers, and to capture the voices of students in documents beyond their transcripts. For the archives, not only do they help to fulfill a mandate in an area difficult to document and collect, but they provide the opportunity to work with students helping them to understand the nature and purpose of archives.

NOTES

1. Heather Briston is now Head of Public Services for Library Special Collections at the UCLA Library.

2. The author wishes to thank Kevin Hatfield, adjunct history faculty, and assistant director for academic initiatives, residence life, faculty instructor of the course; Conor Ross, Betsy Selander, and Matt Villeneuve, student instructors of the course 2007-2010, for their ideas, innovation, collaboration, and hard work in creating and teaching the course, as well as the insights for this case study. The development and teaching of this course was previously presented in part at the Coalition for Networked Information (CNI) in April 2010, and the EDUCAUSE Learning Initiative Annual Meeting, January 2010.

3. Northwest Digital Archives finding aid, http://nwda-db.wsulibs.wsu.edu/findaid/ark:/80444/xv56450

4. Student course evaluation and Web 2.0 survey, HIST 199, "Hidden History," December 2009.

5. Hatfield, Kevin, Prepared remarks for "Rebooting the Past, Uploading the Future: Web 2.0 and the Study of History Through a Living Learning Community," EDUCAUSE Learning Initiative Annual Meeting, Austin, TX January 2010.

6. Scholars' Bank, University of Oregon institutional repository https://scholarsbank.uoregon.edu/xmlui/handle/1794/9984

7. Student course evaluation and Web 2.0 survey, HIST 199, "Hidden History," December 2009.

The Special Collections Laboratory: Integrating Archival Research into Undergraduate Courses in Psychology and Music

Shan C. Sutton

INTRODUCTION

The traditional laboratory, full of beakers, microscopes, and assorted instruments, is one of the most time-honored elements of the undergraduate experience. In the sciences, the lab plays a vital role as a place where students have opportunities to conduct hands-on experiments. As the value of archival collections for undergraduate education becomes more widely recognized, the reading rooms of special collections and archives departments ought to be viewed as archival laboratories for students. These learning spaces offer raw materials (collections), research technicians (staff), and tools (finding aids) that students can use to conduct original research, make discoveries, and test hypotheses just as they do in scientific labs. Even with this combination of impressive resources, however, the special collections laboratory can only meet its full pedagogical potential through effective partnerships with the teaching faculty to ensure widespread use in undergraduate courses.

This approach has been embraced by the University of the Pacific Library's Holt-Atherton Special Collections department in its efforts to integrate archival research into the undergraduate curriculum. Undergraduate research is highly valued at Pacific, and a commitment to information literacy is found within the university-wide student learning objectives. The Special Collections staff is proactive in supporting student research and information literacy through collaboration with faculty in a broad range of academic units to develop archival

course assignments. From 2005 to 2010, an average of eleven courses involving 207 students per academic year have featured assignments using Special Collections. During this period undergraduates at Pacific used manuscript collections to conduct research in Sociology, Religion, Psychology, Music, General Education, and History classes.

Two primary methods for reaching instructors in pursuit of curricular collaborations involve hosting an orientation for new faculty members and making proposals for specific course assignments directly to professors. The case studies presented in this chapter, involving a Psychology course and a Music course, reflect the outcomes of these respective strategies for faculty engagement and student learning in Special Collections.

Each academic year, new faculty members tour the University Library as part of their campus orientation. When they visit the Special Collections department, the professors are informed that its holdings are used in a variety of undergraduate classes, and they are invited to schedule a follow-up meeting to discuss potential uses of Special Collections in their courses. Intriguing examples from the collections, such as letters, diaries, photographs, maps, and rare books are displayed in the reading room during the tour. As these materials are described, their uses in specific courses at Pacific are highlighted. One orientation session inspired a new psychology professor to contact Special Collections about creating new class assignments, which led to the diary analysis project described in this article.

In addition to hosting faculty tours, the Special Collections librarians regularly review the university's course catalog in search of classes that are good candidates for an archival research assignment. Some preliminary ideas are developed based on a course's focus and the holdings of Special Collections, and communicated to the instructor via email or in person. Professors have generally reacted positively to this approach, including the director of the jazz studies program, who adopted a Special Collections research component in the seminar that is the focus of this article's second case study.

One of the keys to success in developing effective student engagement with Special Collections is giving them some degree of freedom within the structure of the assignment. Including an element of choice in the assignments can offer students a sense of ownership in their scholarship, and has led to positive student responses to the archival research projects in both of these case studies. In the Experimental Psychology course, the diaries available for student use have been preselected by the librarian, but students choose the specific ones they want to study. Alternatively, in the Jazz Seminar and Perspectives course, students must research the same topic, jazz icon Dave Brubeck, but are free to select from a wide variety of material types (e.g., audio, video, clippings, and correspondence) in their use of the Dave Brubeck Collection.

EXPERIMENTAL PSYCHOLOGY

The Experimental Psychology course is taken mostly by sophomore and junior psychology majors. In this class students learn about research methods and design as well as data collection and analysis. One of their research projects involves analysis of diaries in Special Collections to study the mental and emotional states of the diaries' authors. In designing this assignment with the instructor, the librarian selected four sets of diaries to capture variation in historical period, life stage, gender, content, and style. The dia-

ries were written by Delia Locke, Jonathan Lyman, Paul Desmond, and Allan Lindsay-O'Neil.

Locke lived on a ranch in northern California from 1855 to 1922. Lyman was a student at the University of the Pacific from 1890 to 1892. Desmond was a world-renown jazz saxophonist from the 1940s to the 1970s. Lindsay-O>Neal was a student leader of the anti-Vietnam War movement at the University of the Pacific in 1970. Together, these diaries offer a variety of people and experiences to analyze, and they enable students to experience the process of discovery in investigating the writers' personalities.

The first step in the assignment involves a class visit to Special Collections where students receive an orientation on how to handle and study the diaries. During this session students also have an opportunity to examine diaries in small groups. Initially, no information is given about the identity of the authors, and students are encouraged to play detective in developing a profile of the writer and evidence of his or her psychological state based on clues within the texts. After allowing the students twenty minutes to explore the diaries, each group presents their findings and the full identities of the respective authors are revealed.

Students offer a wide range of observations in this discussion, including information on the authors> attitudes, beliefs, emotions, and relationships. For example, a group of students examining the diary of Delia Locke noted that she drew connections between her mood and the state of the weather. This observation led to a class discussion of the broader impact of weather on people's moods. At the end of the orientation students are given the diary analysis assignment. It requires each student to return to Special Collections on their own to locate and analyze two diary entries that contain information on the writer's psychology. The entries can either be from the same diary at two points in time, or from two different authors' diaries. Students then write a 1-2 page paper examining the excerpts from the perspective of psychological analysis.

When the assignment is handed in, there is also a class discussion of the students' findings and the pros and cons of using diaries as sources for this kind of study. For example, one student noted that the author did not mean for these diaries to be viewed by the public, and, therefore, he may have been more forthcoming. Others commented on the inherent information gaps found in diaries, which leave the researcher to fill in the blanks. These observations serve as a reminder that in the process of learning course-specific content, archival research can also enable students to develop information literacy skills such as the ability to evaluate the strengths and weaknesses of different information sources. This student learning outcome is also evident in the second case study of this article.

JAZZ SEMINAR AND PERSPECTIVES

The Jazz Seminar and Perspectives course is taken by juniors and seniors in the Conservatory of Music's jazz studies program. In this class students study the careers and styles of major jazz figures as a mechanism for understanding their own styles as musicians. Because the Special Collections department is home to the Dave Brubeck Collection, students have a unique opportunity to conduct in-depth research on his career through a variety of primary sources. Three inter-related assignments make up the archival research component of this course.

First, students select ten segments of videotaped oral history interviews with Brubeck, and write a one page paper on how the content of these interviews resonates with their own personal and musical development. There are thirty-five segments to choose from, and their focus ranges from Brubeck's musical accomplishments to his well-known efforts in support of civil rights. The oral history videos can be streamed from the Special Collections web site, so students can complete this assignment remotely at the time and location of their choosing.

The second and third assignments require students to use the Brubeck Collection in the reading room to research Brubeck's performance and compositional styles, respectively. The librarian first teaches an orientation session that includes opportunities to examine and discuss the variety of materials found in the Collection. In this discussion students discover how different types of sources contain different kinds of information and provide context to each other in the research process. For example, understanding Brubeck's performance style requires analysis of multiple sources such as reviews of his concerts, audio tapes and videos of his shows, and interviews that may be in print, audio, or video formats. Similarly, content on Brubeck's compositional style is contained in his original musical scores, reviews of his albums and album notes, and concert programs from premieres of his orchestral works. Armed with a multi-format research strategy, students return to the reading room on their own to study the sources they select to develop a full picture of the Brubeck style.

Once the students have completed their research they submit two 4–6 page papers, one on Brubeck's performance style and one on his compositional style. Submission of the papers is accompanied by class discussion of their findings and the kinds of archival sources they used. In 2010, the University Library provided the students with an opportunity to present their research at a panel discussion as part of Pacific's annual Brubeck Festival. This event, entitled "Pacific Studies Brubeck," was organized and moderated by the Head of Special Collections, and included presentations by four Pacific students and one professor on their research in the Brubeck Collection. It was attended by thirty people, including Brubeck's daughter and his producer. The event offered a unique opportunity to highlight student use of the collection to representatives of the donor community, as well as the university community and general public.

The students welcomed the chance to publicly share their scholarship and vouch for the value of Special Collections as a resource for undergraduate learning. One student spoke of getting goose bumps as he held an original score of "Strange Meadowlark," a favorite Brubeck tune from his childhood. Another related how seeing several drafts of a musical score with large red X's through them indicated that even the greatest composers must work hard at their craft, an observation he found inspiring as a young musician just beginning his career. These student presentations demonstrated how the "digital natives" that now fill the undergraduate ranks can benefit from encounters with new sources of knowledge in the form of original manuscript materials. This contribution to undergraduate research is an increasingly important role for Special Collections as students enter universities with an understanding of information that is overwhelmingly based on digital formats.

CONCLUSION

Student descriptions of Special Collections as a place of inspiration and goose bumps are surely the stuff librarians dream about. Although the growing importance of Special Collections to undergraduate education may seem self-evident, there remains an ongoing need to solicit student feedback and validation. This may be achieved through a variety of mechanisms, from public presentations in which students describe their experiences, to more quantitative assessment instruments. At the end of the Experimental Psychology course, for example, students rank what they learned from various class activities on a scale from 1 (*next to nothing*) to 5 (*a lot*). The average rating for the diary analysis assignment has been 4.0, making it one of the highest-rated activities in the course.

The case studies presented in this chapter can easily be emulated at other universities. Diaries are found in nearly every special collections and archives department, and the Experimental Psychology assignment illustrates how they can be utilized in innovative ways that transcend purely historical analysis. Although the Brubeck Collection exists only at Pacific, it serves as an example of how large, complex manuscript collections can support assignments that enable students to combine the use of different material formats in the research process. Another lesson from the Jazz Seminar and Perspectives course is the value of providing students with opportunities to present their research outside of the classroom. Special Collections staff should familiarize themselves with campus, regional, and national conferences that focus on undergraduate research and encourage participation by their students. This represents another area ripe for partnerships with professors in support of student learning and achievement.

Faculty collaboration is clearly the key to student engagement with Special Collections. Both of the case studies described here involved instructors who were open to exploring the roles that Special Collections could play in fulfilling their students' learning objectives. These kinds of professors can be found on any campus, but the Special Collections staff must be proactive in making the initial connections. Once faculty partnerships are established, they lay the groundwork for students to experience Special Collections as an archival laboratory where their own research discoveries occur as an important part of their undergraduate education.

Teaching Cultural Memory: Using and Producing Digitized Archival Material in an Online Course

Robin M. Katz

BACKGROUND

The University of Vermont Libraries' Center for Digital Initiatives[2] is a digital library of unique research collections situated under Special Collections. The forthcoming collection *Kake Walk at UVM* will be the CDI's first from the University Archives, its first to include streaming audio and object photography, and its most controversial collection to date.

Kake Walk was an 80-year university tradition based, in part, on minstrel theatre and the turn-of-the-century cakewalk dance craze. The annual synchronized dance competition known as "a-walkin' fo' de kake" was the highlight of Winter Carnival weekend which featured fraternity brothers in blackface and kinky wigs high-stepping to the tune of "Cotton Babes." The event, abolished in 1969, occupies a controversial position in institutional memory, representing, for some, a hallowed legacy of creativity, school spirit, and leadership and for others, overt racism. With only one known scholarly piece on Kake Walk by former UVM professor James Loewen, a credible, well-described digital collection will support much-needed study of this unique cultural phenomenon.

THE COURSE: "CURATING KAKE WALK"

In the summer of 2010, I co-taught a six-week course entitled "Curating Kake Walk: Race, Memory, and Representation" with Dr. Brian Gilley.[3] This case study demonstrates how we utilized an unfinished digitized archival collection in an online class and how students contributed to its production. The first half of the course covered Kake Walk, American racial formation, cultural repositories, and collective memory through daily readings, lectures, and discussions. After the midterm paper, students synthesized and applied these concepts by working *on*—not just *with*—the incomplete *Kake Walk at UVM* collection.

This three-credit ALANA[4] US Ethnic Studies course met asynchronously online to capitalize on the digitized materials and to create a potentially safer space in which students could chose whether or not to reveal their age and/or race. It was offered through Continuing Education to welcome local and remote community members, alumni, and schoolteachers in addition to undergraduates. Seven undergraduates, mostly upper-class humanities or education majors, enrolled (one later dropped). Many took the course to fulfill an Arts & Sciences diversity requirement. Three auditing continuing education students included staff in Alumni Relations, an alumna who attended Kake Walk, and a native Vermonter.

Before class began, a minimally-described collection of 229 items was made available on the CDI's development site, an unpublicized URL similar to http://cdi.uvm.edu. Both instructors selected for digitization a representative sample of the archival collection; I supplied initial metadata. The class was delivered via Blackboard and students were taught to use the CDI's public and development sites through readings and video tutorials.

Using this collection as a "humanities laboratory"[5] helped meet the CDI's outreach goal, stated in our second IMLS grant, of fostering an "open, collaborative environment." When considering similar collaborations, the repository's strategic goals and the course's learning objectives must align. Our learning objectives, measured by quizzes, discussions, a midterm paper, group collaborations, the final project, and reflection papers, were:

- Demonstrate a knowledge of Kake Walk's history
- Present an argument about racial formation and Kake Walk
- Understand the function of cultural repositories and the power they have in constructing cultural memory
- Perform the curatorial duties of selection and description
- Synthesize concepts of memory and representation with respects to *Kake Walk at UVM*

This case study will demonstrate that involving students in curatorial activities is not an easy way to farm cheap labor, but a way to blur the line between producers and users. Dismantling this binary benefits the collection, students, repository, and society at large.

THE FINAL PROJECT: COLLABORATIVE CURATION

The final project engaged students in "the messy work of negotiating power and ideas and memory."[6] Through individual, group, and class activities, students were given three tasks: to select a collection image, write series-level scope and content notes, and recommend Library of Congress Subject Headings for collection items. These assignments were designed as a collaborative learning experience to divide the work, to make apparent the subjectivity of curation, to build in quality control, and to form some consensus around potentially difficult decisions.

The entire class selected the collection image through nominations and voting. Scope notes and subject heading recommendations were completed in groups. The six for-credit students were partnered into three heterogeneous, teacher-formed pairs. The collection was divided and assigned as follows:

Series Format	No. of Items	Assigned to
Newspapers	15	Group 1
Programs	19	Group 2
Photographs	102	Group 3
Music, Artifacts, & Exhibit Materials	5	Group 4 (Auditing Students)
Records	86	Instructor
Secondary Sources	2	Instructor

Pending CDI approval, the groups' series-level scope and content notes would be incorporated into collection-level metadata and subject heading recommendations would be applied. As shown above, I completed the bulk of description to maintain feasible student contributions. Students were frequently reminded that their work would be public; in reflections, they appreciated the "rare and exciting opportunity" to "affect any future researchers who use the collection."[7]

Collaborative work was staged in a managed succession of individual and group assignments. Students first had one week to individually complete the scope note and subject heading assignments. Over the next two weeks, partners reviewed each others' work, discussed the project, and agreed on final versions. Grading rubrics reflected this combined independent/interdependent approach, evenly dividing points between individual, group, and reflection assignments. Participation grades also included peer evaluations.[8]

SELECTING THE COLLECTION IMAGE

CDI collections are represented by 160 pixel square thumbnails appearing on the CDI homepage, the collections browse list, and the About the Collection page. Historically, collection images were chosen quickly and easily on grounds primarily aesthetic. Because of the potentially offensive or shocking nature of

Kake Walk images, this uncontextualized thumbnail needs to match well-defined selection criteria.

At the start of the course, a question mark graphic served as the placeholder thumbnail. Each student was required to determine three selection criteria, to examine the collection's graphic materials, and to select the image which best meets those criteria. Individuals described their process and shared their nominations in a class-wide discussion. Invariably, students nominated an image in the format they knew best, that of their assigned series. There were no duplicate nominations, but everyone suggested materials from the 1950s and 1960s, the most stylized era of Kake Walk. Midway through the nomination period, I proposed two images to provide more voting options and to model selection.

In the subsequent class discussion, students debated whether or not to show blackface and, if shown, whether to use photographs or illustrations. Someone in favor of depicting blackface wanted to "spark a curiosity," but asked, "how do we choose an image that doesn't 'scare' people away?" Another responded, "users should be somewhat uncomfortable… I don't see how it's possible not to be, honestly." A third concurred, "It is only fair and respectful to just confront the issue head-on." In a vote utilizing Blackboard's survey feature, students overwhelmingly favored showing blackface. The winning image (see Appendix 17.1) was the 1963 program cover, an illustration of two walkers mid kick.

In private reflections, a few students voiced dissatisfaction with this decision. One objected to depiction of blackface because "uneducated" users will be "too distracted" by such a "shocking" picture. Conversely, two students felt the illustration did not "go far enough" and preferred "real" (meaning photographic) representations.

Because the collection was pre-selected by instructors, the collection image assignments provided students their only opportunity to set criteria, survey material, and defend a selection. The scale was quite manageable; the entire selection process took one week. The impact of this decision on future researchers is significant, however, as this image is now literally the face of Kake Walk.

WRITING SCOPE AND CONTENT NOTES

To learn to write series-level scope and content notes, students read definitions and examples from *DACS*,[9] the EAD 2002 site,[10] and a Library of Congress manual.[11] I provided minimal feedback to individuals' drafts, explaining, for example, that the word "cataloging" has a technical meaning in libraries or that the number of items in a series is different than the number of images. Based on completeness, conciseness, tone and relevance, the groups' final notes were all excellent.

In reflections, most students revealed that writing concisely was "the most challenging part" of this task . This course required extremely different skills than most university assignments, so students needed to be reassured when experiencing anxieties such as feeling "lost" or "a little confused." Despite perceived struggles, the final notes all approached 100 words. I generally pared them down by another 20% and made very few edits to the public versions.

Most groups imitated the "disinterested" tone of sample scope notes, despite discussing Howard Zinn's admonition that "the archivists' 'supposed neutrality' was 'a fake.'"[12] In the eleventh hour, one group submitted a note including what they termed this "disclaimer:"

> These photographs should be seen not as encouraging racism, but as an opportunity to learn from insensitivities from the past that can help us build a more unified future.

In a reflection, one group member said "it is very important, even essential, to… [let] users know what there is no bigotry involved with the displaying of these materials, and that it is solely for educational purposes."

Had other groups been able to see this innovative suggestion, so incompatible with the others' notes and with professional standards, students could have debated the appropriate tenor of collection-level metadata. Some groups might have changed their notes. In similar assignments, another stage should be added for students to review others groups' work, leading to fewer revisions by librarians and a more unified end product. Students might even write all collection-level metadata together, not just discrete pieces.

In this case, I moved the statement to a different section of the collection overview, ascribed it to one

ASSIGNING SUBJECT HEADINGS

To prepare for subject analysis, students read from Arlene Taylor's *Organization of Information* and watched a lecture I created on controlled vocabularies. Although this lecture compared folksonomies and taxonomies, some students consistently referred to LCSH headings as "tags." Targeted responses to every incorrect use of the term[15] did not break the habit. The lecture also modeled searching subjects, finding authorized headings, and locating control numbers on http://authorities.loc.gov. I demonstrated several searches and completed this sample of the chart required of students:

Item ID	The Subject In Your Words	Authorized LCSH	LC Control Number	Explain Your Decision optional: for interesting or difficult headings
sample001	University students	College students	sh 85028356	
" "	Minstrelsy or Blackface	Blackface entertainers	sh 86002417	Neither "minstrel music" or "minstrel shows" are accurate, as Kake Walk does not belong in these broader cultural traditions. **OR YOU MAY DISAGREE!**
sample002	Fraternities	Greek letter societies	sh 85057168	

group, and asserted that these students' sentiments reflect the convictions of the class. This edit, the only significant revision of student scope notes and a difficult curatorial decision in itself, was intended to maintain the majority tone.

I was surprised students were not more skeptical of supplied information as this collection was pre-selected, minimally-described, and only available online. Just one student questioned the accuracy of a few supplied titles. This finding, combined with the replication of the sample notes' "neutral"[13] tones, suggests most undergraduates are either unquestioning or are reluctant to challenge a librarian's authority—even in a course which critiques library resources as "value-laden instruments of power."[14]

The second column articulates subject analysis. The last column makes apparent the subjectivity of "aboutness" and initiates group discussions. This chart documents item-level assignments, so many headings were frequently repeated. For convenient grading and metadata creation, future students should also submit a consolidated list of all recommended headings.

This exercise required considerable group communication and instructor feedback. In every group, the number of shared revisions and discussion posts about this task was much higher than for the scope notes. In group discussions, I raised issues like item-specific aboutness (was Kake Walk really a college musical?), disambiguation (*Audience (Musical group)* is different than *Audiences*), or how to assess appropriate use of a heading in the absence of a scope note (WorldCat shows *Judges* refers to the biblical book).

Determining the appropriate level of specificity was hardest for students. In reflections, they said the collaborative process and instructor feedback helped them to see "the obvious 'big picture'" or to avoid "tunnel vision." Many students cited consistency as a challenge, but the chart helped student visually ensure most headings were consistently applied.

This course was not designed to train future catalogers, but our makeshift approach, combined with substantial instructor feedback and built-in quality control, led to successful results. This chart records the total number of headings submitted by each student group, the number of headings submitted by students but deemed unusable in the digital collection, and the number of additional headings supplied by librarians (the headings "missed" by students):

	HEADINGS		
SERIES	**Submitted**	**Not Used**	**Missed**
15 newspapers	29	9[◇]	2[◇]
19 programs	7	2[*]	10[*]
102 photos	33	6[+]	2[♦]

◇ Eliminated or added for "aboutness" reasons
* More appropriate in genre/format headings
* Seven of these provided by other groups
+ Three eliminated for "aboutness," one for failure to disambiguate; two replaced by slightly more appropriate headings
♦ Does not include the replacements mentioned above

To compare the undergraduates' performance with new catalogers or paraprofessionals, I informally consulted several catalogers. They described the students' subject analysis as "excellent," "great," and "very good results." Students were graded on completeness, accuracy, and relevance; all groups received 80–100%.

CONCLUSIONS

An interesting polarization among students suggests we successfully challenged the user-producer binary, creating a group of quasi-experts. In reflections,

about half the students considered themselves prototypical users; one explained, "I just tried to think about what I would search for." Others felt that by taking this course, they are now removed from the average user. One student lamented that "not all users will be as well verse[d] in Kake Walk as I am" because "it's always hard to put yourself in the mindset before you knew something." These discrepancies invite further research on the impact of participatory curation on students' perceptions, skills, and knowledge.

Blurring the line between users and producers promotes libraries, and students expressed "new appreciation for the work of librarians." Students became more aware of library resources and services, more competent evaluators of primary sources, and more critical researchers. "[This class has] made me much more conscious of how powerful a role the selector (curator) plays in the creation of an archive," stated one final evaluation.

Steven Lubar demonstrates that as "points of inscription"[16] and "sites of cultural production,"[17] archives are "sites of power."[18] In the case of Kake Walk, allowing students to "*do* the work of culture"[19] also builds consensus for the project. From his experience acquiring KKK materials, Frank Boles advises that "educational efforts" are necessary to defend "controversial collecting decisions."[20] Our students felt this class "inherently avoids" Boles' "problems." By making "the debate about selection and access… a public debate,"[21] this course approached the democratic vision called for by Eric Ketelaar: "an archives of the people, by the people, and for the people."[22]

I believe, as this case study shows, that archives are indispensable in the task of understanding our sometimes difficult past and that students should actively engage in that struggle in a classroom setting.

Kake Walk at UVM *was published at http://cdi. uvm.edu in mid-September 2010. To facilitate community dialogue and informal learning, the well-publicized launch included robust campus programming.*[23]

APPENDIX 17.1. Winning Kake Walk image

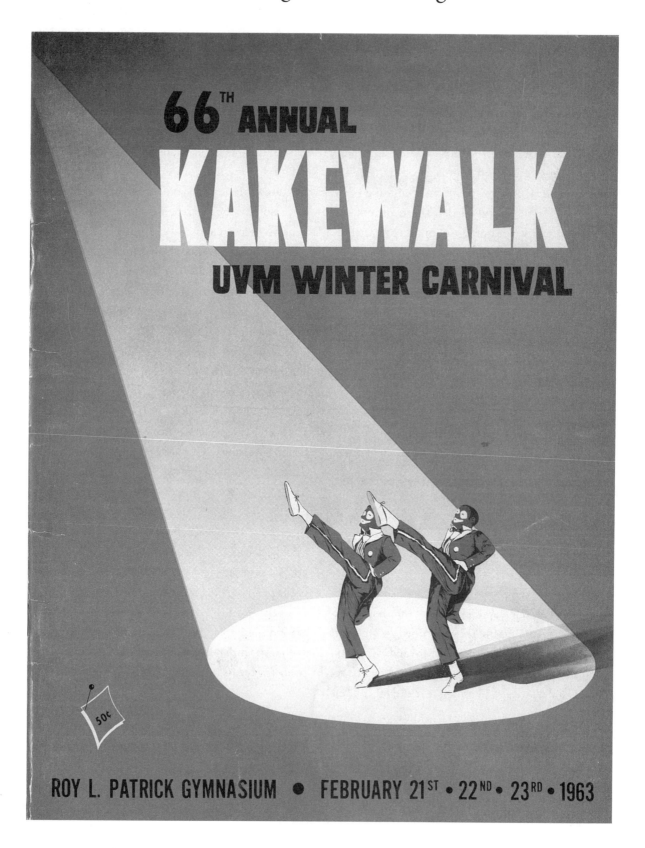

BIBLIOGRAPHY

Boles, Frank. "Just A Bunch of Bigots: A Case Study in the Acquisition of Controversial Material." *Archival Issues* 19, no. 1 (1994): 53–65.

Describing Archives: A Content Standard. Chicago: Society of American Archivists, 2007.

Encoded Archival Description Tag Library, Version 2002. Society of American Archivists. Last modified August 2002. http://www.loc.gov/ead/tglib/.

Loewen, James. "The Black Image in White Vermont: The Origin, Meaning, and Abolition of Kake Walk." *The University of Vermont: The First Two Hundred Years,* edited by Robert V. Daniels. Hanover, NH / University of Vermont: Distributed by University Press of New England / University of Vermont, 1991.

Lubar, Steven. "Information Culture and the Archival Record." *The American Archivist* 62 (Spring 1999): 10–22.

Library of Congress. *National Digital Library Program Writer's Handbook.* Last modified October 2000. http://memory.loc.gov:8081/ammem/ndlpedit/handbook/.

Taylor, Arlene. *Organization of Information.* 2nd ed. Westport, Conn.: Libraries Unlimited, 2004.

Schmiesing, Ann and Deborah Hollis. "The Role of Special Collections Departments in Humanities Undergraduate and Graduate Teaching: A Case Study." *Portal: Libraries and the Academy* 2, no. 3 (July 2002): 465–480.

Jimerson, Randall C. "Embracing the Power of Archives." *The American Archivist* 69 (Spring/Summer 2006): 19–32.

NOTES

1. Katz was formerly at University of Vermont, is now at Brooklyn Historical Society.
2. http://cdi.uvm.edu
3. When Katz was the Digital Initiatives Outreach Librarian at the University of Vermont Libraries' Center for Digital Initiatives, Dr. Gilley was Anthropology Professor and Director of the ALANA US Ethnic Studies Program at the University of Vermont.
4. African-, Latino/a-, Asian-, and Native-American
5. Schmiesing and Hollis, 465.
6. Lubar, 18.
7. All unattributed quotations are anonymized excerpts from student work, discussion posts, or evaluations.
8. Many thanks to Dr. Christopher Hoadley's "Learning Through Collaborative Technologies" Faculty Resource Network 2010 Summer Seminar for tips on instructional design.
9. "Scope and Content Element." *Describing Archives: A Content Standard.* (Chicago: Society of American Archivists, 2007), 35–38.
10. "EAD Elements: <scopeandcontent> Scope and Content," *Encoded Archival Description Tag Library, Version 2002,* Society of American Archivists, last modified May 26, 2006, http://www.loc.gov/ead/tglib/elements/scopecontent.html.
11. "6.7 Scope and Content Note," *National Digital Library Program Writer's Handbook,* Library of Congress, last modified September 1999, http://memory.loc.gov:8081/ammem/ndlpedit/handbook/scope.html.
12. Jimerson, 22.
13. Ibid., 22.
14. Cook and Schwartz in Jimerson, 23.
15. Accompanied by a link to the useful comparison chart at http://www.useyourweb.com/blog/?p=62
16. Lubar, 14.
17. Ibid., 21.
18. Ibid., 15.
19. Ibid., 15.
20. Boles, 59.
21. Ketelaar in Jimerson, 28.
22. Jimerson, 32.
23. Events included a film screening of Spike Lee's *Bamboozled* and a lecture by MIT professor and former Alvin Ailey dancer Dr. Thomas F. DeFrantz. For more information, please see http://www.uvm.edu/~uvmpr/?Page=News&storyID=17016 and http://www.vermontcynic.com/professors-comment-on-the-history-of-kake-walks-1.2361563.

When Did Sacajawea Die Anyway?: Challenging Students with Primary Sources

Rick Ewig

Marcus Robyns, in his 2001 article "The Archivist as Educator: Integrating Critical Thinking Skills into Historical Research Methods Instruction," conducted an informal survey of twelve university archival institutions and their involvement in the teaching of research methods courses at their schools. The common frustration expressed by the archivists was that "a number of faculty members do not share my view that systematic archival research should be an indispensable part of teaching undergraduate history, that is, the lab work of history instruction."[1] This is not the case at the University of Wyoming (UW) as shown by the Archival Research Methods class taught by archivists at UW's American Heritage Center (AHC) through the UW History Department.

The course came about from a discussion between various AHC faculty members, the chair of the UW History Department, and the faculty member from the UW College of Education, an associate professor in Secondary Education and Social Studies Education, who teaches students preparing to be social studies middle and high school teachers. The AHC's three classes on archival administration, taught since the early 1990s, no longer drew many students so a substitute was deemed necessary. It was thought the methods course would not only draw history students, but also education students, who could benefit from researching manuscript collections, evaluating sources, crafting arguments, and writing history, all of which might lead to innovative teaching in the social studies classroom.

The methods course as developed is intended to "provide the student with advanced research strate-

gies with interdisciplinary applications." The class focuses on primary document research based upon manuscript collections at the AHC. The course objectives include learning research techniques as well as gaining experience in analyzing and evaluating primary sources. Additionally, "students will develop higher level interpretive skills and be able to synthesize information from diverse, sometimes conflicting sources."

The course is designed to provide information about several aspects of archival administration, to provide research examples for the students, and to have the students spend considerable time researching manuscript collections and crafting arguments based on collection materials. In the first class, we review the syllabus and assign a short writing exercise. Then the students examine and evaluate sources related to whether Esther Hobart Morris, who lived in gold-mining community South Pass City, Wyoming, during the late 1860s, had anything to do with the passage of the territory's suffrage law in 1869, which granted women full suffrage and the right to hold public office. During the 1920s, former UW professor Grace Raymond Hebard claimed that Morris held a tea or dinner party during which she convinced William Bright, who became the president of Wyoming's first Territorial Senate, to introduce the bill. Only one primary source supports this interpretation, that one written in 1919, fifty years after the fact. However, many Internet sources today support the claim without providing any documentation. A statue of Morris is one of Wyoming's two contributions to Statuary Hall in the U.S. Capitol, not only because she served as the first female justice of the peace in the country, but also because of the afore-mentioned party.[2] Historians today discount the tea party, labeling it a myth. Esther never claimed any credit for the passage of the bill, saying it was due entirely to men. In the class the students evaluate the sources and come to their own conclusions.[3] However, this being the first class, some students are somewhat hesitant to express their views.

The next three classes are devoted to archival administration. Students learn about the appraisal process, arrangement and description of manuscript collections, and reference. These three topics are taught because they inform the research process. The students need to know how and why and what types of materials are collected; how those items are arranged and described; and then how to search for appropriate collections and research materials.

According to educator John Bean, one "way to promote critical thinking is to model it."[4] Through two readings and class lectures we provide examples of research processes. The first book the students read and review is Robert Root's *Recovering Ruth: A Biographer's Tale*.[5] Root, at the time he wrote the book an English professor at Central Michigan University, was intrigued by an 1848 diary of Mrs. C.C. Douglass in the school's library and wanted to find out more about her. His research led him to conclude that the diary, attributed to a Mrs. Douglass (Lydia), was not written by her. His journey to discover all he could about the actual author (Ruth, Douglass' first wife) became quite personal and extensive. The students do not write a typical review of the book, but review his research process: was it productive, creative, too far afield, etc.[6]

The second book is Robert M. Utley's *Billy the Kid: A Short and Violent Life*.[7] This book is used not because of the well known subject of the Old West, but because of Utley's evaluation of sources in the endnotes. Again, students do not review the book, but instead how the author evaluated the sources re-

lated to Billy's life and death. Many authors do not dissect their sources to the depth Utley does and many readers do not bother reading the notes. Utley's notes, however, illuminate why he used some sources while discounting others, and even explain why he used some previously discounted sources to provide context.[8]

Two class lectures also model research processes. In one, we explore the story of purported Western hero Frank Hopkins, featured in the Disney movie *Hidalgo* (which the film studio claimed was a true story). In a number of short articles written in the 1930s and 1940s, Hopkins details his life as a dispatch rider during the 1870s, an endurance racer who never lost a race, and a longtime performer in Buffalo Bill's *Wild West*. However, none of these claims can be verified in any newspapers, Buffalo Bill materials, census records, etc.; this then serves as an exercise in negative research through which we conclude that the exciting life of this supposed western hero is all fiction.[9] The other research model is presented by AHC faculty member D. Claudia Thompson, who has written about the image of Tom Horn. Horn has become a noted figure in Wyoming history because he was convicted and hanged in 1903 for the murder of a fourteen-year-old boy. The discussion of whether Horn actually committed the crime is still ongoing in Cheyenne. Getting beyond the familiar story of Horn and his purported misdeed, Thompson looks at how Horn has been portrayed through the years.[10] She also discusses a letter donated to the AHC several years ago supposedly written by someone who witnessed Horn talking about one of his alleged murder victims and has the students discuss its provenance and validity.[11]

The Archival Research Methods course includes two group projects. Educators and others believe group work is a form of active learning that promotes critical thinking and provides practice in leadership, group interaction, public speaking, and makes the students responsible for designing research questions and formulating their own solutions.[12] The two projects deal with a World War II Japanese internment camp, the Heart Mountain Relocation Center, which was located in northwest Wyoming, and Sacajawea, the well-known Native American who accompanied Lewis and Clark on their expedition during the early 1800s.

The AHC has a number of small, but quite rich, collections dealing with the Heart Mountain Relocation Center. Among items in this collection are a diary of one of the camp's early administrators; letters of the two Wyoming governors who held office during the war; copies of the camp's newspaper, the *Heart Mountain Sentinel*; and the papers of a UW faculty member who studied maternity care at the camp. The class is divided into four groups, each receiving its own collection. The students use one class period (two and one-half hours) to research the materials, but they are expected to conduct research on their own time as well. The end product of this project is a lesson plan, presented to the entire class, based on selected primary sources directed at tenth grade students. The lesson plan includes a title page, a statement of two or more lesson objectives, an introductory essay of one or two pages providing context, a document set of five to ten primary sources for student analysis, three to five discussion questions, and a bibliography of sources used. Through this group exercise, the students enhance their own research skills and develop discussion questions and activities for critical thinking exercises.[13]

One of the most useful and enjoyable exercises is a debate about when Sacajawea died and where she is buried. The class is again divided into four groups. Two research the view that Sacajawea died in 1884 on the Wind River Reservation in Wyoming, using the papers of Grace Raymond Hebard, the chief proponent of the Wyoming version. The other two groups research the interpretation that she died in 1812 in what is today Montana, and use the papers of Blanche Schroer, a local historian from Fremont County, Wyoming, who at first supported Hebard, but changed her mind after researching the subject

on her own.[14] The students again have one class period (in addition to their own time) in which to research the papers and select appropriate sources to craft an argument. Two debates follow in which competitive juices flow and some of the students become quite animated and intense. Winners are not declared, but after the debates the class as a whole discusses the sources. Each group also turns in a five-page paper detailing their argument along with copies of the most valuable sources related to their interpretation. As noted in Bean's *Engaging Ideas*, "...collaborative learning promoted argumentation and consensus building: each student had to support a hypothesis with reasons and evidence in an attempt to sway others. The improved thinking grew out of the practice of formulating hypotheses, arguing for their adequacy, and seeking a reasoned consensus that all group members support."[15]

The class also includes a semester-long research project. This is a document-based research effort culminating in a research paper of fifteen to twenty pages in length (twenty to twenty-five pages for graduate students) and a presentation to be given before an audience during the last few class periods. Most students choose PowerPoint presentations although presenting in the format of a lesson plan is also encouraged. The focus of the research may be biographical or topical. Students receive a list of AHC collections during the second class period from which one is selected. Among the available collections are materials about and from Wyoming,, those related to World War II, to journalism, to the blacklisting of the 1940s and 1950s, and to popular culture. All of the listed collections contain more than enough material for this type of project.[16]

The students are limited in the type and number of sources which can be used in their research. Web-based sources, both secondary and primary, can total only ten percent of the sources. If they used web-based sources they must provide a written evaluation of the authority of the sources. Also, the students can only use other secondary sources totaling another ten percent of the total sources. Primary sources other than those from the web should total eighty percent. The goal of the semester project is for the students to conduct in-depth research and write their paper based mainly on their interpretation of the sources in the collection. Students are given two class periods for their research, although this certainly is not enough research time for such extensive papers. Since this is a semester-long project there are related assignments during the class to ensure students do not wait until the last week or two of class to begin working on the paper. Students need to first select their collection, then provide a preliminary research thesis, then a bibliography, and finally a revised thesis statement.[17]

During one of the classes two students selected the papers of Admiral Husband Kimmel for their research projects. Kimmel was the commander of U.S. Naval Forces at Pearl Harbor at the time of the Japanese attack in December 1941. Both students explored who should bear responsibility for the lack of preparedness for the attack. One student leaned more toward the revisionist interpretation, concluding "the burden of responsibility …does not rest on Admiral Kimmel's shoulders. Due to the evidence of suppressed diplomatic intercepts and President Roosevelt's belligerent attempts to provide a Japanese act of aggression on the United States, the burden of responsibility has to rest higher up the chain of command, namely with President Roosevelt." The other student's interpretation revealed a more complicated matter, finding fault with top officials in Washington, the inability to quickly sort through the vast intelligence gathered, the army and the lack of planes in Hawaii, and Kimmel for leaving the majority of the fleet in port. "What occurred was the result of numerous mistakes committed by the top officials in Washington and the forces at Oahu, not conspiracy." They presented during the same class period which led to an interesting discussion of interpretation. Other topics were wide-ranging and have included a study of medical care along the Or-

egon Trail, the life of a fur trapper who lost his entire family to smallpox, an examination of Carroll Baker's role in the 1950s movie *Baby Doll* and how that challenged the mores of the time, and the reasons behind the suicide of U.S. Senator Lester Hunt in his senate office in 1954.

The Archival Research Methods course has proven to be a success at UW. Attendance has grown each year. During the spring semester of 2010, the class was full at twenty students; about one-quarter of the students were education majors, with the majority of the remainder history majors; in spring 2012, 19 students were enrolled. The class is now a permanent class in the History Department and is included in the Museum Studies program curriculum and is a required course in the Public History Concentration.[18]

NOTES

1. Marcus C. Robyns, "The Archivist as Educator: Integrating Critical Thinking Skills into Historical Research Methods Instruction," *The American Archivist*, 64 (Fall-Winter 2001): 379.

2. The website for Statuary Hall in the U.S. Capitol states this about Morris: "To promote the idea of giving women the right to vote, Morris organized a tea party for the electors and candidates for the first territorial legislature." See http:www.aoc.gov/cc/art/nsh/morris.cfm. Accessed August 1, 2010.

3. For more information about the tea party discussion see Rick Ewig, "Did She Do That: Examining Esther Morris' Role in the Passage of the Suffrage Act," *Annals of Wyoming*, 78 (Winter 2006): 26-34. See also T.A. Larson, *History of Wyoming* (Lincoln: University of Nebraska Press, 1965), pp. 78-94; Michael A. Massie, "Reform Is Where You Find It: The Roots of Woman Suffrage in Wyoming," *Annals of Wyoming*, 62 (Spring 1990): 2-22. When Morris' statue was dedicated at the U.S. Capitol in 1960 a number of dignitaries spoke and supported the idea Morris played a substantial role in the passage of the suffrage bill. Nellie Taylor Ross, who became the first female governor in the country when

she took the oath of office in Wyoming in January 1925, gave credit to Esther; Wyoming U.S. Senator Joseph O'Mahoney also gave credit to Morris and her "notable tea party"; even Vice President Richard Nixon said he believed "all the stories about the tea party that started it all," certainly putting an end to all of opposition to the story.

4. See John C. Bean, *Engaging Ideas: The Professor's Guide to Integrating Writing, Critical Thinking, and Active Learning in the Classroom* (San Francisco: Jossey-Bass Publishers, 2001), p. 172.

5. Robert Root, *Recovering Ruth: A Biographer's Tale* (Lincoln and London: University of Nebraska Press, 2003). Root sees writing history as a "creative process of focus, selection, interpretation, and expression...." p. 7.

6. The review instructions ask the students to evaluate "the author's research process, giving special attention to any notable successes, as well as to omissions, pitfalls, and oversights which appear to have occurred in the research and preparation of the manuscript." In one of the reviews a student wrote the book "is a great introduction to the nature and spirit of research with primary documents."

7. Robert M. Utley, *Billy the Kid: A Short and Violent Life* (Lincoln and London: University of Nebraska Press, 1989).

8. The students in their reviews have to provide "a detailed discussion of the author's evaluation of his sources as reflected in the endnotes of the work. The reviewer should discuss how information provided in the endnotes enhanced or informed their overall understanding of both the text and Utley's research process in preparing the book." One student remarked in her review: "I will be the first to admit that when I see a little number at the end of a sentence that I am reading I will ignore it completely and continue with my reading. However, I suppose I will have to rectify that misdeed because while reading this book I found the endnotes to be informative, entertaining, enjoyable.... Some of what I read in his footnotes will definitely make a difference in how I do my research

in the future."

9. Hopkins claimed he won 400 endurance races all over the world. The "Ocean of Fire" race featured in the film *Hidalgo* is not verified in any sources. There is no record of Hopkins ever being a member of Buffalo Bill's troupe, even though Hopkins claimed he rode with Cody for more than thirty years and attended his funeral in 1917. For more information about Hopkins' writing see Frank Hopkins, *Hidalgo and Other Stories*, edited by Basha O'Reilly (Long Riders Guild Press, 2004).

10. See D. Claudia Thompson, "The Image of Tom Horn," *Annals of Wyoming*, 77 (Spring 2005): 2-11.

11. D. Claudia Thompson, "Tom Horn's Accusers," *Annals of Wyoming*, 77 (Summer 2005): 26-28.

12. Bean, *Engaging Ideas*.

13. One of the groups that had the camp newspapers as well as other newspapers developed some interesting objectives, questions, and activities. Two of the objectives were to educate students about the camp and apply research methods to enhance critical thinking skills. One of the discussion questions was "what did you learn from the newspapers that you might not have learned from a history book?", which was intended for the students to think about different types of sources and to compare and contrast the pros and cons of primary sources. A second question was "why do you think America allowed Japanese internment camps during the war?" with the intent to relate to the motivations of the time. The AHC has digitized its collections related to the Heart Mountain Relocation Center and the documents are accessible on the AHC's website. Since education students are part of the intended audience for the class, having them lead in the creation of a lesson plan in the class may encourage them to use the lesson plan in their future classroom. I put an education student in each of the groups so they can provide leadership in this exercise.

14. Grace Raymond Hebard also wrote a book about Sacajawea titled *Sacajawea: Guide and Interpreter for Lewis and Clark* first published in 1933. The book is still in print. One of the most recent books which discount's

Hebard's interpretation is Thomas H. Johnson, *Also Called Sacajawea: Chief Woman's Stolen Identity* (Waveland Press, Inc., 2007). Hebard's papers (#400,008) and Schroer's papers (#10575) are both held by the AHC.

15. Bean, *Engaging Ideas*, p. 150.

16. The final paper includes a title page, footnotes or endnotes, and an annotated bibliography. *The Chicago Manual of Style* is used in the class.

17. During the research time provided in class, I go around and talk to every student about their collection, thesis, and what sources they are finding most useful. Of course, students often will change their thesis based on the sources they find in their chosen collections.

18. The author is the associate director of the American Heritage Center, University of Wyoming, and the editor of the state's historical journal, *Annals of Wyoming*.

THE
PROGRAM

Faculty Buy-In: Encouraging Student Use through Faculty Stipends

Sarah M. Horowitz and Jamie L. Nelson

Materials in special collections departments are sometimes overlooked by undergraduate students in their rush to find online, full-text answers to questions that might better lend themselves to more thoughtful inquiry. Augustana College Special Collections has designed a relatively inexpensive, yet highly effective, program that encourages the use of Special Collections materials in the curriculum and is easily replicable at other institutions. Because exploring special collections materials and incorporating them into a course can be time-consuming, Augustana College Special Collections acknowledges faculty effort and provides a small stipend as both an incentive and a reward. Fourteen faculty stipends for enhanced access to the collections during the summer months have been awarded since 2001, and the results have been nothing short of amazing.

Using stipends as a way to encourage researchers to work in special collections is a time-honored practice, but these stipends are usually aimed at supporting the personal research of outside scholars. Such grants bring prestige, either through word of mouth or publications, to a special collections department and its holdings. Using stipends to encourage campus faculty to design undergraduate assignments based on special collections materials is a more locally focused program, and one designed to influence how special collections is used and perceived on campus.

Augustana College (Rock Island, Illinois) is a liberal arts college with approximately 2,500 students. Special Collections holds 16,000 printed volumes, 2,317 linear feet of manuscripts in just over 300 collections, and about 60,000 images of various types. We have 2.5 FTE staff (two librarians, .5 support staff; until Fall 2007, there was only one Special Collections Librarian), and rely heavily on student workers. We are open Monday through Thursday, 1:00–5:00, and by appointment. Special Collections taught twenty-eight class instruction sessions in academic year 2010-2011 for faculty in seven disciplines (the greatest use came from faculty teaching first-year general education courses), and completed 718 reference requests from student researchers, with 857 reference requests overall.

In Spring 2001, Special Collections announced its first call for proposals for a faculty research stipend program. The stipend program is open to all faculty at Augustana, including adjunct, tenure-track, and tenured. Stipends of $600 for one week of enhanced access to Special Collections are added to each recipient's summer payroll as taxable income. (Stipends were originally $500; the amount was raised in 2008 in an attempt to keep up with inflationary pressures.)

Information on the faculty stipend program is available year-round on the Special Collections website, but we remind faculty each spring about a month before the proposals are due. We announce the stipend via an email to all faculty, the online faculty newsletter, and the library's blog. Applicants are asked to write a brief statement about the materials they wish to use or what question they want to explore, the course into which these materials might be integrated or the research project they are intended to inform, and dates when they are available to work in Special Collections. The application is available on our website: http://www.augustana.edu/x34663.xml.

Once the announcement has been sent to faculty, the Special Collections Librarians often receive inquiries about whether we have materials related to the interests of various faculty members. While all inquiries do not necessarily lead to applications, faculty do learn more about our collections because of the program's existence and our publicity. Once proposals have arrived, they are reviewed by the Special Collections Librarians. The proposals are evaluated based on the intersection of factors such as: proposed student projects and course level; uniqueness of the materials to be researched; potential impact on the curriculum; feasibility of the research and resulting student projects; and the ability of the faculty member to influence other faculty, directly or indirectly, to consider Special Collections for student use. Not all proposals have been funded; the goal is to award money with discretion and make the best use of limited staff time and funds. The number of recipients each summer has generally depended on the availability of money and librarians and number of proposals received, but it has ranged from one to four. Once the grant recipients have been selected by the Special Collections Librarians, the proposals are reviewed by the library director and the academic dean. These are pro forma reviews, as the director and dean have always concurred with the librarians' selections, but it is a good way to make the program and Special Collections more visible to the general library and the College administration. Furthermore, having the dean serve as one of the reviewers adds prestige to the program in the eyes of faculty.

We inform applicants about the status of their proposals in mid April, and work with them to schedule their research in Special Collections at a time mutually agreeable to the faculty member and his/her librarian partner. While a researcher may work with both Special Collections Librarians, generally one is assigned to be the researcher's primary partner. The nature of the project and availability of the librarians determines partnerships. Assigning faculty members to work primarily with one librarian enables remaining staff to continue other essential activities during the stipend period.

Standard security and use policies are followed during the faculty member's time in Special Collections, and staff are available to assist with research, talk through research questions, suggest resources, and provide reproductions for further study. While this level of service is provided to all researchers throughout the year, the award program provides an incentive for faculty to spend concentrated time periods in Special Collections, and the Special Collections Librarians clear their schedules in order to be especially attentive and available during this time. The librarian partner normally sits down with the researcher at the beginning of his or her time in Special Collections to discuss the research question(s) outlined in his statement of interest and how he would like to proceed on his research. At the end of the week, the librarian generally meets with the faculty member to wrap up and discuss possible assignments, any other work that may need to be done, and the faculty member's experience. Faculty are asked to provide Special Collections with a short summary of their work. While the amount of interaction with recipients will depend on their level of familiarity with special collections materials, it is not unusual for the librarian to spend much of the week collaborating with each researcher.

Special Collections and faculty both reap benefits from this program. Faculty can design new or invigorate existing courses with unique content and generate creative projects for students, while Special Collections reaches new audiences (faculty and student) and gains a deeper knowledge of the materials in our care. Reference and instruction statistics have more than doubled since these stipends have been offered, and while this increase can be attributed to a combination of outreach efforts, it is clear that the stipend program has contributed significantly to this success. Fourteen stipends have been awarded from 2001 to 2011 to faculty of varying ranks from diverse disciplines. The disciplinary distribution is widespread and somewhat surprising: four history (one with joint appointment to Women and Gender Studies); two English (one with a joint appointment to education); and one each from anthropology, geography, art history, religion, math, French, German, and Scandinavian Studies (see Appendix 1.1, Faculty Stipend Recipients).

As stated in the call for proposals, research with a direct tie to the curriculum and student use of the materials is privileged in the selection process. A natural result of this, and an easily measurable metric of success, is the number of instruction sessions scheduled as a result of the stipend research. In the 2000-2001 academic year—the school year directly before the stipend implementation—Special Collections conducted three instruction sessions. By the 2010-2011 academic year, instruction had grown to twenty-eight sessions, tying with a previous record high during 2008-2009 (see Appendix 1.1, Instruction Sessions and Total Reference). Through Spring 2011, 653 students have been introduced to Special Collections through the instruction sessions of stipend-awarded professors.

Not all of this instruction is directly attributable to the stipend program, although thirty-five sessions of class instruction have been requested by faculty stipend awardees since the inception of the program. Of the fourteen faculty awardees to date, twelve have scheduled at least one instruction session in Special Collections post-stipend. From 2001 to the end of the 2011 academic year, these twelve recipients partnered with Special Collections for an average of three classes each. Of the two who have not scheduled classes in Special Collections, one used his research in support of an article (which was his intent at the time of his application), and one has been reassigned to teach courses not related to her research in Special Collections.

These instruction statistics might be higher if the stipend program were limited to tenured faculty. Of the fourteen recipients from 2001-2011, four have been tenured faculty, eight have been tenure-track junior faculty, and two have been adjuncts. Five of these fourteen are no longer in the employ of Augustana College due to retirement (1) and pre-tenure turnover (4). The Special Collections staff time and stipend money spent on these five professors is still a good investment, in that Special Collections Librarians connect with their successors and talk about Special Collections resources investigated by their predecessors and the potential benefits to student learning. Of the replacement faculty for these five, three have used Special Collections for the instruction purposes envisioned by their predecessors. While acknowledging the potential lack of continuity when working with junior faculty, we feel the benefits outweigh the potential costs.

Additional reference and instruction traffic is generated by faculty's enthusiasm for special collections materials. Individual, upper-level students are directed to Special Collections for research in collections examined by stipend awardees. Faculty members who have heard of colleagues' success with special collections-related assignments refer individual students, schedule full classes for instruction, or are motivated to apply for stipends themselves. The stipend program has enabled Special Collections to achieve mainstream status within the array of academic resources available at Augustana. As more faculty use Special Collections as a learning laboratory for their students, momentum grows and demand for our materials increases.

Our success has been coupled with a few challenges, however. While Special Collections celebrates our ever-increasing reference count, the phenomenal growth puts a strain on our small staff. When our total reference count was around 300 at the inception of the stipend program, students could count on lengthy, personalized reference interviews with the Special Collections Librarian. As reference has soared to over 800 interactions per year, Special Collections Librarians can no longer spend as much time with each researcher and student workers have stepped in to assist patrons. The reading room can be packed to capacity when assignment due dates near, with thirty students needing assistance within the space of four hours. Often each student needs reproductions made from our materials, placing an additional burden on our student support staff, as patrons are not allowed to make their own copies. While too many researchers is an enviable problem, the demand does have an impact on the rest of our operations.

Librarians at Augustana have ten-month contracts, and work approximately twenty days during June, July, and August. Summer is often a good time to catch up on projects that have languished over the school year or to get ahead for the fall term. Scheduling one or more faculty stipends in the summer reduces librarians' ability to concentrate on such projects, since at least five of those days are spent with each stipend recipient. Due to demands on staff time, applications were not solicited or accepted for four of the eleven years the program has been in existence. In 2004, Special Collections underwent a major collection reorganization and was closed to all researchers for the summer. In 2007 and 2009, maternity leaves made it impractical to host stipend researchers. In 2011, the installation of new compact shelving necessitated closing Special Collections over the summer. While it is important to build momentum with such a program, staffing is a very practical consideration.

While the faculty stipend program detailed in this article was initially developed within Augustana's framework, it is easily adaptable and relevant to many institutions. Institutions will have to decide the best way to schedule faculty access, how much money to offer each recipient, how to evaluate the proposals they receive, and how to evaluate the success of the program.

The amount of money offered for the faculty stipend should be based on local expectations; librarians might consider the amount of money offered to faculty through other grant programs at their institution. Augustana's $600 stipend is fairly generous, considering that a college summer research grant for junior faculty pays $1800 for the entire summer. The money used for our program comes from gift funds, but this is not the only possible source of income. A faculty stipend program might be sponsored by a library or special collections friends group, be added as a regular budget expenditure, or gathered through departmental fundraising. Some institutions may benefit by funding several small stipends, others by funding one larger, more intensive project.

The stipend program at Augustana has been offered over the summer because there are few summer classes, so the reference load is lighter. Depending on staffing and faculty availability and interest, other institutions might make stipend weeks available over other class breaks, or even during the term. The length of time for enhanced access could also vary. One week is easy for faculty to commit to and does not take up too much of a librarian's time. Other institutions could expand or reduce faculty research time in response to their own staffing.

A faculty stipend program is an excellent way to increase the visibility of special collections among faculty. The stipend can be marketed to attract departments or programs that have underutilized special collections. For instance, publicity could be targeted to faculty who have never used special collections before, to faculty teaching general education classes, to faculty teaching senior seminars, or to new faculty. Augustana College's faculty stipend program deserves some credit for the high patron count and number of classes using Special Collections. With a modest investment of money and staff time, the visibility and use of special collections materials can be dramatically increased.

APPENDIX 1.1. Faculty Stipend Recipients

Year	Department	Status	Classes since award
2001	Sociology**	tt	0
	History	T	2
	French**	tt	3
	English*	T	1
2002	History	tt	3
	Geography	T	2
2003	History	tt	6
	Scandinavian**	tt	1
2004			
2005	Art History**	tt	3
2006	Religion	a	8
2007			
2008	WGS/History	tt	4
	English	a	0
2009			
2010	Math	T	1
	German	tt	1
2011			
			Total: 36
Key *retired **gone T = Tenured tt = Tenure-track a = Adjunct			

Instruction Sessions and Total Reference

Year	Number of Class Sessions	Total Reference
2000-2001	3	295
2001-2002	8	373
2002-2003	6	349
2003-2004	6	340
2004-2005	7	379
2005-2006	10	427
2006-2007	13	479
2007-2008	16	570
2008-2009	28	731
2009-2010	26	815
2010-2011	28	857

Collaboration between the Iowa State University Honors Program and the Special Collections Department (ISU Library)

Tanya Zanish-Belcher, Laurie Fiegel, and Ashley Rosener

The Iowa State University Honors Program is a university-wide program established in 1960 to encourage breadth of intellectual experience and interaction among high ability students from all academic majors. The program is designed to promote an individualized four-year academic plan developed to meet a student's particular needs, interests, and abilities. Shared knowledge is an important component of a well-rounded University education, and collaborative learning experiences provide the means for such engagement. Although this is a flexible program, there are some minimum requirements all students must meet. All members of the Honors Program must enroll in a series of interdisciplinary seminars designed to promote creative exploration. This begins with a first-year seminar where students are introduced to the importance of learning outside the traditional classroom setting. Students in this course experience the broader scope of a Carnegie Research I institution through an in-depth exploration of campus research facilities and lectures. Upper division Honors seminars give faculty members from all academic departments the opportunity to explore new course materials or teaching techniques in a collaborative learning environment. The courses are designed to promote discussion and student-faculty interaction. According to former student Ashley Rosener, "The small class sizes of the honors seminars create a wonderful environment. Everyone grows comfortable with each other, and we're able to share our thoughts and ideas without fear of reproach."

The Special Collections Department of the Iowa State University Library was founded in 1969, and contains over 16,000 linear ft. of archival collections; 1,000,000 photographs; 10,000 motion picture films; and 55,000 rare book volumes, with the earliest dating to 1475. The Department maintains an active program of public service, outreach, and tours for both on and off campus groups, including academic classes, the Center for Excellence in Learning and Teaching, ISU Learning Communities, Extension and 4-H groups, and K-12 student groups such as those participating in National History Day. The University Honors Program is an obvious candidate for curricular outreach, given the program's goal of promoting "an enriched academic environment for students of high ability, regardless of major, who are interested in taking advantage of educational and intellectual opportunities and challenges."

Beginning approximately ten years ago, the Special Collections Department and Honors Program began to collaborate on a systematic program of visits and tours that—though modest in scope—greatly benefits undergraduate students. Building on this foundation, in 2005, the Head of Special Collections submitted a proposal for a one-credit Honors Seminar, "From Incunabula to PDFs: The Future of Libraries," further strengthening the relationship with the Honors Program. Honors seminars can be one- or two-credit courses on current topics, and their purpose is to offer a "crucial atmosphere of intellectual exchange and a high level of student involvement in learning." The original intent of this seminar was to offer a unique opportunity for students to connect personally with special collections materials, and to see how they might be used as part of future learning experiences at the university. It was hoped that these students, after learning more about the collections, would return to use them for their coursework. The second goal was to increase general undergraduate use of special collections by simple word of mouth, throughout the Honors Program and beyond.

Since 2005, this seminar has met one evening a week, from 6:00-8:00 p.m., in the Special Collections Reading Room. The class starts with a general introduction and tour of the Department. It continues weekly with an in-depth topic, such as rare books, artifacts, the basics of archival appraisal and description, working with donors, the history of photographs, and the challenge of electronic records. Each week includes a brief presentation and discussion based on previously assigned readings, as well as one hands-on type of activity. Another feature, early in the seminar, was to have Karen Brookfield's *Book* (a history of printing and early books) available in the Special Collections Reading Room and require each student to come in and read it during the week between class meetings. This exercise was intended to increase student comfort levels with walking in the front door of Special Collections (which, at times, can seem intimidating). The artifacts class focuses on some of the 3,000 three-dimensional objects in the University Archives, specifically showcasing items from the University's history, such as a letter sweater, a death mask, and other objects. The discussion covers the challenges relating to description, housing and long-term preservation of this collection. A class on rare books includes the presentation of "The Making of a Renaissance Book," film and a hands-on session examining a selection of early manuscripts and 16th-18th century herbals. Another class exam-

ines the day-to-day issue of working with donors of personal papers and organizational records and the many difficulties and opportunities provided when communicating with individuals and groups. Later readings include works by Gerry Ham, Mary Lynn Ritzenthaler, other selections from the Society of American Archivists, and even an online digital preservation tutorial. Each year this seminar has been offered, the instructor has retained elements of the syllabus that worked well and fostered discussion, and removed those that did not. The seminar has also involved a number of guest speakers, covering such topics as the history of academic libraries and the work of the Library's Preservation Department. In addition, an early assignment for the participants requires them to select three online exhibits on an archives or special collections topic and analyze their research value.

Over the years, the ISU Honors Program has evolved considerably. One of the central tenets of the program is the importance of peer teaching. After Year 1 of the seminar, the instructor felt the need for a concluding event, or culmination of the course, and an opportunity for each participant to research and share information on a particular topic. By the fourth week of class, students are expected to have selected a possible topic for a research poster and presentation. By Year 4, this assignment had expanded to include a contextual paper and bibliography, as the students appeared to respond better to a certain level of requirement in the coursework. Another addition in Year 5 was a round robin analysis of primary documents and photographs. Each student now spends 5 minutes analyzing a specific item based on guidelines and questions provided by the instructor. The documents can be as varied as a 1950 freshman rule book, an issue of *The Green Gander* (an early campus humor magazine), Civil War letters, or historical newspaper clippings. The instructor adds comments and analysis of the object's origins, meaning, context, and limitations as well.

The results of this collaboration between Special Collections and the Honors Program has had several results, some expected, others not. It offers the opportunity for the Department Head to interact with undergraduate students on a more personal level, to assess how rare and unique materials might be used by them, how they perceive the Department and its role in the university, and to raise awareness about the Department. As of 2011, this seminar has now been offered five times, and student participants have gone on to complete internships in the Department, apply for Library employment, work on library projects, and complete a variety of Honors Capstone projects that are related to archives or special collections. Several have even applied for graduate work in archives and library science.

Many of the Honors students participating in the seminar elected to use Special Collections as a basis for their Capstone Project. One such student is Ian Ringgenberg, currently a graduate student at Iowa State. For his project, he elected to conduct a series of oral history interviews with ISU students from the 1980s, under the auspices and direction of the Department's University Records Analyst. After being introduced to interview techniques and technology, he submitted a proposal to the Honors Program Review Board, adhering likewise to the rules of the University's Institutional Review Board (regarding the use of human subjects).

A number of participating students have also approached the Department about potential employment, and—when appropriate—the students have been hired as assistants for collections processing. Ashley Rosener, a recent Iowa State graduate, not only was hired as a student worker, but also completed an in-depth internship focusing on archives work. Her Capstone project involved digitizing a collection of photographs from the University Archives and then researching the benefits and challenges of digital preservation. In response to these opportunities, Rosener said, "The work I've been able to do with the Special Collections Department and Honors Program has been the highlight of my undergraduate career. I've found an area of study I am truly passionate about." Rosener aspires to be an academic librarian and now attends the University of Illinois's Graduate Program in Library and Information Science.

Students who were part of the Honors Program also have been encouraged to collaborate with Special Collections in other ways. Samuel Berbano, an Honors student during his employment time in Special Collections, focused his efforts on developing an updated tour and podcast on the Library for every student in the Honors Program that is still being used. The Honors Program additionally sponsors a research mentorship. As part of the continuing collaboration, the instructor participated in this program, mentoring a first-year undergraduate in the research process. This included meeting with the student once a week and introducing the student to the basics of research, such as conducting a literature survey and compiling information for an article.

Another unexpected benefit of this ongoing collaboration has been the donation of student-related materials to Special Collections. During the first year of the seminar, several friends living in a first-year Honors Learning Community took the seminar together. As an outcome of their experience, they made arrangements to transfer scrapbooks from their hall, called Harwood House, to the Library. Recognizing the importance of providing a use copy, the Special Collections Department digitized the scrapbooks and provided copies to be retained in the residence hall. The originals are maintained in the University Archives, but the students still have copies to peruse. Similarly, another student group, the Society of Chemistry Undergraduate Majors (also known as SCUM), donated a scrapbook and clippings that documented their outreach activities.

At Iowa State University, the Director of the Honors Program and the Special Collections Department Head continue to explore ways of expanding collaborative projects. One recent proposal has been to develop an in-depth research seminar for the entire Honors Program enrollment. The 2010 seminar had seventeen students enrolled and the instructor incorporated additional hands-on and interactive work. For staff in Special Collections and Archives, opportunities abound for collaborating with their institutional Honors programs. For those at other institutions just beginning a similar journey, consider working with an identified group of chosen students as a starting point. Not only is it more likely that these students will be interested, but a structure and some administrative support will already exist. Approach the Director of the University Honors Program or a program director for any kind of first-year seminar or learning community. Spend some time investigating the specific goals and needs of the program, and ways in which they might intersect with library-related goals, such as:

- Expanding the students' concept and understanding of an academic library
- Revealing the role Special Collections can play on a university campus
- Introducing students to the concepts of primary documents and the time/effort/labor that go into caring for them in perpetuity

The results can be fruitful and long-lasting, for both the Department and the Honors students.

APPENDIX 2.1 HON 321Y
Incunabula to PDFs: What is the Future of Libraries?
Tuesday, 2nd half, 6:00–8:00 p.m., 1 credit.
(Oct. 26-Dec. 7, 2010 | 403 Parks Library)

Instructor: Tanya Zanish-Belcher
tzanish@iastate.edu or 294-6648)

Description: Utilizing the rare and unique collections housed by the Special Collections Department in the Iowa State University Library, students will explore and discuss the various issues relating to the preservation and access of primary sources. We will specifically look at the Department's rare book collection, including incunabula (published between 1475 and 1501); the artifact collection documenting the history of ISU; the photograph collection which numbers over 1 million images; manuscript collections, focusing on the topic of international agriculture through letters and photographs; and a collection of motion picture films created by ISU. How researchers use this material will be discussed, and finally, the class will look at the impact of the digital revolution. What issues does digitizing raise for these materials, in terms of their access, care of the physical object, copyright, reference use, and technological needs of the institution? Class time will be dedicated to presentations based on the topic, care and handling of the objects, and class discussion related to the presentation and readings.

Attendance: Attending each class is highly recommended. Excused absences must be submitted in advance.

OCTOBER 26:
- 6:10-6:30: Introduction and Overview of Class
- 6:30-6:50: Guest Speaker: Ed Goedeken, ISU Library Collections Officer, "Overview of Academic Libraries"

- 6:50-8:00: History and Tour of Special Collections

Reading for next class:

Brookfield, Karen. Book. London: Dorling Kindersly, 2000. (On reserve in Special Collections)

Weiner, Sharon Gray. "The History of Academic Libraries in the United States: a Review of the Literature." (Will be distributed in class)

Assignment: Due November 17 by 5:00 p.m., can be submitted electronically at any time prior

Topic: Review of 3 Special Collections-related (non-ISU) online exhibits on any topic

Length: 2 pages

Structure for Report:
    Institution Name
    Exhibit Title
    URL
    Brief description of topic and research value
    Personal impressions of the technology and visual design
    What worked/what did not

OCTOBER 27

- Readings Discussion
- Collection Development for Special Collections
- Rare Books
    Incunabula
    Reference and Access Issues
    Preservation Issues
    Digital Issues
    Special format books
- Video—*The Making of a Renaissance Book* (20 minutes)

Reading for next class:

Ham, F. Gerald. *Selecting and Appraising Manuscripts*. Chicago: Society of American Archivists,

1993. (Selected Chapters, distributed in class)

NOVEMBER 3

- Readings Discussion
- Working with Donors
- Archives and Manuscripts
    Workflow
    Arrangement and Description
    Reference and Access Issues
    Preservation Issues
    Digital Issues
- University Archives
    Records
    Artifact Collection
    Institutional Repositories
    Electronic Records

Exercise: Examining Primary Documents

Poster Sessions: Discussion of topics for December 8; Topics Due Nov. 17

Each class participant must prepare and give a short presentation and poster session to the entire class. Any topic related to special collections and libraries is welcome. In addition, a one-page paper must be submitted, detailing the following: the topic, a brief bibliography, and overview of the presentation as well any conclusions or observations.

Reading for November 10 class:

Ritzenthaler, Mary Lynn. *Photographs: Archival Care and Management*. Chicago: Society of American Archivists, 1984 (Selected Chapters, distributed in class)

Preservation Issues in Special Collections

NOVEMBER 10

- 6:10-6:20: Readings Discussion
- 6:20-6:30: Preservation-related issues in Special Collections
- 6:30-7:15: Guest speaker: Hilary Seo, Head

of Preservation
- Tour of Preservation Lab
- 7:15-8:00: Special Formats and Visual Materials
  - Scrapbooks
  - Glass Plate Negatives
  - Motion Picture Film/Videos/DVDs
  - Photographs
  - Reference and Access Issues
  - Preservation Issues
  - Digital Issues

NOVEMBER 17

First assignment due
Poster topics due

Outreach
- Exhibits
- Undergraduate and K-12
- History Day
- Internships

Administrative Issues
- Budget
- Personnel
- Library

Reading for November 27 class:
Cornell Tutorial: http://www.library.cornell.edu/iris/tutorial/dpm/eng_index.html

NOVEMBER 24: THANKSGIVING BREAK

DECEMBER 1
- Readings Discussion
- Current Projects:
  - Archive-It
  - Institutional Repositories
- Digital Collections and Electronic Records
  - Collection development
  - Technical aspects
  - Metadata
  - Access
  - Maintenance and preservation

Small Group Exercise: Real World Decision Making in the Digital Landscape

Viewing: Video, "The Story of Home Economics"

DECEMBER 8
Poster Presentations

Building a Book Studies Program at a Liberal Arts College

Laura Baudot and Wendy Hyman

What ought to be the role of Book History and the Book Arts in the liberal arts institution blessed with a strong special collections—but lacking the resources, obviously, of a university? How can a small institution make best use of both its bibliographic and pedagogical assets? What does it take to transform a random group of classes into a curriculum? How can a small group of faculty—with already-full dance cards in their individual departments—effectively staff an interdisciplinary program with an eye to institutional longevity?

These were some of the questions that drew us together to begin thinking about the role and future of Book Studies (a little more about our use of this term shortly) at our institution, Oberlin College. Although we were relatively new to the institution, we quickly came to realize the exceptional resource that Oberlin has in its special collections, and not least for the scholar and student of all things bibliographic. Hired at a time when our department and dean were especially open to bridging the gap between the classroom, libraries, and campus museum, we had institutional support to pursue what was already a shared intellectual and pedagogical interest: bringing students into contact with primary source objects in the service of literary and interdisciplinary bibliographic study. But how to make it happen: should we, and how should we, move from a smattering of courses to a self-defined program of study? As tenure-track faculty with other primary disciplines (in Renaissance and in 18th-century English literature, respectively), we wanted to find ways to explore the curricular possibilities at our in-

stitution without sacrificing the time we needed to devote to teaching and scholarship; we also wanted to build bridges among faculty and create excitement among students, colleagues, and administration, though we ourselves were newcomers here.

Before we detail the steps we are taking to explore the possibility of establishing such a program—and we write in the present tense, as we are still in the middle of the process now—we should say a few words about what we mean by Book Studies, the scholarship and teaching of which is obviously abetted by, but not synonymous with, the mere fact of teaching with special collections and archival holdings. For our use of this term itself reveals how much we must define our project with reference to the particularities of our liberal arts setting. At a large university, The History of the Book (with its historical, sociological, and literary foundations) and the Book Arts (with its connection to studio arts and the world of small press poetry) might well be housed in different departments, if not different schools. But at a small institution, it is crucial to place everyone we can under one generous, if sometimes ungainly, umbrella: the Victorianist who examines periodicals and audience; the classicist who transcribes papyrus fragments; the art historian who works with medieval illuminated manuscripts; the film scholar interested in textual culture; the African-Americanist interested in patterns of orality and literacy in the novel; the linguistic anthropologist who researches emerging and alternative literacies; the East Asian Studies professor incorporating Japanese woodblock prints in courses on literary and filmic aesthetics; the published author and rhetoric professor interested in the materiality of writing—to say nothing of local papermakers, printers, book artists, and more. In other words, we employ the term Book Studies to encompass all of us at Oberlin College thinking about cuneiform or Kindle, textual transmission or consumption, the relationship between medium and message, and the social, cultural, economic, and aesthetic issues that arise from these studies—in almost any form whatever. In other words, by Book Studies we do not always even mean books!

Of course, there are challenges as well as virtues to such a broadly defined area of study. The pleasure of thinking so broadly is that it provides great opportunities for cross-pollination—team teaching, scholarly innovation, networking with colleagues at other schools—among those normally constrained by field and institution. But how broadly can we define this area before it becomes too amorphous to be useful? How do we find a methodological common ground or define a legible identity? What should be the nature of the conversation and institutional structure, if any, around such a diverse group of classes?

As is always the case, actualizing the possible is not about the hypothetical, but about the resources that are and are not at hand. Luckily, at Oberlin, with a strong special collections, a first-rate undergraduate art museum, and artists' books, print 'zines, and mail art collections in the art library (to mention just a few highlights), we have unusually rich resources for studying these fields. The College's first professional librarian, Azariah Root, not only taught bibliography but also vigorously built the library's collections back when rare books were less rare and less pricy. The human resources are also terrific, with several people actively publishing in the field. We have opportunities to collaborate with woodcut artists, papermakers, and printers in Oberlin and Cleveland. Considering that there has been at Oberlin College no programmatic focus in

the field, a surprising number of faculty members have genuine expertise and interest in Book Studies. Crucially, for many years prior to our arrivals, the library director and special collections librarian have collected rare and pedagogically important books, and, ever-willing to host a variety of classes, have taken great pains to encourage faculty use of special collections. This, more than anything, has laid the groundwork for the recent steps taken to build a program. In addition, grants offered by the Friends of the Library committee for the integration of special collections into courses have been very effective in generating faculty interest in special collections. Receiving a grant to revamp a course on British 18th-century fiction to include regular "lab sessions" in special collections is in fact what led one of us to undertake this project of building Book Studies into the curriculum.

Finally, several library-sponsored talks and conferences have helped to generate a certain amount of energy around Book Studies among faculty and students prior to our more recent efforts. In the spring of 2009, for example, the library organized a conference on the "Future of the Book." Faculty from the college served as respondents for talks given by high profile players in the fields of publishing, library studies, and media studies. This conference was very helpful for highlighting the timeliness of Book Studies by revealing the large cultural stakes of the digital revolution. Such conferences draw attention to one of the issues we stress in conversations with other faculty and the administration: Book Studies does not just offer enormous pedagogical opportunities (learning from artifacts; embracing the complexity of cultural objects in their social, aesthetic, historical and economic dimensions). Students also really *need* to be aware of the dramatically shifting landscape of information technology.

While the special collections librarian, library director, and Friends of the Library board at Oberlin have been tireless in encouraging faculty interest in special collections, librarians will be the first to say that for Book Studies to gain real traction in the curriculum, faculty need to take the lead. As the details of our case study demonstrate, for generating ideas, gaining administrative support and wider faculty interest, branching out to other schools, benefiting from bibliographic resources in the area, making structural changes to the special collections room—in other words, the whole host of things that will make a program possible—faculty members and librarians must join forces. This was particularly true in our case, as relatively new untenured faculty. We offer here a narrative of the steps taken between the fall of 2009 and the present, in collaboration with the director of libraries and the special collections librarian, to put Book Studies on the map at Oberlin.

In an informal meeting in the fall of 2009 with the special collections librarian, we decided that the first step in raising the profile of Book Studies and special collections was to measure faculty interest. To that end, we sent a college-wide email inviting all faculty currently teaching or potentially interested in teaching Book History or Book Arts courses at Oberlin to attend a lunch-time meeting. We thought it was best to frame the conversation as inclusively as possible, not least to attract faculty who might already be teaching in the field without even realizing it. We were equally eager to establish the breadth and flexibility of our goals for the meeting. We ourselves were not sure exactly where the meeting would lead but we wanted at least to get a conversation started among faculty about the potential of this interdisciplinary field. So we left things quite open:

Our desire at this point is to gauge interest for further collaboration, from the informal (sharing techniques for incorporating primary sources in the classroom; inviting speakers) to the ambitious: if there is sufficient interest, we might even talk about creating an interdisciplinary program in "Book Studies" at Oberlin.

The meeting was successful for both measuring and generating faculty enthusiasm, and it really gave us a sense that there was a critical mass of interest. Our agenda for the meeting turned out to be relatively simple. We asked faculty to describe the ways they used special collections in their teaching and to brainstorm ways special collections components of their courses could be improved. Suggestions included: master classes for faculty interested in teaching book studies but lacking the knowledge of how to do so; improving the special collections room so that it functioned less as a museum and more as a working classroom space; informally advertising Book Studies courses for students on the Oberlin website; and attracting alumni interest (and possible donations) for a small working press to teach the basics of printing in the hand-press era.

In the week that followed this meeting, we set up a listserv with the names of faculty who responded to our email and/or attended the meeting. Without letting too much time elapse, we then sent a summary of the meeting and requested that faculty send us descriptions of the Book Studies-related courses that they teach or would like to in the future. These two outcomes from the meeting—a listserv and a list of book studies courses, essentially a curriculum in embryo—were crucial for giving coherence to our efforts. The latter was particularly effective for preparing for our next step: meetings with the dean of the faculty and the dean of academic programs.

Several events then happened in quick succession. While we communicated with faculty and strategized about curriculum, grant possibilities, and a web presence, the special collections librarian pursued acquiring a printing press. The library director began conversations with the dean and with the Oberlin architect to see about renovating the special collections room. On a somewhat different front, we jumped at the opportunity to use English department lecture funds to organize a books history speaker series for the spring of 2011 (Anthony Grafton, Adrian Johns, and Leah Price all agreed to participate; the library director mobilized a different grant to also invite Michael Suarez during the same semester). We also worked to follow up on the suggestions of the initial meeting with faculty and to do so relatively quickly. We again wanted to profit from the initial wave of enthusiasm. We thought that being able to point to several projects already in the works would strengthen our case with the deans.

These efforts culminated in a meeting with the library director, the dean of faculty, and director of the office for sponsored programs, which took place in mid-November 2009. Our goal was to bring the enormous potential of this emerging interdisciplinary field to the attention of the dean and to see what he and the director of the office of sponsored programs thought would be the best way to proceed, including how to raise funds, gain administrative backing, and give book studies a formal curricular presence. Their principal suggestion was to apply for a Mellon 23 collaborative workshop grant. These sizable grants support faculty from 23 liberal arts colleges who wish to explore, in collaboration with their colleagues at other liberal arts intuitions, a new area of research or a new approach to teaching a field or discipline. The grant possibility seemed to precisely fit our goal of fully considering the value of this interdisciplinary field in the context of a liberal arts education.

The application process involved writing a proposal and an outline of the discussion topics as well as providing a list of participants from other Mellon 23 schools who wished to be involved. We were enormously assisted in the latter by the library director's contacts at other Mellon 23 schools; this enabled us to quickly generate lists of faculty interested in Book Studies. Once we had a list of interested participants from other schools, we circulated a draft of the workshop proposal for suggestions to participating faculty at the following schools: Amherst, Carleton, Colorado College, Grinnell, Smith, Wellesley, and Vassar. The final proposal for

"Book Studies and the Liberal Arts" and a workshop budget were due in early December. In March we learned that our application was successful. We spent spring and fall semester of 2010 preparing for the workshop, which took place October 29 and 30th, 2010, and also pursuing a curricular home for Book Studies at Oberlin.

In the meeting with the dean that led us to apply to the Mellon 23 workshop grant, we also discussed what would be the most appropriate curricular model for Book Studies at this point. At Oberlin College, the options are major, minor, program, and concentration. Most schools, we imagine, have a similar array of relatively long-standing single-subject and newly-minted interdisciplinary models. The college dean suggested a "concentration" as the best fit and advised we meet with the academic dean to discuss what this would entail. Existing concentrations at Oberlin include Peace and Conflict Studies, Cognitive Sciences, and International Studies. They are interdisciplinary and do not require departments to manage them (unlike majors); they are run by committees and mostly draw from existing courses. This is ideal for an emerging field and for faculty already busy with teaching, research, and service. In March 2010, with news of our grant and equipped with the list of courses, we met with the academic dean to see what she thought about the concentration as a curricular home for Book Studies and what would be involved in establishing such a concentration. She explained that the key elements for gaining approval of the faculty committee responsible for determining the viability of new concentrations are the articulation of a coherent set of curricular goals, a set of core courses that are aimed at achieving those goals, and the demonstration of enough faculty depth in the field to insure that sufficient courses will be available every semester.

Our approach up until this point had been to strike while the iron is hot. With support and enthusiasm coming from so many different directions, we did not want to lose any time. And in retrospect, this was essential for building the right kind of momentum. But the academic dean stressed that we have done as much as we could as two untenured faculty members both in terms of workload and influence with faculty committees responsible for approving new concentrations. To give Book Studies more clout, to share the labor involved in creating a curricular home for Book Studies, even one as relatively flexible as a concentration, we needed the help of tenured faculty. She thus offered to create a Book Studies committee and to officially invite the faculty we would select to join this committee. To create a committee, we targeted by email and over lunch specific faculty we knew (and hoped!) would be interested; we also sent an open invitation to the listserv, soliciting volunteers. We aimed at having faculty from as many departments as possible and to attract faculty interested in non-Western approaches to Book Studies. Our committee so far consists of faculty from the following departments: Art, East Asian Studies, English, and the Oberlin director of libraries. We began meeting in the fall of 2010 both to see us through the Mellon-funded "Book Studies and the Liberal Arts" workshop, and also to discuss the next steps for exploring the possibility of a standing Book Studies concentration here. In the meantime, with the help and support of the English Department chair, we have set up a departmental "focus" in "The History of the Book"—an excellent end in itself, and a possible means to a more interdisciplinary future.

Determining how to insure the interdisciplinary nature of Book Studies, in particular how to attract faculty and students working outside the humanities, was precisely the kind of question we looked to explore during the Mellon 23 workshop. The workshop did indeed generate ideas about reaching out beyond the humanities, for example: collaborations among faculty and students in the humanities with those in Sociology, Psychology, Neuroscience, and Computer Science departments on projects studying the changing reading habits of undergraduates,

and the cognitive differences, if any, between the experience of reading a printed or a digital book. In addition to thinking about ways the field could grow outside of humanities departments, the workshop was enormously helpful for elaborating the practical ways Book Studies can be implemented—both at the macro level of program-building, and at the micro level of designing classroom exercises. The greatest value of Book Studies for liberal arts education, participants determined, is its very ability to combine experiential and theoretical learning, its power to engage both head and hands. The exercises shared by participants were so useful that we discussed, as part of the follow-up goals, putting together a collected volume that addresses different modes of teaching Book Studies. Two participants at the workshop are currently in conversation with a publisher about editing such a collection of essays—with contributors to be drawn, at least in part, from the Mellon 23 workshop.

The workshop was most gratifying and exciting for participants because we had the wonderful sense that we were all working together, even if at different speeds given the differences among institutions, as part of a movement to significantly enrich liberal arts education by developing this new field. Each institution represented at the workshop faces unique challenges and advantages, so it was very clear how much we stand to learn from each other. To this end we have begun planning to create a web presence that would address the specific needs of faculty and students working in the field of Book Studies at liberal arts colleges. (Joining forces with SHARP's—the Society for the History of Authorship, Reading, and Publishing—website seems the most likely route at this point). As we pursue the various follow-up projects from the workshop such as a website and edited collection, we are also busy working locally with the Oberlin College Book Studies committee to submit a formal program proposal in hopes of gaining approval for a Book Studies concentration.

Our efforts began with an informal meeting with the special collections librarian in the fall of 2009 to discuss ways to increase the visibility of book history, book arts, and special collections at Oberlin. A little over a year later we hosted a successful Mellon 23 workshop on "Book Studies and the Liberal Arts"; formed an official Book Studies committee; held a book history speaker series in the Spring of 2011; launched an active faculty listserv for sharing information related to Book Studies and liberal arts colleges. Meanwhile, the library has begun taking action on its own plans to renovate the special collections reading room, and has now already established a small letterpress studio. What remains to be done is finalize our curriculum for Book Studies and submit a proposal to the college-wide committee that evaluates new program proposals.

Our point here is not to pat ourselves on the back for a job well done, not least because the job is not done! We hope, rather, that our case study has illustrated the initial steps that can be taken to set up a Book Studies program, the various players that need to be involved, the necessity of collaboration among faculty and librarians, and the advantages of following up on meetings and ideas relatively quickly. We should also add, in conclusion, the importance of pausing to remember why the dream one is so busily attempting to realize is worthwhile. At various points along the way, we have turned to each other to ask this very question—not for lack of faith in the idea, but out of a sense that our initial conviction of the importance of Book Studies to liberal arts education has been buried under plans for making it happen or lost in sales pitches to deans. The best reminder of the value of this interdisciplinary field in the making is to head back to special collections with a group of students and witness how transformed they are by their encounters with the lives of books.

"The Links in the Chain": Connecting Undergraduates with Primary Source Materials at the University of California

Sherri Berger, Ellen Meltzer, and Lynn Jones

"Monday through Friday I set out on a solo expedition to Westwood in search of any information that might be pertinent to my topic [...] I wanted to immerse myself [in] as much primary information as possible so that I could reconstruct what happened, like a real historian [...] I could not help but get a rush from feeling like some investigator out of a Bond movie."[1]

These are the reflections of a freshman at the University of California, Berkeley who spent her spring break absorbed in documents and case files at the UCLA Library Special Collections. Not only was her research experience—her first with primary source materials—obviously personally rewarding, but it also earned her an honorable mention from UC Berkeley's Library Prize for Undergraduate Research.

How did this student learn to "do history" so well and so early in her career? How do we inspire undergraduate students to use archives and special collections, and how do we support them in doing so? At the University of California (UC), we see several "links in the chain" that contribute to student engagement. This chapter focuses specifically on campus initiatives at UC Berkeley and system-wide projects at the University of California–California Digital Library (CDL) to illuminate a continuum of activities, namely:

- Online access to finding aids and digitized special collections materials
- A supportive undergraduate curriculum

- Dedicated reference librarians working in partnership with faculty
- A library-sponsored annual prize for undergraduate research

DRIVE FOR ONLINE ACCESS

Undergraduate students increasingly demand online access to library materials, and UC meets this need for special collections with the Online Archive of California (OAC).[2] Managed by the California Digital Library since 1998, the OAC website aggregates collection guides and digital objects from more than 150 libraries, archives, and museums at all ten UC campuses and throughout the state, thereby providing integrated access to collections dispersed among many institutions.[3] Institutional commitment at the system-wide level has enabled the OAC to evolve to meet the needs of researchers at all levels, including undergraduates. As of June 2010, it contains over 28,000 collection guides (EAD finding aids contributed by institutions and MARC21 records extracted from UC's system-wide catalog) and 210,000 digital objects (contributed images and texts).

Additionally, the OAC's companion interface, Calisphere, is a useful tool for undergraduates—especially those who are interested in digital reproductions rather than physical records.[4] Launched in 2006, Calisphere is a simpler "face" of the OAC that excludes the finding aids and presents many of the objects (images and texts) in topical and chronological groupings with short contextual essays. Although the primary intended audience for Calisphere is K-12 teachers, the interface and organization of the site has proved to be helpful for undergraduate students. The CDL is considering ways to better market and potentially further tailor Calisphere for undergraduate use.

The digital object collection in the OAC and Calisphere is strong in particular areas that support research by undergraduates. For example, the Japanese American Relocation Digital Archive (JARDA) contains approximately 10,000 digital images and 15,000 pages of electronic texts on the subject, from repositories across the state.[5] JARDA was launched after repositories reported being inundated with reference questions on the Japanese-American internment from students and researchers.[6] Today JARDA is the most visited part of Calisphere. It is popular among undergraduates in a range of fields, including history, sociology, ethnic studies, American studies, and others.

Other digital collections in the OAC and Calisphere that are especially germane to undergraduate research include an impressive regional history collection (currently approximately 20,000 images), hundreds of photographs of postwar West Coast suburban architecture, and almost 6,000 images of people and places in the Pacific Islands—just to name a few. These resources are made available through a combination of grants, partnerships, and the commitment of institutions to make their resources widely available.[7] Whether used exclusively online or as an entry point to the physical materials, the digital collection provides a rich resource for undergraduates throughout UC.

SUPPORTIVE CURRICULUM

"I found that when looking at sources in the library for a limited period of time, I had to think carefully about their significance to my paper; I had to decide the direction of my paper early on in my research in order to select and analyze sources."[8]

A supportive curriculum encourages undergraduates to use primary sources both online and in person. Several large undergraduate courses at UC Berkeley require assignments based on primary sources. These include the History Department's senior thesis classes (which enroll several hundred students each semester), American Studies classes, and classes in International and Area Studies that focus on world history. As scholarship becomes increasingly interdisciplinary, moreover, the use of historical evidence is permeating other fields. For example, in 2010 a Theater class developed a performance piece using the University Archives as its source material. Students in Architecture and Land Use Planning are also known for their use of archival collections. No doubt there are other courses and assignments, as yet unknown to the library, that also drive traffic.

Nevertheless, perhaps the most noteworthy example of supportive curriculum is UC Berkeley's History 7B (US History: from Civil War to Present), which makes learning with primary sources a priority for a mass of students with varying levels of interest in US history. History 7B enrolls approximately 600 students in 35 discussion sections offered each spring.[9] The course is so large because it fulfills several requirements, including American History for history majors and American Cultures (mandatory for all undergraduates).[10] It also has a tradition of being taught by "star" professors with compelling lecture styles. Accordingly, History 7B attracts a broad range of students, some of whom are future history majors, but many of whom will major in the sciences or engineering.

In addition to attending lecture and discussion section, in which the interpretation of sources is consistently modeled, every student is required to write a ten-page research paper based on the analysis of a set of primary sources.[11] While the nuances of the assignment may vary by course section, one feature is ironclad: students are expected to read deeply in a body of primary historical material and interpret it using skills taught in lecture and section, without referring to historiography or secondary research. One of the main goals of the assignment is to motivate students to develop arguments and draw conclusions from the source material itself, rather than find sources that support pre-established arguments. As one graduate student instructor states:

> I'm mostly interested in the students coming away with an idea of what's out there in the source base and how to find it. I'm trying to push the idea that they will arrive at a question and then a thesis by browsing through the sources rather than going into the sources looking to substantiate a hypothesis that they've already formed.[12]

The result is very high undergraduate use of special collections at UC Berkeley. Even while students are now able to discover many special collections online through the OAC and Calisphere, they still use The Bancroft Library, UC Berkeley's primary special collections library, heavily for in-person research; undergraduate students, many of them from History 7B, represent a remarkable 30 percent of its users. Students also visit other repositories, at UC Berkeley and beyond, to dig into the rich collections they find online. For example, the student quoted at the beginning of this chapter discovered collections housed at UCLA that she proceeded to research during a trip home to the Los Angeles area.

While each History 7B discussion section has a theme, and many are devoted to specific collections, the potential topics for the class papers are virtually unlimited, given the long chronological scope of the class (1865-present). Choosing a "doable" topic and narrowing it sufficiently to write something meaningful in only ten pages is a significant challenge for students.

Among the most popular topics are the histories of various ethnic groups in the US, particularly Japanese-American Internment, Chinese exclusion, and the Civil Rights Movement. History 7B is often the first history class students have taken that encourages multiple, alternate retellings of United States history—beyond the major political events—and they frequently use the paper assignment as an opportunity to learn more about their own culture or ethnic history. This can prove challenging. A typical example is the student of Armenian ancestry who wants to use Armenian language newspapers from central California as primary sources, but does not read the language. A very common and important lesson for students is the fact that primary sources are rarely translated.

Other heavily explored themes in History 7B include the Cold War; Vietnam and the anti-war movement; suburbanization; 20th century popular culture; and local Bay Area and California political, social and economic history. Naturally, California topics are most easily researched, to the disappointment of students who want to focus on other areas of the US. But this is also an important discovery about doing history: most of the historical record is in archives, not on the Internet.

Given that libraries collect materials specifically to support faculty research and instruction, librarians might expect to see more examples like History 7B that integrate collections and curriculum. However, despite its great success, the very fact that this course is noteworthy demonstrates how challenging it can be to align curriculum with special collections content. Both the academic department and the library must recognize the potential for using the collections and devote time and effort to making the collaboration successful.

DEDICATED REFERENCE LIBRARIANS

"I was initially intimidated by the fact that I could not simply wander in and browse [The Bancroft Library's] collection, but I found it was remarkably easy to conduct research there after learning how to use the collection. I accepted

my reader's card with the pride of receiving a diploma."[13]

The parameters of the research papers in History 7B and other courses can be daunting for students, most of whom have had little or no prior experience with primary source research. Unfortunately, with the amount of material faculty have to cover in lecture, few ever take the time to explain what an archive is and how it is organized. Even the larger concept of the historical record—what has endured from the past and what has been lost—is rarely introduced.

At UC Berkeley, librarians play a key role in helping undergraduates overcome these challenges by showing them how to locate and navigate special collections. For History 7B, for example, librarians conduct course-integrated instruction: one librarian presents a mini–lecture to the whole class, where students get an introduction to the nature of the historical record and archives, a whirlwind web tour of the many kinds of primary sources they will be using in their papers, and information about seeking reference assistance. In addition, each section has its own librarian who conducts an hour-long session in one of the library's computer-equipped classrooms, focused on locating primary sources pertinent to the section theme or on using specific collections chosen for research.

Library instruction sessions cover conceptual matters, such as topic specification, citation and plagiarism, as well the mechanics of using finding aids, the OAC, library catalog, and primary source databases. In these sessions, students begin to develop a more sophisticated comprehension of primary sources, moving beyond simple recognition towards understanding the strengths and weaknesses of any source as evidence of the past.

Web-based learning objects are posted on the library's website and the campus course management system to support students and library general reference staff in the History 7B paper. A guide to finding primary sources and a web-based History 7B course guide are revised annually to match changes in the class syllabus.[14] Recently, with the introduction of the Library à la Carte content management software at UC Berkeley, course guides customized to individual discussion sections are being produced, including quick videos and tutorials on specific tools. But a need remains for additional learning objects to support use of finding aids and archival collections.

Even this degree of support cannot address all student demand for help with such an unfamiliar and challenging assignment. Consequently, the Library has developed a program of appointment-based reference called the Research Advisory Service.[15] This long-standing program, which enables students to sign up online for 30-50 minute appointments with reference staff, is heavily used by History 7B students. The History 7B librarians offer an annual review for general reference staff on the requirements of the assignment and the themes and collections of each section. History 7B librarians also work closely with Bancroft staff to facilitate the large influx of students during each Spring, for instance, arranging to pre-register students as Bancroft patrons, and teaching students about the protocols of using special collections.

A recent survey of History 7B students indicated that 68% of respondents felt that library instruction contributed "much" or "very much" to their understanding of historical research, while 80% of the graduate student instructors felt library instruction contributed "much" or "very much" to the goals of the course.[16] According to a graduate student instructor:

> Students learned not only how to search Oskicat [UC Berkeley's OPAC], but they also received detailed instructions about navigating both the actual Bancroft as well as the library's on-line finding aids. As a result, I had students visit the 'mysterious' Bancroft

even before our scheduled visit. I credit our librarian for that.[17]

A PRIZE INCENTIVE

"I developed a personal connection to the pictures and writings that I came across. There is nothing more poignant in learning about the past than being able to read and touch original pamphlets: the smell of the old printed paper just confirmed the fact that I couldn't get closer to the past."[18]

Another important undergraduate initiative at UC Berkeley is the Library Prize for Undergraduate Research, which illustrates the significance of institutional support in connecting students with primary sources. Established in 2003 and funded generously each year by the Library administration, the prize raises the visibility of and underscores the value of library research to undergraduate students at all levels of study. The criteria for the prize are:

- Sophistication, originality, or unusual depth or breadth in the use of library collections, including, but not limited to, printed resources, databases, primary sources, and materials in all media.
- Exceptional ability to locate, select, evaluate, and synthesize library resources and to use them in the creation of a project in any media that shows originality and/or has the potential to lead to original research in the future.
- Evidence of significant personal learning and the development of a habit of research and inquiry that shows the likelihood of persisting in the future.

The Library Prize has become a prestigious campus institution. Because of its reputation, faculty in a range of disciplines who assign original research projects encourage their best students to apply. In addition to the honor, the awards—$1,000 for upper division students and $750 for lower division students—provide a substantial incentive for un-

dergraduates. Among the departments that have generated prize winners are Classics, History, Music, Interdisciplinary Studies, Architecture, and Molecular and Cell Biology. A measure of the success of the Library Prize is the number of other academic libraries that have established programs based on the Berkeley model.[19] With even moderate institutional support, this model can be replicated at institutions of all sizes.

EVALUATING THE FRAMEWORK

The student comments quoted throughout this chapter show that UC is doing something right to connect undergraduate students with primary sources. Perhaps the greatest factor in UC's success is commitment, as it ultimately strengthens the chain at every link. Commitment is evident in the system-wide support for ongoing development of the OAC and Calisphere and the content there, the relinquishment of class time for library instruction, the dedication of library staff to assist students, and the allocation of funds for the Library Prize. Each of these represents a single, but significant, commitment on behalf of UC to further undergraduates' access to and use of primary sources.

Nevertheless, there is room for improvement, especially when it comes to coordination between system-wide and campus services. The CDL is funded and operated through the UC Office of the President. While this structure allows the CDL to provide independent and impartial services to the ten campuses, it also means that those services are developed a step removed from library users. It is a communications challenge, on both sides, to translate user needs into new technical features and fixes to the OAC and Calisphere. There is a need to more effectively "close the loop" between what librarians hear from undergraduate students and what changes are made. The CDL team that manages these services is currently thinking of new ways to gather feedback from the front lines that might inform future development.

Another challenge for UC is how to continually improve online search and discovery for undergraduate students. In 2009, the OAC interface was substantially redesigned to address the needs of both advanced users (archivists, librarians, faculty, and graduate students) and novice users (primarily undergraduates).[20] While the new interface incorporates many design elements for novice users, including an accessible interactive Flash tutorial, it can still be confusing and frustrating for undergraduate students. Part of the problem is that this user group typically has little or no prior knowledge about what an archival collection is and how it is organized, so structure and terminology of a discovery tool is equally baffling. Compounding this challenge is the reality that undergraduates may not be communicating directly with librarians, preferring to limit their searching to the web without outside help. They may also have the expectation that all of the resources described in a finding aid are digitized, and can become confused when they discover this is not the case.

The CDL is considering ways to enhance the OAC so undergraduate users more quickly understand how it works and what it can do for them. One idea is to create short tutorials on the OAC that explain the basics of archival organization: the kinds of materials in a collection, how they are grouped, where they are physically located, and other facts that may not be evident to the new researcher. Another area of consideration is the implementation of subject search on the OAC and/or Calisphere, as "many users prefer to learn what collections are about."[21] This, however, presents a significant technical challenge because contributed metadata varies significantly among institutions.

More work also could be done to surface and market special collections directly to undergraduate students and other users. Increasingly, repositories would benefit from the development of marketing strategies to promote use of their holdings—which comprise the most unique and unusual materials in the library—among faculty and students. Descriptions of collections need to be broadly disseminated in the path of the user, whether that is through search engine optimization, the inclusion of links to the OAC, Calisphere, and local indexes in undergraduate course software and pathfinders, blog posts, handouts, or class visits—or all of the above.

Nevertheless, UC's framework shows how a multifaceted approach can be effective in connecting undergraduate students with special collections and archival materials. Each link in the research chain—discovery tools, research assignments, faculty and librarians—plays a part in bringing students to the sources. Together they comprise a workflow that is not unlike the research process itself, described by one undergraduate who appreciated all that it involves:

"I learned that a systematic approach to research is essential, but is not the only strategy necessary for success [...] I began to understand the necessity of various research methods working in synergy. Simultaneously, I read and transcribed manuscripts, consulted hundreds of pages of published primary literature, systematically searched for secondary sources, and serendipitously discovered some important primary and secondary sources [...] For me, the convergence of these processes is what made the research creative and enjoyable."[22]

NOTES

1. Evita Rodriquez, 2004. Unless otherwise attributed, all of the quotes in this chapter have been extracted from student essays recognized by UC Berkeley's annual Library Prize for Undergraduate Research (see http://www.lib.berkeley.edu/researchprize/).

2. http://www.oac.cdlib.org

3. For a more detailed history of the OAC and a bibliography of articles and reports on its development, see http://www.cdlib.org/services/dsc/oac/history.html.

4. http://www.calisphere.universityofcalifornia.edu.

5. This project was funded by the Library Services Technology Act (LSTA). JARDA is available at http://

www.calisphere.universityofcalifornia.edu/jarda/.

6. For additional background on JARDA and other early collection building projects on the OAC, see: Chandler, Robin. "Building Digital Collections at the OAC: current strategies with a view to future uses." *Journal of Archival Organization* 1, no. 1 (Spring 2002): 93-103.

7. For example, the regional history collection is the result of the Local History Digital Resources Project (LHDRP), a multi-year partnership between the CDL, the California State Library, and Califa Library Group since 2000. LHDRP is supported by the Institute of Museum and Library Services under the provisions of LSTA and administered in California by the State Librarian. For more information, see http://califa.org/lhdrp.php.

8. Stefanie Shih, 2005.

9. http://history.berkeley.edu/faculty/Einhorn/H7B/7B.pdf

10. http://americancultures.berkeley.edu/about.html

11. Berg, Ellen. "History 7B: Undergraduates Explore Bancroft Collections." *Bancroftiana*, Volume 119 Fall 2001. http://bancroft.berkeley.edu/events/bancroftiana/119/history.html

12. Jeff Rogers, e-mail message to Lynn Jones, February 21, 2010.

13. Elizabeth Mattiuzzi, 2005.

14. For guide to finding primary sources, see: http://www.lib.berkeley.edu/instruct/guides/primarysources.html

15. http://www.lib.berkeley.edu/doemoff/ras.html

16. History 7B student, in-house assessment, UC Berkeley Library, conducted May 2010.

17. History 7B graduate student instructor, in-house assessment, UC Berkeley Library, conducted May 2010.

18. Elizabeth Mattiuzzi, 2005.

19. Jones, Lynn. 2009. "The Rewards of Research—Library Prizes for Undergraduate Research." *College & Research Libraries News.* 70, no. 6: 338.

20. For more information on the OAC 4.0 redesign, see *R/Evolution of Access: The Online Archive of California Interface Redesign.* Panel presentation at Society of American Archivists Annual Meeting, August 2008. Available at http://www.cdlib.org/services/dsc/publications/.

21. Schaffner, Jennifer, 2009. The Metadata is the Interface: Better Description for Better Discovery of Archives and Special Collections, Synthesized from User Studies. Report produced by OCLC Research. Published online at http://www.oclc.org/programs/publications/reports/2009-06.pdf.

22. Benjamin Botts, 2003.

Books IN History; Books AS History: Teaching Undergraduates in the Toppan Rare Books Library, University of Wyoming

Anne Marie Lane

INTRODUCTION

In this case study, I offer practical tips for teaching undergraduates using rare books, based on my many years of experience in the Toppan Rare Books Library of the American Heritage Center at the University of Wyoming, Laramie. At the American Heritage Center (AHC), we are passionately committed to bringing history alive through first-hand experiences with materials, both in the Toppan Rare Books Library and in the AHC Archives. The AHC's mission statement emphasizes that "… we play an active and creative role in the teaching and research missions of the University." The archives reference area has a classroom of its own where various classes visit to learn about the archival collections,[1] but this case study will focus just on classes in the rare books library.

The approximately 60,000 books in the Toppan Library date from the fifteenth century to the present (with the exceptions of an earlier cuneiform tablet and Book of the Dead fragment). They come from many different countries and comprise many different subject areas. The scope of the collection attracts professors from many departments (both from the University and the local community college), and they bring their classes into the Toppan Library for custom presentations (under controlled circumstances, of course, to protect the books). As the University's sole rare books curator, I also have been teaching semester-long book history courses

in the library for the last fifteen years. These efforts have proved to be excellent ways of introducing students to a hands-on learning environment, using physical materials from the past, which is usually quite new and intriguing to them.

THE IMPORTANCE OF ONE'S OWN CONTINUING EDUCATION: IN ORDER TO TEACH THE STUDENTS WELL

Unless we have a previous education degree, most librarians and archivists are not trained to teach. Starting down that path can be intimidating, so I would like to suggest to others what has helped me: attending sessions on general teaching methods at the Center for Teaching and Learning Excellence here on campus; taking continuing education courses; participating in national conference sessions; and reading professional journal articles. For continuing education, one of the five-day courses offered at the University of Virginia's Rare Book School is "Teaching the History of Books and Printing." Another wonderful experience that connected me with like-minded peers was a seven-day seminar at the American Antiquarian Institute in Worcester, Massachusetts, called "Teaching the History of the Book." Relevant conference sessions on teaching book history included one at the SHARP conference at Colonial Williamsburg, Virginia. The website of this international organization (the Society for the History of Authorship, Reading, and Publishing) contains numerous links to related sites of interest, including useful course syllabi from a wide range of institutions.[2] SHARP publishes an annual volume of scholarly essays called "Book History" that I use as required readings for my semester-long students. RBMS (the Association of College & Research Libraries' Rare Books and Manuscripts Section) has sponsored numerous sessions on teaching book history: e.g., one in Atlanta, Georgia, in 2002, called "Teaching the book: it's not virtual." So, do keep an eye out for future opportunities like the above.

In our professional literature, the ACRL *College & Research Libraries News* had a recent article called "Lighting fires in creative minds: teaching creative writing in special collections," by David Pavelich,[3] and *RBM: a Journal of Rare Books, Manuscripts, and Cultural Heritage* sometimes carries articles related to teaching—with the entire Fall 2006 issue devoted to the topic. Helpful earlier articles include one by Suzy Taraba called "Now what should we do with them?: Artists' books in the curriculum,"[4] which relates success stories from Wesleyan, Amherst College, Mills College, and the Claremont Colleges, where the teaching faculty collaborated with the special collection librarians to arrange class projects. In another article "One day it will be otherwise … changing the reputation and the reality of special collections," Robert L. Byrd suggests several ways to promote greater access and use: such as librarians actively reaching out to educators to invite them in with their classes.[5] In another article "Is there a future for special collections? And should there be? A polemical essay,"[6] Daniel Traister remarked that as an undergraduate he never saw a rare book or manuscript because "… it never seems to have crossed anyone's mind that these might be things a young person would want to see, to touch, perhaps even—God forbid!—to read."[7] Finally, Sidney F. Huttner's article, "Waving not drowning: rare books in a digital age," expresses the concern that young people are growing up in an environment in which books are not appreciated as much as in the past.[8] To help

rectify this situation, he suggests: "We should rather entice all first-year students to hold in their hands a rare book or a very old manuscript. We know that their doing so by itself offers them an opportunity to go on a quest to understand."[9] I have found all of these articles inspirational, and I use their lessons in my own teaching.

PROMOTING THE CLASSES AND COLLECTIONS, ESPECIALLY IN ESTABLISHING GOOD WORKING RELATIONSHIPS WITH PROFESSORS ACROSS THE CURRICULUM

For many special collections librarians and archivists at academic institutions across the country one of our primary responsibilities is to educate students in how to do research. While sometimes frustrating, this is more often an extremely rewarding experience. When taking on actual "teaching," it is important to make sure that the extra work is reflected in your overall job description. Through the years (after seeing how much time it can take), I have increased the percentage of giving presentations to other classes ("Instructional Support") to 15%, and to 20% for my own Book History class (thus, 35% for both forms of teaching), so that my job description now reflects something close to the time actually spent.. I also suggest not taking on more than you can handle. For example, I no longer bring in a lot of classes during the fall semesters when I teach Book History, because I ended up spending too much time evenings and weekends setting up and breaking down all the presentations.

But if you explain this to professors nicely, they understand. In fact, they have been extremely supportive of my efforts; and I would not have been able to introduce so many students to the intellectual stimulation of using older materials without their teachers encouraging it. Plus, the University of Wyoming's rare books library would not have been able (over these last seventeen years since it opened) to prove its value to the University administration without such collegial support. Thus, I strongly encourage others to collaborate with local academics; together, we can make a real difference in the college experience of our students. One way I have done that is to look over the upcoming schedule of courses for classes that would be good candidates for a "field trip" visit, and then contact the teachers. Once you can entice professors in the door, and show them how agreeable you are to working with their students, most happily return in later semesters. In addition to encouraging such personal one-to-one relationships with the teaching faculty, the AHC sponsors "Teaching & Research Grants,"[10] where funding is available to encourage teachers to use the materials here. We also have formed a "Faculty Use Task Force" of AHC archivists in which we brainstorm ways to bring in new professors and classes.

INTERNSHIPS

In addition to building relationships with teachers, internships provide opportunities for working one-on-one with students over a semester. Over the years, twelve interns have worked in the Toppan Library and received credit from History, English, Art History, Women's Studies, American Studies, and the Foreign Exchange Program. Interns' projects can take many forms. A French student translated some vellum manuscripts from the French Revolution that had been "recycled" as bindings on Voltaire volumes and received credit in the Foreign Exchange program. An independent study student researched book illustration history under the joint guidance of an Education Professor and me.

PRESENTATION LOGISTICS FOR CLASSES IN THE TOPPAN RARE BOOKS LIBRARY

At the Toppan Library, we do our best to balance the dual goals of preservation and access. All books in the library are always placed in cradled supports for viewing under supervision from me or my assistants.

The building is temperature and humidity controlled, and a technician checks the library's digital hygrothermograph regularly. To protect from theft, we have color, high definition security cameras in the library that are monitored by security guards present in the building. After hours, any motion-activated live feed is relayed to the University of Wyoming police station.

When the students arrive in the building for a class session in my department, I greet them in the front lobby and have them leave backpacks, jackets, food, drink, and pens in the lockers there, and then wash their hands in the restrooms. It is important to consider the size of the room and how many students can be seated in it comfortably. For the Toppan Library, I try to keep the student number under twenty. I also recommend always photo-documenting each table of book displays. This makes it much easier to set up again if the lecture is repeated (and most are). Depending on the allocated length of the class period, presentations can run from about half an hour to over an hour, with the last 15 minutes or so reserved for the students to look very carefully through the cradled books.

Finding books to bring out for presentations is never a problem. On the contrary, the challenge is limiting the number by selecting the best ones for each particular class. It helps to ask the professors to send a syllabus, so you can pull books by the authors being studied, or about the topics under discussion. Sometimes the educators have the students take notes for later discussions or testing, and occasionally the students have to return later to do an assignment related to the books. Keeping a list of the books shown to a particular class will help identify the materials when students want to see them again.

I recommend publicizing the teaching that goes on in the library to all your constituents, so they are aware of all the ways students are using the facility. In these days of accountability, one should not be modest about such achievements. For example, after just one year of teaching, I wrote a short article called "Toppan Library Popular with Classes,"[11] for the AHC *Heritage Highlights* newsletter that goes out to our donors and others. To make it eye-catching, we included a photograph of Clara Toppan (provider of our endowment money) in the library, and another photo of an entomology professor showing a fly fishing book to two students.

EXAMPLES OF CUSTOM PRESENTATIONS TO INDIVIDUAL CLASSES FROM VARIOUS DEPARTMENTS

Book history encompasses many disciplines, and a particular library's collection affects the types of classes that can best make use of those materials. However, most academic special collections libraries possess tens of thousands of books, if not hundreds of thousands. Even with the Toppan Library's fairly small collection of approximately 60,000 books, we are able to accommodate numerous courses in a variety of disciplines.

The Art Department consistently brings the most classes to the Toppan Library: e.g., printmaking (every semester), Islamic Art history, Medieval Art History, Nineteenth-century Art History, Life Drawing, Two-dimensional Design, and Color Theory (every semester to see our Josef Albers' *Interaction of Color* portfolio). The preponderance of art classes relates to my academic background: a Bachelor's and a Master's degree in Art History. After all, it is easy to talk about books when we can tap into our own subject strengths. My overall attitude about books is greatly influenced by those degrees and an additional eight years working in archaeology. In addition to the importance of books as carriers of information, I see them as historical, and often artistic, artifacts from which we can learn a great deal about their original social context.

English Department classes have included Research Methods, Creative Writing, Book Culture, Western Writing, The Bible as Literature, World Literature in Translation, and different periods of both American Literature and English Literature. One item that is always a big hit is the London-printed "Political Magazine" of March, 1783, with George Washington's ownership signature on it[12]). History, American Studies, and Anthropology professors have brought in classes such as American History, Ethnohistory, European History, Native American Studies, Public History, Medieval History, and Western Americana classes. The Education Department has brought in Visual Literacy, Pedagogy, and children's literature classes. Religious Studies classes look at Jewish, Islamic, Christian, and Buddhist books. For international students in ESL classes, I also bring out books representing a variety of religious traditions.. We welcome students taking classes at the local Latter Day Saints Institute, showing them historic books such as our first edition Book of Mormon.

In recent years, the University has begun to offer interdisciplinary classes that are cross-listed in multiple departments.. These courses include Gender and the Humanities, Native American Culture and Literature, Book Arts, and Victorian Women's Lives: their Art, Literature, and Culture. In addition, we have had occasional visits from other departments for courses in pharmacy, zoology, music, costume design (Drama department), clothing history (Family & Consumer Science department), geology, mass media & communications, aquatic entomology, and general humanities.

To give just one example of how to relate a specific book to a topic: in presentations that focus on diversity in literature, I always include examples of prejudice in children's books. The juxtaposition of the intended audience of children and the negative representations of people of color makes a strong impression on students. They are always shocked when I show (without speaking) the title page from a story in a 1922 book *Mother Goose and her friends: tales told by the gander.*[13] They see visual documentation that publishers could get away with using the "n" word (in a story about ten little children) because a tradition of white superiority had become established in children's books of the previous century. In the same vein, we also look at and discuss depictions of race in nineteenth-century geography books.

THE SEMESTER-LONG BOOK HISTORY COURSE

This semester-long History of Books class was born from my desire to utilize the Toppan Library's collections even more than in just the single presentations. At the University of Arizona, where I received the M.L.S., my favorite class was the Book History course taught by Professor Margaret Maxwell. She taught it in a normal classroom, sometimes using slides. At that time, I had a graduate student job in the University of Arizona Special Collections, and watched as the director Louis Hieb, and the rare book curator Theresa Salazar, showed actual books to different classes—by working off a cart and then putting each book on a table after they talked about it.

After starting here as the University's first rare books curator, I suggested to the AHC director the idea of combining these two methods into one: that is, a semester-long class AND using the books in my custody as examples for discussion. He liked the idea and in 1996, an Education Professor on the AHC Board of Faculty Advisors let me try it as a pilot project, as a "Special Topics" Education course, to see if it worked. It did, and is now part of the permanent curriculum in the History Department. (Efforts to get it offered through the English and Art History Departments were unsuccessful, because I do not have a doctorate.) The History Department Chair, however, understood that an M.L.S. combined with my master's degree in Art History, and the daily experience of working with the books, qualified me to teach about them.

Upper-division undergraduates (usually about 15) comprise most of the class; graduate students (usually just two or three) can also take it. Students receive three hours of credit. It was previously a one-semester overview from ancient times to the present, but that caused much moaning from students about the large quantity of material presented in such a short time. So it was then divided into two semesters. Students still felt it was "too much." They are much happier now with the "Special Topics" format. It is also more manageable for me to teach. The first special topic was nineteenth-century books from different countries; the second was the Renaissance (using both manuscripts and incunables); the third was, on nineteenth-century American books; and the current course is on nineteenth-century British books.

Students can choose to write scholarly research papers or do creative projects, like making book illustrations or bindings in the style of the time. We study both the content of the books and the books as physical artifacts. As of last December 2010, 221 students have been enrolled in my book history courses. Each student has spent a full semester experiencing all the wonderful textual and visual expressions of the past that this rare books library—like every other one—has to offer. Twenty students are enrolled for the fall semester 2011, and they represent a melting-pot mixture of majors, including History, Art, and English, plus three library staff and an archivist taking it for continuing education. I encourage students from different backgrounds because the varied perspectives result in more lively class discussions.

Through books, newspapers, and other materials (such as sheet music and almanacs) we attempt to understand the complexities of the much larger historical picture. While this type of long-term instruction certainly is intensive, the special collections library is the ideal environment in which to discuss how books fit into world history: past, present, and future. As students read the words of long ago, they come to understand better the attitudes of people in different places, at different times, and with different religions, politics, and traditions. We study materials "within their historical contexts," by discussing how specific books fit into social, religious, political, artistic, and literary contexts. This includes being aware of aspects such as gender (when do we start seeing more women readers and authors?); class (what forces during the Industrial Revolution encouraged greater middle-class and lower-class literacy?); and age (what do we see in children's books that reflects how the parents and teachers of the time wanted them to think?).

CONCLUSION

Special collections libraries contain an amazing wealth of books and other materials for students to experience. It is just a matter of students realizing it. That realization occurs as they are brought in on class trips, or as they participate in semester-long classes or internships. I would like to end my case study with the words of two Book History students. On the 2009 Renaissance Books final, Stephanie Loehr beautifully explained that "Before this class, I knew books and I knew history, but I did not know book history. …This class has been my own personal Renaissance. It has brought me exploration, knowledge, joy, and taught me to appreciate a book for its cover, and then whatever else is on the inside." Richard Glantz articulated in his final essay from 2005: "These old books have some kind of weird power that pulls me to them." Such individualized student responses make us smile. We smile with the satisfaction that we have succeeded in making meaningful connections between books and students. That's why we put our hearts and souls—not to mention long hours and careful planning—into teaching undergraduates with rare books.

NOTES

1. For an additional faculty archivist's experiences with classes visiting the archive section of the American Heritage Center (besides that of Associate Director Rick Ewig's case study in this book), contact the Archives Reference Department Manager, Ginny Kilander, at ahcref@uwyo.edu.

2. At http://www.sharpweb.org/

3. David Pavelich, "Lighting fires in creative minds: teaching creative writing in special collections," in *College & Research Libraries News,* vol.71, no.6, June 2010, pp.295-297, 313

4. Suzy Taraba, "Now what should we do with them?: Artists' books in the curriculum," in *RBM: a Journal of Rare Books, Manuscripts, and Cultural Heritage,* vol.4, no.2, 2003, pp.109-120

5. Robert L. Byrd, "One day it will be otherwise … changing the reputation and the reality of special collections," in *RBM: a Journal of Rare Books, Manuscripts, and Cultural Heritage,*vol.2, no.2, 2001, pp.163-176)

6. Daniel Traister, "Is there a future for special collections? And should there be? A polemical essay," in *RBM: a Journal of Rare Books, Manuscripts, and Cultural Heritage* , vol.1, no.1, 2000, pp.54-76

7. Ibid, p.58

8. Sidney F. Huttner, "Waving not drowning: rare books in a digital age," in *Rare Books and Manuscripts Librarianship* vol. 13, no.2, 1999, pp. 97-108

9. Ibid, p.103

10. For further information on the American Heritage Center's "Teaching and Research" grants, go to http://ahc.uwyo.edu/eduoutreach/trgrants/default.htm

11. Anne Marie Lane, "Toppan Library Popular with Classes," in the American Heritage Center's *Heritage Highlights* newsletter, June 1995, p.1.

12. You can view this on the Toppan Library webpage, under the "Highlights" section. The Toppan Rare Books Library's website can be found at http://ahc.uwyo.edu/about/departments/toppan.htm

13. Maud Radford Warren and Eve Davenport, *Mother Goose and her friends: tales told by the gander* (N.Y.: George H. Doran Co.), 1922, pp.205-256

Where Do We Go From Here?: Evaluating a Long-Term Program of Outreach and Making it Better

Suzy Taraba

Over the past dozen years, Wesleyan University's Special Collections & Archives has played an active role in the institution's undergraduate curriculum. Through a targeted program of outreach to faculty across the disciplines, each year hundreds of Wesleyan students visit Special Collections & Archives (SC&A) to learn about primary sources and the rich and varied holdings of the collections. This case study presents three very different class assignments that engage undergraduates in the use of Wesleyan's special collections. Each assignment can be readily adapted for use in other collections. The chapter offers an analysis of the strengths of these approaches, as well as the challenges inherent in sustaining a broad, ambitious program of class instruction with a small staff.

Wesleyan's Special Collections & Archives holds over 30,000 rare books, more than 8,000 linear feet of archives and manuscripts in all formats, and significant local history collections. While some parts of the collections have been held by the University since its founding in 1831, the impetus for active building of an outstanding collection of rare materials dates to the opening of Olin Library in 1928 and the Centennial of the University in 1931. Particular strengths include incunabula and early imprints, British and American literature and history, travel and exploration, history of science, Methodistica, 19th century Americana, German and Austrian literature from the turn of the 20th century, poetry, and artists' books. We hold the papers of Henry Bacon

(architect of the Lincoln Memorial), avant-garde composer John Cage, William Manchester (historian and author of the *Death of a President*), and many Wesleyan faculty. Twentieth-century United States legal history is well represented through the Collection on Legal Change, a group of several archival collections that document such significant issues as abortion, prohibition, and civil rights, among others. The department's staff is comprised of two full-time professional librarian/archivists, one 2/5-time cataloging librarian, one half-time paraprofessional, a second paraprofessional who works just a few hours per week in the department, and several student workers. The instruction program is the responsibility of the two full-time librarian/archivists; all staff except students serve in a rotation at the SC&A reading room desk.

Wesleyan's intensive use of special collections in the undergraduate curriculum began in 1998, in response to the department's marginalization and low use of the collections, despite their many strengths. Very few professors brought their classes to SC&A; those who did, came to the department on their own, with little or no attempt at outreach from within the library. The approach of the Special Collections & Archives staff was a traditional one—certainly the norm for its time—emphasizing collection development and stewardship of the collections as the department's primary missions. Implicit in this approach was the idea that research and class instruction in special collections and archives was perhaps not appropriate for many or most undergraduates. The collections were superb, but very few people were using them.

When I became Head of Special Collections & University Archivist in 1998 (after a year as University Archivist), I feared that the department would become increasingly marginalized if we continued with the status quo. That year I began an intensive, perhaps even aggressive, approach to bringing classes into SC&A. The first step was to find a close connection between our holdings and Wesleyan's curriculum. To do this, I studied the course catalogue carefully and matched holdings to what was being taught. I wrote detailed letters to each faculty member whose course seemed to connect well to our holdings; although I used the same basic form for each letter, I tailored each one with a specific list of items I would show to the class if they would come in for a visit. In the first year alone, this effort resulted in twenty-four class sessions for nineteen different courses and a total of 276 students. Of course not all interested faculty responded right away: more than two full years later, one professor of Romance Languages dropped by the department, with the letter in hand, to inquire about scheduling a class session.

As the program has grown, certain trends have emerged. Perhaps not surprisingly, the largest number of requests for class sessions come from the American Studies, English, and History departments. Faculty in African American Studies; Classical Studies; Feminist, Gender, and Sexuality Studies; Music; Romance Languages and Literatures; Science in Society; and Studio Art are regular participants as well. From time to time, we've hosted classes in astronomy, atomic theory, computer science, dance, German, government, and sociology. Over the past dozen years, we've worked with upwards of 100 different faculty members (including visitors and non-tenure track faculty) to bring classes to Special Collections & Archives.

With very few exceptions, the earliest classes involved a traditional "show and tell" model, with an array of materials related to the topic of the class presented by the librarian/archivist leading the session and some comments by the professor. Today, many class visits to SC&A still take this approach. While it is a tried and true method of presenting unfamiliar and complex materials, it is not always the best way to engage students. No matter how compelling the items shown may be, students can lose interest when too many items are presented and described. A passive "show and tell" session can be easily enlivened by asking the students questions and by inviting them to read out loud from the sources presented. A particularly effective approach is to have students analyze imagery in archival photographs, elaborate 16th and 17th century architectural title pages, or authors' portraits, such as the famous image of Phillis Wheatley that adorns the first edition of her poems.

An in-class exercise we often use is the "mystery book exercise," which was developed jointly with a faculty member teaching the history of science. "Mystery book" is a fun, fast-paced, in-class exercise that trains students to evaluate an unfamiliar source quickly and teaches information literacy skills using books or documents connected to the subject of the course. Students work individually or, for larger classes, in teams of two or three, to size up a document or book they've never seen before and answer ten questions about it. (See Appendix 6.1 for questions.) Only seven to ten minutes are allotted for this, so students understand right away that they can't read the whole book, but must focus on such sometimes ignored paratextual apparatus as the title page, table of contents, introductory matter, and index. For many, especially those trained to do close textual study or who are new to academic research, this is an eye-opening experience. When time is up, each student or team reports very briefly (2-3 minutes) to the class about the source.

This is an active exercise that requires the participation of every student, not just evaluating the book, but also speaking in class. It requires demonstration of information literacy skills, including identification of the author's point of view and intended audience. It is also good training for the experience of more in-depth use of special collections or archives, since browsing at the shelf is not an option. The "mystery book" exercise is readily adaptable to a wide range of primary sources. Materials used need to be accessible enough that students can at least begin to get a handle on them in a few minutes, but rich enough to spark their curiosity. We have employed this exercise successfully in classes as varied as Nineteenth Century American Utopias (using works by utopians, as well as their detractors), Perspectives in Dance as Culture (using photographs, documents, and clippings from Wesleyan's ethnomusicology and dance programs), and Cryptography: The Art and Science of Secret Writing (using nineteenth- and early twentieth-century shorthand instruction books).

"Mystery book" is an almost foolproof activity. Even so, its success hinges on careful selection of mystery items and on allowing enough time for all students or teams to report on the book or other source they have analyzed. Rigorous timekeeping is essential, since many students find it difficult to stay within the allotted time, especially as they report out to the class.

A more complex, ongoing undertaking is the "book as object" assignment. This is an intensive, half-semester project, in which students learn how to "read" aspects of the book that are not the text, including type, binding, and provenance. They also gain experience in researching the publication history of a particular text and its author. Developed initially by Magda Teter, Professor of History at Wesleyan, for her classes on Early Modern Europe and on Jewish History, this assignment has gone through several iterations and revisions. (See Appendix 6.1 for its most recent version.) Sometimes the requested final product has been a traditional research paper, other times a mock exhibition, encyclopedia entry, or website. In each case, the stu-

dents come to Special Collections & Archives for a class session early in the semester. They receive an introduction to the history and technology of early books and printing, along with guidance on identifying and analyzing various aspects of the physical book and how to prepare a basic publication history for a specific title. Because the class has already experienced reading assignments and in-class lectures about the history of the book, they are well-prepared for the visit to SC&A. Viewing examples of the kinds of materials they have learned about helps to reinforce the readings and make them more concrete. After the session, each student signs up for a book from a preselected list; that book will be the focus of the student's inquiries for much of the rest of the semester's work on the "book as object" assignment. (Of course there is another part of this assignment that requires each student to analyze the content of the book s/he is working on and to set it in the context of its historical period, but it relies more on reprints or electronic editions of the texts than on the holdings of Special Collections & Archives and is therefore not discussed here.)

The "book as object" assignment requires students to learn a new vocabulary and set of concepts related to aspects of the book that they have rarely considered before and to apply what they have learned to a specific, often not clear cut, example. They develop their understanding of primary sources and move beyond that to the physicality of the book and what they can learn from it. It is an intensive assignment that can be very rewarding. It often raises many questions for students, and it can require a significant amount of one-on-one assistance by the staff of Special Collections & Archives when students come to the reading room individually to examine their chosen books and continue their research. Challenges inherent in this assignment include the wear and tear on the books studied, the relationship of the size of the class to the size of the staff of Special Collections & Archives, and the significant amount of time that students need to spend in the SC&A reading room to complete the assignment well. The approach works best with a relatively small class, ample time to work on the project, and staff members who are themselves experts in all the aspects of the "book as object." Since each book offers different features, and most of the identification skills asked of students are new to them, an important lesson students learn in this assignment is how to look closely at elements of the book that have little or nothing to do with the text. This analysis can be complex and subjective, and there are often no easy answers. Some students find this frustrating, while others grasp immediately that the process of examining the book for clues about its past is at least as important as the specific outcome of their analysis.

A third class module is regularly used by English Department faculty in the gateway course, The Study of Literature. The "*Othello* assignment" introduces textual editing concepts and praxis while putting the student in the shoes of the editor, allowing him/her to make choices about the "best" version of the text. The aim of the assignment is for each student to produce her/his own "edition" of a single line of *Othello*. Students must choose how they will present the text itself (e.g., old spelling or modern) and what kind of textual apparatus they will have. They must then write a paper explaining their decisions and how they affect the reading of the play.

Developed by Natasha Korda, Professor of English at Wesleyan, and adopted and adapted by several other English faculty members, the *Othello* assignment is a short-term project with a deadline one to two weeks after being assigned. First, the class visits Special Collections & Archives for a session on the publication and editorial history of Shakespeare. Because Wesleyan's Shakespeare holdings are so rich, we are able to show nearly all of the most important editions: quartos (in facsimile), all four folios, many of the major 18th century editors (such as Rowe, Theobald, Malone, Stockdale, and others), 19th century versions (including the infamous 1804 *Family Shakespeare*, from which the salacious parts

were excised by its editor, Rev. Bowdler), modern fine press editions, and artists' books that use the bard's work as a jumping off point.

For the assignment, students return to SC&A on their own time. They choose one of a small number of preselected cruxes in the text, places where textual variations in different editions of *Othello* have resulted in complex, interesting readings and divergent meanings. Working from several different editions that span the centuries from Shakespeare's time to our own, they study and analyze the passages in question, write about the variations and their meanings, and posit their own editorial views on which is the "best" reading and why. This assignment introduces the idea of textual variations, and makes it clear that even texts as canonical as Shakespeare's plays have evolved through editorial interpretation. While it would be possible to create a similar assignment using online versions of various editions of *Othello*, the requirement of handling books from earlier time periods, some with evocative marginalia and other unusual features, adds an extra dimension of authenticity to this project.

These three assignments—mystery book, book as object, and *Othello*—are examples of the variety of approaches used by Wesleyan faculty and librarians to teach undergraduates with the resources of Special Collections & Archives. A 2002 online exhibition, "Old Books, New Pedagogy: Special Collections and Archives in the Curriculum," highlights these and other class assignments and in-class exercises that have helped to make Wesleyan's program successful. A link to the exhibit can be found at: http://www.wesleyan.edu/libr/schome/exhibit/index.htm

As Wesleyan's program has matured, refinements have been made. While teaching undergraduates using the resources of Special Collections & Archives clearly benefits students, faculty, and librarians alike, an ambitious program of class instruction and assignments that bring students to the department can easily overwhelm a small staff.

After the first few years of Wesleyan's program, it gained momentum, and it was no longer necessary to spend a lot of time and effort encouraging faculty to bring their classes to SC&A. Instead of ongoing marginalization, we found that juggling the number of requests and balancing class instruction with our many other duties became evermore challenging. To cope with the increase in class visits and assignments generated by our successful program, we have developed some strategies to help make it more effective and manageable. With thirty-five to fifty SC&A class sessions reaching 500-600 students each academic year, effective time management is essential for success. Most classes require at least three (and sometimes far more) hours of preparation by the librarian to work with the faculty member, familiarize herself at a basic level with the topic of the class, and select books to show and/or use in class exercises. Time must also be allotted to pull the relevant materials from the SC&A stacks, set them up for class, and put them away afterwards. Of course, repeat visits of the same or similar courses require less preparation time.

However tempting it may be to try to reach every undergraduate before graduation, it is important to target classes appropriately. The best class experiences with Special Collections & Archives are good fits because of a variety of factors. Naturally, it is important to match the content of the course with the holdings of the department, as has been recognized from the beginning of Wesleyan's program. But other factors are also crucial for success; these became apparent through trial and error. When targeting classes, it's important to pay attention not only to content and its relation to the collection, but also to the size of the class and its format. In general, smaller classes (in which all students can participate actively) and a seminar or discussion-focused approach, rather than larger lecture classes, work best. (There are notable exceptions, such as the huge introductory astronomy class that visited in several smaller sections to see early classics in the field, 19th century texts used at Wesleyan, and astronomy-influenced artists' books—a successful experience, by all accounts.) It almost goes without saying that an engaged faculty member is essential, whether or not she or he will be the primary teacher of the class on the day (or days) of the SC&A visit. The faculty member should be present at the class session whenever possible. In the few cases that the faculty cannot accompany his/her class to SC&A, we have found that a short assignment to be handed in at the next class meeting for review, but not necessarily a grade, encourages students to reflect on the intellectual value of rare materials and serves to debrief the faculty member about the session he or she missed. These assignments are often focused on what the student took away from the session, an especially intriguing item that was encountered, or how the visit may have changed her/his perspective. The first such assignments were developed by faculty who were concerned about having to miss the class. More recently, this approach has been recommended by librarians as a way to ensure the success of the class even without faculty presence, and faculty have readily agreed to use it.

To help manage the increased reading room activity after classes requiring or encouraging students to use special collections materials outside of class, we are beginning to work with faculty to stagger assignments so that they won't all fall at the same time in the semester. Not surprisingly, not all syllabi can be flexible enough to adapt easily to the scheduling issues at hand. In some cases, we offer extra reading room hours (in addition to the regular schedule, and usually in the evening) exclusively for students in a specific class with an assignment requiring the use of SC&A materials. This approach has been especially successful with the *Othello* assignment, with its limited timeframe and small number of items students are required to use. All of these strategies help keep our small reading room from becoming chaotically crowded, and they provide a better experience for both students and staff.

We often work very closely with faculty to develop assignments using our materials and to ensure that the assignment is clear and manageable for students and the SC&A staff who will be monitoring the reading room and answering questions. We have found that a preselected list of materials to work on can help students understand and focus on the strengths of the collection rather than setting them up for disappointment if they choose a topic that our holdings don't support well. When we find that students from a class that has not visited as a group are coming to SC&A to do their research, we contact the faculty to get a copy of the assignment so that we know what is expected of the students. In these cases, we also encourage faculty to consider a class session so that all students in the class can receive the same introduction to our holdings and how to use them, rather than having each student learn this individually when s/he comes in to begin the assignment.

Wesleyan's active program of class instruction in special collections has been a dozen years in the making. In large part due to this program, Special Collections & Archives is well known and highly regarded on campus. This visibility benefits not only our department, but the whole library. The program, which continues to evolve, is rewarding for students, faculty, and librarians, despite some challenges for our small but dedicated staff. Since its inception, the program has more than doubled in size. In 2010/11, we taught forty-two classes in SC&A, reaching more than 600 students; during several academic years, as many as fifty class sessions have been conducted in SC&A. Students who have visited SC&A with a class often bring family and friends to departmental events, especially our open houses during Reunion/Commencement and Homecoming/Family Weekend. After their initial encounters with SC&A, many students use our resources for their other classes and extracurricular activities. Some have written superb honors theses based on our holdings. Several have become student workers in the department, and a few have gone on to careers in librarianship and archives. Our program enjoys considerable positive publicity through faculty and student word of mouth, as well as more formal promotion including a joint faculty-librarian presentation to Wesleyan's Board of Trustees (November 2006) and an in-depth article in the alumni magazine about student research in the department (*Wesleyan: The University Magazine*, 2006:II). Despite some challenges, our program is definitely successful, and we continuously seek to improve it.

APPENDIX 6.1: Special Collections & Archives Exercises

QUESTIONS TO CONSIDER
(aka Mystery Book Exercise)

1. Who is the author?

2. What is the title?

3. When and where was the book published? Is the publisher a commercial firm or a private person or a religious organization (or something else)? [Note that in earlier periods commercial firms were often named for their founders or owners.]

4. What type of text is it? (some possibilities include first person accounts, secondary sources, novels, etc.)

5. Who is the intended audience of the book?

6. What is the author's point of view and/or his or her relationship to the topic?

7. Is the book illustrated? How do the illustrations relate to the text?

8. Can you tell anything about former owners of this copy of the book or how or when this copy of the book came to Wesleyan?

9. How would this book inform your research?

10. What else would you like to know about this book and how would you go about finding out more about it?

S. Taraba rev. 10/5/04

THE BOOK AS OBJECT

This assignment requires you to think about a book in a way that may be unfamiliar to you: not as a text, but as an object. Physical books (as opposed to virtual or online books) carry meaning beyond the texts they contain, offering clues to the circumstances of their production, distribution, and use. They evoke earlier readers. By looking carefully at the concrete, physical aspects of a book—its format, type, illustrations, binding, and provenance—you can understand aspects of its history that will never be revealed by its text. Research into the printing and publishing history of the text and careful study of apparatus of the book will help you set the book in the context of the history of printing, publishing, and readership. Below you will find tips and questions to help you think about your book as an object. Note that it is not necessary to be able to read the language in which the book is written to be able to understand the book as an object.

Look carefully at the title page, colophon, and other apparatus of your book:

1. Study the definition of **colophon** from Carter's *ABC for Book Collectors*.

2. Use the title page and colophon to determine the book's title, author, place of publication, printer and/or publisher, and date. Check your work by finding the record for the book in Wesleyan's online catalog. Note that Latin titles are often intertwined with the author's name and other information. Unless you've studied Latin, the online catalog record will be especially helpful in identifying the information found on the title page or colophon.

3. If you haven't used roman numerals since grade school, visit these websites to learn how to convert roman to Arabic numerals. Each site has its strengths. Spending some time with both of them will be worth your while.

    http://www.yourdictionary.com/crossword/romanums.html

    http://www.lib.auburn.edu/serials/docs/training/manual/roman.html

Identify the format of your book:

1. Study the definitions of the following terms (from Carter's *ABC for Book Collectors*): **format, folio (def. 3), quarto, octavo, laid paper, chain lines, wire lines, watermark.** Further clarification may be found in Glaister's *Glossary of the Book*.

2. Use the folded paper models available in Special Collections to determine whether your book is a folio, quarto, octavo, or some other format. If these tools are not enough, consult McKerrow's *An Introduction to Bibliography for Literary Students* or Gaskell's *New Introduction to Bibliography*.

3. Once you've determined the format of your book, think about what the format might tell you about the book's cost (to produce and to buy), the impression it makes on the reader, its suitability for the content of the book, and anything else that might have been a factor in the printer's decision to use that format for this book.

Look at the type used in your book:

1. Study the definitions of the following terms (from Carter's *ABC for Book Collectors*): **gothic type/gothic letter, italic type, roman type.** Further clarification may be found in Glaister's *Glossary of the Book*.

2. Determine which of these kinds of type are used in your book. It is not necessary to try to identify the specific name of any typeface used in your book—stick to the three general kinds of type. Are different kinds of type or different sizes of type used to distinguish parts of the text or to help the reader in some way? Can you posit some reasons why a particular kind of type might have been used deliberately by the printer to convey something about the text? What is appropriate about the use of this type in this book? If there are many different kinds and sizes of type used in your book, answer these questions for just the type of the main text and two other parts of the book.

Look at the decorations or illustrations in your book, if there are any:

1. Study the definitions of the following terms (from Carter's *ABC for Book Collectors*): **head-piece, tail-piece, vignette, fleuron or printer's flower, rules.** Read about **woodcuts, copperplate engravings,** and **handcoloring** in Gascoigne's *How to Identify Prints*.

2. Does your book have any of these decorative or illustrative elements? If so, identify them and indicate how they are used.

3. If your book has illustrations (rather than just decorative elements), use Gascoigne to determine whether they are woodcuts or engravings and, if they are colored, whether this was printed or done by hand. Once you've determined the what kind of illustrations your book has, think about what they might tell you about the book's cost (to produce and to buy), the impression it makes on the reader, its suitability for the content of the book, and anything else that might have been a factor in the printer's decision to use the illustrations for this book.

Look at the binding of your book:

1. Use Greenfield's *ABC of Bookbinding* to learn what you can about the materials, style, and approximate time period of the binding of your book. Because books were routinely sold in sheets (i.e., not bound) until the late 18th century, each copy of a book had a different binding, usually chosen by the purchaser. Books are sometimes rebound many times from the time of their publication to the present, so it is very common for the date of publication to be much earlier than the period of the binding.

2. Write a simple, one or two sentence description of the binding of your book that includes the following: material used for the covers (leather, vellum, wood, something else?), endpapers, style or decorative features. If there are easily identifiable clues that would help you determine a date

for the binding (even a decade or a century), explain them.

Look for provenance evidence, marks of ownership, or annotations in your book:

1. Study the definition of **provenance** from Carter's *ABC for Book Collectors*, with the proviso that scholars (as opposed to rare book collectors) are as interested in evidence of ordinary readers as famous people.
2. What provenance evidence, marks of ownership, or annotations can you find in your book? What do they tell you about former owners, readers, or how the book was used?

Look for information about other editions of this work and other books printed by the same printed or publisher:

1. Search WorldCat, available from the library's homepage.
2. Search the *National Union Catalog of Pre-1956 Imprints*. (This is the nearly 800 volume set of large green books on the shelves outside the Interlibrary Loan Office in Olin.)
3. Search for your book in at least one subject or genre or author bibliography.
4. Analyze how your book fits into the context of other books printed by the same printer or publisher and other books written by the same author.

S. Taraba 2/10

THE
WORK

Real Objects, Real Spaces, Real Expertise: An Undergraduate Seminar Curates an Exhibition on the Medieval Book of Hours

Marianne Hansen

In Fall 2007, the author (curator of rare books and manuscripts at Bryn Mawr College) collaborated with an art history faculty member to lead a semester-long undergraduate seminar on the medieval book of hours. During the class the students created the Library's Spring 2008 exhibition. The exhibition was accompanied by a keepsake flier, a website, and two events: a panel discussion with student curators and a lecture by a manuscripts scholar. The class and exhibition were supported by the Friends of the Bryn Mawr College Library. This essay emphasizes student work on the exhibition, which I supervised, rather than the academic study of medieval manuscripts, supervised by the faculty member and essentially similar to classes which do not include an exhibition component.

We hoped to have about fifteen students; twenty-six attended the first day. We explained the class was going to be a lot of work, requiring a paper as well as full participation in the exhibition. We warned the students that they were going to have to criticize and be criticized by their classmates. Neither of these reduced the prospective class size appreciably, so we handed out a questionnaire that covered interests in, and previous experience with, art history, history of religion, and the Middle Ages, and finally chose the students for the class based on their responses.

In the first month, the class focused on books of hours and other medieval manuscripts. The required texts included Wieck's *Painted Prayers,*

Brown's *Understanding Illuminated Manuscripts,* and de Hamel's *The British Library Guide to Manuscripts,* with readings in *Time Sanctified, Image on the Edge,* and other standard works. The faculty member led the historical and theoretical discussions, while I talked about manuscript production methods and introduced the students to our books.

At the end of September, we added the exhibition component to the class. I had difficulty identifying useful readings which could serve to rapidly introduce the students to issues in creating an exhibition, but settled on the following:

- Lindauer, Margaret. "The Critical Museum Visitor." in Marstine, *New Museum Theory and Practice,* 2005.
- Serrell, Beverly. *Exhibit Labels: An Interpretive Approach.* Alta Mira Press: Ca, 1996
- Clarkson, Christopher. "The Safe Handling and Display of Medieval Manuscripts and Early Printed Books." *The New Bookbinder: Journal of Designer Bookbinders.* v. 19, 1999.

We designed an exercise to get the students thinking about exhibition design—they visited our current show on the history of the College's archaeology department, then discussed how their readings helped them understand the show's design and audience, and its overall strengths and weaknesses. They also started to consider how our space could be used in their own exhibition, including the layout of the show, paths a visitor might take through the exhibit, and visual aspects of the display. Throughout the class we found it productive to work in ways that made the physicality of the books and the space an integral part of the students' experience; they tended to let theory surmount other concerns if they were away from the objects and the exhibit hall. This exercise revealed for the first time an issue that affected our work flow and decision-making throughout—fifteen students were too many to truly agree on anything.

An essential part of this class was extensive and repeated contact with the books themselves. The first assignment was to thoroughly study one book and report on the contents, illustrations, decoration, and any other topic addressed in the class or readings. At the next class meeting we elicited a list of topics that interested the students, and began discussing the show's focus. The possible themes covered a wide gamut, but as the students prepared their next assignment—a written proposal for the show—topics of general interest emerged. Because we met only once a week, we used course management software (Blackboard) for out-of-class discussions and to present reports and suggestions. (As the semester progressed, we also use it to build a preliminary website for the exhibition, using its wiki so all the students could load text into the site structure.) Using the shared workspace provided by Blackboard, the students then commented publicly on one another's proposals and began negotiating what we should do. A second issue surfaced at this time: although the College's collection is extraordinary for a small institution, we have no books of hours of the quality ordinarily shown in art history classes, and we could not support an entire display on many of the topics that interested the students. For example, although like many scholars they were excited about the role of women in the production of hours—and fascinated by ownership by women—neither could be illustrated with our holdings.

Similarly, the hall has fourteen wall cases and a long built-in case, as well as several movable vitrines, but we have only eleven books of hours, half

of which are fully illuminated. We required the students to use only works in our collection, so some points had to be illustrated by reproductions from books on display in other cases. We were, fortunately, able to provide additional books and objects and the final exhibition included two breviaries, a psalter, a Mariale, three printed hours, a pair of sixteenth-century sculptures, and a plaster cast (a "fictile ivory") of a thirteenth-century sculpture. There was also a facsimile book of hours, with a medieval-style chained binding as an interactive display. But the problem of making a coherent statement with the artifacts at hand was difficult for some students. We did emerge from the discussion of the proposals with an overall theme—the use of books of hours in acts of personal devotion. A popular suggestion was made early, even before the topics solidified: that the cases be arranged in the ordinary order for a book of hours, and this turned out to fit the chosen theme and formed the basis for our display.

Although this theme was far from groundbreaking, I was impressed with how many of the students understood from their own experience points I have known older curators to ignore. They said:

"I don't think that many individuals outside of our class or other medieval studies courses know what a Book of Hours is"

and

"I want the exhibition to have a structure that is clear enough that anyone who is completely new to the subject can grasp the exhibition."

and

"Too much text and too little mental and/or physical engagement in the exhibit is definitely a concern. Having to stop at a station for long periods of time to read a display card (rather than moving around visually and mentally stimulating cases at a quicker pace) can really bog down an exhibition."

The next assignment was to examine the books more closely. Each student was assigned a section of the book of hours (the calendar, matins, prayers for the dead, etc.) and required to look at that section in every available book, exploring how the sections might illustrate our chosen topics. Those topics included the cult of the Virgin, marginalia, production techniques, reader response, and other issues commonly addressed in the literature. Based on their findings and suggestions, I matched the topics with relevant sections of the books, and assigned each combination to a student. So, one student would curate the part of the show covering the Office of the Dead, and also address death, and reader response. As soon as the topics were assigned, the students began research and writing.

From the beginning of November through the end of the semester, successive drafts of the label text were due every week, as were responses to classmates' texts. We hoped the students would experience what it was like to be a curator of a small collection, the excitement as well as the exhaustion, but some were more troubled by normal difficulties than their professional counterparts would be. As the show developed we had to drop sections and change assignments. For example, students were interested in the use of hours to teach literacy in the medieval home, but we could not illustrate this with our collection. Early enthusiasm for exploring parallels between pictorial storytelling in books of hours and in comic books was set aside when the topic failed to fit into the overall theme we settled on. A professional who is juggling ideas and artifacts expects to have to reject topics and shift focus, but students who had done preliminary work on issues that were deleted were disconcerted. Many also struggled with balancing their recently acquired knowledge with the brevity imposed by a label. I finally had to advise them: "A guideline I use is to write what I would tell a friend who is pleased to see the item, but not interested in hearing more than two minutes worth of info about it."

We printed out draft labels and taped them on the exhibition cases, then went around reading, commenting, and rearranging. This physical approach to the exhibition highlighted the experience of the viewer and helped identify weaker sections. Students were able to hear and evaluate criticism of their work, and they made necessary changes promptly. This layout technique was indispensable the day we matched the books (represented by printed images) and topics with the cases they would occupy.

The students were also responsible for other tasks. Based on a survey of interests, I assigned students to teams: graphics (visual identity, label design, and advertising), publicity and programming, displays (fixtures and also interactive displays), publications (website and keepsake), and editing. Most students had little experience in these areas and staff instructed and coached them or, in a few cases, took over a task that was too complex. For example, I taught the display team to make book supports, but when they envisioned creating a replica book of hours for visitors to page through, I did the binding.

Choosing the title was the most difficult negotiation the group engaged in. It is a task that experienced teams have trouble with and the varying sensibilities of the students made it harder. We tried open discussion, brainstorming by writing titles on slips of paper presented anonymously, communicating on a discussion board. We never did reach unanimity—when we finally voted on the top dozen contenders, each student listed their three top choices and also one title they truly disliked. One title (*Like the Virgin*) received seven favorable votes and four utter rejections. We finally chose *Intimate Devotion: The Book of Hours in Medieval Religious Practice*, a title one student had criticized on the grounds that it made her think of underwear.

The end of the semester saw a flurry of activity: labels, comments on other students' drafts, revisions. The editing team had the worst of it, because they could not start until everyone else was nearly finished—and the curators were slow to respond to their suggestions. But by the end of the semester the books were chosen; supports made; reproduction images identified; label text written and revised; posters, postcards, and keepsake designed; opening event with a panel of student curators planned; speaker invited; and website started. The instructor had dropped the paper requirement when it became clear how complex and time-consuming the exhibition was.

Because Bryn Mawr's semester ends in December and the show opened in January—and because there was an exhibition in the gallery through the fall semester, the class finished before we were able to install the exhibit. Throughout early January, while the students were on break, the instructor, other staff members, and I worked to make the exhibition reality. We corrected final errors in the text. We laid out the labels according to the students' design, and had them printed and mounted. We sent the poster design to our graphics shop, and the postcard design to the printers.

When the students returned, we installed the show; about half the students assisted. We taught them to hang signs and bind books into supports, and let them deal with the esthetics of placement of books in cases and reproduced images on walls. The opening event was a panel discussion, and five of the students reflected on their experiences. We were pleased to hear that several were more interested in working in museums or libraries than they had been—and resigned when one said frankly that it had helped rule out these careers. An unusually large number of students attended, most drawn by invitations from class members. The panel was followed by a reception and supper for the students. A second event mid-semester brought Kathryn Smith, a prominent art historian from NYU, chosen by the

students from a list of eminent scholars, who spoke on royal female patronage of a book of hours.

Three major problems attended the class: First, some students did not meet deadlines nor fulfill the requirements of the class and exhibition. This is common, of course, but in this case every failure inconvenienced fifteen people. We met once a week, and if I did a class like this again, I would argue strongly for twice: many of the students worked best in class, and would have benefited from more contact time. We also met on Mondays; many routinely left things until the last moment and since Special Collections is closed weekends, they did not have access to books or advice when they wanted to work.

We also had trouble with the course management software. Blackboard supports e-mail communication, a bulletin board, and a wiki. The students disliked the bulletin board, and nearly all struggled with the wiki, which I personally spent too much time trying to manage. A shared workspace is essential for this sort of project, but we had the wrong one.

Finally, the group was too large to hold a fully participatory discussion, too large to work as a single team, and too large to easily come to agreement on different issues. A smaller group of more expert students (a graduate seminar for example) might avoid this problem. Or an undergraduate class where the instructor took more control could build an exhibition quicker. But you would lose the autonomy of the students in shaping the show, and their involvement in other parts of the planning and decision-making.

Overall, though, the seminar was extremely successful. The participants were apprentices and students, but they were also, in a real sense, curators. They had as much authority and autonomy as we could give them (or as much as they would take). They determined the theme of the show and its layout, wrote the label text, did the work of support staff, and dealt with a complex communication project. They handled books of hours and wrote about them so frequently that most became genuinely fluent in the terminology and adept in the basic issues to an extent I have never seen in ordinary classes. The panel discussion gratified the college administration, since the seminar represented the remarkable student experience that Bryn Mawr, uniquely among institutions of its type, can support with our collections of rare books, manuscripts, and art objects.

An important part of the success of this experience depended on the people involved. My colleagues, Eric Pumroy and Barbara Ward Grubb, were indispensable, both in moving the project along and as models for the students of timely, friendly, expert cooperation. And the entire project would never have existed without the professor, Martha Easton, whose cheerful willingness to experiment, to let others take the lead at times in her classroom, and to tolerate ambiguity underlay everything we accomplished.

The web version of the exhibition is at http://www.brynmawr.edu/library/exhibits/hours/.

Exhibiting Artists' Books: Three Perspectives from a Curatorial Seminar

Laurel Bradley, Kristi Wermager, and Gabriel Perri Silberblatt

In this article, three authors describe their roles and experiences in a curatorial seminar offered winter term 2010 at Carleton College. Laurel Bradley, Senior Lecturer in Art and Art History, Director of Exhibitions, and Curator of the Carleton College Art Collection, provides an overview of the seminar and describes her strategies for engaging students with artists' books and the curatorial process. Kristi Wermager, Curator of Special Collections in the Gould Library, describes the challenges attendant upon providing student access to the artists' books. Gabriel Perri Silberblatt, a seminar student, writes about his experience in the course and highlights special challenges and learning opportunities. The course description sets the stage for three points of view put forth in this article.

Curatorial Seminar: Artists' Books course description. Artists' books, representing a dynamic, non-traditional format for contemporary artists, comprise a collection within Carleton College's Gould Library Special Collections. This curatorial seminar challenges a small group of students to immerse themselves in the collection, develop a set of organizing ideas and themes, and orchestrate an exhibition to be staged in the Art Gallery spring term 2010. In addition to working with primary materials, students will recommend a new acquisition to the collection and collaborate with the Special Collections Librarian on refining goals and developing curricular uses for artists' books.

Laurel Bradley, Director of Exhibitions and Curator of the College Art Collection

As Director of Exhibitions and Curator of the College Art Collection, I teach a curatorial seminar every other year at Carleton College as a way to give students a taste of the curatorial process, and to directly "use" the art collection for teaching and learning. In 2010, I reached beyond the art collection under my care to another important campus resource—Artists' Books in the Gould Library. Kristi Wermager, Curator of Special Collections, embraced the course and resulting exhibition as an excellent means to realize her goal of incorporating the collection into the curriculum; we sought to groom students as advisors and ultimately to "exploit" them as advocates for the collection and its use.

Curatorial seminars present tremendous challenges to students, most of whom are art history majors. In order to curate an exhibition within our short ten-week terms, students must quickly acquire at least a superficial mastery of a specific field before conceptual and practical work can begin; familiarize themselves with college holdings within that field; engage with curating, an entirely new method of knowledge production and analysis; perfect the art of writing museum labels for public consumption; and navigate the complexities of a group project even while making high-quality individual contributions.

The course outcome was not a paper exercise, but a real exhibition mounted in the art gallery spring term. I therefore restricted enrollment to six so that participants had time to cohere as a working group, and could meet with me individually as many times as necessary toward the end of the term. Course work progressed through a series of practical exercises to develop curatorial skills. Simultaneously the students refined their definition of "artists' books," and used the exercises to collectively brainstorm toward possible exhibition themes. After I cautioned that catch-all "Cool Stuff" themes such as "Treasures," or "Highlights" were insufficiently intellectual or historically based, the students proposed umbrella concepts including: Artists Books and the Upper Midwest; Book Arts and the Liberal Arts, Artists' Books as Social Critique; Revolutionary Tomes; The Codex and Beyond; Reading for Pleasure. Woven through many proposals was an interest in the radically experimental nature of form, and artists' books as vehicles for revolution and reform. The final title, then, became *Artists Books: Radical Messages, Revolutionary Means*. Within the two major sections, subthemes included Radical Messages: Stories of Struggle, Engaging the Environment, and Identity; and Revolutionary Means: Predecessors, *Livres d'Artistes*, The Democratic Multiple, Institutional Critique, Out of bounds, and Free Verse.

Mid-term brought a sense of urgency to class proceedings. Even though the group had logged rich experiences by visiting other artists' book collections, continuously explored Carleton's holding through bi-weekly sessions in the Special Collections classroom, engaged with a visiting librarian about using artists' books across the curriculum, and experimented with exhibition label formats, a long list of tasks remained. Texts, when written, were barely out of first draft phase. And final object choices proved elusive. Finally, Kristi and I cut off access to books not on the exhibition checklist in order to force the fledgling curators to focus and begin to refine thinking through writing. The final checklist comprised 54 books, and a few framed photographs, unbound sheets, and other artifacts to complement the book objects.

And then, during week six, one of the most exciting "real life" assignments came due. "Pitching an Acquisition to the Gould Library Special Collections" charged students with browsing the online marketplace for artists' books, then selecting a single object (or group of related objects) and pitching this work as a potential acquisition to a panel of distinguished individuals. Each student had five minutes and was limited to a budget of $1000. In addition to introducing the object and artist, class participants had to contextualize the acquisition within the existing collection, and define how it would work in the upcoming exhibition. Students rose to the challenge, giving impressive performances grounded in sound selections. The mock trustee committee (comprised of a Dean, a Librarian, a faculty bibliophile, and a studio art faculty member) was able to support two acquisitions, instead of only one, as the two winning proposals came in under $500 each.

The course text, in addition to a survey history of artists' books, was Beverly Serrell's *Exhibition Labels: An Interpretive Approach*. Serrell's "Big Idea" is a powerful tool to force a succinct project statement, which must then resonate within every other supporting text, including the introductory statement, the thematic labels, and the individual object labels. "A Big Idea is a sentence—a statement—of what the exhibition is about. It is a statement in one sentence, with a subject, an action, and a consequence."[1] Research and writing responsibilities were divided among students. Those charged with orchestrating the general didactic labels, including the introductory statement and the two major section labels, had to submit their prose repeatedly to their classmates, so as to accurately represent their ideas. Each student took responsibility for several groups of books, and had to produce labels of approximately 100 words for each object. These were edited up to 3 or 4 times, in individual meetings with the instructor, until text quality rose to a level I judged "proper for public consumption."

Exhibitions are more than a selection of riveting objects complemented by interpretive labels. In the last weeks of winter term, students addressed public programs, publicity, the website and ways to bring books alive in a "do not touch" exhibition setting. However, the actual design of the space and rhythmic placement of objects proved beyond the scope of the course. The gallery staff took on the complicated tasks surrounding installation during spring break after grades had been submitted and students had left campus.

Reflecting back on the seminar, the rewards included a deepened knowledge of the collection for all parties, the pleasure of collaborating intensely with another campus curator, and delight in watching young curators blossom. *Artists Books: Radical Messages, Revolutionary Means* was more difficult to realize than previous collection-based exhibitions because of access issues. When planning a print or photography exhibition, one can rely on facsimile images to stand in for the real objects. But this project required that the books, in all their quirky 3-dimensions, be consulted directly under terms of restricted access. Even if the library database had included images for each object record, the complexity of these books would not collapse into a single image. Finally, the goal of using students to re-write a set of collection goals awaits realization. The Special Collections curator is currently engaged in drafting a statement inflected with the students' passions and targeted interests discovered over ten weeks in winter 2009.

Kristi Wermager, Curator of Special Collections

At the Gould Library, Special Collections participates actively in the learning and teaching mission of Carleton College. Each academic year between 35 and 50 classes visit, integrating primary resources and visual materials into coursework. Most classes come for one or two structured sessions, but occasionally have longer-term projects, including small exhibits mounted in the Library.

The *Curatorial Seminar: Artists' Books* offered an opportunity to expand existing models for curricular involvement. Using the collection as a "laboratory" would further develop this curricular resource and the exhibition would focus attention on Special Collections. I welcomed the opportunity to collaborate with another campus curator. And I saw great value in working with highly motivated students to develop strategies for serving their interests within the Special Collections program.

As preparations for the seminar progressed, several challenges demanded attention. The discovery tool for finding artists' books within the library collections was clearly inadequate. Up to that point, patrons had relied on OCLC generated catalog records from our on-line catalog and on pre-existing knowledge of the Artists' Book Collection. Patrons seeking artists' books on certain topics or using particular print processes were doomed to frustration, until they turned to the curator. I emerged as the essential guide to the collection. Recognizing this fact, I decided to improve my own knowledge by examining and *reading* all of the books in the Collection. It was a valuable process, reacquainting me with forgotten books and introducing me to others.

It was time, however, to move beyond the human search engine and enable seminar students to discover books on their own! Grounded in knowledge of each object, I enriched an Access database with my own supplementary search terms. However, although we introduced this tool to the students early in the seminar, they rarely used it, preferring to discover books through browsing or personal recommendation. We had not yet created an effective discovery tool.

Providing student access to the collection also challenged usual Special Collections practices. Browsing was necessary to fulfill the course requirements. Yet the stack area housing Special Collections could not accommodate this activity. Fortunately, there is ample space in the classroom adjacent to Special Collections. To provide full access, we devised the solution of re-shelving the collection on four carts that were easily moved back and forth between the classroom and the secured stack area. A temporary new classification system simplified re-shelving items onto the carts after each class visit. Our artists' books are classified and shelved using Library of Congress call numbers. The numbers are complicated and difficult to differentiate, causing errors in shelving. Our solution was to inventory the collection ahead of time and assign each book a simple numerical shelving designation from 1-495. The inventory process doubled as a security measure, ensuring that all of the books in the database were in the collection at the start of the term.

Finally, security and control issues stretched our usual practices and boundaries. Classes that use Special Collections materials are always supervised by library staff. During the seminar, Special Collections staff attended only some of the class sessions, ceding some control. Control was also an issue in the exhibit, mounted in the Art Gallery across campus from the Gould Library. While book exhibits in the library are always housed in locked cases, this exhibition displayed objects both in cases and on open surfaces. "Do not touch" signs accompanied exposed books and gallery attendants monitored the exhibit during open hours.

Looking back on the experience it is clear that Special Collections realized all four major goals: increased use; students engaging actively with the collection; collaboration with another campus curator; and a raised profile on campus for the Artists' Book Collection and Special Collections in general. Further benefits followed from the growing realization that the artists' books, because they are art objects, require a level of attention different from more traditional Special Collections materials. Whereas standard library discovery tools rely on text to describe books and facilitate access, artists' books, as visual objects, are best accessed through a combination of relevant search terms and images. Having witnessed the limited success of our non-visual Access

database, Special Collections is now in the process of creating an improved discovery tool, using Content-DM software. In addition to exporting existing bibliographic information and search terms from on-line catalog records and the Access database, we are adding two images from each artists' book. From now on, all new artists' books will be carefully analyzed, read, photographed and entered into a visually enhanced discovery tool. We are also exploring ways to link this tool with our on-line catalog.

I believe that collaboration, at the heart of the students' seminar work, was also the most valuable feature of my experience. As a curator, I was excited to work with the professional Art Gallery staff and to see many of our artists' books exhibited beautifully in a gallery setting. My thinking about artists' books in general and artists' books at Carleton was expanded by interactions with Laurel and the seminar students. Their reactions to physical objects and thematic content confirmed some assumptions and challenged others. Students were, as expected, drawn to books with strong social and political messages. What the seminar showed me, however, was that students also valued books of a whimsical, poetic, or esoteric nature. Throughout the seminar, Laurel and the students made suggestions and posed questions that broadened my thinking about the purpose and future direction of the collection. Students pointed out a lack of sculptural books, for example. Although we had avoided such complicated objects because of storage issues, we are now filling that gap with new acquisitions.

Gabriel Perri Silberblatt, Carleton College student, class of 2011

As a junior enrolled in the curatorial seminar, I gauged the success of the class by how unlike it was from the rest of my undergraduate experience. The seminar stood out in two fundamental ways: it provided opportunities to work directly with art objects in the classroom as well as new productive challenges to my academic writing.

A unique physicality grounded in actual objects was perhaps the most edifying aspect of the course for me and for my peers. We students of art history had come to expect departmental seminars to be heavily laden with abstract ideas, theory and historical context. The curatorial seminar quickly developed into a refreshing counterweight to these classes.

Having had the experience of two summers working in museums, I am familiar with the advantages of what museum educators call "object-oriented learning." The complex visual character of all kinds of art is engaged through long, careful, and first-hand contemplation. Every artwork, be it concrete or conceptual, has *form*; object-oriented learning addresses formal analysis to a degree that is simply not possible in a slide-based lecture. For example, the first time I sat down with Caren Heft's *The Core of James Farmer*, a book from our collection, I spent nearly an hour reading and re-reading its carefully printed pages. I touched its delicate blood-red deckled edge, and somberly admired the surgical-like stitching of its binding. With careful looking, the book slowly reveals the painful history of civil rights activist James L. Farmer and his Freedom Riders of the 1960s. Heft's work beautifully captures the tragic tensions implicit in the march toward racial equality in America. The book's powerful and subtle messages cannot be grasped from slide images, or from my cursory description here; they come only from careful observation and first-hand experience. These ways of looking were not just encouraged, but absolutely required by our curatorial seminar.

Directly engaging with objects for close formal analysis teaches us as much about *what* we see, as *how* we see. The course, therefore, laid bare how I make very subjective decisions about quality and effectiveness in a work of art. Charged with the daunting task of curating 50 artists' books from a collection of over 450, class members were forced to deal with the material—visually, experientially,

and intellectually. Having to justify or deny an object's relevance to a thematic exhibition to a group of peers will remain one of the most difficult and meaningful experiences of my undergraduate career.

The curatorial seminar also placed unique demands on my writing. As undergraduates, we learn a very specific academic prose style. Writing is defined as a very solitary endeavor: we write alone, and pitch our writing to a single highly informed reader, the professor. Ill-conceived ideas or obscure textual constructions frequently go unchallenged when we 'write for the professor'; the assumption is that her knowledge of the topic and shared experience in the classroom will fill any gaps in our arguments. The curatorial class, by contrast, required a departure from this "usual" kind of academic writing. Writing for an exhibition, we learned, means writing for a public—for a reader who may or may not be informed, and whose interest and willingness to engage varies enormously. Writing for the artists' book exhibition, each student had to cater to this heterogeneous group of viewer/readers, while at the same time constructing a coherent narrative for the show.

Writing for the "public" posed several productive challenges as we began drafting texts. For example, we could not simply assume visitor fluency with specific art historical ideas such as 'the democratic multiple,' or 'institutional critique'. We were also very wary of becoming overly didactic or providing too much information. The writing process was one of concision through reduction. After drafting a wall label, each of us had to ask, "Can I do this in 500 words? 250? Two sentences?" The prose might sound more elegant in 700 words, but when that text is placed on the wall with art nearby, a reader can be lost with even 50 unnecessary words.

The group came together frequently to read aloud and collectively scrutinize texts. This workshopping activity, although at times frustrating, was ultimately a truly rewarding experience. Six sets of eyes pulling apart every sentence exerted hundreds of pounds of pressure on every word. Writing and editing together, in fact, amounted to a "close formal analysis" of one's own writing. At the end of the day, this sometimes stressful and aggravating activity became an unexpected source of growth for me as a writer and editor. This seminar, a collaborative course predicated on a group of peers looking, learning and writing together, provided a unique opportunity for experimental and experiential learning in a familiar setting.

NOTES

1. Beverly Serrell. Exhibit Labels: An Interpretive Approach. Walnut Creek: Altamira Press, 1996, p. 1.

Finding Value and Meaning through Work/Study in the Archives

James W. Gerencser

THE QUESTION

Managing undergraduate work/study employees can be both challenging and rewarding. Some students may be particularly engaged in their assigned tasks, while others may be more cavalier about their work. Training and supervising students can be quite time consuming, but at the same time students can contribute a great deal and help to advance the work goals for the college or university archives. At their best, student employees are valuable and productive members of the team; at their worst, they are a drain on resources and a serious distraction.

In my own experience, I have been blessed with quality undergraduate workers year in and year out. Over the past decade they have processed hundreds of linear feet of archives and manuscripts; they have transcribed thousands of pages of handwritten text; they have organized and identified thousands of photographs and slides; they have examined and evaluated rare books; they have prepared dozens of exhibits; they have spent countless hours performing original research; and they have assisted with innumerable mundane photocopying, filing, editing, shelving, and inventorying tasks. It is frightening even to think about how much less we would have accomplished without their contributions.

In thinking about all that our undergraduates have done, I began to wonder about their perspectives. We certainly appreciate their efforts, but do they themselves consider their work to have been time well spent? How do they view their hours of processing, transcribing, scanning, filing, and researching? Do they feel that they learn anything

useful or valuable? Does the work that they do in the College Archives have any larger impact beyond being just another job?

THE SURVEY

At the annual meeting of the Society of American Archivists in San Francisco in 2008, I attended a session in which panelists were discussing how we, as a profession, educate and prepare the next generation of archivists. As I listened to the speakers, I began to think about my own experiences with work/study employees, interns, and volunteers. I started making a list of former students who I knew were now pursuing careers as information professionals. In a short time I had jotted down more than a dozen names.

Dickinson College is a liberal arts institution with an enrollment of 2300 undergraduates. The Archives and Special Collections Department generally employs eight to ten students during each academic year, and many students work there for more than one year during their academic careers. All undergraduate employees are required to apply for work in the College Archives through the library's standardized student employment process, and interested applicants are interviewed prior to being hired. For a relatively small repository with so few work/study students overall, a dozen former students pursuing information careers seemed like a large number to me. Throughout the remaining days of the conference, I asked colleagues if they knew how many of their former undergraduates were working in the field. Most responded that they could only think of one or two. This left me wondering if my experience with work/study employees was particularly unique, and if so, in what ways was it different.

I decided that it might be useful to develop a survey as a means of soliciting feedback from my former undergraduate workers. I hoped to learn from them what they had found worthwhile about their employment, what kinds of tasks they had been responsible for during their employment, what courses they had majored in and what their career plans had been at the time, and what they felt would have improved their job experience. With the assistance of colleagues at the college, I developed a series of questions and prepared a survey using the Survey-Monkey online service in order to solicit input from work/study students from the past ten years

The survey was composed of fewer than 30 questions that were broken up into four sections. The first section of the survey asked respondents what types of materials they had worked with and what kinds of work they had performed. Multiple choice options were provided in order to help students recall whether they had worked with books, papers, or with photographs, whether they had used word processing software to transcribe documents or maybe used photo editing software to scan slides. As much as anything, these initial questions were designed as a memory aid, helping people recall and reflect on the work they had done as many as ten years earlier.

The second section of the survey focused on the positive and negative aspects of employment. These questions were open-ended, allowing the former employees to share their thoughts in their own words. Respondents were asked how they came to apply for the job. They were then asked to discuss what they liked and didn't like about their work, as well as what they found useful or not so useful. In an effort to solicit feedback on how the job could have been better, the section finished with a question about what the former employees might have enjoyed doing, but never had the chance.

The third section of the survey focused on work experience before and after employment in the College Archives. Individuals were asked if their work had had any impact on their career decisions, and if so, how. They were also invited to reflect on whether they felt they had learned anything useful that could be applied to their current jobs or everyday lives. Finally, the respondents were asked if they would recommend such work to others, as well as what they might suggest for ways to improve the work experience.

The fourth section of the survey sought information about the majors and career paths the students had planned when they first entered college. Subsequent questions asked what majors had ultimately been pursued, what graduate schooling they had obtained (or expected to obtain), what kinds of jobs they currently held, and what career goals they had now set for themselves. Finally, respondents were offered the opportunity to comment on the survey itself.

In order to test the survey, I piloted it with two professional archivists who had graduated from Dickinson College at an earlier date than the students who were the target population for the survey. In response to their feedback, some adjustments were made to the survey, including clarifying the language for a number of questions and adjusting the order. Early in 2009, the survey was ready for distribution. (See Appendix 3.1.)

THE RESULTS

For this survey, I wanted to focus on those undergraduates who had been traditional work/study students. I felt that students who chose to arrange internships for college credit or who had volunteered their time without pay were a more self-selected group who had already had encouraging archives experiences and knowledge that led them to seek such opportunities in the first place. It seemed that such interns and volunteers who were intrinsically motivated to seek work in the archives might paint a rosy, biased picture and might influence the survey results in a more positive direction, compared to those students who were perhaps less well-informed about working with primary sources and were more exploratory in having chosen to apply for employment in the College Archives.

The survey pool included all work/study students who had spent at least one semester as employees in the College Archives, and who were members of the ten graduating classes from 1999 through 2008. (The move to a new facility during the summer of 1998, combined with a change in management for the department, led quite naturally to changes in the kinds of work student employees were being asked to perform. Thus, the earliest students to work under these new conditions would have been members of the class of 1999.) Of those 52 individuals identified, 49 email addresses that were believed to be active were acquired through the database maintained by the Alumni Affairs Office as well as through personal connections among the current employees of the College Archives. For the remaining three individuals, paper copies of the survey were prepared and were mailed to their last known addresses. Ultimately we received completed surveys from 30 individuals within one month of distribution, a response rate of 57.7%.

Section one of the survey revealed that personal papers, books, photographs, and college records were each handled by more than half of the respondents, and the most common tasks included processing and inventorying, transcribing, and performing original research. Most students primarily used word processing software for their work, but fully a third used scanners and image editing software.

When asked in section two about their primary motivation for work in the College Archives, 56.7% indicated a general interest in history or in rare books and other special materials. Only 10% indicated that they had prior knowledge about archives, while 23.3% became interested after being introduced to archives through their coursework. Since relatively few undergraduates typically have

experience with rare and special materials, exposure through their college classes clearly can have a positive impact on encouraging further exploration of these materials.

Fully 100% of the respondents felt that their employment in the College Archives was a positive experience overall. Though only 16.7% indicated that they had worked in an archives or special collections repository prior to college, 63.3% reported such work after college. Perhaps even more striking, 56.7% of the respondents confirmed that work in the College Archives influenced their career decision, and fully 100% mentioned that they would, or did, recommend employment in the College Archives to others.

Section three of the survey asked participants whether they had learned something through their work in the College Archives that they found useful in their chosen career, and 86.7% responded in the affirmative. For those who have decided to pursue a career in some information or history-related profession, such an answer was not unexpected. Among those who pursued careers in other fields (including law, science, and business), improved research skills and analytical reasoning, as well as better organizational and presentation skills, were mentioned as benefits of their work experiences in the College Archives.

As to whether participants felt they had learned something useful that did not relate to their careers, 83.3% responded in the affirmative. Some mentioned that they developed a greater appreciation for history, and others described how they feel better equipped to manage their own historical records as well as their family's papers. A few respondents cited the value of the general organizational skills they had acquired through their College Archives employment. Learning how to work well with a variety of people with different backgrounds and viewpoints was also mentioned.

When asked what recommendations they might make to improve the work/study experience of undergraduates, the respondents offered a number of helpful suggestions. The idea mentioned most often was to vary the tasks assigned as much as possible so that students could explore different types of materials and ways of working with them. Along with that idea, one person suggested several shorter projects rather than just a few long ones in order to facilitate broader exploration. A number of people would have liked to visit other archival repositories as part of their experience, and one individual mentioned that it would be helpful for students to have the chance to share with one another what they were working on, since the work can sometimes seem isolated and unrelated to work being done by others. One person recommended that students be allowed to design at least one work project on their own, both to encourage greater individual engagement as well as, potentially, to increase the variety of subjects being explored. Finally, one person suggested having students keep a journal and set individual goals.

Only 40% of respondents reported that they had intended to major in History, but 76.7% ultimately graduated with a History degree; English and Anthropology were the next two most popular completed majors. More than half, 56.7%, reported having received a degree beyond the bachelor's degree, and 16.7% indicated that they were currently enrolled in a graduate program. In addition, 66.7% indicated an interest in pursuing graduate study at some point in the future, an indication that many of those who already had masters and other advanced degrees planned yet more schooling down the road. All respondents but one (a stay-at-home parent) indicated that they were employed, and 73.3% reported that they were employed in their intended permanent career field.

Nearly half of the respondents, 46.7%, reported working in an information-related field; those individuals are currently employed in a variety of government and academic libraries and archives, as well as private museums. The next most popular field was law, with 16.7% of the respondents. Other current fields of occupation included education, publishing, social services, business and finance, academic administration, and ecology.

THE FUTURE

As one might well imagine, the results of this survey were particularly heartening. Students had clearly taken with them not only fond memories, but also knowledge and skills that they considered valuable. They applied what they learned not only in other jobs, but also in their daily lives, and their work experiences had, for more than half of the respondents, influenced their career choices. The survey demonstrated that, for most individuals, work/study in the College Archives amounted to more than just another job.

The positive results notwithstanding, there is always room for improvement. In describing aspects of the job that they liked least, respondents revealed issues that can be addressed, like making sure that more tedious and routine tasks—generally unavoidable in any work situation—are evenly spread among employees. In addition, the suggestions and recommendations that past employees made to improve the work experience were all practical and worthy of being explored. Being sure to vary the types of work assigned to students is certainly reasonable, and visits to other repositories can easily be arranged when desired.

Interestingly, while the respondents shared many of the same concerns with regard to least enjoyed aspects, there was great variety revealed by those things most enjoyed. While some preferred to spend time transcribing older documents, others were fond of organizing visual images; while some liked processing manuscript collections, others favored creating exhibits and displays. Moreover, some preferred to be given a lot of direction and to receive regular feedback on their efforts, while others liked to pursue their work with only minimal instruction; some enjoyed working as part of a team, while others found it preferable to work independently. Thus, what the survey revealed—which should not come as a surprise to anyone—is that everyone has unique interests and learning styles. What naturally follows is that tailoring the work, as much as possible, according to the individual interests of the undergraduate employee, and providing training and instruction in a variety of ways, can help to ensure a productive work experience for both employee and employer.

The Archives and Special Collections Department at Dickinson College houses a wide variety of materials, both in terms of format and content. I like to think that there is something there of interest to everyone. The challenge, then, is to make connections between the work/study employees and those things that interest them. The parallel challenge is to guide the pursuit of those interests in ways that will support the needs and goals of the department. If those two challenges can be well met, then I think we may continue to benefit from successful employment experiences.

No student chooses what college or university to attend based on the employment opportunities afforded through the work/study program. This does not mean, however, that such work cannot potentially be a valuable part of the undergraduate learning, growing, and maturing process. Surveying past employees as a means of assessing the quality of your work/study offerings is one way to help ensure that your efforts as an instructor and supervisor of students will continue to have a positive impact well beyond their undergraduate years.

APPENDIX 3.1: Survey Questions

SECTION 1

1. What kinds of materials did you work with while employed in the College Archives? (check all that apply)
   - Personal papers (e.g. letters, diaries, notebooks, postcards, memorabilia, etc.)
   - College records (e.g. committee minutes, student transcripts, office files, etc.)
   - Photographs
   - Books
   - Pamphlets
   - Artifacts
   - Slides
   - Cassettes or video tapes
   - Other

2. What types of work did you do while employed in the College Archives? (check all that apply)
   - Checked online catalog records of books and pamphlets
   - Processed or inventoried collections of personal papers
   - Transcribed handwritten letters or diaries
   - Organized and cataloged photographs
   - Performed original research
   - Scanned photographs, books, or other materials
   - Inventoried, organized, and sorted college records
   - Prepared exhibits or displays
   - Edited OCR'd texts
   - Added materials to, or weeded materials from, drop files
   - Provided reference assistance to on-site patrons

3. With what kinds of software did you work? (check all that apply)
   - Word processing software (Microsoft Word, WordPerfect, etc.)
   - Spreadsheet software (Microsoft Excel, etc.)
   - Optical character recognition software (OmniPage Pro, etc.)
   - Photo editing software (Photoshop, etc.)
   - Web authoring software (Netscape Composer, Dreamweaver, etc.)
   - Other (please specify)

4. With what kinds of hardware did you work? (check all that apply)
   - Desktop computer
   - Scanner
   - Digital camera
   - Other (please specify)

SECTION 2

5. What was your primary motivation in seeking employment in the College Archives? (select one)
   - Applied for work in the library and was assigned to the Archives
   - General interest in history
   - General interest in rare books and other special materials
   - Became interested after being introduced to the College Archives through a class assignment
   - Knew about archival work from experiences prior to entering Dickinson College
   - Other (please elaborate)

6. Overall, was your employment in the College Archives a positive experience?
   - Yes
   - No
   - Please elaborate.

7. What did you find MOST enjoyable about your employment in the College Archives?

8. What did you find LEAST enjoyable about your employment in the College Archives?

9. What did you find MOST valuable or useful about your employment in the College Archives?

10. What did you find LEAST valuable or useful about your employment in the College Archives?

11. Are there any activities you would have like to do, or skills you would have liked to learn, but did not have the opportunity while you were employed in the College Archives? If so, please elaborate.

SECTION 3

12. Did you work, volunteer, or intern in an archives or special collections repository BEFORE working in the College Archives?
    - Yes
    - No
    - If yes, where did you work?

13. Did you work, volunteer, or intern in an archives or special collections repository AFTER working in the College Archives?
    - Yes
    - No
    - If yes, where did you work?

14. Did your work in the College Archives influence your career decision?
    - Yes
    - No
    - Please elaborate.

15. Did your work in the College Archives teach you something you have found useful in your current career?
    - Yes
    - No
    - Please elaborate.

16. Did your work in the College Archives teach you something you have found useful in your life unrelated to your career?
    - Yes
    - No
    - Please elaborate.

17. What recommendations would you make for ways to improve the work/study experiences of undergraduates employed in the College Archives?

18. Would you (or did you) recommend employment in the College Archives to others?
    - Yes
    - No
    - Please elaborate.

19. Are there any additional comments about your work experience in the College Archives that you would care to make?

SECTION 4

20. When you first enrolled at Dickinson, what field of study did you intend to pursue as a career?

21. With what major(s) did you graduate from Dickinson?

22. In what year did you graduate from Dickinson?

23. Have you earned any post-undergraduate degrees?
    - Yes
    - No
    - If yes, what degree(s) have you earned, and from institution(s)?

24. Are you currently enrolled in a graduate program?
    - Yes
    - No

- If yes, what degree(s) are you currently pursuing?

25. Would you like to attend graduate school in the future?
    - Yes
    - No
    - If yes, in what field(s) of study? If already completed or currently in attendance with no immediate plans for future study, please proceed to the next question.

26. Are you currently employed?
    - Yes
    - No
    - If no, in what field of work was your last employment, what was you job title, and with whom were you employed? If yes, in what field are you employed, what is your job title, and with whom are you employed?

27. Are you currently employed in your intended "permanent" career field?
    - Yes
    - No
    - If no, in what field would you ultimately like to be employed?

28. OPTIONAL: Please provide your name and current address. Information will be used for internal purposes only and will be kept strictly confidential.

29. Do you have any comments about this survey?

Social Networking Software in the Archives: Using Blogs to Engage Students with Primary Sources

Malinda Triller

INTRODUCTION

Dickinson College (Carlisle, PA) is a private, liberal arts college chartered in 1783 and located in rural central Pennsylvania with a current enrollment of 2,300 undergraduates. In the fall of 2009, the institution celebrated the 125th anniversary of the matriculation of its first female students. In preparation for this occasion, the staff of Archives and Special Collections assembled a team of students to gather information about the history of women at the college in order to support the events, publications, and exhibit that would mark the anniversary year. The project coordinators wished to capture the results of this research in a way that harnessed the power of collaboration and made the students' findings accessible to the public. As a solution, they created the "Women's Experiences at Dickinson College" blog (http://itech.dickinson.edu/coeducation) using Drupal, an open source content management system. This electronic resource continues to grow and serves both as a research guide and as a tool for members of the campus community to communicate about their shared history. (See figure 4.1.)

DEVELOPMENT OF THE BLOG

In 2007, the staff of Dickinson's Archives and Special Collections began employing blog posts as access points for that department's collections. Using Drupal, members of the staff had developed one blog that allowed for on-demand cataloging of materials requested by researchers (http://itech.dickinson.edu/archives/) and had experimented with another as a delivery mechanism for a digital photo archive. As the 125th anniversary of Dickinson's transition to coeducation approached, the staff recognized that the resources contained in the college's archives would be critical in the development of programming for that occasion. The special collections librarian and the college archivist subsequently made arrangements to engage a team of student researchers to scour the records for materials relevant to understanding the experiences of the institution's female students, alumni, faculty, and staff. Based on the Archives and Special Collection Department's earlier experiences with Web 2.0 technology, a blog focused on women's history appeared to be a natural mechanism for gathering and distributing the information the students discovered. In fact, a blog format seemed particularly suited to this project, as it would allow the students to view their findings and share them with the public in real time, making it immediately useful in preparing for the anniversary.

The special collections librarian and college archivist developed the women's history blog with the assistance of a member of Dickinson's Instructional and Media Services (IMS) Department. They chose to build this new tool using Drupal, because they had found it flexible and easily customizable in previous project work. They also hoped that using a uniform software platform would allow them to merge their various Web-based resources more easily in the future.

Figure 4.1. The Women's Experiences at Dickinson blog features stories discovered in the college archives by undergraduate researchers.

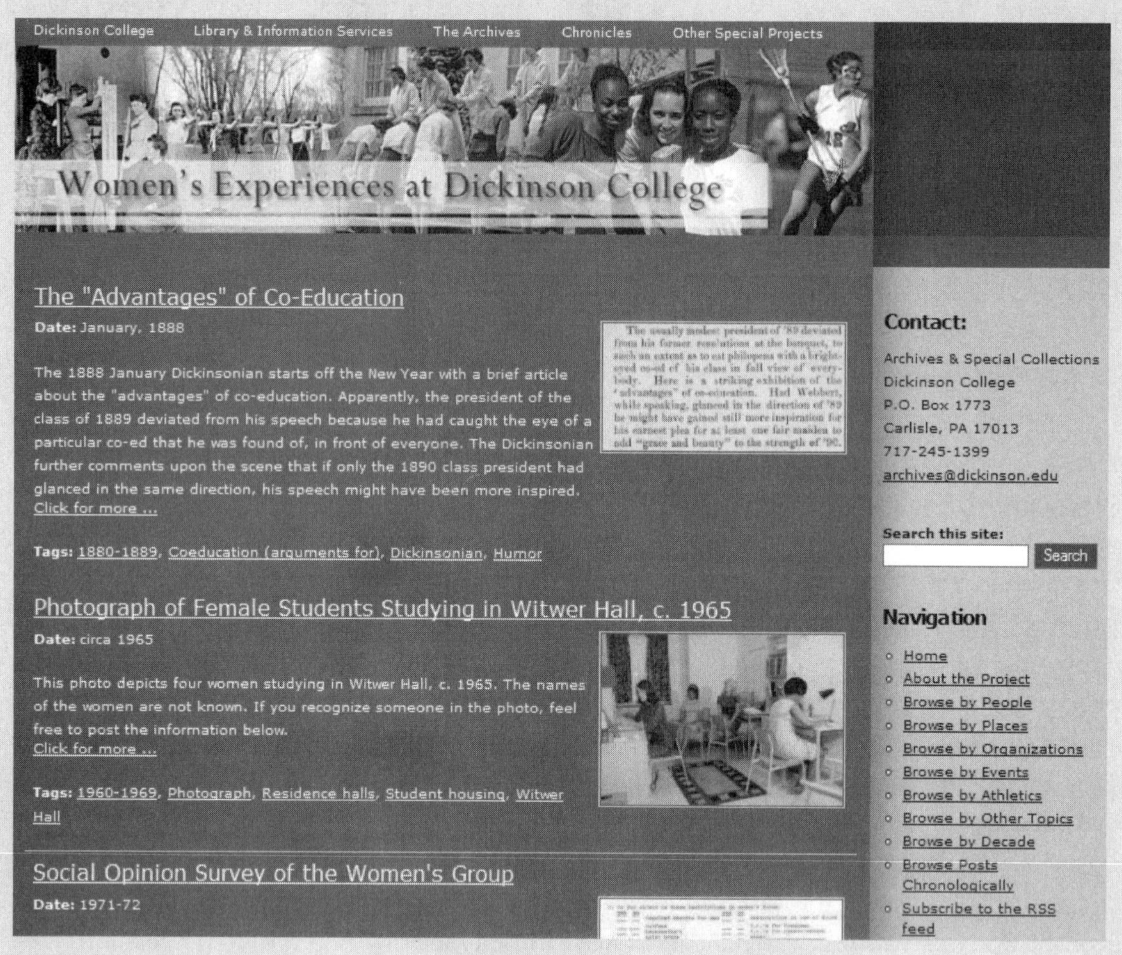

The special collections librarian and archivist envisioned the blog as a cataloging tool that would capture metadata at a level of detail much greater than that possible with a traditional finding aid. According to this model, students could create at least one blog post, or item-level record, for each document, but also have the ability to compose multiple posts to highlight facets of lengthier or more complex documents, such as memoirs. In order to allow student participants to focus their energies on analyzing primary sources, rather than on mastering technology and cataloging principles, this blog needed to be easy to populate. As a first step, the special collections librarian and archivist identified the pieces of information they wished to capture about any document the students might consult in the course of the research project. They decided to record the original date of creation, a short summary of each item's contents, the shelf location for the original material, and a one-page scan of every document to create a zoomable thumbnail for each post. In addition, they determined that each post would include a title (or headline) to be determined by the students, as well as tag fields that would generate convenient browse lists for various subjects such as people, places, organizations, events, athletics, or other topics represented in the archival materials. The IMS representative built a data entry

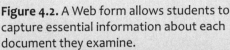

Figure 4.2. A Web form allows students to capture essential information about each document they examine.

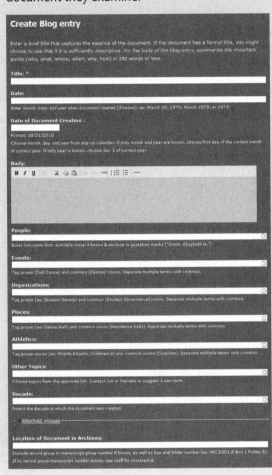

form based on these selected fields, and an Archives and Special Collections intern tested it prior to the launch of the project to ensure that it functioned properly and was intuitive to use. (See figure 4.2.)

PROJECT WORKFLOW

Once the blog's data structure met with their approval, the special collections librarian and archivist assembled the research team, which included paid interns sponsored by the college's Research and Development Committee, work-study students, and volunteers recruited with the assistance of academic departments and campus women's organizations. Over the course of several semesters, 18 students

(and several faculty) contributed to the blog. The participants represented a variety of majors and, in most cases, they had not visited the Archives and Special Collections Department prior to embarking on this venture.

Before blogging commenced, the special collections librarian distributed two short essays about the history of women at the college to all of the participants in order to provide them with a sense of historical context. Each student then had the opportunity to select an aspect of women's history that was of personal interest, such as the experiences of women of color, the role of Greek life, the development of women's athletics, or the impact of World War II on gender roles. The special collections librarian located materials appropriate to each topic, in some cases uncovering resources that staff had not known existed or that had sat on the shelves unexamined for many years. As a result, the students utilized a wide variety of documents dating from the nineteenth and twentieth centuries, including student newspapers, yearbooks, faculty and trustee meeting minutes, student essays and orations, photographs, the records of student organizations, oral histories, and correspondence between administrators and trustees.

As most students had no previous experience with scanners or blogging software, the special collections librarian provided a series of 30-60 minute training sessions for all participants during which she demonstrated the necessary workflows and proper usage of equipment. Team members then created practice posts with the guidance of the librarian before embarking on their individual research pursuits. The students quickly became proficient with the scanners and data entry form and were able to work on their own to a large degree. The Archives and Special Collections Department has eight computer workstations equipped with scanners, so bloggers could come and go during business hours as their schedules permitted. Archives staff were readily available to answer questions and to provide the student researchers with background information on the historical context or document genre of the primary sources supplied to them. For handwritten materials, staff also made transcriptions available whenever possible and helped students decipher nineteenth-century script as needed.

CHALLENGES

As this project was fueled in large part by student energy and enthusiasm, the staff gave students a large amount of latitude in selecting their topics and in identifying which elements of an individual document to highlight in a blog post. The special collections librarian and archivist did serve a basic editorial role, however. One of the most challenging aspects of the blogging process was the creation of consistent tags for each post. Drupal software does offer an auto-complete feature that remembers and suggests tags entered in earlier posts, improving the chance that once a student has entered a term (e.g., Meredith, Josephine), that subsequent individuals will be less likely to enter an alternative form of the term (e.g., Meredith, Josephine Brunyate). Variant spellings inevitably entered the system, however, often because the terms were not spelled consistently in the original documents themselves. In other cases, students chose different synonyms to describe concepts (e.g., African American women vs. women of color), leading to browse lists that failed to bring together all the documents under one term. The special collections librarian and archivist wanted the students to focus more on writing descriptive summaries of their documents rather than agonizing over issues of controlled vocabulary, so they created a short handbook listing approved terms to help minimize discrepancies. They also accepted that a certain number of inconsistencies and typographical mistakes were inevitable. To ensure quality, the project leaders regularly read through new posts with an eye to correcting those types of errors.

The project leaders also needed to commit sufficient time to locating appropriate resources for the bloggers to examine, and those items needed to accord with the department's access policies, especially with regard to the protection of student/alumni privacy. In some instances, staff found it difficult to locate items relevant to a student's chosen topic. In those circumstances, in consultation with the particular blogger, they would either locate records indirectly related to the selected theme or help the student identify an alternate area of study based on personal interests. In order to assist in selection of resources and to avoid having more than one student blog the same document, the special collections librarian maintained a spreadsheet tracking each item or collection as it was used.

BENEFITS

Over the course of approximately one year, this team of students created more than 1,000 blog posts based on their original research, with numerous resulting benefits. The bloggers represented a wide range of majors, including women's and gender studies, history, English, medieval and early modern studies, theatre and dance, psychology, and American studies. Many of these individuals, who were predominantly women, dedicated time to this project because of their interest in women's history or because they viewed their participation as a form of feminist social action. "Women's lives and experiences throughout history are not documented as well as those of men. This project provides a voice to a history, culture, and experience that has been silenced and overshadowed," reflected one intern. For the majority of the participants, this project provided them with the opportunity to work with original historical sources for the first time, and, with guidance from the special collections librarian and archivist, they learned to identify and analyze documents in a variety of formats that previously had been unfamiliar to them. One researcher described the project as an "incredibly … rewarding experience. I believe that it has helped me understand the history of the school, as well as the methods behind archival research." The students also became very engaged in their research, regularly noting the connections they made between the past represented in the documents and both their own student experiences and the feminist theory they had learned in the classroom. Several of the students were so excited about the opportunity to explore Archives and Special Collections that they brought classmates and friends to the department for behind-the-scenes tours.

The blog itself has, and continues to serve, a number of purposes. A team of interns used this resource to inform the creation of a physical exhibit featuring photographs, artifacts, and documents telling the story of women's lives at the college. A member of the Alumni Relations Department repurposed stories and facts captured in the blog to build a PowerPoint presentation in order to take the 125th anniversary "on the road" to alumni clubs. Students search the blog to aid in research for course assignments, and in a few instances, alumnae have made use of its comments feature to remark on existing posts and to contribute their personal memories. The stories shared in this blog have subsequently inspired faculty to incorporate oral history projects into their classes, projects in which alumnae and students have participated with enthusiasm. The Archives and Special Collections staff consults this electronic resource to respond to reference requests, and the blog itself has generated new requests from members of the public who have discovered it through search engines. In fact, one individual in Europe contacted the staff after a Google search led him to a post about a long-lost relative for whom the family had no other historical record.

Overall, this project heightened awareness of the Archives' resources and services, especially within the campus community. Faculty embraced the initiative by collaborating with the special collections librarian to develop instruction sessions and assignments using the college's historical records. The members of a local sorority, wishing to include their story in this celebration of women's contributions, proudly presented the Archives with a scrapbook documenting the group's establishment. The alumnae of a long-standing women's honorary society conceived the idea for a reunion event during which members could participate in oral histories and donate memorabilia to the archives. Members of the college community have also responded to the stories contained (and not contained) in the blog, by posing new questions, especially in regard to women of color, sexual identity, and sexual violence, questions that will fuel future exploration as this blog continues to grow.

APPLICATIONS

The Women's Experiences at Dickinson blog demonstrates one approach for engaging undergraduates with primary sources in a way that leverages the collaborative and interactive nature of Web 2.0 technology. Faculty, archivists, and librarians could apply this approach as a way to organize and preserve student contributions to group assignments, to prepare for exhibits, to document the findings of research-based internships, or to develop guides for archival and manuscript material. While the staff at Dickinson chose to utilize Drupal to develop a customized blog with many carefully defined fields, a more streamlined approach using a simple WordPress blog or comparable tool would yield similar results. The goal is to provide a vehicle for students to capture and share the results of their research in a way that facilitates the process by which they learn to make connections between individual documents within a broader historical context.

Using a blog in this way also provides students with a visual representation of the method by which one document yields clues or raises new questions that lead to the discovery of additional resources. For example, one blogger examined a folder from the college president's office containing a Social Opinion

Survey distributed in 1972 by a women's group that the Archives staff had not known existed. A careful combing of other administrative files yielded memos and correspondence regarding the group's advocacy for more female faculty positions and gynecological services on campus. These subsequent discoveries resulted in a better understanding of the chronology and nature of feminist activism at the college that informed future searches through the student newspaper and the records of other women's organizations.

The very nature of blog technology makes a collaborative research project such as this extremely flexible. Any number of individuals can contribute, and they can do so in an asynchronous manner, as access to equipment and archival materials allows. Unlike physical or electronic exhibits, which generally exist for a finite period, a blog can persist and continue to grow as long as research continues and the technology remains supported. Once a template and workflow exist, they can then be adapted to support new projects. The public nature of a research blog also allows students to contribute to scholarship in a visible way that a traditional paper, which is a private exchange between student and faculty, does not. As the experience at Dickinson demonstrates, when students have the opportunity to share their work in a digital environment, others can benefit and build upon their efforts, in essence creating a synergy in which student research actually begets student research.

CONCLUSION

For the past decade, archivists have been digitizing their resources so that researchers, such as undergraduates, can enjoy easier access to their collections. Dickinson's blog model offers an alternative approach in which the students themselves build the electronic resource as they examine primary sources in their original formats. In this way the process of historical research and analysis has the potential to become a dynamic, public exchange with a global audience. As the students sharpen their own information literacy skills, they also bring to light the human stories hidden on the archives' shelves, facilitating future exploration and discovery for their peers and others. According to this model, both the research process and the final product serve to broaden students' understanding and usage of archival materials.

Waiting to Excel: Undergraduate Research Partnerships in Special Collections at Lafayette College

Diane Windham Shaw

What college or university special collections librarian wouldn't want collections processed, exhibits mounted, and important events in the institution's history documented—and all paid for out of someone else's budget? This is the promise of Lafayette College's Excel program, designed to foster collaborative research between students and faculty members. To become an Excel Scholar, students are nominated by a faculty mentor to play a substantive role in a research project. Proposals are reviewed by the Faculty Committee on Academic Research, with final approval by the provost. The program is open to sophomore, junior, and senior students in all disciplines, who have at least a 3.25 GPA. Excel Scholars can work full time during summer and interim sessions and up to ten hours per week during the fall and spring semesters. They receive a higher rate of pay than regular student assistants and free college housing during the summer and interim. As touted by the college's website: "The program is central to Lafayette's dedication to providing unique academic opportunities and promoting the personal mentoring of students by faculty. It began in 1986 with 14 students. The program now has an annual budget of over $500,000 with more than 160 students participating each year. The success has made the program a model for other colleges and universities."

By virtue of their faculty status, Lafayette's librarians are eligible to participate in the Excel program. The librarians have faculty status, but not rank or tenure, and so there was initially some con-

fusion as to whether or not they could participate as faculty in the Excel scholars program. When the Excel program was first introduced, the special collections librarian's eligibility was questioned by the assistant provost charged with its oversight. A formal ruling by the provost affirming the librarians' eligibility settled the matter, but there were other hurdles. One noteworthy example was the stipulation that the work of the Excel Scholars could not be "clerical or bibliographical in nature." Although the latter prohibition was meant to keep students from checking bibliographies *ad nauseam*, it appeared to negate any potential project relating to rare books. The librarians did not succeed in getting that clause amended, but it was eventually understood that projects that involved books would be acceptable.

Since 1986, the baker's dozen Excel Scholars that have come through special collections have proved beyond a doubt the value of the program. Our students have helped create our historical photographs and college sports collections; they have analyzed the physical characteristics of our rare book collection; they have interviewed many of our first women students who arrived on campus in the fall of 1970; and they have documented the remarkable story of two Louisiana slaves who were sent to Lafayette in 1838. Through the Excel program, special collections has benefitted enormously from the work of some of the college's most talented students, a few of whom have gone on to careers in library and archival work. This case study will describe and evaluate Lafayette's experiences with the Excel program.

Like most special collections, much of the work at Lafayette's special collections is project based or can easily be positioned as such. Activities like arrangement and description of manuscript collections, preparation and mounting of exhibits, and development of web exhibits and other web resources all involve research. Decisions about what to put forward as an Excel proposal usually were based upon whether the project could contribute to resolving our most pressing needs or move us forward in a way that would be beneficial to our mission. Thus, for instance, an important early project focused on gathering up all of the college's historical photographs, giving them proper housing, and preparing a finding aid. Years later, we were able to be more proactive in selecting projects, and used the Excel program to help us prepare for the 40th anniversary of coeducation by developing a historical website. Project conception and making the case for its research value were the relatively easy parts of an Excel proposal.

Sometimes the harder challenge was to find the right student partner. A number of our students were selected for Excel work after spending some time with us as regular student assistants. Those that seemed like they would be an especially good fit were invited to be part of an Excel project. Other times when we had a worthy project, but no student in mind, we would seek advice from the faculty. Some of our most outstanding students came to us this way. With students we did not already know, we always conducted personal interviews. Since any Excel scholar had to have a 3.25 GPA, we knew all potential candidates were academically talented. So we evaluated them on less tangible attributes such as level of enthusiasm for the project, degree of interest in the materials, and indications of a strong work ethic. I will never forget the response of one of our oral history students when I called to ask if she would be interested in coming in for an inter-

view. "Would I ever!," she said, "This is my ticket to stardom."

Once hired, our Excel scholars received training that emphasized not only the skills needed for the particular project, but also provided background on the holdings and mission of the department in general. Students were given an in-depth tour of the department and its collections, as well as an opportunity to meet one-on-one with department members to learn about their roles. Each student was given general readings about archives and special collections, which were to be discussed with the special collections librarian. These readings have changed over the years, but have usually included articles on the profession, reference and security, and arrangement and description. More specialized readings germane to the project were then introduced, often SAA manuals and workbooks on archival processing. For processing projects students were also asked to review good examples of finding aids from Lafayette as well as other repositories. Finally, training for certain projects required special expertise. For the photograph project, the special collections librarian and the Excel Scholar attended a day-long workshop on identification of photographic processes and preservation housing for photographs. And for the oral history project, an archivist from a repository with an active oral history program was brought in to give a workshop to the special collections staff and Excel Scholars.

From the very first project in 1986, the arrangement and description of several series (fifty cubic feet) of the papers of Lafayette alumnus and former Secretary of the United States Treasury, William E. Simon, a number of Excel projects have involved some type of archival processing. Other projects have involved assembling and processing collections that were dispersed across campus. The college's photographic archive was essentially created by our Excel Scholar, who gathered together photographs from multiple campus locations, organized them into series, gave them preservation housing, and wrote a finding aid for what ultimately proved to be some 50,000 images. We promoted the conclusion of this project by mounting an exhibit of 130 years of college photographs. Still another such project involved the dismantling of a defunct political science museum on campus, and incorporating its collections into special collections. Our Excel Scholar processed the resulting collections and again we mounted an exhibition to call attention to these rediscovered materials.

Other projects have helped to further improve access to our holdings. In conjunction with the construction of a new recreation center and the renovation of our field house, we proposed a sports history survey and inventory project to facilitate the development of exhibits on Lafayette athletics in the new facility. Our Excel Scholar created a sports history vertical file, a timeline of all sports played at the college, and a compendium of sports highlights. She also inventoried our athletic film holdings and processed thirty-six cubic feet of athletics communications records, which included the documentation of our first women's teams. Another project involved increasing access to small manuscript collections. The Excel Scholar was charged with providing concise, comprehensive descriptions of the materials and recommendations about access points from which our cataloger could create collection-level MARC records. In preparation for the retrospective conversion of our rare book cataloging records, we proposed an Excel project that would enhance information about the physical characteristics of the books. Our Excel Scholar undertook an analysis of the collection, noting specific aspects of printing, binding, paper, illustrations, provenance, collation, and condition.

The Excel Scholars have been a boon to our exhibits program, as many of them have worked on exhibits both physical and online. One large project involved not only the archival processing of the papers of an alumnus artist, but also the mounting of two exhibits on his work—one for special collections in the library and the other for the college art gallery. The Excel Scholar was selected to present her work on the artist at the National Conference on Undergraduate Research. Other exhibit-based projects involved Excel Scholars with exhibits on the Marquis de Lafayette's farewell tour of America in 1824-25, books written by foreign visitors to America before the Civil War, and the history of social dancing at Lafayette College. The same student who worked on the latter two exhibits, a multi-year Excel Scholar, was also responsible for bringing major projects on the Marquis de Lafayette to the web in 2001-02. Using web authoring tools, she coded the extensive finding aid for our Marquis de Lafayette holdings (manuscripts, prints, and memorabilia) for our first website. Nicely designed, with more than fifty images, her version is still in use today. She also produced our first digital collections, scanning Marquis de Lafayette-related sheet music and printed ephemera for the website. And she created two of our earliest online exhibits, designing a web version of a physical exhibit on the Marquis de Lafayette and slavery and developing her own small web exhibit on Lafayette's captivity in Austria, 1792-97.

Projects to document aspects of the college's history have provided some of the most interesting research experiences for Excel Scholars. In 2009, we used an Excel Scholar to help locate existing records on two former Louisiana slaves who were in residence at Lafayette College, 1838-44. The Excel Scholar read microfilm, transcribed letters, accompanied me on research trips to the Presbyterian Historical Society and the Schomburg Center for Research in Black Culture, and spent his spring break in Louisiana where he looked at collections of the slave owner's papers at Tulane University and Louisiana State University. He and I gave several joint presentations on the project.

Our most ambitious undertaking was an oral history project designed to document the experiences of our pioneering women and African American students at Lafayette in the late 1960s and early 1970s.

Three Excel Scholars were involved with the project between 2002 and 2004. More than fifty interviews with alumni, faculty, and administrators were conducted and transcribed by the Excel Scholars, who also presented on the project at a regional women's studies conference. Two of the Excels scripted and produced a full-scale theatrical show using the oral history project's first-hand accounts of Lafayette's transition to coeducation. The play, complete with decorated set, period music, and historical images, had a three-night run in the college's student center, where it drew an audience of nearly 300. To prepare for the fortieth anniversary of coeducation at Lafayette, a new Excel Scholar created an extensive website that included a historical timeline, resource documents, photographs, and sample transcripts

and audio files from the oral history project, as well as video clips and the full script from the play. The Excel Scholar made several presentations to alumni groups and to classes which were using the website. In 2011 our original play on the beginnings of coeducation was reworked by the Theater Department and presented on the main stage of the arts center.

After twenty-five years of mentoring Excel Scholars, I can look back on an overall record of great success. Although some projects were not as fruitful as they might have been, the majority surpassed all expectations. In addition to the significant amount of work in special collections that these scholars accomplished, there were a number of intangible benefits for both the students and the repository. For our students, being selected as an Excel Scholar car-

Figure 5.1. Lafayette College Special Collections Librarian Diane Windham Shaw and her Excel Scholar Sarah Shuster '12 hold up the 1970 recruitment poster for the college's first class of women. The poster was designed for double duty; it could also be used as a book cover.

ried a certain amount of prestige; they became part of an elite community. During the summer, there were special forums and social events held just for them. As is almost always the case with students working in special collections, the Excel Scholars felt privileged to work there and the things they learned about the institution's history connected them more closely with their alma mater. Finally, for some, the Excel program was not only a resume builder, it was a direct career path. Among our Excel progeny can be found one rare book dealer, one librarian, and two archivists.

For special collections, the Excel program enabled us to have the services of some of our most intellectually capable students for an extended period of time. Unlike semester-long internships for academic credit, which we also offer, the Excel Scholars could work up to three years on one or more projects. I often likened the nature of their work to that of graduate assistants. Our use of the Excel program also sent a positive message to the faculty about the level of research and type of work undertaken in special collections. All proposals had to pass muster with the Academic Research Committee and all our projects were listed in the year-end report of the committee, which is seen by all faculty. Finally, and most importantly, through the Excel program we have been able to realize one of our core goals of contributing to the teaching and learning mission of the institution.

The Swing Around the Circle

Sarah Dauterive and Ryan P. Semmes

Many exhibits begin simply by accident. An archivist stumbles upon a previously undiscovered document or object, and, through curiosity starts down a research path that evolves into an exhibition that is both informative and unique. Such is the case with the "Swing Around the Circle" exhibit at the Ulysses S. Grant Association offices in the Mississippi State University Library.[1] A student worker's discovery of a curious photograph resulted in an exhibit project which utilized primary and secondary source materials and, though small in size, was informative and well-received.

The *Papers of Ulysses S. Grant* collection offers a unique opportunity for students who work for the Ulysses S. Grant Association. Though the editors continue to utilize the materials for the publication of the written works of Ulysses S. Grant, the Association was interested in making the project files available to other researchers. This has led to an enormous amount of work in processing the collection and organizing the materials into a variety of series: Subject Files, Unpublished Correspondence Files, Published Correspondence Files, Scrapbooks, Photographs, and Family Correspondence, among others. The exhibit project was an outgrowth of the Photograph Series description project. Our student assistant, Sarah Thornburg, a history major and aspiring archivist, was creating item-level descriptions of the various images in the Photograph Series of the *Papers of Ulysses S. Grant* project. The organizational structure of the series—subject headings—was previously in place; however, given that the materials encompassed only 3 linear feet, the

decision was made to describe each item individually. While organizing images of Ulysses S. Grant posing with other individuals, Sarah came upon a small *carte-de-visite* of General Grant, Secretary of the Navy Gideon Welles, and President Andrew Johnson. On the verso of the CDV were the names of the three gentlemen, the date that the image was taken (August 31, 1866) and the location—Auburn, New York.

We quickly realized the uniqueness of the image and became interested in the event that had brought Grant, Welles and Johnson together. We found, in *The Papers of Ulysses S. Grant*, a letter written by Grant to his wife, Julia (from Auburn, New York), on the day the image was taken. The letter stated, in part, "I am getting very tired of this expedition and of hearing political speaches [sic]. I must go through however." The "expedition" was what became known as "The Swing Around the Circle," a publicity tour organized by President Andrew Johnson to sell his Reconstruction Plan to the people of the North. Our curiosity piqued, I tasked Sarah with researching the expedition and to consider anything she found for possible inclusion in an exhibit featuring the image.

As Sarah began her research we decided that this was a great opportunity to show her some of the challenges that archivists, particularly those in small institutions, face when creating exhibits. Sarah was tasked with creating an exhibit around the Grant image and the context for the photograph. She was also tasked with researching Grant and Johnson's expedition utilizing primary and secondary sources found within our collections, with conceptualizing an exhibit that accurately portrayed the historical significance of the expedition, and with physically creating an exhibit that was visually pleasing, yet capable of being displayed in our one available display cabinet. It was our hope that, despite the exhibit limitations in our area, Sarah would be able to create an exhibit with a defined thesis, and that her understanding of the use of primary and secondary resources in historical research would be enriched.

There are a number of difficulties inherent in mounting such an exhibit. Our exhibit space is limited to two small cases and only one was available at the time. That case is a refashioned department store glass display, not constructed to archival standards, and having no lock. With one glass shelf and dimensions of 17" x 30" x 60" the amount of space would be limited to around eight or nine documents of approximately 8" x 10" size. Secondly, our budget for exhibits was equally limited. We did, however, benefit from the Mississippi State University Library's Instructional Media Center, which provides software and printing capabilities for campus students, faculty and staff.

Utilizing our in-office scanner, Sarah was able to digitize all of the materials she intended to use in her exhibit. This provided many important benefits. First, we were able to expand the size of the CDV from a 2" x 4" card to an 8" x 10" image. Secondly, maintaining digital copies of exhibited materials would enable us to create an online version of the exhibit. Finally, because of the unsecured nature of our exhibit case, it was important for us not to exhibit any original materials. What follows is an account of our student's research findings and her experiences with creating the exhibit, as well as lessons learned from conducting research utilizing primary sources and secondary sources.

SARAH'S FINDINGS
[Text in **BOLD** taken from Exhibit Text Block Transcripts]

In August of 1866, President Johnson set out to promote his Reconstruction plan to the American people on a trip that came to be known as the "Swing Around the Circle." Johnson's plan had been rejected by Congress, so he hoped to gain the support of the people by bringing several popular American figures along, including General Grant. Grant was so popular that the people would yell his name instead of Johnson's to the point that it made Johnson angry.

The two pieces I chose to display first on the top shelf were a newspaper headline and a map. The newspaper headline read, "The President's Tour. Johnson's Speeches on the route from Chicago to Springfield. He Becomes Incensed at the Repeated Cheers for Grant."[2] I liked this headline because the large, bold words "The President's Tour" acted as another title for the exhibit. The newspaper clipping revealed Johnson's anger at the people's cries for Grant, setting the tone of the trip. This headline put the rest of the presented information into perspective for the person viewing the exhibit. The map[3] depicted stops Grant and Johnson made on their tour. The placement of the map was important because it showed not only where the President and Grant went, but also the date of the tour.

Grant did not appreciate Johnson's attempt to use Grant to promote his Reconstruction plan. In a letter to General William S. Hillyer, Grant asked that his name no longer be used to influence the votes of the people. Grant wanted "every man to vote according to his own judgment..." Just a few months later, Grant would begin to publicly oppose Johnson's plan, as seen in the clipping from the New York Times from November 1866.

The next pieces on display were the letter written by Grant to General William S. Hillyer[4] and an article in the *New York Times*[5]. Both documents served to provide insight into Grant's reaction to Johnson's harsh treatment of the American people and his Congressional opponents by outlining the rapidly declining support Grant offered Johnson. Grant's presence on the tour provided the public support Johnson wanted, although Grant privately opposed the plan. However, just days after the tour had ended, Grant wrote a letter to Hillyer in an attempt to disassociate himself with Johnson's Reconstruction plan. The *New York Times* article, written just ten weeks later, shows Grant's further attempt to distance himself from the plan by publicly opposing the President.

Pictured from left to right are General Ulysses S. Grant, Secretary of the Navy Gideon Welles, and President Andrew Johnson. This picture was taken in Auburn, New York on August 31, 1866 on the porch of Enos Throop, the former governor of New York, just a few days into the trip. On the same day, Grant wrote to his wife, Julia, and said he was "very tired...of hearing political speaches [sic]." Grant would come to dislike both of these men.

Displayed on the left side of the bottom shelf were the CDV[6] and the letter Grant wrote to his wife, Julia.[7] In terms of the sequence of the exhibit, the letter fit well here as it followed the documents which described Grant's deteriorating support for Johnson. In the letter, Grant reveals that he is not happy on the tour but feels he must continue. The "sense of duty" tone that his letter evokes sheds light on his reasons for participating in the tour, despite his reservations concerning Johnson's plan. The letter and CDV together provide insight into a typical day on the tour for Grant. The CDV is the only image in the collection taken while on the "Swing Around the Circle." The well-preserved and rarely seen photograph is a treasure of the collection and warranted highlighting in the exhibit.

Figure 6.1. Grant, Welles and President Johnson

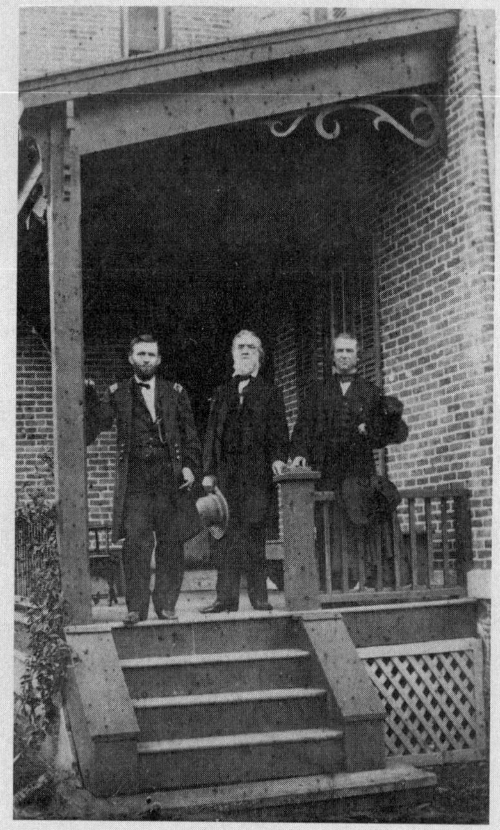

Figure 6.2. Letter to Julia Grant from Grant, August 31, 1866

Mr President Johnson
Auburn, N.Y.
August 31st/66

Dear Julia,

I am getting very tired of this expedition and of hearing political speaches. I must go through however. I only write now to give you a letter each day as near as I can. Love and kisses to you and the children.

Ulys.

Ac. No. 12068

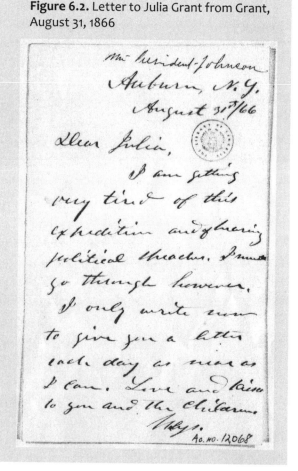

I next added a second newspaper clipping on the shelf to supplement the information already revealing Johnson's jealousy towards Grant's reception by the American people. The headline, which reads, "A. Johnson. Progress of the Egotist from Detroit to Chicago…He Speaks Often and is Hissed Frequently…Johnson Meets with a Decided Snub—The People Cry Aloud for Grant, and do not want to hear A.J.," portrays the people in a very hostile mood towards Johnson.[8] It should be noted, however, that the *Chicago Tribune* had an obvious bias against Johnson. While Johnson did have the support of some of the media—the *New York Times* described Johnson as being "greeted with enthusiastic cheers" when speaking—I only included the material that portrayed the public's disgust, due to the fact that the accepted historical opinion is that Grant and the majority of the American citizens did not support Johnson.[9]

Figure 6.3. Johnson is greeted by protesters

Johnson's Reconstruction plan was not well received by the public. Prior to his trip, there were bloody riots in New Orleans and Memphis. Johnson was critiqued for his leniency towards Reconstruction as seen in the two pages from Harper's Weekly, a popular newspaper during and after the Civil War. Many felt the riots in New Orleans and Memphis were proof that Johnson's plan was not strict enough to put the country back together.

The final pieces I chose to include were cartoons from Harper's Weekly. These cartoons emphasize the majority opinion — that Johnson's Reconstruction plan was too lenient towards the former Confederates.

The first cartoon uses images from the race riots in Memphis and New Orleans to insist that Johnson's plan would not solve America's problems. Johnson plays the role of the evil Iago, and an African American Union soldier appears as the Moor Othello from Shakespeare's play, *Othello*. Johnson plots to take away the soldier's new-found freedom, granted to him by the "Honorable Discharge" papers in his hand and signed by Grant. The second cartoon portrays Johnson giving a speech while on the tour in Cleveland, Ohio. Johnson's words are presented in a satirical way, implying a tough policy towards the South, which Johnson had no intention of carrying out.[10]

SARAH'S CONCLUSIONS

During my research, I had to find primary and secondary sources that helped to elucidate the story of the CDV in a brief manner. Building this exhibit forced me to take the skills I developed in my undergraduate career and use them in new ways. My background as a history major provided me with the basic research skills necessary to complete this project, but the project also required me to expand my use of primary sources, something I had not previously experienced. And the project demanded that I be more selective in order to find suitable material that would not only illustrate my thesis, but would also work well inside the exhibit case. Many newspaper articles were multiple pages with no headline. Likewise, books with appropriate material for the exhibit that might cover multiple pages were also difficult to display. These materials still played an important role, however. Because I was not aware of the event known as "The Swing Around the Circle" prior to discovering the CDV, these articles and books that were not displayed were still useful and informative. They led me to other valuable resources by providing me with additional search terms and a general understanding of the historical context of the "Swing Around the Circle." I expected that my lack of knowledge of this subject and period of American history would be the greatest challenge in creating this exhibit. However, I found locating material that best told the story around the CDV and fitting all of the information into the small case to be more difficult than I ever imagined.

For undergraduate students, creating an exhibit can provide an opportunity to use the skills learned in a classroom setting in a unique way. A better understanding of the research process and using primary sources can be a valuable tool for students in other undergraduate classes and those that continue with post-graduate education.

PROJECT CONCLUSIONS

Sarah's conclusion illustrates that she understood the objectives of the assignment and will be able to put her lessons into practice at another institution. It is important to see primary sources as not only tools for research, but as objects that give us a glimpse into the past and, when placed in their correct context, can tell a story that may have otherwise gone untold. Creating the exhibit instilled in the student the idea that these materials are the building blocks

of historical research. Utilizing primary sources as the theme of the exhibit, with secondary sources providing context, we were able to create a concise and accurate exhibit on an often-overlooked event during the Reconstruction period. It is also important that students understand that by using proper sources and providing the best possible information they will always overcome the persistent problem of limited space and resources that archivists often find in their institutions.

NOTES

1. The Ulysses S. Grant Association moved to Mississippi State University in January 2009. The Grant Association has collected copies of every known Grant document and it continues that effort, making possible evaluations of his life and career based on documentary evidence. The Mississippi State University Libraries assist in the publication of *The Papers of Ulysses S. Grant* and maintain the records of the Grant Association and the publication project. These records are available to qualified researchers.

2. *Chicago Tribune,* 8 September 1866.

3. "Johnson's Swing Around the Circle, August-September 1866," ed. Paul H. Bergeron, *The Papers of Andrew Johnson* (Knoxville, TN: The University of Tennessee Press, 1994), V. 11, 656.

4. Letter from General Grant to Brevet Brigadier General William S. Hillyer, 19 September 1866, ed. John Y. Simon *The Papers of Ulysses S. Grant* (Carbondale, IL: Southern Illinois University Press, 1988), V. 16, 310.

5. *New York Times,* 29 November 1866.

6. Photo courtesy of the Ulysses S. Grant Presidential Collection, Mississippi State University.

7. Letter from Ulysses S. Grant to Julia Dent Grant on 31 August 1866. Ulysses S. Grant Presidential Collection, Mississippi State University.

8. *Chicago Tribune,* 6 September 1866.

9. *New York Times,* 9 September 1866.

10. *Harper's Weekly,* 27 October 1866.

The American History Textbook Project: The Making of a Student-Centered Special Collection at a Public Liberal Arts College

Christina Connor and Stephen P. Rice

Ramapo College of New Jersey is a public four-year college in northern New Jersey with an enrollment of approximately 5,000 undergraduate students. From its founding in 1969 the college has maintained the identity of a liberal arts college, having been formally designated as "New Jersey's Public Liberal Arts College." Among the undergraduate majors associated with the liberal arts, history is one of the largest, with an average enrollment of around 230 students over the last four years. In the fall of 2007 a new 200-level course in historiography was added as a requirement of the history major. The purpose of the course is twofold. First, it seeks to ensure that students—ideally at the sophomore level—are familiar with the principles of historical research, including knowledge of essential primary and secondary source databases, and of the conventional citation and bibliographic style. Second, it introduces students to the field of historiography, which considers how historical writing has a history of its own. Here, students can see that the treatment of certain subjects by historians—the American Civil War, for instance—has in fact changed over time, helping them to understand that the historical accounts we read (and produce) are themselves bound up in their own historical moments. The hope is that once students learn to appreciate the subjectivity of historical writing, they will become more critical readers of both primary and secondary sources, and pay closer attention to the potential biases of their own work.

When Stephen Rice (who is a professor of American Studies, and who routinely teaches history courses) taught the historiography course for the second time in the spring of 2009, students wanted to use old U.S. history textbooks as primary sources for their final paper assignment. This assignment required them to trace how historians' treatment of one of several selected subjects in American history—including labor, women, the West, and the American Revolution—have changed since the mid-nineteenth century. The assignment followed an in-class case study that focused on how historians have treated the subject of American slavery since the period before the Civil War. For primary sources students found some useful out-of-copyright books on Google Books (including various editions of George Bancroft's classic studies of American history), but they mostly relied on scholarly articles available on JSTOR, which provides full text access to selected academic journals dating back to the nineteenth century and earlier. While utilizing JSTOR as a primary source database was eye-opening to students, there was relatively little to work with for some topics, even with Google Books as an additional option for sources. At the same time, students who were seeking teacher certification were very interested is seeing how these subjects were or were not taken up in American history textbooks. They found, though, that such books were difficult to locate, either as print copies in libraries or as digital copies on-line. At the end of the semester a group of students who would be returning in the fall met and agreed to work with Professor Rice to see about collecting old textbooks for use by future historiography students and anyone else interested in using textbooks as primary sources.

What quickly became evident was that such a collection would help illuminate the social context of education more generally, as textbook content has long been debated among politicians and educators. At the center of this debate most recently was the 2010 Texas textbook controversy over the inclusion and exclusion of material within textbooks as decided by the Texas School Board of Education. While once confined to the correction of factual errors, in the past decade Board members began arguing that they should "consider as factual error omissions—in which partial information on a topic could lead to inaccurate interpretation—or facts that are presented with an inherent bias."[1] Texas is the second-largest textbook buyer in the country and has historically influenced publishers on content that then gets distributed nationally.[2] However, as publishing technology has evolved, publishers may more easily alter content to suit different markets, curriculum shifts, or school boards' biases.[3] Digital textbooks or textbooks containing digital components are becoming the desired direction for more school districts since they can more easily "reflect changing education policy,"[4] as well as regional input through tailored content. Furthermore, they may allow for more rapid updates and other features such as linking to supplementary information and online note-taking.

While textbooks remain in print, students and historians are able to trace historiographical change over time. They are able to see and compare the content in these works and draw connections and better understand the context that might have shaped a particular interpretation of historical events. With digital textbooks, this comparison may become increasingly difficult. While the advantage of a digital copy is the ability to easily change or update con-

tent, this is also a disadvantage. Once a digital copy is updated and the newer copy replaces the original, the student is likely to have difficulty accessing other versions.

The future of textbooks is an interesting discussion for current history students. From a historiographical perspective, digital textbooks and the controversy surrounding revisions provide students with the opportunity to deeply understand how current events can shape textual content in secondary sources. While the textbook collection can serve to document these political controversies, it can also address another issue. Given the increasing likelihood of the disappearance of the traditional print textbook, the collection will serve to preserve these works for future study.

ESTABLISHING THE COLLECTION

In the fall of 2009, then, the American History Textbook Project (AHTP) was formally inaugurated. At the beginning of the semester, around eight students and two project advisors, Stephen Rice and Alexander Urbiel (the head of the college's Teacher Education program and a member of the history faculty specializing in the history of education), met to develop a project plan. One student reported that over the summer she had found at her old high school more than 20 textbooks that were no longer being used (some were decades old) and that might be appropriate for the collection. In reviewing those titles, it became clear that the group needed to establish criteria by which books would be added to the collection. After some discussion the group decided to limit the collection to textbooks published through to the end of the Cold War, a stopping point that would allow for some distance between the books in the collection and our own time. It was decided to focus on books that provided a general survey of U.S. history and that were designed for use in the high school classroom. Books that were clearly intended for elementary school students, or that focused more on civics, or on a particular period or region (a history of the Civil War, for instance, or a state history), would generally fall outside the collecting criteria. The group also discussed possible sources for books, such as used bookstores, on-line book dealers, public library book sales, and schools, should they be willing to donate books that were no longer being used.

With this first meeting it also became clear that one or two students needed to be put in charge of coordinating the group's activities and ensuring that progress was being made. Dr. Rice applied for and received a small grant from the School of American and International Studies (the academic unit where the history major is housed) that made it possible to hire a student to work as an AHTP intern for the remainder of the semester. This student readily located two bibliographies of United States history textbooks that would help identify the potential corpus of textbooks to be collected. These bibliographies were distributed to the project group members who were asked to begin looking for books on eBay and other on-line venues, and to keep an eye out for books when at used bookstores or garage sales. The intern also began compiling biographical and bibliographic information on the authors of textbooks that had been located up to that point, and she created a system for inventorying books as they were collected. In the meantime, Drs. Rice and Urbiel received a second grant from the Ramapo College Foundation to hire another student to work as an intern during the spring semester. Given that searches of used bookstores and other "on the ground" efforts had yielded only two books, the project group decided that the best strategy for developing the collection was through purchase from online book dealers. Therefore, the new intern went through the more substantial of the two textbook bibliographies and checked the books listed against Abebooks, an on-line consortium of used book dealers. A second student did the same with another on-line book distributor, Alibris. Both found that a significant number of books were indeed available for purchase, many for $10.00 or less. A donation of $100, and a subsequent additional grant of $300, made it possible to begin making purchases, which the group did collectively over the course of several meetings. At those meetings the group searched for specific titles on Abebooks and discussed the merits of purchasing one book over another, taking into consideration various factors including the year of publication, the edition of the book, the price, and the book's condition. By the end of the semester, approximately 30 books had been purchased. These include Charles A. Goodrich, *A History of the United States of America, from the Discovery of the Continent by Christopher Columbus to the Present Time* (1833); John Andrew Doyle and Francis Amasa Walker, *History of the United States* (1876); Susan P. Lee, *New Primary History of the United States* (1899); Wilbur Fisk Gordy, *A History of the United States for Schools* (1916); Sisters of the Third Order of St. Francis of the Perpetual Adoration, *The Cathedral History of the United States* (1923); and William A. Hamm, *From Colony to World Power: A History of the United States* (1953).

LIBRARY INVOLVEMENT

As students acquired the initial assortment of textbooks, Dr. Rice used his office as a storage space. Soon, though, as the collection and its potential use outside a single class grew, it became clear a more appropriate space was needed. Dr. Rice approached Library Dean Elizabeth Siecke about permanently housing the textbook collection in the George T. Potter Library at Ramapo College, specifically in the College Archives, as a special collection. The archives collection within the Potter Library was originally established with the primary mission to serve as the institutional memory of Ramapo College. Its purpose was to house, preserve, and make available materials authorized by or related to the college that have historical, research, legal, and administrative uses. Over the years, the archives have expanded to include signed copies of books from speakers on campus, as well as books deemed too fragile for the

Figure 7.1. Images of text books

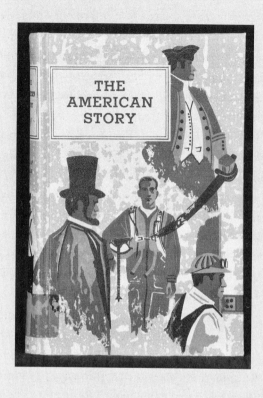

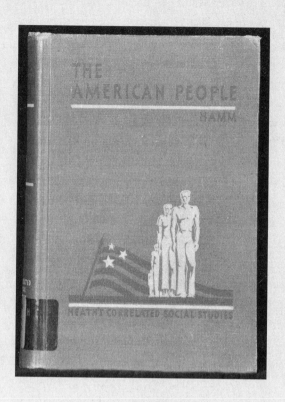

circulating collection. After some discussion, Dean Siecke agreed to house the collection in the library, and the Instruction and the Emerging Technologies Librarian Christina Connor was appointed the library liaison and coordinator for this project.

The main concerns regarding the textbook collection for both Dr. Rice and library faculty were security and access as well as preservation and collection management. Library faculty agreed that the archives provided an available, protected environment for this collection because the area could be locked when not in use. The College Archives has never been an "open collection," nor was it a monitored one, but it was important for students using the textbooks to have easy access to materials. In the past, librarians or circulation staff would pull items in the archives if someone wanted to use ma-

terials. AHTP required librarians to rethink access since students needed to be able to pull and work with multiple volumes at a time, if not the whole collection. Therefore, Ms. Connor arranged with circulation and the College Archivist that students using the collection were permitted to check-out an archives key for a period of time, let themselves in the space, "self-serve" while reviewing books, and return the key when finished. Since the archives key is barcoded, Ms. Connor can see who is using the collection and when. While this offers some help with security since it provides a record of students accessing the space, it also assists Dr. Rice in making a stronger argument for monetary support on campus because demonstrates the popularity of the collection. In addition, students are encouraged to sign-in at the work desk near the textbooks and document why they are using the collection (see Appendix 7.1). Again, this helps illustrate that use of the textbooks is not limited to Dr. Rice's historiography class. Space was allocated within the archives next to the textbooks for students to comfortably sit at a work station and use the collection. Finding aides and signage were also created to assist students in finding what they need. At the same time, rules were established for using AHTP and were posted at the work station. Unlike some materials in the archives, which can be loaned at the discretion of the College Archivist, textbooks in the collection are restricted to the archives room (unless a student needs to make a photocopy). Textbooks are treated as "artifacts," and students are asked not to draw in the books nor remove any objects (such as notes, bookmarks, etc.) from them.

While there are many unique aspects of this collection, from a library standpoint it has been crucial to have the input and assistance of Dr. Rice and his student interns. In addition to their responsibility for selecting and acquiring texts, Dr. Rice's interns were shown how to use WorldCat.org (a global catalog of library collections) to find bibliographic records for the textbooks. They also learned how to set up a system for the library to receive and process books for the collection. The Potter Library is relatively small, with 1 full-time cataloger to process books. With AHTP interns providing important information, librarians are able to accelerate the process of making books available (see Appendix 7.2). The instruction slip created by Ms. Connor explains to the library's cataloger if special processing is needed (such as protective archival boxing or minor repairs) as well as if there is limited OCLC information and therefore a unique record needs to be created.

In addition to the books collected by Dr. Rice and his students, books within the library's circulating collection that met the project's collection criteria were relocated to the archives to be included in the American History Textbook Project. In the fall of 2009, the project's first intern went through the library's catalog and compiled a list of materials in the general circulating collection that met the project's criteria. In the spring of 2010, librarians reviewed the books listed and agreed that they should be part of the new special collection. While the items were important for historiographical purposes, they no longer properly supported general research projects.

CURRICULAR USES

Although the AHTP collection is still very new, students and others have already begun to appreciate its value. Students involved in the project who have read through books acquired for the collection have met on a number of occasions to discuss aspects of the works that seemed especially interesting. In some cases the bias of an account was particularly evident. John Bach McMaster's *A School History of the United States* (1897), for instance, observes of "the Indian" that "he was never so happy as when, at the dead of night, he roused his sleeping victims with an unearthly yell and massacred them by the light of their burning home."[5] Twice since the beginning of the project students have hosted an evening "showcase" event where people came together to peruse and discuss textbooks arrayed on different tables. These have been very successful at spurring interest in the collection. In addition, Drs. Rice and Urbiel conducted a fall 2010 workshop on the collection at the College's Faculty Resource Center, to introduce faculty from across the College to possible projects that could be conducted with the collection. The collection has also already given rise to a focused student research project. In the summer of 2010 an independent study under Dr. Rice had a student examining marginal notes and other pen and pencil markings that were found in a number of the books. In the student's work she distinguished among several kinds of markings—notes, doodles, and defacement—and suggested what they reveal about how these books were used. Finally, Dr. Rice developed and implemented new assignments based on the collection in both his fall 2010 Introduction to U.S. History I course and his spring 2011 Historiography course. At the same time, the entire history faculty at the College has been kept apprised of the collection's development and may consider using it in their relevant courses.

While it is evident how this collection will be useful within historiography and other history classes, Ms. Connor has found it useful as an aid for Information Literacy sessions. Often students understand how to create a traditional research paper, but the concept of a historiographical essay is generally something new. Since Ramapo College was founded in 1969, it is a fairly young school with a young library collection. In addition, many libraries now face the problem of limited space and the need to weed what some consider "out-dated" materials. Therefore, it becomes difficult to show students examples of the changes over time in how a particular topic has been treated by historians when a complete representation of a topic is not available, particularly for the period before the 1950s. Ms. Connor is able to use the collection to provide numerous examples on a broad range of historiographical coverage in lessons while keeping the discussion manageable for an hour-long workshop.

With Dr. Urbiel's active involvement, interest in this unique collection has expanded to include Education faculty members. This is particularly true of faculty teaching Social Context of Education, a required course for all students in the Teacher Education program. Some faculty have begun assigning research projects centered around the textbooks, and Ms. Connor now has frequent requests to set up library sessions devoted solely on the collection.

LOOKING TOWARD THE FUTURE

In order to ensure that the collection continues to expand both in its content and in its use, several initiatives are currently being planned. First, participants in the project will be working with Drs. Rice and Urbiel to develop a system for soliciting and receiving book donations from schools, as this seems like a potentially rich source for locating books for the collection. In addition, the group will plan to systematically collect each edition of a particular book, so that students can trace precisely what content was added, amended or deleted from one edition to the next. In addition, Drs. Rice and Urbiel will seek additional outside funding to expand the collection and its use, including possible funding to use the collection for a professional development program for area high school teachers. Finally, Ms. Connor, with the help of Dr. Rice, is beginning to construct a webpage for the collection to be included on the Potter Library's website. As the collection continues to expand and gain interest, the library looks forward to meeting the needs of those who use it.

APPENDIX 7.1. American History Textbook Project

American History Textbook Project			
Please Sign-In			
Date	Name	Major	Reason for Using Collection (e.g. assignment? special project?)

APPENDIX 7.2. AHTP Book Instructions

AHTP Book Instructions		
	Standard Processing	
	Special Processing	
		WorldCat Information Limited
		WorldCat Information Not Found
		Fragile—Needs Box
Additional Notes:		

NOTES

1. Kathleen K. Manzo. "History repeats itself in Texas for textbook-review process." Education Week 21, no. 43 (2002): 11.

2. Ibid.

3. "Textbook Wars." *Chattanooga Times Free Press*, 26 May 2010, sec. Free P, p. B7. Kate Alexander. "Plan for social studies gets OK." *Austin American Statesman*, 13 March 2010, sec. A, p. 1.

4. Alyssa Sunkin. "Schools react to textbook trends: More districts look for online components." *Times Herald-Record*, 21 June 2010.

5. John Bach McMaster, *A School History of the United States* (New York: American Book Company, 1897), p. 69-70.

The Early Novels Database and Undergraduate Research: A Case Study

Rachel Sagner Buurma, Anna Tione Levine, and Richard Li

Traditionally, the classroom has been associated with the canon as opposed to the library, with the idea that a special subset of texts selected as both especially excellent and representative (of the literary tradition, say, or a specific cultural moment) are all one can or should teach given the time constraints of traditional college classes and the goals of the liberal arts education. Making the library—even the special collections library—into a classroom in the way our bibliographic database project does therefore raises obvious challenges, ranging from the procedural problem of training undergraduates to do competent descriptive bibliography and library cataloging to the ethical and pedagogical issues surrounding the involvement of undergraduate students in work that many might consider the province of the graduate education. Our case study—co-authored by the database's faculty director Rachel Sagner Buurma and its undergraduate researcher-catalogers Anna Tione Levine and Richard Li[1]—describes a database project to which undergraduate researchers have made a significant and ongoing contribution, and suggests that even projects involving such relatively technical and specialized work have a role to play as part of a liberal arts education.

THE EARLY NOVELS DATABASE: A DESCRIPTION[2]

The Early Novels Database (END) is a bibliographic database based on the University of Pennsylvania's Rare Book & Manuscript Library's extensive collection of fiction in English published between 1660 and 1830. Produced by the collaborative effort of Penn li-

brarians, information technology specialists, faculty from Swarthmore College and Penn, and Swarthmore College undergraduate researchers, the completed database will include richly descriptive records of more than 3,000 novels and fictional narratives, from the very canonical to the almost unknown, from fictions that clearly announce themselves to be novels to the works of fiction (fable, travel narrative, romance) that formed part of that genre's notoriously murky origins. Users will be able to perform both keyword and faceted searches across bibliographic records containing both edition-specific and copy-specific information about each novel.

We have designed END to complement the extensive existing full-text facsimile archives that contain early novels (such as ECCO, GoogleBook, and the Internet Archive). One of the most significant problems with recent large-scale book digitization projects has been the loss of edition-specific and copy-specific structured metadata—of information *about* and describing the book—of the kind often available in library card catalogs. The absence of this data can make it difficult for scholars and other researchers to find particular novels or sets of novels they are interested in, because even as our archive of digital texts from the seventeenth, eighteenth, and nineteenth centuries has expanded exponentially, our ability to access them in precise, controlled, and complex ways has diminished. While recent projects have begun to take on this challenge—Brian Geiger's (University of California, Riverside) and Ben Pauley's (Eastern Connecticut State University) Google-sponsored effort to automatically match ESTC (English Short Title Catalog) records to GoogleBook items is a notable recent example—our project seeks to use human eyes and brains and hands to create and control bibliographic descriptions in ways that computers cannot. For example, we tag each noun, adjective, person name, place name, and object mentioned in the title of each novel; the resulting information can be keyword searched but also appears as a set of "facets" that display how often a given word in each category appears. Therefore, researchers can not only perform traditional keyword searches of the title field to turn up relevant items, but can also see the entire array of nouns appearing on all title pages sorted alphabetically or by frequency. We also include in-depth information on other aspects of the novel's paratexts, describing the prefaces, introductions, dedications, indexes, tables of contents, copyright statements in both controlled and more discursive vocabularies.

A scholar interested in the genre of "history," to take a hypothetical example, can not only instantly call up all 189 records of novels with this noun in the title; she also, at the click of a button, can see that of the records of novels with "history" in the title, 27 of them also include the adjective "young"; that 56 of them have prefaces; that the majority of them are written in the third rather than the first person; and that four of them profess to be written by women but were in fact penned by men. She can sort and unsort them by year and decade of publication, and notice that most of them are published in London, but that after 1787 many of them also are published in Dublin; she can pull up records of all novels that contain prefaces, and click on each record to see the individual idiosyncratic titles of each one. She can find out instantly that 134 of them have epigraphs on the title pages, and by looking at the authors of those epigraphs she can determine at a glance how many are by "ancient" and how many by "modern" authors. And she can do all of this work in seconds, rather than in the weeks or even months it would take for her to generate this information herself. So while as a bibliographic tool END does not itself make a claim about literary history, or even represent to its users the "insides," or texts, of the novels it includes, it makes possible the writing of new, alternative histories of the novel.[3]

THE WORK OF THE UNDERGRADUATE RESEARCHER

The great challenge—and promise—of this kind of project is that it unites the bibliographic description

Figure 8.1. Screenshot of the database front page

of books produced in an extraordinarily idiosyncratic genre and publishing moment with the necessity to "control" the descriptive terms we use in order to make searches across large numbers of records possible and meaningful. To this end student researcher/catalogers Anna Levine and Richard Li have been involved in the process of creating a bibliographic template of information we want to capture, developing a cataloging protocol for the project, writing the glossary, guides to searching, and other website text, in addition to actually cataloging the books. We have had to ensure that Anna and Richard learn "professional-quality" descriptive bibliography, think about bibliographic description and control in sophisticated ways, and manage their time effectively all while engaged in work that can sometimes be mindnumbingly, eyeglazingly boring. At the same time, we've had to try to make sure that their work on the project is valuable as a part of a liberal arts education. As we theorize it, this value has to do with the very practical and immediate way the project foregrounds the necessity to aspire to some kind shared and transparent standard of description while simultaneously acknowledging (and even being suspicious of) the difficulty or impossibility of this as a perfected project.

To work on the Early Novels Database, to spend a summer (or two summers) of days creating detailed bibliographic descriptions of novels as Anna and Richard have, is to be involved in an ongoing demonstration of the impossibility of reducing even the paratext of the novel to a standard formula, and a continual rediscovery of the singularity (and resistance to full description) of the material text. Working on the database also required that Anna and Richard not only to do research themselves (for example, to determine epigraph's author, to verify book format, to authorize a name), but also that they learn to imagine what kinds of searches in which researchers using the database might be interested. The process of creating the bibliographic template offers one example. Anna and Richard not

only helped decide what information to enter in the database, but even worked to make decisions about standardized terminology, format, and design. The necessary work of familiarizing themselves with existing conventions and how they exist in the novels we are working with has been both a challenge and a learning opportunity. In some cases, this is a mere matter of learning new terminology in order to be able to identify and name half-titles, for example, or subscriber lists. In other cases, terminology is complex, ambiguous, or nonexistent; in these case the project team worked together to create terms that are intuitive and transparent to researchers as well as faithful to the books surveyed. A classic example of a conflict between an "intuitive" classification and a "faithful" one arises in the case of recording the titles of the paratextual essays appearing in each novel. Since the terms that early novels' paratexts use to name themselves (for example "advertisement," "dedication," and "postscript") are often idiosyncratic (even by eighteenth-century standards) and inconsistent, we want to capture that variation and diversity. Yet we also need researchers to be able to quickly sort books by the types of paratexts they contain. We solved the problem by creating three related fields: a field containing a controlled set yet expandable set of terms early novels use to describe their paratextual essays, a notes field offering less expert database users a "translation" when necessary, and a field that gives the title of each essay verbatim. But the creation of controlled terms is—problematically—never-ending; since each book cataloged potentially enlarges the range of types of paratextual essays we know about, Anna and Richard must be able to make on-the-spot decisions about adding new terms. And, of course, they have to know when and how to ask expert advice—from a librarian, a professor, a reference work—when necessary.

END's design, as we quickly discovered, offers wide latitude for the undergraduate researcher to explore her own interests without introducing unwanted clutter, since it is possible for us to tag characteristics of books in the bibliographic records which our program and web editor can then exclude from the website display. Anna Levine took full advantage of this built-in opportunity to experiment without consequences. After becoming interested in the historical relationship between epistolary fiction and third-person narration in her first-year seminar at Swarthmore, she decided to create a field that tracks the narrative form of each novel (as determined—admittedly imperfectly—by a few minutes of scanning). Under the guidance of Rachel, Anna organized the experimental narrative form field into two main subfields: the first, $a, denotes the primary narrative form of the text (if one exists), while the second subfield, $b, contains narrative forms within the volume that are not expressed in $a. This categorical system has proven itself useful in many cases: if a novel is written completely in letters, for example, but between the fictional exchange of letters there exists third-person narration (as in Richardson's *Pamela* to take the most canonical example), we would note in $a that the primary narrative form is "epistolary"; we would then record the existence of third-person narration in $b. In this situation, the subfield system is quite useful: $b allows and highlights narratorial exceptions, while $a honors the preeminence of the primary narrative form.

Because of the room for experimentation that the END inherently allows, we found that it was easy to incorporate Anna's experimental field into the project without compromising any other aspects of the END. We have also found, after working closely together to develop a comprehensive set of terms to define the narrative intricacies of early novels, that the narrative forms field seems relevant enough to the project to make it into a facet on the website. In these ways and in many others, END's undergraduate researchers continue to make significant contributions to the shape of the project while learning ways of thinking and skills that hopefully have relevance to life beyond END.

NOTES

1. Anna and Richard's work on END has been made possible by the generous support of Swarthmore College's summer humanities research grant program and by a Hungerford grant from the office of the Provost at Swarthmore

2. END would not have been possible without the unwavering support and concerted efforts of the following individuals: Lynne Farrington Curator of Printed Books, Rare Book and Manuscript Library, University of Pennsylvania; Michael Gamer Associate Professor of English, University of Pennsylvania; Heather Glaser, Curator and Assistant Fine Arts Librarian, Fisher Fine Arts Library, University of Pennsylvania; David McKnight Director, Rare Book and Manuscript Library, University of Pennsylvania; Dennis Mullen, Web Developer and Designer, Van Pelt Library, University of Pennsylvania; Jon Shaw Head, Research, Training and Quality Management, Van Pelt Library, University of Pennsylvania; Laurie Sutherland, Metadata Specialist, Van Pelt Library, University of Pennsylvania; Leslie Vallhonrat, Web Managing Editor, Van Pelt Library, University of Pennsylvania. View the database at: http://hdl.library.upenn.edu/1017/88396

3. While END is in many ways a database of information designed to give researchers a "middle distance" view of the novel (as opposed to enabling the kind of "distant reading" of visualized large-scale sets of information about the novel which Franco Moretti and others are interested it), some of the types of macroscopic information included may eventually lend itself naturally to graphical representation. (See Franco Moretti, *Graphs, Maps, Trees: Abstract Models for a Literary History* (London; New York, Verso), 2005.) 2005. Eventually, for example, END may be able to map the frequency of epigraphs against a timeline, or even more specifically, the frequency of quotations from Shakespeare used as epigraphs against a timeline.

TULANE UNIVERSITY

Amistad Research Center Case Study

Christopher Harter

Following Hurricanes Katrina and Rita in 2005 and the loss of seventy percent of its staff, the Amistad Research Center, an independent non-profit special collections library/archives housed on the campus of Tulane University in New Orleans, Louisiana, underwent a reorganization of staffing and institutional priorities with emphasis placed on increased use of technology, improved donor relations, and expanded access to its collections. Since 2009, the Center has embraced the trend within libraries and archives of exposing its "hidden collections" by taking advantage of its role as a community partner in Tulane's service-learning component of its undergraduate curriculum. This case-study examines the development of this partnership and the successes and lessons learned from two class-based projects involving the supervision of multiple students assisting in the processing of archival collections.

The Amistad Research Center is the nation's oldest and largest independent archives/special collections library that chronicles race relations and ethnic history within the United States and the African Diaspora. Founded in 1966 as an outgrowth of Fisk University's Race Relations Department, an early civil rights training ground, the Center incorporated as a 501(c) 3 non-profit organization in 1969, and today resides on the campus on Tulane University in New Orleans, Louisiana. Originally founded as a repository for the archives of the American Missionary Association, a Christian abolitionist organization that later worked to found schools for the Freedmen following the Civil War, the Center expanded its collections into the areas of race rela-

tions, the Civil Rights Movement, the Harlem Renaissance, and the other aspects of the history and culture of African Americans and other minority groups.

This expansion was based in part on an aggressive acquisitions policy that focused on the collecting of materials documenting underrepresented peoples at a time when such collecting was not widely emphasized by cultural institutions. However, budgeting and staffing for this non-profit organization did not always allow for the arrangement and description of these collections according to professional archival standards. During its existence, the Center has become a well-established research center on the topic of minority history. However, a significant portion of its collections have been underutilized by scholars and the general public due to lack of processing, which has limited access to the Center's holdings.

Coinciding with Amistad's embrace of a hidden collections agenda, was its development of a more formal student internship and mentoring program—one that sought, in part, to introduce students from underrepresented populations to library and archival work. Since the development of this program, students from area historically Black institutions, Dillard University, Southern University-New Orleans, and Xavier University, as well as students from non-HBCUs, Tulane University and Loyola University and a local high school, have completed internships and volunteerships at the Center. This student assistant recruitment program has allowed the Center to pursue its focus of expanding access to unprocessed archival collections—and the accompanying workload involved with such—while maintaining a reduced staffing level due to budget constraints.

Following the storms of 2005, Tulane University instituted a service-learning component to its curriculum. As part of this component, students and faculty partner with a community organization, often one that is topically-related to the course, in order to provide community assistance to that organization. During the course of each class, students are required to provide 20 individual hours to the community partner. The Amistad Research Center has leveraged its unique status as an independent non-profit housed on campus to partner with Tulane's Center for Public Service to provide internships and class-based projects to undergraduate students interested in gaining experience in archival/library settings. Specifically, the Center's staff has partnered with faculty from Tulane's Department of History to offer intensive course-focused projects that provide students with an introduction to archival studies, instruction in the preservation of primary sources, and a better understanding of the need to preserve and make accessible the historical record of underrepresented peoples. These projects have been led by the Library and Reference Services department, which typically oversees outreach at the Center. In each case, students have received instruction and supervision from the head of that department with additional staff assisting from time to time.

THE CLASSES AND THEIR PROJECTS

During the Spring 2009 semester, Amistad embarked on its first partnership with Dr. Elisabeth McMahon, who taught a course on primary source research in contemporary African history. With input from Amistad staff, the syllabus for this class outlined a project involving student volunteer hours at the Center, intended to lead to the development of research

papers for the class based on their work at Amistad. In order to stress the important role that archives play in preserving the historical record, the class was first invited to the Center for a tour and introduction to all aspects of the Center's operations. This broad introduction was cited by students as aiding them to understand the importance of their assistance to the Center and its mission even while performing such mundane tasks as indexing correspondence and removing rusted staples from documents. At this time, the students were also provided with a detailed description of the project they would be working on and numerous examples of the issues they might face. Following lectures by Amistad staff on the nature of archives, arrangement and description, and how archives provide access to materials, students assisted staff in the indexing of correspondence from the American Committee on Africa (ACOA) Records and the inventorying of the vast amount of printed ephemera from that collection using a series of spreadsheets.

ACOA was a New York-based organization founded in 1953 with the goal of supporting anti-colonial and anti-apartheid movements in Africa. The records at Amistad measure approximately 146 linear feet and include administrative records, program records, and printed works collected by the organization from various institutions and groups involved with and interested in African affairs. Although the ACOA records had been previously arranged in 1983, the resulting finding aid was not sufficient to provide access to the myriad of letters, speeches, brochures, periodicals and other publications that comprise the bulk of the collection. Lack of deeper access to the collection had long been an issue for the Center and researchers.

The ACOA records provided an ideal trial project for a course-based undergraduate learning experience: 1) Amistad staff had identified the need to index and inventory portions of the collection as a project that could not be undertaken without assistance due to staff levels and 2) students would work on a large, but singular, collection, which would provide an opportunity to discuss similar issues and methods during their work. The class of 12 students concentrated on the files that documented ACOA's activities in various African countries and each student was allowed to select their country of interest. Throughout the course of this project, the students worked closely with Amistad staff to answer questions such as how to cite particular pamphlets or reports, or how to solve riddles such as illegible names and undated letters. However, the time the staff spent with students at the beginning of the project, as well as documentation about the typical issues confronted when processing an archival collection were valuable to both groups. The understanding derived gave the students greater confidence in completing assigned tasks and relieved the staff of the need for continuous supervision of the students.

One issue arose, which had not been anticipated by Amistad staff. As different students worked at different speeds and staff members were not always available to communicate with them directly at the end of each work session, keeping track of each student's progress became somewhat problematic, especially when a student would finish with material in one box and need to request another before their next work session. Also, although staff and students had constructed a calendar for their work sessions, this calendar quickly fell by the wayside as student schedules changed and other priorities took precedence. The project needed a simple way for each student to track their work and requirements and leave questions and comments for staff. This issue would be successfully addressed with the second service-learning class hosted by Amistad during the Spring 2010 semester.

By the end of the semester, the students had completed the indexing and inventorying of approximately 60 linear feet of records, leaving about 15 linear feet to be completed by Amistad staff. The work of the students needed little editing. The remaining unprocessed collection was small enough that staff

members were able to easily integrate the additional work into their daily schedules. Ultimately, the information obtained from this project will be used to expand the finding aid, which will be entered into the Center's online finding aid database.

Based on the success of this initial partnership, the Center hosted a second class on Modern African American History taught by Dr. Rosanne Adderley during Spring 2010. Rather than work on one collection, the five students in this course were each assigned a small collection (under .8 linear feet) of personal papers in need of preservation treatment and arrangement. Examples included the papers of musicians Elliot Von Joseph Beal and Fletcher Henderson and civil rights activists Charles Hatfield, Charles Sherrod, and Lillie M. Carroll Jackson. Amistad staff compiled a preliminary list of collections, and students were again allowed to select collections that most interested them. In addition to arranging and describing the collections, students also conducted research in order to write drafts of the biographical and scope notes for each collection. In total, the students processed seven collections and drafted collection and biographical notes, which the staff entered into the online finding aid database.

As with the first class, these students received an initial introduction to the Center and its mission, as well as a detailed project description. Based on communication issues between staff and students in the previous class, Amistad developed the use of "work" journals for each student in the second class. These journals (simple composition books purchased at the university bookstore) allowed students the space to make notes on their work, keep track of work completed, and leave questions for staff at the end of each work session. Students cited the journals as beneficial to organizing and charting their work at the Center. Some students used the journals simply as a way to inform staff of what they had accomplished during a given day, while others used the journals to keep detailed notes on the collections and the individuals documented within. The use of the journals also provided staff with an opportunity to examine how different students approached the processing of archival collections.

SUCCESSES AND LESSONS LEARNED

As a non-profit institution with a small staff, the Amistad Research Center often prioritizes the processing of archival collections based on projects that are grant-funded, an approach which leaves a number of significant collections lower on its processing priority list. The increased use of undergraduate student assistance, as well as partnerships with the service learning classes has allowed the Center to arrange and describe collections that would not have been completed in the near term given current staffing and work on grant-prioritized collections. Work completed thus far on the ACOA records has greatly increased access and reduced staff time needed to answer reference queries regarding those materials. Greater access to other newly-processed collections on the topics of the Civil Rights Movement and school desegregation have led to increased donor philanthropy (primarily from the donors of those collections themselves) and more opportunities to provide public programming utilizing those collections. In addition, student assistance has allowed Center staff the opportunity to complete online finding aids for all the collections processed.

Apart from the benefits of providing students with an introduction to archival principles and receiving assistance in processing these hidden collections, Amistad staff have used these two trial partnerships to refine methods of instruction, communication, and supervision for course-based projects. Having gone beyond simply providing a venue for class-based projects, the Center has been able to integrate its collections and mission into courses and provide students with the experience of not only conducting research using primary sources, but assisting in the preparation of those sources for use by other researchers.

Although both classes were based on the same concept of exposing archival methods to undergraduate students, each class offered a unique lesson in the effective management and supervision of such course-based projects. Amistad's partnership with the first class demonstrated that supervision of student groups does indeed take a greater amount of coordination and supervision on the part of staff than does supervision of individual student workers or interns. Use of work journals for the initial (and larger) class would have assisted in maintaining an efficient level of communication between staff and the class and among the students themselves. The development of the work journals for students in the second class allowed for an "open-door" method of communication even when students and staff could not touch base at the end of each work session. Such journals will be an integral part of similar course partnerships in the future.

Throughout the semester of the first course, Amistad staff did receive feedback from students via reflection journals submitted to their professor, which were forwarded to the Amistad supervisor. Examples of student feedback on their work included:

"Working with these documents is such a rewarding experience because I feel like there is so much to be learned, a whole side of history that I could not grasp in this way from just reading a book about this topic. It is also rewarding in the fact that I feel like I can really make a difference in helping to shape the way historians for years to come will find access to this material. "

"It is interesting to think about the fact that, if there were not people to organize and to create finding aids for these resources, in many cases it would be virtually impossible for historians to know what was out there or to gain access to it."

"All of the experience I have been gaining through the readings we have done and the through the work and research I have begun in the ARC has really brought new aspects to my understanding of archives and how they function."

The level of integration of the service learning aspect into the larger class structure was another essential difference between the two courses and affected the calendar of work at the Center. The requirement that students base their final course research paper on their work with the ACOA records required students to begin their work at Amistad early in the semester and ensured that the work was done in a timely manner. The lack of such a direct tie-in between their work at Amistad and a related research project during the second course resulted in a last minute rush at the end of the semester to finish the processing of assigned collections by some of the students. Procrastination by the students then forced Amistad staff to alter their own priorities to ensure adequate oversight of the students' work and obtain needed supplies, often further delaying the students' work. One particular student was forced to complete the majority of his 20-required hours in the last two days of the semester in order to fulfill his graduation requirement for the university. In the future Amistad staff will work closely with students and faculty to stress the time management skills required during the processing of archival collections.

Apart from increasing access to its collections, the Amistad Research Center has measured the success of these service-learning classes by the number of students who have returned to the Center to complete individual internships or work-study positions following their work with the course-based projects. A history and theater major from the first course returned to process the papers of African American soprano, Anne Wiggins Brown, and a music business major from the second course returned to a work-study position and assisted with the processing of the papers of New Orleans jazz musician, Harold Battiste. Based on its previous work with the History Department at Tulane University, the Center is also currently working to formalize an agreement with the department through which the Center will host an annual undergraduate course on research methods, which will include instruction by Center staff on archival theory and methods and allow the Center to host students on a regular basis as part of their service-learning requirements.

APPENDIX 9.1: Example of processing spreadsheet

Sender	Recipient	Date of Letter	Box	Folder	
ACOA	Cabral, Luis	1974, 8-30	88	32	Congrats of successful UN Vote
Pereira, Aristides	Houser, George M.	1974, 12-30	88	32	
Houser, George M.	Pereira, Aristides	1975, 1-14	88	32	Headquarters now in Bissau, hope to visit soon
Pereira, Aristides	Houser, George M.	1975, 1-24	88	32	
Houser, George M.	Pereira, Aristides	1975, 2-6	88	32	Met with Julio Semedo, checks for 25 grand didn't go through, voiding and reissueing
Houser, George M.	Pereira, Aristides	1975, 2-11 enc.	88	32	
Houser, George M.	Pereira, Aristides	1975, 3-6	88	32	
Houser, George M.	Vieira, Herculano	1975, 4-11 enc.	88	32	NY times article enclosed, written by Houser
Houser, George M.	Boal, Maria da Luz	1975, 3-27	88	32	10 grand to come, reports to raise additional funds, want ed. Plan, funds for new schools, new equipment, vehicle...?
Houser, George M.	Boal, Manuel	1975, 3-27	88	32	Videos,
Houser, George M.	Boal, Manuel	1975, 7-8	88	32	
Houser, George M.	Boal, Maria da Luz	1975, 7-22	88	32	trying to order as much equipment for boarding schools with the 10 grand, in cooperation with Church World Service
Lovink	Houser, George M.	1975, 7-30	88	32	Houser now executive secretary for the Africa Fund
Tourinho, Maria	Houser, George M.	1975, 7-29 enc.	88	32	Note enclosed about sizes and quantities of shows for the friendship institute
Houser, George M.	Boal, Manuel	1975, 9-10	88	32	10 grand from Africa Fund for Solidarity Hospital
Houser, George M.	Boal, Maria da Luz	1975, 9-16	88	32	list of purchased materials, tried to get shorts and shirts, too expensive, did order 100 footballs too
Boal, Maria da Luz	Houser, George M.	1975, 10-6	88	32	
Boal, Manuel	Houser, George M.	1975, 10-20	88	32	got the money, will be going to many things—schools, listed
Kleinschmidt, Horst	Houser, George M.	1976, 7-1	88	32	
Houser, George M.	Boal, Maria da Luz	1976, 1-20	88	32	Check from Africa Fund for 4200
Houser, George M.	Boal, Maria da Luz	1976, 2-6	88	32	Shipment inventory

Sender	Recipient	Date of Letter	Box	Folder	
Houser, George M.	Boal, Maria da Luz	1976, 4-20 enc.	88	32	
Davis, Jennifer	Borjes, Dulce	1976, 5-21	88	32	Material for English language courses, pamphlets
Duarte, Jose	Houser, George M.	1976, 5-22	88	32	
Executive Committee of PAIGC	Houser, George M.	1976, 8-24	88	32	
Boal, Manuel	Houser, George M.	1976, 9-7	88	32	
Houser, George M.	Executive Committee of PAIGC	1976, 9-10	88	32	
Boal, Maria da Luz	Houser, George M.	1976, 9-16	88	32	
Houser, George M.	Camara, Almani Alan M.	1976, 10-18	88	32	
Houser, George M.	Tavaris, Lucette	1976, 10-18	88	32	
Camara, Almani Alan M.	Mane, Maneebo	1976, 10-23	88	32	
Houser, George M.	de Andrade, Mario	1976, 11-3	88	32	
Houser, George M.	Araujo, Jose	1976, 11-3	88	32	
Houser, George M.	Tavaris, Lucette	1976, 11-10	88	32	
Houser, George M.	Camara, Almani Alan M.	1976, 11-22	88	32	
Davis, Jennifer	Houser, George M.	n.d.	88	32	
Houser, George M.	Instituto Amizade	n.d. enc.	88	32	

Learning As Doing: Undergrads Using Special Collections for Conservation and Material Culture Studies

Deborah C. Andrews, Vicki Cassman, and L. Rebecca Johnson Melvin[1]

The Special Collections Department in Morris Library at the University of Delaware (UD) has enhanced undergraduate learning on campus through conventional bibliographic presentations targeted for many disciplines, traditionally history and literature, as is the case for many academic libraries. In addition, the rare books, artists' books, and graphic art collections at UD have supported assignments in art and visual communication classes, where students design and produce their own works through the operation of a campus letterpress. Librarians have promoted collections for creative assignments: art students have consulted an extensive bookplate collection before designing their own bookplates, and cultural geography students researched manuscript recipe books to select an item to prepare for a class banquet. Student discovery of primary sources found in Special Collections is a fundamental component of information literacy for an increasing number of academic programs, important to librarians and faculty alike. Inclusion of the infinitely varied "other formats" of primary sources found in archival collections considerably enlivens this discovery process.

This chapter highlights an engaging approach to student learning that emphasizes the process of *working with* special collections rather than simply extracting informational content *from* them. While Delaware's graduate programs in art conservation, material culture studies, and museum studies are internationally known, the development of undergraduate courses in these fields, along with UD's

promotion of service learning,[2] has fostered new collaborations among faculty, librarians, and community members in Newark, whose history is intimately intertwined with the University's.[3] These collaborations teach undergraduate students about collection management for a variety of primary source materials, raise awareness of career options and shared values among cultural heritage institutions, and offer students a chance to fulfill UD's undergraduate service learning requirements.

STRENGTHS IN UD SPECIAL COLLECTIONS

Special Collections at UD have great strengths in American, English, and Irish literature; Delawareana and historical sources related to the Greater Delaware Valley and the Mid-Atlantic region; the history of technology and chemistry; the history of printing, papermaking, and the book arts; horticulture; and fine and decorative arts. The Library's holdings complement those in nearby private institutions with whom UD offers renowned graduate programs: the Hagley Museum and Library (history of technology and business history); Winterthur Museum and Country Estate (early American decorative arts and conservation); and Longwood Gardens (horticulture and landscape design). While graduate students have long taken advantage of these regional resources for dissertation research and internship opportunities, undergraduate use has typically been limited to honors students, faculty-directed studies, or one-time visits. In this chapter, we briefly review three case studies of longer-term projects for undergraduate students that have challenged them to discover context for objects within collections. At the same time the students are learning about provenance, ongoing significance of cultural memory within communities, and cross-disciplinary professional responsibilities of preservation, interpretation, and use of collections.

Introduced to Special Collections through class presentations, art conservation majors have eagerly sought positions as student assistants in the department in order to learn more about collections care and handling. As Coordinator of the Manuscripts Unit, Rebecca Johnson Melvin has worked with several of these students to identify special cleaning, housing, and study projects which students often add to their undergraduate portfolios. One student intrigued by the inherent problems of scrapbooks, for example, wrote a paper on such preservation challenges as binding structures, paper quality, adhesives and other attachments, and reactions of laid-in items. Another student surveyed the cleaning and mending needs of a collection of architectural drawings, and yet another student performed an extensive mending, cleaning, and housing project for multiple albums in an important genealogical collection that receives frequent use.

Special Collections benefits from the work of these committed students as they develop special skills; in addition, students spread the word to classmates and faculty about what they are learning and share information about their curriculum and available internships with librarians. Students have become a vital link in communication between faculty and librarians; their engagement enhances UD's learning environment for all concerned.

Vicki Cassman, director of Undergraduate Studies in Conservation, developed a more formal service learning program to provide the hands-on internship experiences vital for training art conservation students, who go on to varied material culture- and preservation-based careers within librar-

ies, museums, and galleries. The program was developed in conjunction with the local all-volunteer Newark Historical Society (the Society), where 30 years of casual collecting required some immediate policy, inventory, and rehousing work. Many of the Society's collections are considered of an archival nature and several of Cassman's conservation students have used Special Collections as a reference point to generate ideas for what the Society might achieve on an extremely limited budget. Since 2007, approximately 45 students have worked at the Society on short-term projects, full semester internships, or summer work projects. The continuum of student involvement began with a conservation assessment survey of the Society undertaken by the 30 students in the core sophomore course in 2007-2008. The students worked in teams each of which completed one aspect of the survey: housekeeping, pest control, temperature and relative humidity, security and access, rough estimates of types of collections and their numbers, and the like. This initial assessment made clear that intellectual control of the Society's collection was a management priority; collections housing came in at a close second.

Once the short- and long-term goals were identified, a desktop computer was donated and Past-Perfect Software was purchased for the Society. As collection documentation began, Cassman and her students turned to Special Collections for examples of proper storage and an established collection management program. In a behind-the-scenes tour of Special Collections, Johnson Melvin highlighted storage and housing options for the richly varied "other formats" of archival collections: works on paper or parchment, photographs, maps and oversize documents, artwork, scrapbooks, ephemera, audiovisual media, electronic records, and objects. Johnson Melvin, Cassman, and the interns discussed the pros and cons of various storage methods and materials, exploring the range from minimal housing to optimal conservation treatments. By identifying the vulnerable physical properties of the sources, weighing the inherent preservation risks with environmental threats, and discussing other factors such as use and value of the sources, the students learned about cost-effective options, phases of treatment and housing, and the principles of "do no harm" and "make it reversible."

One particularly challenging aspect for the students was what to do with the Society's oral history audiotapes from the 1980s. Time-based media present one of the greatest preservation challenges, given the relatively short longevity of CDs, and unknown duration of MP3 or WAV files. Students felt that since many of the interviewees were no longer alive, tape preservation was a high priority for the Society. For the Society's audiotapes, the class developed a preservation strategy based on MP3 files that would be stored on CDs, as well as on a hard drive that would be stored off-site. In addition, the students decided that all tapes needed to be transcribed and the resulting documents stored on acid-free archival paper. Students also recommended that MP3 files and transcript copies should remain with Special Collections in the Library as an off-site backup (with improved public access), but the Society was reluctant to allow copies of their unique holdings to be housed at another site. The students utilized equipment housed in the Library's Student Multimedia Design Center in order to reformat the audiotapes to MP3 and the process continues with new interns. Special Collections, along with Cassman, provided guidance and helped students develop a preservation policy beneficial to the Society, supporting UD's mission to contribute to the community.

COLLECTING AND CREATING NEW DOCUMENTATION FOR THE COMMUNITY

A second collaboration among Special Collections, Cassman, an art conservation honors student, and a community organization centered on a decomposing monument begun in 2005 and built in honor

Figure 10.1. The deteriorating condition of this outdoor sculpture was the original focus of Katelyn Uehling's undergraduate honors thesis in art conservation. The monument was originally intended to celebrate the traditionally segregated African-American neighborhood, known as the New London Road/Cleveland Avenue community, in Newark, Delaware.

of the traditionally segregated African-American community at the northern border of the campus. The student, Katelyn Uehling, undertook a project to restore the monument that eventually led her in a quite different direction. UD has physically and economically encroached on this neighborhood, known as the New London Road/Cleveland Avenue community, for the last fifty years. The community, settled first in the 1830s, exists today, but in reduced population and geographic size. The monument, built by a UD visiting artist, was meant to recognize and celebrate the community (see figure 10.1). Instead, in the opinion of many community members surveyed by Uehling, the monument turned out to be of debatable aesthetic appeal, in addition to being structurally unsound, thus failing as a gesture of good will. Stakeholder meetings that Uehling organized made clear that the monument did not resonate with residents of the community and its loss would not be mourned. Uehling asked community members to suggest some other memorial that the University could create that might be more meaningful to the community. Members of the local Black Heritage Committee proposed a pamphlet and a walking tour of the remnants of their neighborhood so that current residents, descendants, and, most importantly, new UD students might be made aware of the struggles of this community and the injustices it faced. Two seminars in material culture studies had earlier recorded oral histories of some of the residents and privately published two books about the community.[4] Uehling's research prompted the transfer of the interviews and book files to Special Collections, where the sources are now available to the public.

At Uehling's community meetings (see figure 10.2), photographs were shared and scanned, stories

told, and key community members identified for additional oral histories, which were digitally recorded by Uehling, and then transcribed. These materials, too, are in Special Collections. The project is continuing with the community members contributing text for proposed state historic markers and for video podcasts to accompany a walking tour. Special Collections provided a secure but accessible location for these new resources about the local community. Johnson Melvin's interest in Uehling's work extended beyond completion of the honors thesis. As program co-chair of the spring 2010 Mid-Atlantic Regional Archives Conference in Wilmington, she invited Uehling, then completing her first year of employment at the Center for Conservation of Art and Historic Artifacts in Philadelphia, to present a paper in a session on community documentation projects.

MATERIAL CULTURE STUDIES STUDENTS LEARN EXHIBIT SKILLS

In another collaboration, Johnson Melvin and Deborah Andrews, Director of the Center for Material Culture Studies, developed a project for students in Andrews's capstone seminar for minors in the field.

In teaching material culture, Andrews emphasizes the importance of learning from and with objects and she addresses the concept of collecting as a major topic in her course: why people collect, how they manage and display their collections, how collections move from private to institutional hands, and how institutions select, manage, and display the various collections in their care. To illustrate these concepts in her capstone seminar she and her students *researched* the context and management of numerous objects from the extensive Littell family papers and ephemera donated to Special Collections by Jeanie Morse Littell Winslow. In visits to Special Collections, the seminar students learned how to appropriately handle objects, photograph them, write about them, and install a selection of them in an onsite public exhibit, as well as an online exhibit.

Figure 10.2. Uehling (standing, right) held community meetings with residents of the New London Road/Cleveland Avenue community and discovered their interest in creating a new memorial project: a pamphlet and walking tour documenting landmarks in the historic neighborhood.

The Littell collection includes items mainly from 1830-1930, formerly possessed by a family that traces its roots to some of the early 18th century European settlers in the greater Delaware River Valley and whose 19th century ancestors flourished as publishers, clergymen, and amateur botanists, among other activities. The photographs, scrapbooks, souvenirs of missionary work in China, needlework samplers, cases for calling cards, jewelry, playing cards, silver award goblet, and other *realia* in the collection provided clues for the students to aid their understanding of the rich historical context of family life as it intersected with major currents of production and consumption, of social and political life in the trans-Atlantic and trans-Pacific worlds during the periods represented by archival sources and material objects preserved by the family.

In introducing the Littell family papers to the seminar students, Johnson Melvin emphasized the importance of donor relations, collection integrity, provenance, and archival context—using textual evidence from documents and photographs in the collection to establish meaning for the varied objects that were preserved with the papers. She opened a slideshow family history with the poignant photograph of the donor and caretaker of the family memories as a child (see figure 10.3). This grainy photograph captivated the students and became a kind of motif as they learned about the Littell family and its objects and in particular about the women who preserved these items. The photograph also anchored the homepage of the virtual exhibit. At the end of the introductory class, students examined each of the objects on display to select the one they wanted to study in detail. Their selections reflected personal and academic interests: for example, a lover of games selected a triangle puzzle game; a history major was intrigued by a section of the Atlantic Cable fashioned into a pendant by Tiffany's; an art conservation major was drawn to a silver goblet; a photographer wanted to investigate a daguerreotype in the collection. Handling the object, writing about the object in its presence, and photographing the object were each important components of their research, as was reading archival content for background about the family and researching secondary sources about the time in which their object was acquired.

Based on their research, each student wrote an essay profiling their object. As they developed their essays, the students also took on a second role as curators of the two exhibits. Sitting around a seminar table, the class debated the exhibit's title and theme, selected the items to display (not all could be includ-

Figure 10.3. Jeanie Morse Littell Winslow, born in 1918, lost her mother later that year in the Great Influenza Epidemic. Mrs. Winslow became keeper of the family history, donating the family archives and small objects to the University of Delaware Library. Photograph from the Littell family papers.

ed), and composed text for an introductory statement and for individual labels. A team of two students took on final responsibility for designing the exhibit and installing the labels and objects in a glass-enclosed case within the Special Collections reading room (see figures 10.4 and 10.5). Publicized across campus, the exhibit lasted two months and drew many visitors, including undergraduate peers who had never been in Special Collections before. Photographs of the exhibit became part of the students' portfolios.

The debate about the best title for the exhibit reinforced rhetorical theories discussed in the class about defining and describing objects and drawing visitors' attention to them. The seminar students ultimately decided on the title "A Family Keeps," with these further lines of introduction:

> Through generations, they keep together
> Over time, they keep the special things that enter their lives
> Women are the major tenders of the family keep, its storehouse
> One part of the Littell family keep is now here…

The role of women as collectors and keepers of family treasures was particularly emphasized, inspired by the unforgettable first impression of Mrs. Winslow photographed as a care-giving child.

Students also felt that the term "material culture," which made sense to them, might puzzle visitors, so they added this text:

> As students and teachers of material culture we are often asked the simple question: what is it? Here are some answers that shaped our study of this collection:

> *The things we make reflect our beliefs about the world; the things around us affect the way that we understand the world. There is an unending circularity to this that implies less a circle and more a kind of wheel moving.*—Lance Winn

> *Material culture is the history and philosophy of objects and the myriad relationships between people and things.*—Bernie Herman

Figure 10.4 Undergraduate Anne McBride was on the installation team for the exhibit of objects selected from the Littell family papers in Special Collections. The exhibit was on display in the reading room of the Special Collections Department at the end of the semester, but the seminar's online exhibit remains available at http://quimby.english.udel.edu/rworley/littell/

Figure 10.5. The Material Culture Studies seminar students learned to select objects for an exhibition, interpret the selection with a title and coherent label text, and present the objects in an appealing manner within the confines of a physical space.

Material Culture is the unpacking or mining of both historic and everyday objects to find the embedded ideas and concepts that define the surrounding society. —Joyce Hill Stoner[5]

To develop the online version of the exhibit from their objects and essays, the seminar collaborated with students from another class on web design. The seminar became the client of a project team in that class. Workshop discussions between the seminar and the web design team surfaced questions about adapting text and images from the physical display to one for the web. A major concern was how to capture the physicality of a three-dimensional object in onscreen images. The web designers also had their own opinions about which objects were most screen-worthy. Another concern was how to edit the core text to accommodate the sequencing and layering in the online exhibit as opposed to the way it was displayed on labels in exhibit cases.

Through this experience with objects from a family's collection, once private and probably scattered but now housed together, students had the opportunity to touch the past. They gathered data not only from what they could see and read, but from the special small objects that remained through generations of a family's sorting, discarding, losing, and cherishing their stuff. The students were pleased to have a tangible outcome of their work in the form of the onsite exhibit, displayed during the end-of-the semester period when family and friends came to campus for graduation and other events. This model should be easily adaptable to any problem-based/project-based class that addresses objects as evidence and entertainment. Students selected objects that were attractive, puzzling, storied, and reminiscent of their own experiences. The spring seminar had hoped to complete a catalog of their essays and images of the objects the art department's hand letterpress, but summer and graduation intervened. The online exhibit, too, was not quite finished by the end of the semester. The seminar has now been moved to the fall term for its next iteration, with the hope that students might continue exhibit work into the next semester if necessary.

LEARNING BY DOING

Centers for the study of the book, book arts, and the history of print culture have supported teaching about the materiality of rare books in special collections libraries. Art conservation and material culture studies faculty at UD, in partnerships with librarians, have fostered new opportunities to teach about the physicality of manuscript materials and objects found inside archival collections and the ongoing cultural significance of collection contents to the communities they serve. "Things," or *realia*, are not the norm in the collecting focus for manuscript curators in Special Collections, but many small objects, such as those preserved in the Littell family papers, have meaningful context and enlighten the history to be discovered in such collections. Teaching skills of physical observation, description, and interpretation of objects in balance with archival evidence from collections allows special collections librarians and faculty to engage students in exciting ways with primary sources. Preservation awareness—why we collect, what we collect, and how we care for what we collect—a core value shared by professionals in a wide range of cultural heritage settings, is also at the heart of these teaching goals for undergraduates In these case studies, librarians and faculty at the University of Delaware guided student opportunities to interact with special collections as "things." The student acts of "doing something" with the objects—whether providing conservation treatments, curating exhibits, talking to communities about how they respond to public monuments, or helping collect new documentation—gave students great opportunities to learn. Finally, it is important to note that these projects afforded the librarians and faculty learning experiences, too. Campus collaborations enrich professional relationships, stimulate teaching skills, and make the most of library resources, especially special collections.

NOTES

1. Deborah C. Andrews, Professor, English, and Director, Center for Material Culture Studies, University of Delaware. http://materialculture.udel.edu/ Vicki Cassman, Ph.D., Assistant Professor, Art Conservation, and Director of Undergraduate Studies in Art Conservation, University of Delaware. http://www.artcons.udel.edu/school/people/cassmanv. L. Rebecca Johnson Melvin, Librarian and Coordinator, Manuscripts Unit, Special Collections, University of Delaware Library. http://www.lib.udel.edu/ud/spec/

2. "Service-learning is designed to expose students to the needs of the larger society, engage them in addressing those needs through community service, and connect what they learn in the classroom to real-world conditions through faculty-directed reflection." http://facsen.udel.edu/sites/DLE%20Learning%20Outcomes%20and%20Requirements%20for%20Service-Learning.htm

3. The Academy of Newark, later the College and then the University of Delaware, was chartered in 1769, eleven years after the town of Newark received a royal charter from King George II.

4. *People were close* (2005) and *Food always brings people together : recipes, poems, and stories from the New London Road community, Newark, Delaware* (2006); both, Center for Material Culture Studies and Raven Press at the University of Delaware.

5. Lance Winn (Art), Bernard Herman (Art History), and Joyce Hill Stoner (Art Conservation) are interdisciplinary faculty associated with the UD Center for Material Culture Studies.

UH-Hilo & the Christensen Photographic Collection: Preserving a Piece of Hamākua's History

Kerri A. Inglis and Helen Wong Smith

In an effort to diversify and expand the under-graduate history program at the University of Hawai'i at Hilo (UH-H), opportunities were sought to enhance our course offerings, provide relevant experience within the discipline for students, and foster connections between the university and the local community. We were especially interested in introducing our students to public history as this field provides an excellent avenue to work with communities.

The National Council on Public History has described public history as "a movement, methodology, and approach that promotes the collaborative study and practice of history; its practitioners embrace a mission to make their special insights accessible and useful to the public."[1] Public history can also be described as the conceptualization and practice of historical activities with one's audience foremost in mind. Public history courses generally take place in settings beyond the traditional classroom and we knew providing such a course could broaden student interest and participation in the history department's curriculum.

Practitioners of public history often see themselves as mediators between the academic practices of history and non-academics whose diverse interests in society seek to foster historical understanding. Our goal was to develop a course to introduce students to the possibility of careers in public history while providing practical experience to understand the demands of the field and its desirability as

a graduate discipline. Further, we wanted students to understand that "public history is more than an alternative field within the discipline," but rather assumes "a central role in fulfilling the profession's responsibility to engage society in understanding its past."[2]

The design of a new course in public history focused on service-learning as its major component. Awarded a Diversity and Equality Initiative (DEI) Grant from the University of Hawai'i system in Fall 2008 we prepared for the first course offering. The impetus for applying for the DEI grant was the knowledge that the North Hawai'i Education & Research Center (NHERC), a satellite campus forty miles distant, received a "donated" photo collection which could be the focus of our service-learning component.[3] The grant of a few thousand dollars enabled hiring two student assistants for a semester. This allowed for the initial organization of the collection, preparing for the collection's role as part of the course, and conducting the necessary research for the course and training in working with archival photographic collections.

THE COLLECTION

Seldom do we who teach history have the opportunity to work with a collection which is interdisciplinary in nature, provides unique learning experiences for our students, provides research and publication opportunities for faculty and students, while connecting us to our local community, but such is the case with the "Christensen Photographic Collection".

The Christensen Photographic Collection is estimated to consist of seven to eight thousand images (photographs, negatives, and slides) taken mainly from the 1930s through the 1970s. The collection extensively captures sugar plantation operations throughout the Hamākua district, on the eastern side of the island of Hawai'i, and other facets of life in rural Hawai'i. Paul Christensen learned his photographic skills while serving in the U.S. military at the Kīlauea Military Camp located within the Hawai'i Volcanoes National Park. He was then employed by the Honoka'a Sugar Company as *luna* (boss, overseer) in Hamākua district in 1933. While the collection covers these aforementioned areas and the county seat of Hilo, it reveals the ethnically diverse working community of east Hawai'i Island as well as the impact of World War II on the island and the repercussions of its status under martial law.

The availability of the collection for student *practica* was key to the success of our service-learning component. As one historian has noted, "Because of the need for a broad intellectual perspective on the discipline and the importance of the availability of local professionals who can be invited to give guest lectures in classes or to supervise in-class and internship practica, public history programs most frequently provide specialization in those fields in which there is a professionally staffed independent institution accessible nearby."[4] In other words, service-learning is limited to what is already available within the community, and while we are striving to develop relationships with the two small museums in our town, their limited resources precluded us from access to a collection the magnitude of the Christensen Collection. The acquisition of these materials made the collection, to be processed at one of our satellite campuses, accessible to the entire class, an essential component of our overall course project.

Simultaneously, NHREC staff requested the UH-H Hawaiian Collection librarian[5] who is also a certified archivist, to advise them in processing and digitizing the collection. Unfortunately, the original order of the collection was lost because the

Figure 11.1 and 11.2. Images from The Christensen Photographic Collection

NHERC staff imposed their own subject headings and separated the images despite their format.[6] The staff failed to inform the Archivist that the collection would be used for the public history course. This and the staff's imposed arrangement had an impact on the processing of the collection.

THE COURSE

The course as developed explores the history of Hawai'i (pre-European encounters to contemporary times) through the use of public history venues on the island. Formal classroom instruction was limited to the start of the semester and to discussions of initial readings on the theories and methodologies of public history and basic archival principles, as well as basic guidance from the archivist on best practices for photographic collections and digitization standards. Remaining classes were held "in the field" once a week and were scheduled to allow students to participate in day-long activities when necessary. Three National Historical Parks/Sites and two museums were visited in addition to sites where historical memories of place have been inscribed onto plaques or removed from public remembrance all together (facilitating discussion on the role of history in our daily lives).

The requisite reading and writing adhered to historian Constance B. Schulz's counsel, "The common *purposes* of public history education are to prepare historians trained in the traditional historical skills of research, interpretation, and writing to apply those skills in a broad variety of public settings in order to bring an understanding of the past to bear on the issues, problems, and enjoyment of the present, and to preserve the sources that make that understanding possible."[7] The service-learning component within the course was intended to give students practical learning experience and skill development, while serving as a conduit for bringing the academic side of history into the public context.

Sixty percent of the course involved reading and writing assignments, and field trips to public history sites around the island, with an emphasis on Hawaiian and "local" history. The other forty percent of the course was dedicated to the service-learning component. Upon receipt the Christensen Collection filled six banker boxes with albums, smaller boxes of negatives and slides, and hundreds of loose prints. Of the fourteen students enrolled in Fall 2009[8] course not all fulfilled their service-component hours, but in total the class contributed over 200 hours of work on the collection: approximately 5000 images (60 % of the collection; prints, slides, and negatives) from the collection were placed in protective sleeves recommended by the archivist; digitizing stations allowed students to experiment with scanning and organizing digital images and by the end of the semester some 400 images were scanned into the digital collection. Each student gained some experience in every aspect of this service-learning project. Digitizing is the primary task in the 2010-11 academic year, while the majority of cataloging will be conducted in the Fall 2011 semester.

Several students expressed a desire to continue working on the collection following their initial involvement in the public history course in 2009. Internships or independent study opportunities resulted in two history majors, one geography major, and one sociology major working on the collection during the Spring 2010 semester. Combined, they contributed over 400 hours of work on the collection completing the task of re-housing the entire collection in protective archival sleeves and digitizing an additional 2000 images. Over twenty searchable subject categories have been assigned to the digital collection and a basic finding aid describing the collection was created. Enhancement of the finding aid will include a content list/inventory of the print collection. As a result of our success with the collection coupled with its community significance we successfully secured additional funding to employ these four, now well-trained students, to continue working with the collection for the next year. This funding also allowed for the acquisition of a scanner capable of digitizing variable size negatives. We are now confident we will complete digitizing the entire collection and aspire to make it available to the public via the internet.

When the public history course is next offered (Fall 2011) we plan to conduct it on a new community project following a similar approach applied to the Christensen Collection (i.e. preparation, methodology, practical experience). We concur with Prof. Schulz that "...becoming a public historian can be both an absorbing pursuit, and the doorway to a lifetime involvement in the study and practice of history where it matters profoundly: in neighborhoods and communities".[9]

THE CHALLENGES

It should not surprise anyone that despite our successes with our new public history course and our service-learning project there have been challenges. Some challenges dealt with the practical side of logistics, supplies, and methodological choices. For example, in developing a finding aid for the collection, we are still grappling with our organizational schema of categories and index terms, trying to find an appropriate balance between Library of Congress subject headings and more "google" intuitive terms often utilized by digital image collections.

The greater challenges resulted from working with the "donation" recipient (NHERC) and with the local residents who have close ties to the collection and its photographer. Initially, we were unaware that the collection was donated with the intention of generating usage fees for the donor. This stipulation introduced us to the legal concerns of ownership, fair use, and the use of public funds to provide access to a quasi-private collection. Eventually we reached an agreement with the owner (who inherited the collection from his uncle, the photographer) transferring ownership rights of the images to the University for research and publication purposes. Further,

Figure 11.3. Image from The Christensen Photographic Collection

working in a small community, there were misunderstandings as to what our group was doing and/or planning for the future of the collection. To enhance communication, dispel misunderstandings, and seek much needed help with identification of the images, we published a photo each month in a local newspaper (*Hamakua Times*) asking for community assistance identifying people and places. This approach proved extremely successful—community members have not only identified individuals and events in pictures, some have volunteered to help with the identification of other images in the collection. Our outreach to the community is leading us toward a partnership with a local history group who specializes in community oral history.

Unfortunately, some of these challenges (especially those involving politics and people) diverted our time and energy from the actual processing of the collection. But overall, the course and our service-learning project have been an inspiring success. As one student intern stated, "… I definitely found myself interfacing between community goals and academic objectives with respect to the photographic collection, so I certainly was exposed to the significance of public history from both the community's point of view and the academic perspective."[10] Another student reported "This project has given me a new respect for the work that Public Historians put into their jobs every day. A strong point of this experience is that I still have the desire to do more of this kind of work in graduate school. Of all the lessons that I learned from this project, I think that the issues of ownership, organization (including multi-tasking and time management strategies), and friendly relationships with affiliated organizations are the most important knowledge I have taken away from this project."[11] We also, one an historian and the other an archivist, have learned a great deal through this project—the pleasure of working together on an interdisciplinary project, hands-on experiences *with* our students, our ability to deal with the unexpected, and the joys of connecting our work to our community.

CONCLUSION

The ultimate goal of this project is to produce an internet-accessible, digitized version of the Christensen Photographic Collection that will foster further research, primarily in the area of Hawai'i Island's plantation history, and in that respect the work continues. As we continue to digitize the Christensen Photographic Collection for access and preservation purposes, introducing our students to practical archival and public history experiences—we expect it will provide for a variety of educational, research, and publication opportunities benefiting our UH-Hilo faculty, students, and our local community for many years. The benefits this project has produced for us have far out-weighed any of the challenges:

> We learned about the intricacies of archival work; we developed working relationships with each other; we faced challenges related to our relationship with NHERC; and we took the collection from several unorganized boxes of loose images to an organized, labeled, and digitized collection that we can all be proud of."[12]

We hope that lessons learned from the project will aid others, thus before accepting a private collection with the intent of making it available for public distribution we suggest that the following checklist be consulted.

Checklist

status of collection	be sure the selected collection for your service-learning is a clear donation; if not, copyright, and the owner's right to profit from your efforts are at issue
proper equipment and supplies	in order to properly process your collection you will need proper equipment and supplies (they don't come cheap!); secure funding before your project begins and think *long-term* (your project will likely take longer than expected)
clearly articulated goals	be sure your goals, the local community's goals, and anyone else involved in the acquisition and use of the collection's goals are clearly communicated before you begin; if objectives are divergent, you will have to deal with complications later, often after the work has commenced
define roles	clearly define who represents different entities, their responsibility, and their authority
determine audience and possible collaboration	when planning an online presence consider the audience, their level of expertise with digital collections and the possibility to contribute to digital consortia—this will determine format and metadata at the time of digitization avoiding duplication or unnecessary work later

NOTES

1. See *National Council on Public History*—http://ncph. org/cms/.

2. James B. Gardner and Peter S. LaPaglia, eds., "Part I: Introduction," in *Public History: Essays from the Field*, (Malabar, Florida: Krieger Publishing Company, 2004), 3.

3. At that time, NHERC had accepted the Christensen Collection under a temporary agreement and did not secure proper ownership/copyright permissions as is normally done with archival donations. The then owner of the collection, allowed us to work with the collection for the purpose of archival training; recognizing the historical value of the collection he transferred ownership and copyright to the University of Hawai'i in July 2010.

4. Constance B. Schulz, "Becoming a Public Historian," in *Public History: Essays from the Field*, Gardner and LaPaglia, eds., (Malabar, Florida: Krieger Publishing Company, 2004), 37.

5. Currently archivist at Hawai'i Volcanoes National Historical Park.

6. Format i.e. colored slides determines storage environment.

7. Schulz, 32.

8. We had to cap the course at 14 as our transportation for our field-trips was limited to a 15 passenger van.

9. Schulz, 38.

10. Sarah Anderson, "Final Report, Internship, Sociology 391," 29 April 2010, 2. (Copy in author's possession.)

11. Robert Franklin, "Student Evaluation of Christensen Collection Archive Project," 12 May 2010, 1. (Copy in author's possession.)

12. Holly Miller, "Final Report—the Christensen Photographic Collection Internship," 7 May 2010, 1. (Copy in author's possession.)

"Science Circa 1859: On the Eve of Darwin's *On the Origin of Species*": A Class-Curated Exhibit

Robin E. Rider

In 2009 exhibits—many and varied in size and objective—honored the 200th anniversary of the birth of Charles Darwin and the 150th anniversary of the publication of *On the origin of species*.[1] Some exhibits in libraries took a biographical tack; others incorporated natural history specimens alongside books and manuscripts. Some investigated the publishing history of Darwin's writings; others explored the influence of Darwin's work both in scientific fields and beyond. Many were coordinated with local lectures, programs, and events organized in conjunction with the anniversaries in question.

In consultation with colleagues in the Department of History of Science, in which I hold a faculty appointment, I proposed teaching a one-time undergraduate course[2] entitled "Science Circa 1859," aimed at producing a full-scale library exhibit for the Department of Special Collections in Memorial Library at the University of Wisconsin-Madison. My goal was to mount an exhibit curated by students in the class, one that complemented rather than overlapped exhibits at other institutions. The exhibit theme could accommodate varied student interests as well as showcase mid-19th century holdings in Special Collections and other campus libraries.

The result was "Science Circa 1859: On the Eve of Darwin's *On the Origin of Species*," *on* exhibit in Special Collections November 23, 2009, through March 12, 2010. It showcased holdings of campus libraries and honored the 150th anniversary of Darwin's path-breaking book by exploring the state of science in the decade prior to the publication of *On the origin of species* in 1859. Students enrolled in my course (Topics in History of Science: Science Circa 1859) in fall semester 2009 served as guest exhibit curators. The thirteen students, all but one of whom were undergraduates, cast their net widely in selecting visually appealing books and writing thoughtful captions; and the result took full advantage of the holdings of Special Collections, rare book collections in several of the campus science libraries, as well as other library collections across campus. The exhibit, housed in horizontal exhibit cases, occupied a space of some 1750 square feet in the Department of Special Collections. Many of us in departments of special collections have long involved individual students, both graduate and undergraduates, in the preparation of exhibits, enlisting their assistance in larger projects and guiding them through various phases of curating an exhibit. And I have included various writing assignments designed to produce shorter or longer exhibit captions in undergraduate courses I have taught on history of science as well as in graduate courses on special collections administration in the school of library and information studies. For this course, however, the exhibit served as occasion, objective, and product,[3] all on a tight timetable. The exhibit "Science Circa 1859" needed to open on or before November 24, 2010, the 150th anniversary of the publication of the first edition of *On the origin of species*; the class met just once a week, and the vagaries of our academic calendar in fall 2009 meant we had eleven weeks for research, selection of books, and writing of captions.

Each student was responsible for one horizontal exhibit case (generally 42 inches square) on a single, if elastic, topic pertinent to science on the eve of Darwin's book. To jumpstart the process of selection, I supplied a fairly long list of topics from which the students each chose one; I also pre-selected at least one exhibit-worthy book[4] for each topic; each student then chose two more books[5] on his or her topic, and wrote a case caption exploring the content and significance of all the books in the case. The books or journal issues to be exhibited were to have been published in the 1850s, and the UW-Madison library system needed to own a copy of the actual publication. Digital surrogates would not suffice. The students in the course settled on topics of astronomy, botany, chemistry and industry, experiment and popularization, exploration and expeditions, science education, fossils, the human sciences, museums and other scientific institutions, science and power, scientific instruments, and taxonomy and classification. As it played out, the students' searches and selections drew upon subject-specific collections across campus, not all of them in special collections per se; some of the books they chose were neither rare nor even medium-rare.

The students, most of them juniors or seniors, hailed from many majors, not just history of science. The variety of majors fostered a breadth of subject matter for the exhibit itself, although some students were unaccustomed to historical research and to styles of writing in fields like history and history of science. A number of the students, including some non-majors, achieved considerable sophistication in their research and analysis.[6] All found the experience of reading (and handling) mid-19th century books a novel one.

The sequence of written and oral assignments was structured carefully to ensure students' ability to complete them on time. All of the assignments contributed to the final products of the course: a descriptive case caption for every case, bibliographical information concerning the books exhibited, research files containing relevant secondary literature and research notes shared with other students in the course, and a joint gallery talk about the contents of their cases.[7]

The whole process involved a significant amount of student writing.[8] Bradley Hughes, director of the UW-Madison Writing Center, provided invaluable advice as I considered the shape and sequencing of writing assignments, ways of modeling effective research and writing, incorporation of revision strategies, and opportunities for oral and written feedback, both from fellow students and from the instructor.[9]

The exhibit, by design, showed chronological unity, even if some students strayed a bit from the strict boundaries of the 1850s. Although it lacked a unifying narrative, themes such as the expansion of the scientific enterprise and aspects of print culture helped link the individual case topics. While the cases were in general not author-based, prolific authors like Asa Gray and William Hooker figured in several cases. Students' selections drew from varied genres—textbooks, manuals, guidebooks, catalogs, children's books, institutional reports, descriptions of instruments, and technical monographs—aimed at different audiences for scientific writing in the middle of the 19th century. Most selections tended toward books rather than articles from scientific journals or other periodicals of the period. Not surprisingly, the items selected were exclusively Anglophone.

Several students, recognizing that the small illustrations in their books lacked the impact of larger illustrations, asked for digital enlargements, which we printed out on appropriately cream-colored paper and mounted for display alongside their books. All told, the illustrations they chose represented a variety of reproduction processes; and a few students picked up on references to the novelty of the illustrations in their books, as in the "photo-stereographs" illustrating C. Piazzi Smyth's account of high-altitude astronomical observations in Tenerife.[10] Most felt keenly the constraint of choosing only one page opening for display, and welcomed the opportunity to specify additional images for inclusion in an online version of the exhibit.[11]

The monochromatic character of most of the exhibit was relieved by several hand-colored illustrations and maps, as well as by a gilt illustration on a publisher's binding and colorful samples of cloth dyed with aniline dyes. One student took special delight in the leaves she found pressed in her book,[12] asked that they be encapsulated for display, and related them to specific pages in the textbook in question.

The course requirement of submitting and sharing research files[13] was intended to impress upon students the importance of solid research and accountability as well as to alert their classmates to secondary literature of possible relevance. Citations for these sources were then combined into a wide-ranging collective bibliography to supplement the online exhibit. The students' research files and written assignments afford evidence of the extent to which they actually consulted their fellow students' choices of secondary literature, and to what benefit. Their submissions also illuminate ways in which these particular undergraduate students discovered and deployed primary and secondary sources, consulted digitized books, relied on MadCat (our OPAC), and used Google searches, library reference resources in print, and bibliographical and full-text databases as they explored the content and context of their exhibit choices.

Our discussions of museum practice and online exhibits[14] early in the course showed the students to be insightful (and frequent) museum visitors. Their sense of space and appreciation of design were also evident as we wrestled with which topic went where in the actual exhibit: many of the students pointed out connections between "their books"—note the gratifying sense of ownership—and works in other cases. They were particularly alert to visual analogies—in the look of diagrams, the organization of information on the page, and the use of color. They also considered carefully which cases, topics, and books were most likely to attract a visitor's attention.

Not only did the students work together in deciding which case went where in the overall exhibit organization, they provided detailed case layouts for their own cases. Because of time pressures and the need for consistency, the Special Collections staff printed out the case captions and installed everything in the cases, although a few members of the class lent a hand; all of them observed the installation of several cases and seemed surprised at how much hand work was required.[15]

Class discussions throughout the course emphasized the public nature of the exhibit, in which both the items chosen for display and the students' captions would bear close scrutiny. The students readily appreciated the need to select interesting books (and page openings to show). The understanding that the audience for their writing might extend far beyond me and their fellow students lent special value to accuracy and well-supported general statements in their captions. The students seemed to appreciate that library administration supported our undertaking; I certainly saw the support from library administration, colleagues in the library, and the history of science department as critical to our success.

The exhibit and the class' work enjoyed relatively high profile on campus. As a full-scale exhibit for the Department of Special Collections, it was announced in library publications and on library Web pages. Early discussions of plans for the course and exhibit prompted Jenny Price, a writer in University Communications, to sit in on one class. I also prevailed on her to offer advice to the class concerning writing and revision.[16] Her substantial news story on the course and exhibit[17] was featured for a time on the main campus Web page.

Each student also spoke briefly about his or her case topic and book selections in a collective gallery talk attended by friends, colleagues from the library and the history of science department, and board members of the Friends of the UW-Madison Libraries. To say the least, the students were not uniformly comfortable with this course requirement,[18] but all showed esprit de corps and admirable support for one another.

Compared to earlier printed sources, mid-19th century books—the medium-rare books we have long been discussing in special collections—are perhaps easier for students to read because they feature more standard orthography and book appearance (and they lack the dreaded long S). But, by the same token, they perhaps hold less intrinsic appeal because they are wordy and printed in small type, often with only small illustrations to break up the page. Though they seem (and are) fragile, they are perhaps less quaint than books from the hand-press era. They are more readily available on Google books, and at Madison they tend to be scattered among various campus libraries and shelving facilities. It is not obvious to students why some are in Special Collections and some are not. Interestingly, we did decide to transfer more than one exhibit book from a circulating collection to Special Collections once the exhibit came down.[19]

The students in the course, like the rest of us, looked to digitized works, especially in early stages of their research. But they were occasionally caught off guard by differences between the version of a work in Google Books or the Hathi Trust and the copy, sometimes in dim storage, on our own campus. How, and indeed whether, digital surrogates are linked to catalog records for print books in our collections complicated matters further. That different editions, compilations, and translations could pose problems of interpretation and attribution also seemed to surprise most of the students in the class.[20]

Although most of the students required considerable encouragement to troll their mid-19th century books for lively quotations revealing something of the spirit of the age, several went further and mined the copious review literature of the period via electronic resources like *American periodicals series online* and *British periodicals*. There they found, for example, pointed comments on the general "dullness of museums" and a prescient critique of the effects of colonization on what we would now call biological diversity.

Anyone who has incorporated substantial student use of primary sources into undergraduate teaching knows not to underestimate the time and effort required.[21] But effort devoted to identification of promising materials in special collections, refinement of assignments, construction of guides and tools for students, and individual guidance is essential if undergraduate students are to make profitable use of special collections holdings. Such undertakings constitute a worthy investment in the creation of learning opportunities, not just learning objects.

NOTES

1. http://darwin-online.org.uk/2009.html lists many exhibits, events, and publications associated with these anniversaries.

2. Under the rubric "Special Topics in History of Science."

3. I took inspiration from Roxanne Nilan's course in the Stanford history department in the mid-1990s, in which undergraduate students produced as part of their course work a library exhibit on women in California history, drawing heavily on the holdings of Special Collections.

4. From either Special Collections or Memorial Library, the principal circulating library collection on campus.

5. Or three books, for those students taking the course on an honors basis.

6. The course schedule afforded little time for readings in common, though we did read an excerpt from David Knight, *The age of science: The scientific world-view in the nineteenth century* (New York: Basil Blackwell, 1986). To help each student focus on critical issues and produce well-researched and well-written exhibit text, I identified one secondary source (generally an article or chapter from a monograph or collection) germane

to his or her case topic. The students were responsible for finding other relevant secondary sources; and we spent considerable class time together exploring bibliographies, full-text databases, and other reference works likely to be profitable.

7.   The writing assignments were constructed to make sure that the student workload and the level of their engagement with a broad subject were both appropriate for a 3-unit class. It would certainly have been easier to require just individual item captions rather than a synthetic case caption.

8.   The course was not, however, structured explicitly to meet the requirements of a writing-intensive course within the rubrics available.

9.   Cf. Hughes' generous account of the course in *Time to write. The newsletter of the L&S Program in Writing Across the Curriculum*, v. 13, no. 2 (spring 2010), pp. 4-5.

10.   Charles Piazzi Smyth, *Teneriffe* [sic]*, an astronomer's experiment: or, Specialities of a residence above the clouds* (London: L. Reeve, 1858).

11.   The prospect of an online exhibit allowed us to discuss more general questions of intellectual property and its reuse, and the students all signed a memorandum of understanding governing incorporation of their case captions in such a Web-based product.

12.   Asa Gray, *Botany for young people and common schools* [etc.] (New York: Ivison, Blakeman, Taylor, 1858).

13.   Shared through UW-Madison My WebSpace group directories, as described at http://www.doit.wisc.edu/mywebspace/mywebspace_grpdir.asp .

14.   Including http://www.rbms.info/committees/exhibition_awards/submissions/evaluation_criteria.shtml.

15.   To fill out the space in our exhibit area, we used additional cases for books, manuscripts, and printed ephemera illustrating the place of science in the Great Exhibition of 1851, the phenomenon of nature-printing, and other aspects of popular science at mid-century. These were case topics on the master list, but no students chose them. In particular, I used the example of the Crystal Palace to model the process of selection, emphasizing breadth of research, the importance of outlining, and careful bibliographical citations. The University Archives kindly supplied materials for a case on science at the University of Wisconsin in the 1850s.

16.   Price's very useful comments to the class included suggestions about writing long and then cutting, reading one's writing aloud to pinpoint awkward phrases, and allowing ample time for revision. Good advice for all of us!

17.   Jenny Price, "Exhibit explores state of science at time of Darwin's book, " Nov. 23, 2009, http://www.news.wisc.edu/17388.

18.   I for one would have been unnerved by such an assignment during my own undergraduate years.

19.   E.g., Smyth, *Teneriffe, an astronomer's experiment*, op. cit.

20.   To be sure, some of the works exhibited some bibliographic complexity. E.g., Campbell Morfit and Clarence Morfit, *Chemical and pharmaceutical manipulations* [etc.], 2nd and enlarged ed. (Philadelphia: Lindsay and Blakiston, 1857); Robert Bunsen, *Gasometry: Comprising the leading physical and chemical properties of gases*, trans. Henry E. Roscoe (London: Walton & Maberly, 1857); Auguste de La Rive, *A treatise on electricity: In theory and practice* (London: Longman, Brown, Green, and Longmans, 1853–1858), vol. 2–3 of 3 translated for the author by Charles V. Walker; Jacob Abbott, *Rollo's museum*, new ed., rev. by the author (New York: T. Crowell, 1855), bound by the publisher with *Rollo's experiments*.

21.   Recent local examples include Florence Hsia's use of various editions of the venerable text of Sacrobosco in an undergraduate course on the Scientific Revolution (http://specialcollections.library.wisc.edu/exhibits/sacrobosco/index.html) and Theresa Kelley's sophomore seminar on images (and descriptive metadata) appropriate for inclusion in Romantic Circles, a "refereed scholarly Website devoted to the study of Romantic-period literature and culture" (http://www.rc.umd.edu/).

ABOUT
THE
AUTHORS

About the Authors

Linnea M. Anderson is the Assistant Archivist, Social Welfare History Archives and Research Services Coordinator, Archives and Special Collections at the University of Minnesota. Helping scholars of all backgrounds and abilities connect with and understand the past through primary sources has been one of the most exciting and fulfilling aspects of Linnea's work as an archivist.

Deborah C. Andrews, Professor of English at the University of Delaware, directs the University's Center for Material Culture Studies. She teaches courses in rhetoric and editing, in researching and interpreting objects and sites for public understanding, and in American literature from 1865 to 1945. She has published several texts on professional communication.

John Anzalone is Professor of French and Class of 1948 Distinguished Chair at Skidmore College.

Sarah Arkebauer graduated from the University of Pennsylvania in 2011 with a degree in English. She works for the international poetry and poetics journal *Jacket2*, and plans to pursue graduate study in the near future.

Laura Baudot is Assistant Professor of English at Oberlin College. She holds a BA from Wellesley and a PhD from Princeton. Her research and teaching interests center on eighteenth-century British literature and include history of science, eighteenth-century British art, and book history.

Ryan Bean is the Reference and Outreach Archivist, Kautz Family YMCA Archives, University of Minnesota. Through instruction either in the form of workshops, classes or exhibits Ryan has discovered the joy in seeing users interact with the past and uncover the hidden stories found in our collections.

Sherri Berger is Program Coordinator for Digital Special Collections at the California Digital Library. She provides outreach, planning, and project management support for the Online Archive of California and Calisphere.

Stephanie Boone is the director of Student Writing Support Services and a senior lecturer with the Institute of Writing and Rhetoric at Dartmouth College. Since arriving at the College in 1988, she has trained and supervised the writing center's peer tutors and taught first-year students. In "Thin Skin, Deep Damage: Addressing the Wounded Writer in the Basic Writing Course" (*Arts and Humanities in Higher Education*, July 2010), she explores the challenges of teaching first-year writers.

Toni Bowers, PhD, is Professor of late-seventeenth- and eighteenth-century British literature at the University of Pennsylvania. She teaches courses on literary history and cultural theory, and especially enjoys teaching women's writing, epistolary fiction, and the works of Samuel Richardson. She is the author of *Force or Fraud: British Seduction Stories and the Problem of Resistance, 1660-1760* (Oxford U.P., 2011) and *The Politics of Motherhood: British Writing and Culture, 1680-1760* (Cambridge U.P., 1996). She co-edited a new abridgement of Richardson's *Clarissa* for undergraduate classrooms with Prof. John Richetti (Broadview P. 2010), and with Prof. Tita Chico she has edited a new volume of essays called *Atlantic Worlds in the Long Eighteenth Century: Seduction and Sentiment* (forthcoming 2012, Palgrave-MacMillan).

Laurel Bradley has served as Director of Exhibitions and Curator of the College Art Collection at Carleton College since 1996. She previously taught art history at the School of the Art Institute of Chicago and was the founding director of Gallery 400, University of Illinois at Chicago. Dr. Bradley, who holds a PhD from New York University's Institute of Fine Arts, loves the challenge of curating across the curriculum, using art and exhibitions to stimulate dialogue in a liberal arts college setting.

Peterson Brink, Assistant Archivist, University Libraries, University of Nebraska-Lincoln, is a member of the Academy of Certified Archivists.

Heather Briston is Head of Public Services for Library Special Collections at the UCLA Library. Formerly the Richard and Mary Corrigan Solari University Historian and Archivist, University of Oregon Libraries, Briston has taught credit courses in research and writing using primary sources, and collaborates extensively with faculty using primary sources in their instruction. Her professional research explores legal issues and archives, as well as the use of primary source materials in teaching.

Janet Bunde is Assistant University Archivist and Archivist of the John Brademas Congressional Papers at New York University Archives. Janet works with faculty and instructors to integrate use of archival materials into courses. She earned her MA in History and certificate in Archival Administration at NYU.

Rachel Sagner Buurma is Assistant Professor of English Literature at Swarthmore College, where she teaches and researches in the history of the novel, Victorian literature and culture, the history of the book, and twentieth-century literary criticism. She is finishing a book on Victorian print culture's dreams of collectivity.

Vicki Cassman, Assistant Professor, Department of Art Conservation, University of Delaware, is director of the undergraduate program. Vicki teaches preventive, textile and anthropological conservation.

Elizabeth A. Chase is Coordinator for Research Services at Emory University's Manuscript, Archives, and Rare Book Library. As the head of Research Services, Chase manages the Library's instruction program for graduate, undergraduate, and secondary students. Her research interests include the design and assessment of undergraduate courses built around archival materials. Chase is also a PhD candidate in English at Emory, with a specialization in twentieth century fiction by Irish women.

Christina Connor is the Instruction and Emerging Technologies Librarian at Ramapo College of New Jersey. In addition to holding a Masters in Information Studies from the University at Albany, she also holds a Masters in History. Her research interests include information literacy in the disciplines and American Revolutionary War-era book publishing and culture.

Ruth Copans is the College Librarian and Special Collections Librarian at Skidmore College.

Lauren Corallo is a member of the Class of 2012 at the University of Pennsylvania. She is majoring in Comparative Literature and German, and is currently studying Bertolt Brecht in Berlin.

Sarah Dauterive is a recent graduate of the University of Alabama's School of Library and Information Studies program. She is the Assistant Librarian at East Mississippi Community College in Scooba, Mississippi.

Gabrielle Dean, PhD, is the Curator for Modern Literary Rare Books and Manuscripts and the Librarian for English and The Writing Seminars at Johns Hopkins University. Her research and teaching focus on 19th- and 20th-century literature, print culture and archive formation. She is currently planning several new classes that will take advantage of the George Peabody Library's unique history and collections.

Mary Ellen Ducey, Associate Professor, University Archivist and Special Collections Librarian, University of Nebraska-Lincoln Libraries, oversees collections relating to University history, Willa Cather, Great Plains history and literature, quilt studies, and regional natural history. She is a faculty fellow for the Center for Great Plains Studies and the International Quilt Study Center & Museum.

Deena Engel is Clinical Associate Professor and Associate Director of Undergraduate Studies for the Computer Science Minors programs, Department of Computer Science, New York University. Deena is on the faculty of the Computer Science Department and teaches undergraduate programming and web development courses. She earned an MS in Computer Science at NYU and an MA in Comparative Literature at SUNY-Binghamton.

Eoin Ennis is a senior English Major at Penn; he will graduate in Spring 2012.

Rick Ewig is the associate director of the American Heritage Center, a manuscript repository at the University of Wyoming. At UW he currently teaches two classes through the History Department, Archival Research Methods and Introduction to Public History. Previously he taught the History of Wyoming at Laramie County Community College and was a co-instructor for three archival management courses also taught through the UW History Department. Since 2003, Ewig has served as the editor of *Annals of Wyoming*, the state's historical journal.

Paula Feid, Undergraduate Librarian, New York University Libraries, teaches basic research skills to undergraduates in writing classes and freshmen honors seminars and coordinates the Libraries'

term paper research service. She earned her MLS at University of Rhode Island's Graduate School of Library and Information Science and her MPS in Interactive Telecommunications at NYU's Tisch School of the Arts.

Laurie Fiegel is the Administrative Director of Iowa State University Honors Program. Laurie is an alum of Southeastern Louisiana University, where she earned both a Bachelors of Arts and a Master's Degree in History with a concentration in recent American history.

Rivka Fogel received a BA in English and Creative Writing from the University of Pennsylvania in 2011. Rivka is currently working and writing in New York, where she will soon begin an MFA in poetry at the New School.

Jim Gerencser is the College Archivist at Dickinson College in Carlisle, PA, heading up the Archives and Special Collections Department since 1998. He holds an MLS from the University of Pittsburgh and an MA in History from Shippensburg University.

Julie Grob is Coordinator for Digital Projects & Instruction, Special Collections, at the University of Houston Libraries, where she works with faculty to introduce students to primary source materials and provides oversight for the development of digital collections. She curates collections in the areas of literature, the USS Houston (CA-30), and Houston hip hop. She has published articles in *RBM: A Journal of Rare Books, Manuscripts, and Cultural Heritage* and *portal: Libraries and the Academy*.

Marianne Hansen is the Curator/Academic Liaison for Rare Books and Manuscripts at Bryn Mawr College. She was originally trained as an anthropologist at the University of North Carolina - Chapel, Hill, but during graduate study and employment in the libraries at Cornell University transformed herself into a historian of the late medieval book. She holds the MLS from Syracuse University.

Christopher Harter is the Director of Library and Reference Services at the Amistad Research Center in New Orleans, Louisiana. He received his MLS from Indiana University in 1996 and has worked as a librarian/archivist at the Indiana Historical Society, Indiana University's Lilly Library, and the University of Illinois. His work with Dr. Elisabeth McMahon of Tulane University to integrate student assistance and greater access to the American Committee on Africa records at the Amistad Research Center was awarded a Primary Source Award from the Center for Research Libraries in 2010.

Earle Havens is the William Kurrelmeyer Curator of Rare Books & Manuscripts in The Sheridan Libraries of Johns Hopkins University. Dr. Havens is also an Adjunct Associate Professor in the Department of German & Romance Languages & Literatures at Johns Hopkins, and he teaches undergraduate and graduate courses focused on the history of the book from the late Middle Ages to the Renaissance. His most recent research and published work has dealt with illicit printing, book smuggling, and scribal culture within the Roman Catholic underground in Elizabethan England.

Sarah M. Horowitz is Special Collections Librarian at Augustana College, Rock Island, Illinois. She is particularly interested in the effects of introducing undergraduate students to special collections resources, and how we can best convey the importance of these resources in a digital age.

Wendy Beth Hyman is Assistant Professor of English at Oberlin College, where she teaches Renaissance Literature and History of the Book. She is the editor of the collection, *The Automaton in English Renaissance Literature* (Ashgate, 2011). Her article on Spenser's *Faerie Queene* appeared in *English Literary*

Renaissance, and an essay on Thomas Nashe and early modern authorship is in *Studies in English Literature.* She is completing a manuscript on the philosophical engagements of Renaissance seduction poetry.

Kerri A. Inglis serves as Associate Professor of History at the University of Hawai'i at Hilo where she teaches courses in Hawaiian and Pacific history.

Andrew Jewell is Associate Professor of Digital Projects, University Libraries, University of Nebraska-Lincoln. Andy is a faculty fellow of the Center for Digital Research in the Humanities at UNL, the editor of the Willa Cather Archive (http://cather.unl.edu), and the co-editor of *The American Literature Scholar in the Digital Age* (U of Michigan Press, 2011).

Eric J. Johnson is Assistant Professor and Associate Curator of Rare Books & Manuscripts at The Ohio State University Libraries, where he is responsible for—and regularly teaches with—medieval, Reformation, Renaissance, and Early Modern books and manuscripts. He holds a PhD from the Centre for Medieval Studies at the University of York (UK) and an MLIS from Rutgers University.

L. Rebecca Johnson Melvin is Librarian and Coordinator of the Manuscripts Unit in Special Collections at the University of Delaware Library. Her writing interests mirror her collection responsibilities: regional history, literary manuscripts, contemporary congressional collections, and scrapbooks and other "life writing" genres. She was co-chair for thirteen years of the ACRL RBMS Manuscripts and Other Formats Discussion Group and is also professionally active in the Society of American Archivists with the Congressional Papers Roundtable, the Manuscripts Repositories Section, and the Women's Collections Roundtable. Johnson Melvin organized "Outside the Archival Box: Cultural Heritage Collaborations" for the Mid-Atlantic Regional Archives Conference in Spring 2010, inspired in part by experiences with UD faculty such as her co-authors, Deborah C. Andrews and Vicki Cassman.

Carolyn Jones is currently a student in the University of Pittsburgh graduate program in Library and Information Science. She received her BA and MA in English from Wake Forest University and is planning a career in special collections and archives.

Lynn Jones is an instruction librarian at the University of California, Berkeley. She teaches an average of 1,000 students a year how to do historical research.

Robin M. Katz worked as Digital Initiatives Outreach Librarian / Assistant Library Professor at the University of Vermont Libraries' Center for Digital Initiatives until February 2011. She is currently the Outreach and Public Services Archivist at the Brooklyn Historical Society, where she is working to bring faculty and students into the archives.

Jessica Kim is a rising senior at the University of Pennsylvania, majoring in Political Science and English with a concentration in eighteenth- and nineteenth-century British Literature. A native Californian, she enjoys finding evidence of Samuel Richardson's influence in other works and hopes to be able to study literature further.

Anne Marie Lane was hired in 1994 as the first Rare Books Curator at the University of Wyoming, and has been teaching a variety of semester-long Book History courses for the past fifteen years. The Fall 2011 course is on nineteenth-century British books; the Fall 2012 course is scheduled to be on exploration and travel books. She also regularly gives national and international conference presentations, the most recent being *"Memory's gift: The role of rare book libraries in keeping the love of the physical book alive,"* at the International Conference on the Book, held at the University of St. Gallen, Switzerland (Nov. 7, 2010); and *"Sounding out a text with pictorial symbols:*

the 1789 Dublin edition of 'A Curious Hieroglyphick Bible,'" at the annual conference of the Irish Society for the Study of Children's Literature, held at Trinity College, Dublin, Ireland (March 5, 2010).

Steve Lawson is the Humanities Liaison Librarian at Colorado College in Colorado Springs. He hopes to help expand students' understanding of the current information age by increasing their knowledge of the history of books and printing. His blog is "See Also…" at stevelawson.name/seealso.

L.K. Gypsye Legge is an archival consultant and advocate. Her practice has a special emphasis on creating increased access to collections with digital access.

Anna Tione Levine is a rising senior at Swarthmore College. She is pursuing an Honors degree in English Literature and Interpretation Theory, and is currently organizing an undergraduate conference on the Digital Humanities to take place in Spring 2011.

Victoria Lindsay Levine is an ethnomusicologist whose research focuses on Native North American musical cultures. Since 1988, she has taught ethnomusicology and Southwest Studies at Colorado College, where she serves as the Christine S. Johnson Professor of Music.

Richard Li graduated from Swarthmore College with High Honors in English and Statistics; he currently attends Washington University Law School.

Barbara Losoff is an Assistant Professor, Chemistry and Life Science Librarian at the University of Colorado, Boulder. Ms. Losoff teaches library instruction in the sciences including chemistry, biology, medicine, and the environment.

Doris Malkmus, Archivist and Processing Coordinator, Special Collections Library, Pennsylvania

State University, did extensive archival research for a doctorate in American women's history (University of Iowa, 2001). After earning an MSI degree (University of Michigan, 2005), she worked as an archivist at The Pennsylvania State University Special Collections Library.

Michael Masciandaro is a senior studying History and English at the University of Pennsylvania. He is working on an Honors thesis on eighteenth-century British intellectual history.

Barbara S. Meloni is the Public Services Archivist at the Harvard University Archives. She has served in various capacities at the University Archives and elsewhere at Harvard since 1981. Barbara received her MA in history and MLS from Case Western Reserve University.

Ellen Meltzer is Information Services Manager for the University of California—California Digital Library. Information Services provides direct and indirect user support for CDL programs and services. She also takes the lead in the areas of general CDL education and outreach to the UC campus libraries.

Eleanor Mitchell became Director of Library Services at Dickinson College in August, 2005. Prior to that, she was Head of the Undergraduate Library at UCLA since 1995, and Director of the Information Literacy Initiative there from its founding in 2001 through 2004. She served on the editorial board of *Reference Services Review* since 1998, becoming co-editor in 2005. She has worked in libraries at Arizona State University, Westchester Community College, Vassar College, and *Newsweek* magazine. Her undergraduate degree was in English, from Skidmore College; her MLS was from SUNY Albany. Eleanor thinks, writes, and speaks about undergraduates and libraries frequently.

Megan Mulder is Special Collections Librarian at the Z. Smith Reynolds Library, Wake Forest Univer-

sity. She holds an MA in English from the University of Virginia and an MS in Library and Information Science from the University of North Carolina at Chapel Hill. Integrating special collections materials into the undergraduate curriculum is one of her research interests, and she is currently planning Wake Forest's first for-credit History of the Book class.

Jamie L. Nelson is Special Collections Librarian at Augustana College in Rock Island, Illinois. She was charged with increasing the undergraduate student use of the archival and rare book collections when she joined the campus in 2000. Approximately one quarter of Augustana's student body has conducted research with special collections materials each of the last three years.

Elizabeth Newsom is an Instruction Librarian in Special Collections at the University of Colorado, Boulder. Ms. Newsom has provided Special Collections instruction in a wide variety of subjects, and is now developing digital initiatives for the department.

Dr. Marilyn McKinley Parrish is Special Collections Librarian & University Archivist at Millersville University. Over the past several years she has developed an active instruction program in collaboration with faculty colleagues from a variety of departments. Her research interests include women and learning in social movements, oral history, and libraries as locations for interdisciplinary collaboration and learning.

Michael J. Paulus, Jr., is University Librarian and Associate Professor at Seattle Pacific University. Previously, he was head of archives and special collections at Whitman College. Paulus holds an MLIS from Rutgers University and an MDiv from Princeton Theological Seminary.

David Pavelich is Head of Research Services in the David M. Rubenstein Rare Book and Manuscript

Library at Duke University. Previous to this, he was Reference and Instruction Librarian and Bibliographer for Modern Poetry in the Special Collections Research Center, University of Chicago Library.

John Pollack is Library Specialist for Public Services at the University of Pennsylvania's Rare Book and Manuscript Library. He is the editor of *"The Good Education of Youth": Worlds of Learning in the Age of Franklin* (Oak Knoll Press/University of Pennsylvania Libraries, 2009).

Jessy Randall is Curator of Special Collections / Archivist at Colorado College. She and Steve Lawson co-teach a half-credit course entitled The History and Future of the Book. She is also a poet and novelist, and she blogs about library shenanigans at http://libraryshenanigans.wordpress.com/.

Tatum Regan is an English and French major at the University of Pennsylvania. She very well may pursue a career as a brilliant screenwriter.

Matthew Reynolds is the Public Services Librarian for the Verona Joyner Langford North Carolina Collection at East Carolina University. His research interests include bibliographic instruction in special collections settings and the impact of the digitization of rare materials on the same.

Stephen P. Rice is Professor and Convener of American Studies at Ramapo College of New Jersey. He teaches Introduction to American Studies, Introduction to U.S. History I, Historiography, and a variety of upper-level courses on different aspects of U.S. social and cultural history in the nineteenth and early twentieth centuries. He is author of Minding the Machine: Languages of Class in Early Industrial America (2004) and co-editor of A Cultural History of the Human Body in the Age of Empire (2010). His current book project is on illustration and commercial wood engraving in the nineteenth century.

Robin E. Rider heads the Department of Special Collections in the General Library System, University of Wisconsin-Madison. She is senior lecturer in the Department of History of Science and also teaches in the School of Library and Information Studies at Madison. Her research addresses issues at the intersection of history of science and history of print culture—e.g., "Perspicuity and neatness of expression: Algebra textbooks in the early American republic" (in press).

Dr. Carla Mary Rineer is an assistant professor in the English department and Women's Study Program at Millersville University. Her teaching and scholarship reflect her longstanding passion for primary, archival sources. Her research interests include 19th century American periodicals, early American crime broadsides, 20th century pulp magazines and their portrayal of women, and women writers.

Ashley Rosener is completing her master's degree in Library and Information Science from the University of Illinois, Urbana-Champaign. She currently works as a graduate assistant for the University of Illinois Residence Hall Library System. She received her BA in English from Iowa State University and graduated from the University Honors Program.

Blythe E. Roveland-Brenton is the University Archivist, Head of Special Collections and the Associate University Librarian for Collections at St. John's University, NY. She holds a BA in Anthropology and German from Binghamton University, MA and PhD degrees in Anthropology from the University of Massachusetts, Amherst, and an MLS degree from St. John's University.

Tyler Russell is a 2011 graduate of Penn, where he majored in English. Ty works in the healthcare industry.

Jay Satterfield is the head of Dartmouth College's Rauner Special Collections Library. Since arriving at Dartmouth in 2004, he has worked to integrate Special Collections into the intellectual life of the College. He received his PhD in American Studies from the University of Iowa in 1999 and is the author of *"The World's Best Books": Taste, Culture and the Modern Library* (Amherst: University of Massachusetts Press, 2002).

Dale Sauter is the Manuscript Curator for the Special Collections Division at East Carolina University. His research interests include the twentieth-century American South, as well as American advertising and manufacturing.

Claudia Sbrissa is a visual artist and an assistant professor in the Fine Arts Department at St. John's University. She received a BFA from York University, Toronto, Canada, a BA in Education from Queen's University, Kingston, Canada, and an MFA from Cornell University, Ithaca, NY.

Nova M. Seals is the librarian for special collections and archives at Connecticut College. In addition to an MLS from Simmons College, she holds a Bachelor's in Government from the United States Coast Guard Academy and an MA in American and New England Studies from the University of Southern Maine. Her research interests reflect her current work experience and focuses on developing creative methods of incorporating primary sources in academic curricula.

Douglas Seefeldt is Assistant Professor of History and Faculty Fellow, Center for Digital Research in the Humanities, University of Nebraska-Lincoln. Doug is the Senior Digital Editor of The William F. Cody Archive <http://codyarchive.org>, author of the digital history project Envisaging the West: Thomas Jefferson and the Roots of Lewis and Clark <http://jeffersonswest.unl.edu>, and co-editor of the website Digital History <http://digitalhistory.unl.edu>.

Peggy Seiden has been College Librarian at Swarthmore College since 1998. Prior to joining Swarthmore, she directed the Skidmore College Library, the library at Penn State, New Kensington and worked in various capacities at Carnegie Mellon University. Her research interests and publications are focused on user behavior and library organizational dynamics. She is a past president of ALA's Reference and User Services Association and served on a number of committees in ACRL. She currently chairs the ALA-APA Certification Review Committee for the Library Support Staff Certification program. Her interest in Special Collections stems back to her graduate work in Medieval Studies. At the University of Toronto she had the opportunity to study Paleography under the tutelage of Father Leonard Boyle who subsequently became the Vatican Librarian. She also has a masters in Library and Information Science (Rutgers University); her undergraduate degree is from Colby College.

Ryan P. Semmes is the Assistant Archivist at the Congressional and Political Research Center of the Mississippi State University Libraries. He holds both an MLIS and an MA in Public History-Archives from the University of South Carolina.

Diane Windham Shaw is the Special Collections Librarian and College Archivist at Lafayette College in Easton, Pennsylvania. She received her BA and MLS degrees from Emory University, where she spent the first years of her career as an archivist. She has been active in the field, serving for more than a decade as a member of the Pennsylvania State Historical Records Advisory Board, as a member of the Steering Committee of the Mid-Atlantic Regional Archives Conference, and as chair of the Privacy and Confidentiality Roundtable of the Society of American Archivists. At Lafayette College, she has taught a course on the Art and History of the Book, and in 2007 she was named Lafayette's Administrator of the Year.

Gabriel Perri Silberblatt is a recent graduate of Carleton College where he majored in Art History and English. He now lives and works in NYC, providing administrative and programming support for the Architectural League of New York. He may be reached at gsilberblatt@gmail.com.

Caroline Sinkinson is an Assistant Professor, Instruction Coordinator and Undergraduate Services Librarian at the University of Colorado, Boulder. Ms. Sinkinson coordinates the information literacy component of the first-year writing class, which is a requirement for all incoming freshman.

Helen Wong Smith's experience with archival collections commenced in the 1980s while earning a BA in Hawaiian Studies. Focusing on archival management while earning a Master's in Library and Information Studies in 1991, she became a certified archivist in 2001 while working as a solo archivist for private, government, and educational institutions. Currently the Archivist for Hawai'i Volcanoes National Park, she is responsible for park archival collections throughout the Pacific.

Sandra Sohn will graduate from the University of Pennsylvania in 2012, with Bachelor's Degrees from two Schools: the College of Arts and Sciences (English with an emphasis on Creative Writing) and the Engineering School (Computer Science). While finishing her degrees, Sandra is writing a screenplay and applying to medical school.

Mary Kate Stopa is a member of the class of 2012 at the University of Pennsylvania. She is entering her final year of study toward a bachelor's degree in English with a focus in Creative Writing.

Jessica Sutro is an English Major in the Class of 2012 at the University of Pennsylvania. She focuses on Medieval literature.

Shan C. Sutton is Associate Dean and Head of Special Collections at the University of the Pacific Library in Stockton, California. His areas of specialization include the integration of information literacy and archival research into the undergraduate curriculum, and the digitization of manuscript collections. He holds a master's degree in Library Science from the University of Arizona, and a master's degree in Humanities from Wright State University.

Ellen D. Swain is Archivist for Student Life and Culture in the University Archives at the University of Illinois at Urbana-Champaign where she administers the Archives' Student Life and Culture Archival Program. She holds an MA in American history from Indiana University and an MS in Information Science from the University of Illinois at Urbana-Champaign. Her archival research interests include oral history, documentary strategies, and outreach methods.

Suzy Taraba is Director of Special Collections and Archives at Wesleyan University. She holds BA and MALS degrees from Wesleyan and the MS in Library Science from Columbia. Before returning to her *alma mater* in 1997, she held special collections positions at the Bakken Library of Electricity in Life (now the Bakken Museum), Columbia, Duke, and the University of Chicago. Suzy is a former chair of ACRL's Rare Books and Manuscripts Section. Fostering undergraduate excitement about special collections and archives is one of her favorite parts of her job.

Malinda Triller serves as special collections librarian and liaison to the Women's and Gender and American Studies departments at Dickinson College in Carlisle, Pennsylvania. She has contributed to a number of digital projects, including the James Buchanan Resource Center and the Slavery and Abolition in the U.S. sites, both LSTA-funded projects involving the digitization of nineteenth-century publications. Triller has also been involved in an initiative to make Special Collections images available through Flickr. She holds an MLIS from the University of Pittsburgh and an MA in applied history from Shippensburg University.

Valeria Tsygankova majored in English at Penn and graduated in 2011. She is currently doing graduate work in the History of the Book at the University of London, and plans to study contemporary poetry as a PhD student when she returns to the U.S.

Julia Walworth is Research Fellow and Librarian at Merton College Oxford. Her dual role allows her to combine research interests in medieval manuscript books, library history and the history of the printed book with responsibility for the oldest surviving college library in Europe.

Kristi Wermager: I have been Curator of Special Collections at Carleton College for the past eleven years. During that time I have worked to integrate our materials into courses across the curriculum of the College. I have also worked with interested faculty to develop an artists' book collection. I am particularly interested in exploring ways to encourage undergraduates to engage actively with Special Collections materials.

Tanya Zanish-Belcher is the Head of Special Collections and University Archives at the Iowa State University Library. She received her BA in History from Ohio Wesleyan University and her MA in Historical and Archival Administration from Wright State University. She is a past president of the Midwest Archives Conference and a Fellow of the Society of American Archivists.